Best Escapes
South India

CONTENTS

Plan Your Trip 6

Need to Know 8
This is South India 12
South India Map 16
15 Top Experiences 18
Getting Around 28
Eating in South India 32
Shopping Guide 36
Travelling with Kids 40
What's New 42
Get Inspired 44

South India's Best Trips 46

South India at a Glance 48
● **Karnataka** 50
  Map 52
  Top Highlights 54
  Bengaluru 56
  Mysore 78
  Bandipur & Around 86
  Coorg 98
  Chikmagalur & Sakleshpur 112
  Belur & Halebidu 124
  Mangalore, Udupi & Around 130

Gokarna, Karwar & Dandeli 150	● **Andhra Pradesh**.......................**446**
Badami, Pattadakal, Aihole........170	Map 448
Hampi...180	Top Highlights...........................450
● **Kerala** **188**	Visakhapatnam & Araku Valley 452
Map 190	Vijayawada & Around 466
Top Highlights...........................192	Hyderabad 472
Thiruvananthapuram, Kovalam & Varkala 194	Srisailam 492
Alappuzha, Kumarakom & Kollam.....................................216	Tirupati.......................................498
Kochi & Around.........................234	**Index**................................506
Munnar & Periyar Tiger Reserve............................256	**Acknowledgements**......................520
Kozhikode & Wayanad 270	
Lakshadweep.............................282	
● **Tamil Nadu**.............................**290**	
Map 292	
Top Highlights...........................294	
Chennai & Around 296	
Mamallapuram & Puducherry ..316	
Thanjavur & Kumbakonam.......336	
Tiruchirappalli...........................350	
Chettinadu.................................358	
Madurai & Rameswaram 370	
Kanyakumari 386	
Kodaikanal 392	
Coimbatore & Valparai.............402	
Ooty, Coonoor & Kotagiri..........414	
Andaman Islands 434	

HOW TO USE THIS BOOK

1
Plan Your Trip

- Written specially by our Indian authors who have travelled extensively across the states.
- Our suggestions for the best things to do and see.
- Advice on everything you need to travel around, shop, eat and keep the family happy.
- Need to Know: A 'quick reference guide' for all the key information you will need.

2
South India's Best Trips

- Highlights of the main regions, covering the best attractions and activities in all the states.
- Expert recommendations tell you about not-to-be-missed highlights.
- Reviews of accommodation, restaurants, nightclubs and shopping by Lonely Planet authors.
- Easy maps for each state, with clearly marked and numbered destinations.

Trip Planner

At-a-glance information for each destination

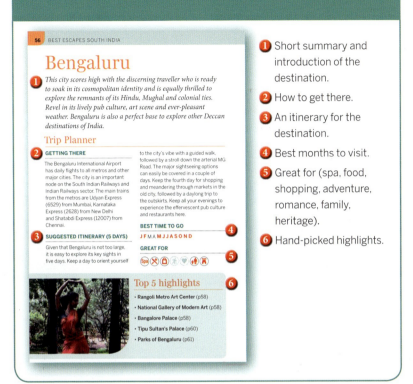

1. Short summary and introduction of the destination.
2. How to get there.
3. An itinerary for the destination.
4. Best months to visit.
5. Great for (spa, food, shopping, adventure, romance, family, heritage).
6. Hand-picked highlights.

Special information

Look for these boxes to help you get the most out of your trip:

- ✓ *Top Tip* – insider advice
- ♥ *If You Like* – themed suggestions
- ₹ *Value for Money* – money-saving advice
- ↗ *Detour* – off-beat trips
- 📷 *Snapshot* – interesting facts
- TOP CHOICE *Top Choice* – our top picks

OUR REVIEWS

Lonely Planet writers have visited every hotel, restaurant, shop and activity in this book. They don't accept any freebies and favours, so you can be sure our recommendations are unbiased.

PLAN YOUR TRIP

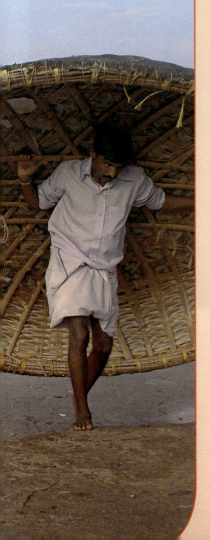

- Need to Know 8
- This is South India 12
- South India Map 16
- 15 Top Experiences 18
- Getting Around 28
- Eating in South India 32
- Shopping Guide 36
- Travelling with Kids 40
- What's New 42
- Get Inspired 44

▪ Bamboo coracle rides on Tungabhadra River are popular in Hampi

Need to Know

🛈 Quick Facts

LANGUAGES
Kannada, Telugu, Malayalam and Tamil are the main languages spoken in Karnataka, Andhra Pradesh, Kerala and Tamil Nadu respectively. However, a smattering of Hindi and English can make you go a long way in all four states.

MONEY
ATMs of ICICI, HDFC, SBI and Federal Bank (in Kerala only) are easily accessible in the bigger cities, but it's better to carry sufficient cash when you are travelling to smaller towns, especially if you are planning to shop there. Most hotels accept credit cards, but check with homestays on how they take payments.

MOBILE CONNECTIVITY
All major cities have mobile connectivity and service from chief operators like Airtel, BSNL, Vodafone, Idea and Aircel.

INTERNET ACCESS
Most hotels have business centres or offer free wi-fi facility (except some hotels in Andhra, especially Vijayawada). But, you may not find internet access in homestays.

Bharatanatyam dancer at a festival in Mamallapuram

When to Go

In all four states it can get really hot and humid during the summer months, except in the hill stations. The best time to travel is during the autumn–winter period.

- **October–February; high season:** This is the best time to explore all four states. With fairly pleasant weather and no rain dampening travel plans, you can enjoy sightseeing and also go for adventure activities such as trekking and microlight flying in Coorg.

- **March–May; mid-season:** These are the hottest months of South India, but are likely to be busy with local tourists on summer vacation. Temperatures in Andhra Pradesh are very high in May; it's advisable to avoid the state in this month unless you are visiting the Eastern Ghats.

- **June–September; low season:** For those who love the monsoons, the Western Ghats are at the greenest in these months. This is also the right time for rafting and to visit famous waterfalls.

First Time in South India

If you are travelling here for the first time, the suffusion of culture, food and historical sites will overtake your senses. Even though the southern states offer great travel experiences, here are some things to keep in mind.

ADVANCE PLANNING

- **Two to three months before:** If you are planning to travel by train, this is when you should be booking the tickets. You can even get a good flight fare. A rough itinerary can be drawn up right now, keeping festivals and weather in mind. Booking accommodation ahead during the peak season (for example New Years in Kerala) is imperative as there is a heavy influx of travellers from not only India, but across the world.

- **One month before:** Chalk out a more specific itinerary as per your places of interest. If you are out on a wildlife, trekking or festival-specific trip, check for timings and access; adventure activities like rafting, trekking, microlight flying and more, maybe closed during the rains.

- **One week before:** Make your calls to hotels/homestays to confirm bookings and spend your time packing optimally in this period. Stock up on medicines you need. Arrange for pick-ups at airport or station, or car rentals.

HEALTH & SAFETY

- **Travelling alone:** Though the South is often spoken of as one of the safest regions to travel alone in India, be on your guard at night, and make sure that you book your stay ahead if you are arriving late in the evening. Have emergency numbers handy and be discerning about trusting strangers, as you would in your city. Most of the time, travelling in overnight buses or trains does not pose any problems and people go out of their way to help travellers.

Dos and Don'ts

✓ Try to learn a few words of the local language. It will take you a long way.

✓ A thank you and smile for drivers, waiters and others who help will be appreciated.

✓ Respect all religious views: the southern states have a fair population to represent the diversity in our country.

✓ Most homestays insist that you leave footwear outside, as it is normal practice to roam barefoot.

✓ Observe meal practices in homestays; many people serve food with their right hand only. Eating on a banana leaf is common.

✓ Carry a hand sanitiser and tissues. Public toilets on the roads are best avoided.

✓ Cameras are not allowed inside several temples. Please check beforehand.

✗ Don't ridicule words or accents you don't understand.

✗ Abstain from sharing derisive opinions on food and culture as someone may take offense.

✗ Don't litter wildlife parks or talk loudly during safaris.

✗ Don't bargain too much, especially with local craftsmen.

- **Hygiene and medical aid:** Most hotels and homestays suggested in this book are clean, serve hygienic food and are fit for family travel, unless mentioned. If you need to make a trip to the hospital, expect decent standards. Large cities like Bengaluru, Hyderabad, Visakhapatnam, Chennai and Cochin are your best bet for speciality hospitals and complex medical treatments.

WHAT TO PACK

- **Strong mosquito repellant:** The greener the destination, more the mosquitoes.

- **Comfortable walking shoes and flip-flops:** Comfortable sneakers may be good for plantations and hiking trails, while beach destinations demand airy flip-flops.

- **Warm clothing:** A light jacket may be necessary in the evenings, but something more wind resistant is needed in the months of October–February in the hills.

- **A heavy-duty umbrella:** Make sure you pick up a sturdy umbrella if travelling in the months of July–September.

- **Leech socks:** Some plantation areas and trekking routes are breeding grounds for leeches during wet weather (July–September). You may want to invest in leech socks or just carry packets of salt to make the leeches drop off once they bite.

- **Prescribed medication:** Carry enough for your trip as you may not find exactly what you need in smaller towns.

- **Dark glasses, sunscreen, a big scarf to cover your face and head, caps or hats:** It is extremely important to avoid getting sunburnt both during summer and winter so carry these with you.

Train journeys provide an excellent opportunity to explore the real South India

NEED TO KNOW

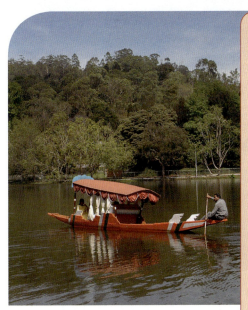

Boating at Kodaikanal Lake is a popular activity in the quaint hill station

DRIVING

The well-maintained national and state highways network in the southern states makes it easy to drive around. Highway stops are in plenty, especially the Kamat chain of restaurants in Karnataka, and a host of small dhaba-like establishments, which have reasonably clean loos, all across the region. The coastal stretches on both the eastern and western side are particularly scenic. The East Coast Road (ECR) from Chennai to Puducherry is one to be earmarked in the itinerary. You may want to check on routes that close for the night if you are expecting to drive along forested areas (usually 6pm–6am is closed on routes that cut across national parks).

TOURIST INFORMATION

Department of Tourism has small information kiosks in all high travel destinations, but the head offices are situated in the capitals – Bengaluru (080 2235 2828), Thiruvananthapuram (0471 2321132), Chennai (044 25368358) and Hyderabad (1800 42545454).

Quick Facts

PRICE RANGES

Throughout this book, reviews use the following price ranges. Rates quoted in this guide do not include taxes, unless otherwise specified.

KEY TO RATES

₹₹₹ over ₹7000
₹₹ ₹3000–7000
₹ below ₹3000

ABBREVIATIONS

The following abbreviations are used to describe the room types given in this book.

s single rooms
d double rooms
ste suites

TAXES

Taxes are additionally charged on the room tariff. Hotels charge between 12.5% to 19.92%. Homestays usually add a 5% tax component.

SEASONAL PRICING

The tariffs are sensitive to high traffic tourist seasons. Peak season can command up to 40% higher tariffs.

FLEXI TARIFF

Some hotels do not reveal the tariff in order to keep it flexible; they can then offer the best deal depending on their bookings.

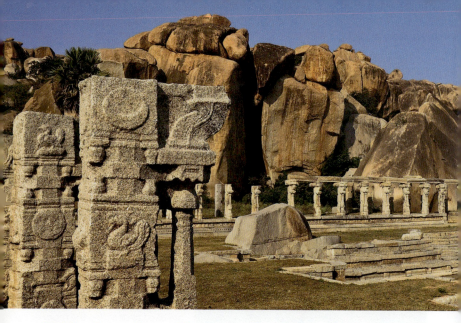

This is South India

The southern states of Karnataka, Kerala, Tamil Nadu and Andhra Pradesh offer an inimitable flavour of unique traditions, rich culture, architectural grandeur, vibrant performing arts and spicy cuisine. Bordered by three seas, a beach is always close by. Move inland for an encouter with coconut groves, plantations and forests, giving green respite.

Karnataka

With a legacy of powerful dynasties, a multitude of landscapes ranging from beaches to the Western Ghats, and an infusion of cosmopolitan life, Karnataka offers some of South India's best attractions. Its rich historical heritage can be seen in the Mysore Palace, ruins of the Vijayanagara capital at Hampi, grand Hoysala temples, Chalukyan monuments of the Pattadakal–Badami–Aihole loop and even the more recent Bangalore Palace. These destinations are an absolute treat for history lovers.

For those inclined towards the outdoors, Karnataka is brimming with wildlife reserves, trekking trails, frothy

Boulders form a dramatic backdrop to Hampi's ruins

rivers to raft down, unexplored surfing sections along the Konkan Coast and scuba diving spots. Set the compass in any direction and you are bound to find something travel worthy.

Kerala

It is amazing how this slim strip of land along the southwestern coastline of India can hoard such a variety of experiences and landscapes. From pristine beaches skirting the Arabian Sea, to its network of backwater canals, and lush forests teeming with wildlife to the tea-carpeted hills of Munnar, the state's stunning topography unfolds seamlessly from one end to another. Between these exotic locations lie layers of history etched over centuries by the spice trade that lured traders from world over.

Travellers have the choice of interspersing visits to heritage monuments with more relaxed activities like cruising leisurely in houseboats, getting an Ayurvedic massage or watching the sun go home from the coastal beaches.

Located close by is the stunning cluster of small idyllic, palm-fringed islands: the Union Territory of **Lakshadweep**, where the waters are crystal clear, tropical fish are aplenty and city living is clean forgotten.

Tamil Nadu

Centuries-old temples with grand architecture, spread across places like Madurai, Rameswaram, Kanchipuram, Thanjavur, give Tamil Nadu a unique identity on the country's travel map. But the state has a lot more on offer – from the beaches of Kanyakumari to the hill stations of Ooty, Coonoor, Kotagiri, Valparai and Kodaikanal, it is rich in natural beauty, giving you a chance to come close and personal with nature. Food is another speciality here. Whether it's the Kongunadu cuisine of western Tamil Nadu or the well-known Chettinadu cuisine, there is always something to tickle your taste buds. And the final ingredient to make your holiday extra special is the opportunity to shop, especially for the legendary Kanjeevaram silk saris.

Close by is the Union Territory of **Andaman and Nicobar Islands**, sparkling like jewels in the middle of the Bay of Bengal. It offers plenty of water sports and stunning colourful corals. This is the closest to tropical heaven you'll get along the coast.

Andhra Pradesh

Steadily etching a place for itself on the travel map of India, the boundaries of this state enclose a wealth of historic, scenic and cultural attractions, enough to excite the offbeat traveller. Apart from Hyderabad's streets replete with character, and Visakhapatnam's untouched coastline, there is much more waiting to be explored: weaving and craft hubs, temple trails and pretty coastal stretches.

The state has some of the most popular pilgrimage centres like Tirupati and Srisailam. For a break from the spiritual, trawl around the villages of Pochampally, Kondapalli and more to see splashes of colour unfold in reams of cotton and silk saris and quaint wooden toys. And for those looking to sink into a happy state of doing nothing, the cool hills of Araku Valley offer the perfect setting.

(At the time of going to press the Indian government had initiated a move to carve the separate state of Telangana from Andhra Pradesh, however we have treated the state as a whole).

Charminar, the iconic symbol of Hyderabad, is in the Old City

South India Map

SOUTH INDIA MAP

⭐ *15 Top Experiences*

❶ Backwaters of Kerala (p216) Float past sprawling plantations and villages, or spend the night in a boat.

❷ Nilgiri Mountain Railway, Ooty (p419) Admire the stunning mountain scenery as the train snakes over bridges and chugs past picturesque stations from Ooty to Mettupalayam.

❸ Konkan Coast Drive (p132) Still raw and untouched, the pristine coastline from Gokarna to Mangalore has several worthy stops.

❹ Scuba Diving & Snorkelling in Havelock (p436) Dive into the stunning blue waters and see the amazing colourful marine life.

❺ Sri Venkateswara Swamy Temple, Tirupati (p498) A trip to the hilltop temple of one of India's wealthiest gods is a fascinating experience.

❻ Coffee in Coorg (p108) Sip your cuppa as you stay on a plantation estate and learn about the brew.

❼ Kerala Ayurveda Treatments (p201) Don't leave the state without trying an authentic Ayurvedic massage.

❽ Hyderabad Biryani Trail (p485) To have authentic biryani make your way to the Charminar area.

❾ Sunset at Kanyakumari (p389) Watch the three seas meet at the tip of the country.

❿ Meenakshi Temple, Madurai (p372) This elaborately carved temple is considered an architectural marvel in South India.

⓫ Bengaluru's Beer Culture (p72–3) Head to the beer capital of India that is home to a number of breweries.

⓬ Puducherry French Quarter (p317) This part of the town has charming cobble-stoned streets and white and mustard-coloured villas.

⓭ Chettinadu Cuisine (p365) If hot and spicy non-veg food is what you like then Chettinadu cuisine would be right up your sleeve.

⓮ Wall of Wonder, Kavaratti, Lakshadweep (p284) This underwater cliff made of soft corals is teeming with marine life in all sizes and colours of the rainbow.

⓯ Periyar Tiger Reserve (p261) Cruise along the Periyar Lake or go for a jeep safari to spot wildlife.

15 Top Experiences

1 Backwaters of Kerala

It is not every day you come across scenery as sublime as Kerala's backwaters: 900km of interconnected rivers, lakes and glassy lagoons lined with lush tropical flora. And if you do, there is no better way to experience it than a few serene days spent on a teak and palm-thatched houseboat. Float along the water – while nibbling on seafood so fresh it's still almost wriggling – and forget about life on land. The distinctive houseboats cluster around the main hubs of Alappuzha, Kumarakom and Kollam (p216).

2 Nilgiri Mountain Railway, Ooty

The historic Nilgiri Mountain Railway (p419) is a must-see for lovers of locomotives. The toy train, a Unesco World Heritage Site, is steeped in old-world charm. Sit by the window, and enjoy the ride from Ooty (p416) to

Mettupalayam as the train snakes over bridges, goes through small tunnels, and chugs past small and picturesque stations. The journey from Coonoor (p419) to Mettupalayam (41km) has delightful views; so try not to miss this glorious stretch.

3 Konkan Coast Drive

The coastal stretch of Karnataka is breathtaking, especially if you drive along its beaches. Still raw and untouched, the pristine coastline has several worthy stops. Start from the northern-most beach destination, Gokarna (p150) and wind your way down the coast, making pit stops at Murudeshwar, from where you can detour to Netrani Island, Baindur, Maravanthe, Malpe in Udupi (p137) and Tannir Bavi close to Mangalore (p136). From rocky outcrops to large stretches of clean brown sand, busy beaches to secluded spots, the topography is charmingly diverse.

4 Scuba Diving & Snorkelling in Havelock

There is no water adventure as delightful as scuba diving (p439) at Andaman's Havelock Island (p436). Venture into a magical world full of tropical fish, colourful live coral, sea turtles, stingray and other wonders. For those who fancy staying above the surface, snorkelling is a great option. With the crystal clear waters of the Andaman coast, you can catch a vivid glimpse into the fascinating world beneath the sea.

5 Sri Venkateswara Swamy Temple, Tirupati

If not for the destination's spiritual significance, the sheer fervour of thousands of devotees is enough to draw you to Sri Venkateswara Swamy Temple (p498) in Tirupati. A trip to the hilltop temple of one of India's wealthiest gods is a fascinating experience. Follow shorn heads in snaking lines to the sanctum, only to be shoved out hastily by ushers. Watch priests counting stacks of money inside a glass-walled hall or scribble your wishes on a sacred stone. Many weigh themselves on a massive scale and offer equal quantities of grain or gold.

6 Coffee in Coorg

The low Coorg hills, covered with thick clumpy bushes of coffee, offer a refreshing green holiday. The best way to learn about the aromatic beverage is to stay at a plantation estate and gather first-hand information about the cultivation on walks and tasting sessions. As you walk along coffee-flanked trails, also see pepper vines and other spices curve up trees in the shade of this thick foliage. There is a wide array of plantation homestays to choose from (p108).

7 Kerala Ayurveda Treatments

Kerala's long association with Ayurveda, has propelled the state into fame for international and Indian travellers. While the entire state (particularly around Kovalam and Alappuzha) is dotted with small establishments, choose a trustworthy practitioner for your massage or treatment. Santhigiri (p281) is one such chain found all over the state, which promises reliable treatments. Manaltheeram (p209) is a good resort in the Kovalam region. Other good places are Amruthum Ayurvedic Village Resort (p204) in Thiruvananthapuram and Kadaltheeram Ayurvedic Beach Resort (p201) in Varkala.

8 Hyderabad Biryani Trail

Insulated from the infusion of modern methods of making this famous rice dish, Hyderabad's oldest joints may be shabby in ambience, but you will not encounter tastier biryani anywhere else. Old Hyderabad or the Charminar area (p485) offers at least three well-known haunts – Pista House is the most popular. Madina and Shadab don't fall too far behind in dishing out aromatic versions of the rice, meat, egg and spices concoction. Further away from this area, Paradise, Cafe Bahar and Bawarchi satisfy queues of hungry biryani lovers every day.

9 Sunset at Kanyakumari

Triveni Sangam (p389) in Kanyakumari is packed with excited travellers as the sun descends into the meeting point of the three seas – Bay of Bengal, Indian Ocean and Arabian Sea. Naturally, the scene is not much different at sunrise. If it gets too crowded at the southern-most tip of the country, a better way to view the sunset is from the Beach View Park or the Viewing Tower, which start getting crowded after 5.30pm, but have ample space to accommodate hundreds.

10 Meenakshi Temple, Madurai

The magnificent Meenakshi Sundareswarar Temple (p372), built over several centuries, dominates the city of Madurai with its four nine-storey rajagopurams (towers) and is visible from most parts of the city. While the religious minded come and offer prayers to Goddess Meenakshi (an avatar of Goddess Parvati), others are awe struck by the architectural beauty of its sculptured pillars and intricately painted ceiling. The thousand-pillar hall within the temple has been converted into a museum and its sculptures and idols are worth seeing.

11 Bengaluru's Beer Culture

Bengaluru has sustained its moniker as the 'Beer capital of India' right from the time when British soldiers popularised the beverage in the late 17th century. MG Road is lined with many pubs within a radius of less than a kilometer. The enthusiasm for a lager in the afternoon, accompanied by some rock music, is still intact. Bengaluru has paved the way in India for safe social drinking in atmospheric pubs sprinkled across the city. New recipes of pale to full bodied ales, from homegrown breweries are what young Bangaloreans crave these days, but the waning sheen of old bars and pubs is upheld by the older generation.

12 Puducherry French Quarter

When the word 'rue' instead of 'road' is unwittingly used by Tamil-speaking residents of a town, you know you are in the heart of the French Quarter (p317) of Puducherry. Tall grey or yellow buildings with minimalistic windows, shadowed by pink bougainvillea, flank the cobble-stoned streets of the 'White Town', lending a charming ambience to the erstwhile French colony. This is the section which is skirted by the beach and cut off from a canal on one side, to segregate the Tamil Quarters. Most hotels, restaurants, shops and cafes that interest travellers lie in these few lanes that make up the French Quarter.

13 Chettinadu Cuisine

If you like your food hot and spicy and have a weakness for non-veg, you can't leave South India without trying Chettinadu food (p365–67), the regional cuisine of the Chettiars hailing from southern Tamil Nadu. Try chicken chettinad and uppu kari (a dry mutton dish) with plain rice or biryani, or ask for a full meal where you will be served at least 10 to 12 dishes on a banana leaf. Vegetarians need not worry as there is sufficient variety for them as well, including unusual ones like mango pachadi (a combination of mango and jaggery) and molagu kolumbu (green pepper curry).

14 Wall of Wonder, Lakshadweep

With a landscape made up entirely of iridescent waters and powder-white sands, Lakshadweep has plenty of allure. But go underwater – 12m to be precise – and you will find even greater treasures. The Wall of Wonder (p284) at Kadmat and Kavaratti is an endless underwater cliff made entirely of soft corals teeming with marine life in all sizes and colours of the rainbow. Divers agree that it is one of the top dives of the world.

15 Periyar Tiger Reserve

One of the best-managed wildlife experiences for travellers in India, Periyar Tiger Reserve (p261) gives you your wildlife fix in South India. The sanctuary houses a scenic manmade lake, around which the forest sprawls for 925sq km. Cruising along the Periyar Lake is a unique way of seeing the jungle as deer, elephants and wild hogs roam the edges for a drink. And if you are lucky, you may even spot the elusive tiger. You can also take a jeep safari to explore this biodiversity hot spot teeming with birdlife and fascinating creatures like the lion-tailed macaque.

Getting Around

With a good network of trains, airports and highways, travelling within South India is simple and affordable. What is starkly different from other parts of the country is the safe overnight bus culture.

Karnataka

TRAINS

The robust network of **South Western Railway** (www.swr.indianrailways.gov.in) connects all the major South Indian destinations to remote towns. The **Konkan Railway** (www.konkanrailway.com), as well as the **Southern Railway** (www.sr.indianrailways.gov.in) network provide travellers with further options. For more information on trains that connect one city to another, refer to opening pages at the beginning of each chapter.

BUSES

The state-run **Karnataka State Road Transportation Corporation** (KSRTC) provides great connectivity by AC Volvos and ordinary buses across Karnataka and its neighbouring states. This is one of the best networks in the south. Bookings can be done on www.ksrtc.in. The other alternative is www.redbus.in, which is an aggregator, but their operators may not always be reliable.

Scenic train rides are synonymous with Kerala

TAXI

Taxi rates range from ₹7–12 per km (depending on AC/non AC cabs and the kind of car), with a minimum run of 200–300km per day and driver's daily allowance (also known as bata) of ₹200–300 per day.

AUTORICKSHAWS

Autos charge a minimum fare of ₹17–19 in different places of Karnataka, but it's safe to assume that you will have to pay ₹20 for a short ride. If you are taking the auto for a longer distance, negotiate the rate before.

Kerala

TRAINS

Trains travelling along the Kerala coast cover many key destinations across the state from Thiruvananthapuram, in the south, to Kasargod up north. Trivandrum Express (16348), Malabar Express (16630), Parasuram Express (16649), Maveli Express (16603) and Ernad Express (16605) run daily on this route. Check the websites of **South Western Railway** and **Southern Railway** for more information on trains.

BUSES

You will see plenty of **Kerala State Road Transportation Corporation** (KSRTC) buses plying within the state. These are reliable and timely, but overcrowded and not recommended for children and elders. You can book through www.keralartc.com. Else, book your seat at the bus depot an hour in advance of your journey.

TAXI

This is the best option to get around in Kerala at your own pace. Cabs will charge you by the km (₹7–12 per km) with an additional amount for the driver's daily allowance (₹200–

🛈 *Quick Facts*

- **Trains:** Book trains on www.irctc.in at least 2–4 months in advance to ensure availability. Tatkal tickets can be booked a day in advance.

- **Bus:** The state-run bus services are www.ksrtc.in, www.keralartc.com, www.tnstc.in and www.apsrtconline.in. Various private operators are www.redbus.in and www.travelyaari.com and can be used to book Volvos with AC and push-back seats or sleepers.

- **Taxis:** Average taxi rates range from ₹7–12 per km, for a minimum run of 200–300km per day and daily driver allowance of ₹200–500, with additional tolls and parking.

300). There is a decent range of cars to choose from. In hilly areas, only day charges are applicable.

AUTORICKSHAWS

These are easy to hire and make perfect sense if you are sightseeing in a city. Minimum fare in most cities is ₹20 but may swell at night. If you are in the hills (especially Munnar and Wayanad) autos charge according to the sightseeing spot and don't go by the meter.

> Autos are easily available in most big cities of South India

FERRY

The backwater region of Kerala is well connected by government ferries; this includes Ernakulam, Kochi, Kollam and Kumarakom. The journey might be slow, but experience at least one trip during your stay to see the lush countryside along the canals. The Kochi islands have regular ferries connecting each other and charge only ₹2.50 per head.

Tamil Nadu

TRAINS

Chennai has two stations – Chennai Central catering mostly to trains travelling outside Tamil Nadu, and Chennai Egmore for trains to a destination within the state. All the big cities and many smaller towns in Tamil Nadu have a rail connection to Chennai. Check the website of **South Eastern Railway** (www.ser.indianrailways.gov.in) and Southern Railway for more details.

BUSES

The bus network in Tamil Nadu is extremely efficient. **Tamil Nadu State Road Transportation Corporation** (www.tnstc.in) runs both public and private buses. Though private Volvo buses are more expensive, they are much more comfortable than other buses.

TAXIS

Cabs usually charge betwwn ₹9–15 per km plus the driver's allowance which is ₹300–500. In some cities such as Coimbatore, you are charged a fixed rate of ₹1500 daily for the vehicle and driver, plus diesel cost.

AUTORICKSHAWS

Although autorickshaws are easy to hire they refuse to go by the meter so you need to bargain. In smaller towns, autos are larger and you have to share them with other passengers.

Andhra Pradesh

TRAINS

With more than 200 railway stations in the state, the **South Eastern**, **South Central** (www.scr.indianrailways.gov.in) and **East Coast Railway** (www.eastcoastrail.indianrailways.gov.in) networks provide many options. You can reach most places with a combination of a train journey and a short drive.

BUSES

Though the state-run **Andhra Pradesh State Road Transportation Corporation** (APSRTC) connects all parts of the state, private Volvo buses are more comfortable.

TAXIS

Taxis charge ₹7–12 per km with the driver's daily allowance of ₹200–300. There is also a daily minimum run, which can range from 200–300km. Discuss rates before, as some of the day trips are not calculated by kilometer.

AUTORICKSHAWS

Minimum fare in most cities is ₹20, but autos charge a premium at night and early morning.

Individual state tourism buses ply across different parts of South India

Eating in South India

Banish the conventional association of only 'idli-dosa' with these four southern states and dive into a world of fabulous ethnic cuisines from its many regions. Each state has distinct specialities within different regions and are best tasted in local eateries.

Idlis and vadas are common breakfast items in all four states

Karnataka

Depending on where you are travelling in Karnataka, there is a wide array of cuisines to choose from. Pandhi (pork) curry and other non-veg delights of Coorg are just as special as the crisp dosas of Udipi and vadas from Maddur. Don't discount staples such as chirroti (fried puffy pastry usually served with milk), bisi bele bhath (a lentil and rice combination), akki rotti (rice pancake), khara bhath (semolina upma), kesari bhath (sweet semolina) and ragi mudde (millet balls).

If you are skirting the coast, try the famous sol kadi (kokum-yoghurt drink) and bamboo shoot pickle. The more familiar idli, sambhar and dosas complement the diverse Kannadiga dishes. A red tamarind paste is usually smeared inside the dosas, along with the potato filling, creating the famous Mysore masala dosa.

The best way to experience the local food is by staying at homestays, where you can also learn about recipes and indigenous ingredients. If you are on the road, Kamat restaurants on highways are good for a snack or a meal. Multi-cuisine restaurants are in plenty in bigger cities.

Kerala

From elaborate vegetarian sadyas (a large feast) to the legacy of non-veg delights from Syrian Christian homes and Mappila food from the coast, Kerala's cuisine can't be compartmentalised into one category. Starting at breakfast, you can spend hours at the table with favourites like puttu (steamed rice flour and coconut), kadala curry (black gram), idiyappams (string hoppers), idlis, dosas, sambhar and the classic appam-stew combination.

Lunch usually consists of veg and non-veg meal combinations served on banana leaves. These are easy to find at basic street-side restaurants if you are travelling. You can add some zing to the food with an additional fish curry or dry chicken. The large coastal stretch of the state offers a vast array of fresh catch; shrimp, crabs, cuttle fish, sardines, mackerel, tuna, prawns, rays and even shark (although its being hunted to extinction). With a large Christian community in the state, cakes are a part of Kerala households and festivals.

You will often find warm water with a tinge of red being served in restaurants; this is a herbal concoction (with the bark of the Pathimugam tree) to make the water safe to drink. But nothing refreshes more than coconut water. If you are adventurous, try the locally tapped coconut alcohol, toddy.

 Quick Facts

OPENING HOURS

Most restaurants in all the four states open at 11am for lunch and close at 3.30pm. Dinner timings are 7–11pm. Those that also serve breakfast open at 7am. Most large chains open as early as 6am for breakfast.

PRICES

Ranges used in this book are based on prices of mains for two people.

Key to Rates

₹₹₹ over ₹500

₹₹ 200–500

₹ under ₹200

TIPPING

In larger restaurants, you can check for service charge and choose to pay over and above that. In smaller places, there are no particular rules, any amount of change is gratefully accepted by the restaurant.

Tamil Nadu

Vegetarians and non-vegetarians alike can savour an assortment of dishes from different types of pongal (a rice preparation) to chicken, mutton and fish cooked in spices common to that region. Pure vegetarians need not worry while travelling through Tamil Nadu. You can try a variety of flavoured rice, from lemon, coconut to tamarind, or have set meals that comprise rice, sambhar, rasam, kootu, poriyal, curds and pappadam. While the local restaurants may not be much to look at in terms of ambience, the food is hygienic, tasty and served on fresh banana leaves.

Contrary to popular belief, you cannot spend your holiday in Tamil Nadu gorging on idli, dosa and vada thrice a day. Idli is available only for 'tiffin' or breakfast, generally from 7–10am. Dosa is available for breakfast and dinner, while vada is an evening snack, best had at tea stalls between 4–6pm as an accompaniment to piping hot tea.

The fiery cuisine of the Chettinadu region in southern Tamil Nadu is known all across the country. While you must try it when in Chettinadu, you can also get a taste of it in Chennai where there are several restaurants serving this cuisine. The food is both spicy and aromatic and while the cuisine is primarily non-veg with chicken Chettinadu and uppu kari (a dry mutton dish) being very popular, there is sufficient variety for vegetarians as well. Try the mango pachadi and molagu kolumbu (a green pepper curry).

Layered parottas and appams are a must-try in Kerala

Andhra Pradesh

The first dish that comes to mind when one talks of Andhra cuisine is the aromatic biryani from Hyderabad; the spicy 'meals' are a close second. But there is more to Telugu dishes than these two hooks alone. Regional classification of the food can be done as per the different regions of the state: Andhra, Telangana, Rayalaseema and Hyderabad.

The northern Andhra food has heavy flavours of fenugreek, mustard, sesame and onions. This emulates the Orissa style of cooking in many ways. Both Tamil Nadu and Karnataka influences are found in the Rayalseema region or southern Andhra, with use of ragi, jowar and rava in the preparation of food. The paper-thin pootharekulu (crepes of rice flour with jaggery stuffing) sweet is famous. Food made in the Deccan region or Telangana would well suit a Maharashtrian palate with use of bajra and jowar.

Arab and Persian cuisines made their way to Hyderabad through the Nizams of the state and are still celebrated for their aromatic, mouth-watering meat dishes and breads. Iftar during Ramzan is particularly famous in the city, with haleem being stirred in massive cauldrons and downed with Irani chai. On the coastal edges, the food largely comprises the fresh catch of the sea, accompanied by tamarind rice, lentils, greens like okra, broad beans and jackfruit.

> Hyderabadi biryani is synonymous with Andhra cuisine

Shopping Guide

Each state in South India has unique shopping items on offer, from a variety of handicrafts, antiques, textiles, saris and natural produce. In each destination you are sure to find something that will appeal to your taste and suit your wallet as well.

Karnataka

- **Handicrafts:** Souvenirs from Karnataka include wooden inlay work in the form of paintings, bric-a-brac in sandalwood, stone carvings and metal work from coastal Karnataka. If you are looking for a single shopping stop, visit **Cauvery Emporium** (p76) in Bengaluru. Just 60km from the capital, the unassuming town of Channapatna is a great stop for children. Here, a few households make colourful wooden toys, a Persian craft introduced in the days of Tipu Sultan.
- **Coffee:** Chikmagalur, Coorg and Sakleshpur are the coffee stalwarts of the state and you can pick up fresh and fragrant coffee from here.
- **Saris:** Mysore is famous for its silk saris. It is the hub of sericulture in the state, with ancillary processes set up in nearby villages. You can find a large variety of sari shops in this town, as well as Bengaluru.

Brightly painted wooden masks are famous in Kerala

Places to shop

- **Cauvery Arts & Craft Emporium, Bengaluru** (p76) You can find all handicrafts of Karnataka under one roof.
- **Jayalakshmi, Ernakulam** (p253) One of the most renowned names for colourful silk saris.
- **Nalli Silks, Chennai** (p314) There is no way you can ignore this grand-daddy of silk shops in the state.
- **Kedarnathji Motiwale, Hyderabad** (p490) Head here for the finest quality pearls in the city.

Kerala

- **Handicrafts:** Local knick-knacks made from coir, wooden elephants and snake boat models, replicas of 'nettippattom' (ornaments worn by elephants during festivals) and Kathakali masks are the most popular picks in souvenir shops across the state. One of the most exotic things to pick up is the Aranmula Kannadi (mirror), made from a special mix of metal and alloy. You will find these only in bigger shops like branches of **Kairali** (p254) in Kochi and **SMSM Institute** (p214) in Thiruvanthapuram. **Uravu** (p281) in Wayanad promotes creative and modern bamboo craft in the form of lamps, earrings, paintings and more. Another traditional souvenir is the bell metal lamp, locally known as Nilavilakku.
- **Art and antiques:** If you are an art aficionado, a print of Raja Ravi Varma's paintings is hard to resist. You can find these in antique shops across the state. The Jew Town in **Mattancherry** (p255) is a good pick.
- **Saris:** It is easy to succumb to the temptation of buying Kerala's typical white cotton saris with golden borders. Known as the 'Kasavu' sari, these are best picked up from the small town of **Balaramapuram** (p198), off Thiruvananthapuram, which has streets full of weaving families. If you are looking for more colourful stuff, Ernakulam and Thiruvananthapuram have many sari shops. For other textiles like durries, bedspreads and towels, weaving cooperatives in Kannur and around are a good bet.

Kanchipuram silk saris are a popular pick across Tamil Nadu

- **Food items:** Kerala's aromatic spices, rich coffee, Kozhikodan halwa and tea from Munnar come in attractive packages perfect for gifts. The typical banana, tapioca and jackfruit chips are another popular buy.

Tamil Nadu

- **Saris:** It is almost impossible to visit Tamil Nadu and return without purchasing a sari. **T Nagar** (p314) in Chennai, with a large number of stores like Nalli, Kumaran Silks, Pothys and RMKV, is ideal for sari shopping.

  While Kanjeevaram silk saris are famous, Tamil Nadu also offers a wide variety of silks from regions like Arani and Dharmavaram. You can also buy beautiful cotton saris with traditional motifs of flowers and peacocks. Kanjeevaram silk saris can be purchased directly from weavers in **Kanchipuram** (p314).

- **Food items:** In the Nilgiris you can pick up a variety of tea – from green tea, black tea, and leaves of various strengths. Ooty and Kodaikanal are also famous for homemade chocolates (p401, 430).

- **Jewellery:** Tamilians love their gold jewellery and that is evident from the large number of gold shops in any city you visit. Even if you are not buying gold ornaments, it is worth visiting a store just to see the huge variety of designs available. Designs are intricate, such as the unique Nakkash jewellery of Coimbatore. You can also check out temple jewellery, which is generally made of silver with gold plating and worn by Bharatanatyam dancers. Sukra at Mylapore in Chennai is synonymous with dance jewellery.

- **Antiques:** The antique market in **Karaikudi** (p362) and numerous shops on the Chennai–Puducherry stretch are great for bargains on antiques. Apart from unique furniture, you can also pick up Raja Ravi Verma prints and Tanjore paintings in an antique finish. If your budget permits, splurge on a genuine Tanjore painting.

Andhra Pradesh

- **Handicrafts:** You can plan an entire trip on a crafts trail of the state. Bidriware (inlaid metal), Nirmal paintings, brassware, textiles, wooden toys and curios all form the vast repertoire. The government handicraft outlet, Lepakshi, is located all over the state and is the best place to pick souvenirs at a reasonable price. You even can stop in villages to get first hand insight, **Pochampally** (p481), **Uppada** (p465), **Mangalagiri** and **Pedana** (p469) can be done by detours from Hyderabad, Visakhapatnam and Vijayawada.
- **Wooden toys:** Visit the small village of **Kondapalli** (p468), where wooden toys and bangles are hewn out of soft wood. **Etikoppaka** (p465), also famous for its bright wooden toys, lies on the same route and makes for a quick stop.
- **Textiles and saris:** Andhra handlooms come in beautiful weaves and patterns. Kalamkari, made with hand-printed vegetable-dye patterns, is the signature textile of the state. Amongst saris, Venkatagiri, Dharmavaram and Gadwal are popular weaving styles and can be found in sari shops across the state. The prices at the showrooms are likely to be at least 40% higher than at the weaving villages.
- **Pearls:** In Hyderabad, visit the Old City for an array of cultured pearls. Old stalwarts like **Mangatrai Ramkumar** (p490) will help you select pieces, studded in gold or silver as per your budget. If you are looking for something exquisite, the 'Basra' pearls are unmatched in lustre, smoothness and colour, which are the intrinsic characteristics of pearls.

An array of quality pearls are available in Hyderabad

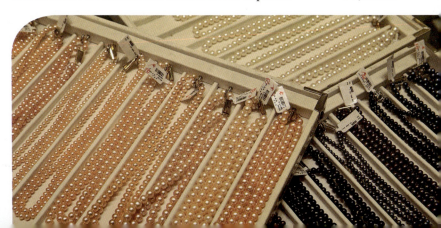

Travelling with Kids

A family trip in South India promises a safe and fun experience, as the infrastructure is reasonably good. But some places may be a historical overdose for youngsters, so plan carefully to intersperse your itinerary with attractions that suit the entire family.

Marina Beach is popular among families

Outdoor Attractions

- **National Parks:** The reserve forests along the Western Ghats work like a charm for youngsters. The lure of seeing animals at close quarters in guided jeep safaris can keep kids engaged for a long time. Parks like **Periyar Tiger Reserve** (p261) have multiple options for a trip into the jungle, of which the bamboo raft promises a unique experience. **Bandipur** (p88), **Nagarhole National Park** (p91) and **BRT Wildlife Sanctuary** (p92) are other good options for kids.
- **Adventure:** The entire Western Ghats stretch and beaches along both the coasts have plenty of water sports and adventure activities. Surfing, scuba diving, canoeing, rafting and camping opportunities are popular with kids. Make sure that you discuss their suitability with organisers.

In forested and hilly areas, easy hikes, camping, rappelling, rafting and rock climbing can be fun for children. Places like

Coorg (p106), **Badami** (p170) and **Dandeli** (p168) are packed with such activities.

- **Boat Rides:** A houseboat ride in Kerala can be a good way to wind down after sightseeing. However, if the lazy pace does not match the energy levels of kids, opt for a speedboat ride to **Pathiramanal** (p219) in the Vembanad Lake, close to Alappuzha. A cruise on the Godavari in Andhra Pradesh or a short boat ride in the Kaveri is equally thrilling.
- **Elephant Interaction:** Pachyderm friends are what the kids might remember for a long time. At **Carmelgiri Elephant Park** (p268) in Munnar and **Elephant Junction** (p262) in Kumily, you can feed and bathe the huge creatures. **Dubare Elephant Camp** (p104) near Madikeri is also a good option.
- **Theme Parks:** Take a break from sightseeing and spend a day at **Wonder La** (p239) in Ernakulum, **Ocean Park** (p489) in Hyderabad or **Maharaja World** (p405) in Coimbatore.
- **Folk Performances:** Abridged folk performances are a lively form of evening entertainment. There are venues in all four states where you can enjoy these shows, like **Greenix Village** (p252) in Fort Kochi and **Kishkinda Trust** (p187) in Hampi.
- **Beaches:** Arm the young ones with a pail and a plastic shovel to build sand castles in the flat sandy stretches of **Lighthouse Beach** (p202) in Kovalam, **Marina Beach** (p299) in Chennai or **Rushikonda Beach** (p456) in Visakhapatnam. Beaches along Karnataka's coast are also good.

Quick Facts

- **Cribs and high chairs:** Most restaurants have high chairs for toddlers, and some have cribs that can be used for infants, while you eat.
- **Food:** The good thing is that you will find plain rice and curd or idlis and dosa anywhere in the four states.
- **Medical facilities:** While bigger towns and the capital cities have good medical facilities, keep prescription medicines and a basic medical kit handy. Many hotels provide a doctor-on-call facility.
- **Hygiene:** It's best to carry a toilet paper roll, liquid soap and hand sanitisers. The quality of highway loos is not top-notch.

Family Hotels

Ask for family rooms or suites to accommodate extra beds for children. This is an economical option. Most of the large resorts ensure supervised game rooms, easy hikes, sightseeing trips and cultural shows. Choosing a homestay is a good way to understand the culture of a place.

What's New

Though deeply rooted in its ancient culture, the southern states are not averse to change. Attractive additions, from malls, pubs, museums and festivals to fresh travel activities are being added every year.

A popular paragliding festival is held at Vagamon

Karnataka

• **Microlight Flying, Coorg (p106):** A two-seater open plane takes you to a height of 3500 ft. This one is certainly not for the faint-hearted.

• **Bangalore Boulevard (p58):** Stripped off its green cover while the metro rail was being constructed, the boulevard along Bengaluru's MG Road has been redeemed. It's now a kilometre-long stretch of art galleries, play areas, craft corners and community spaces. Visitors to Bengaluru will enjoy this new avatar of the historic street.

Tamil Nadu

• **Summer Swell Challenge, Puducherry:** Brothers, Juan and Samai Reboul, initiated the Summer Swell Challenge for surfing enthusiasts. The competition began in 2012 with surfers from around the world. In 2013, it took place in August and was more like a cultural festival with surfing taking the main stage.

• **Phoenix Market City Mall, Chennai:** The latest addition to the mall scene of the city, the Phoenix Market City Mall has the best of shopping, dining and entertainment on offer. It's located in Vellacherry, near the airport and when fully constructed will be the largest mall in the city.

Kerala

• **Malabar River Festival, Kozhikode:** A white-water kayaking festival was launched in August last year near Kozhikode in the Iruvanjhipuzha and Chalipuzha Rivers. It had thrilling

competitions like Giant Slalom, Boater Cross, Free Style and Down River Race.
- **Paragliding, Vagamon:** An annual paragliding festival launched in March 2013 has been a huge success in this town.
- **Spice Coast Open, Kovalam:** A three-day surfing festival was launched along the clear sands of Kovalam in May 2013 and is expected to be regular on the calendar.
- **Keralam, Museum of History & Heritage, Thiruvananthapuram (p196):** Keralam was opened in February 2011. It has a range of exhibits starting from the Neolithic age, murals, sculptures, coins and more.
- **Lulu Shopping Mall, Ernakulam (p254):** A trip here is going to be much more than a shopping expedition. India's largest mall, that opened in March 2013 has a skating rink, gaming zone, a 12-lane bowling alley and a 5D cinema experience.
- **Kochi-Muziris Biennale:** A multi-venue three month-long contemporary art festival showcased the work of 90 artistes from 24 countries across the world. The exhibits were displayed across Ernakulam and Fort Kochi and this is expected to be a regular event.

Kochi is home to the country's largest mall, Lulu

Get Inspired

Books

God of Small Things (Arundhati Roy, 1997) Booker winner for the year, Roy's story of seven-year-old fraternal twins is based in Aymanam village off Kumarakom.

A Century of Tales From City & Cantonment (Peter Colaco, 2003) A light hearted nostalgic account of 'Bangalore' as it was back then by the late Peter Colaco. If nothing else, you will be able to relate to the city instantly.

Where the Rain is Born: Writings About Kerala (edited by Anita Nair, 2002) The book is a compilation of stories, essays and poems written by some of the most esteemed modern English and Malayalam authors of India. It is a journey into the variety of experiences that Kerala has to offer.

Life of Pi (Yann Martel, 2001) In this fantasy adventure novel the protagonist Pi, is a Tamil boy from Puducherry.

Films

Chennai Express (2013) The Shah Rukh Khan and Deepika Padukone starrer that traces SRK's journey from Mumbai to Rameswaram is set in Tamil Nadu, with shooting taking place in Rameswaram, Vattamalai Murugan Temple and Munnar.

Rowdy Rathore (2012) Akshay Kumar and Sonakshi Sinha can be seen gyrating to the song *Dhadang Dhang* in the Vithalla Temple of Hampi.

7 Khoon Maaf (2011) Parts of this movie which showed Priyanka's long journey, were shot at Neemrana Hotel in Coorg, Mysore Palace, Mysore Race Course and Puducherry.

Karthik Calling Karthik (2010) The psychological thriller starring Deepika Padukone and Farhan Akhtar drifts from Mumbai to Kerala, when the protagonist (Akhtar) is looking to detach himself from his ladylove. Parts of the movie were shot in Fort Kochi.

Raavan (2010) Mani Ratnam shot parts of the film at Athirappally Falls. Abhishek Bachchan, playing a bandit, chooses to capture and torture Aishwarya Rai, a policeman's wife, here.

3 Idiots (2009) This Aamir Khan starrer, that shows his journey as a student was shot in the campus of the Indian Institute of Management (IIM), Bengaluru.

Nishabd (2007) The older Bachchan starrer, Nishabd, was shot in Munnar. The neat tea lined hills are a refreshing backdrop to the unconventional love story.

Life of Pi is a novel about a young boy from Puducherry in Tamil Nadu

The song *Jiya Jale* from Mani Ratnam's *Dil Se* was filmed in Kerala

Guru (2007) The song, *Barso Re*, with Aishwarya Rai was shot near the Athirappally Falls. Yet another Mani Ratnam film.

Dil Se (1998) Kerala with its backwaters and houseboats became the location choice for the Shah Rukh Khan-Preity Zinta song *Jiya Jale* and the famous song *Chaiyya Chaiyya* is shot on top of the Mettupalayam-Ooty route on the Nilgiri Mountain Railway.

Websites

Karnataka (www.karnatakatourism.org) Important contacts and thematic information under heads like Beach, Heritage, Nature and more are the highlights of this website.

Kerala (www.keralatourism.org) A comprehensive platform to plan your trip as per festivals and experiences of the state.

Tamil Nadu (www.tamilnadutourism.org) Complete information of state run tours and guesthouses can be looked up here.

Andhra Pradesh (www.aptdc.gov.in) An exhaustive list of things to do can be seen on this government website.

A scene from *Raavan*, shot at Athirappally Falls in Kerala

🎬 *The Hollywood Connection*

THE MYTH (2005) Parts of this Jackie Chan and Mallika Sherawat starrer were shot in the ruins of Hampi.

LIFE OF PI (2012) The initial part of this recent blockbuster, was shot in Puducherry, as the protagonist Pi Patel spent his childhood here before the epic journey at sea.

BEFORE THE RAINS (2007) Nandita Das and Linus Roache make the atypical couple as a village woman and a spice baron, in the period drama. The movie is set in the 1930s in the Malabar region. *Before the Rains* won the Best Theatrical Feature at the World Fest in Houston.

COTTON MARY (1999) An Ismail-Merchant production, the movie is about a British woman living in India. Fort Kochi was the ideal backdrop to this period film.

SOUTH INDIA'S BEST TRIPS

- Karnataka 50
- Kerala 188
- Tamil Nadu 290
- Andhra Pradesh 446

▌ Pamban Bridge leading to Rameswaram is the second longest sea bridge in the country

South India at a Glance

With their ability to inspire, thrill and confound all at once, these four states present an extraordinary spectrum of travel experiences. From a gorgeous coastline running thousands of kilometres, lush landscapes, tea and coffee plantations to ancient temples with grand architecture they will leave you spellbound.

KARNATAKA P50
Karnataka offers culture, history and art, and doffs its hat to modernity with a chilled beer.

KERALA P188
From backwaters, beaches and historic towns to spice and tea plantations, Kerala's exotic locations are a treasure to explore.

Thiruvanathapuram

SOUTH INDIA AT A GLANCE

ANDHRA PRADESH P446
With unexplored beaches, hills, ancient temple towns, handicraft hubs and buzzing cities, Andhra Pradesh presents a huge variety.

● Hyderabad

● Bengaluru

Chennai ●

TAMIL NADU P290
Temple towns, historic beaches, traditional arts and famous cuisine – sample the colours and taste of Tamil Nadu.

Karnataka

Why Go?

With diverse landscapes and a rich history of ancient kingdoms, Karnataka offers a variety of experiences. The capital, **Bengaluru**, infuses a dash of cosmopolitan flavour, while keeping its easy paced charm intact.

Follow the trajectory of the Wodeyar rulers and Tipu Sultan in **Mysore**, closeby. Go back in time to the state's most glorious period in architecture by exploring Vijayanagar ruins in **Hampi** and visiting Hoysala temples in **Halebidu and Belur**.

Karnataka's hilly, coffee stalwarts **Coorg**, **Chikmagalur** and **Sakleshpur** have lots in store for nature lovers – from plantation life, trekking trails, birdwatching to outrageously green landscape. The same goes for wildlife hotspots like **Bandipur**, **Kabini** and **Dandeli**. On the other hand the relatively unexplored coastal stretch of **Mangalore**, **Udupi**, **Gokarna** and **Karwar** give visitors access to the most pristine beaches, a vibrant cultural coastal life and secret surfing spots.

Getting There & Away

Air: Bengaluru and Mangalore are the two international airports in the state with daily flights to all metros and major cities. Other important airports are in Mysore and Hubli though they both have limited connectivity.

Train: With a robust network of trains, the Southern Railways manages to connect most of the key travel destinations of Karnataka by multiple options. Only a few places need to be further accessed by road. Important nodal stations include Bengaluru, Yesvantpur, Hospet for Hampi, Hubli, Mangalore and Udipi for the coast, and Mysore for places like Bandipur, Coorg and other southwestern destinations. Book two months in advance on www.irctc.com.

■I The Mysore Palace is beautifully illuminated every Sunday

Karnataka Map

⭐ 10 Best Trips

① **Bengaluru** (p56) Pub crawls, coffee shops, and a burgeoning alternative vibe, this is Bengaluru for you.

② **Mysore** (p78) This town hoards vast history in its palace and other monuments.

③ **Bandipur & Around:** (p86) Bandipur, Masinagudi, Kabini-Nagarhole and BRT Wildlife Sanctuary are the wildlife stalwarts of the state.

④ **Coorg** (p98) Surrounded with coffee plantations, Coorg offers many adventure sports.

⑤ **Chikmagalur & Sakleshpur** (p112) While Chikmagalur has plenty of options for adventure lovers, Sakleshpur stuns with gorgeous mountain scenery.

⑥ **Belur & Halebidu** (p124) These temple towns mesmerise with intricate workmanship in the temples.

⑦ **Mangalore, Udipi & Around** (p130) Skirting the Arabian Sea, Udipi and Mangalore have buzzing beaches and isolated spots as well.

⑧ **Gokarna, Karwar & Dandeli** (p150) Gokarna and Karwar are dotted with scenic beaches, while Dandeli is great for rafting.

⑨ **Badami, Pattadakal & Aihole** (p170) Cliffs in Badami and temples in Pattadakal and Aihole make for a great visit.

⑩ **Hampi** (p180) Explore the ruins of over 20 temples in this Unesco World Heritage Site.

Coorg is a great place for camping in the state

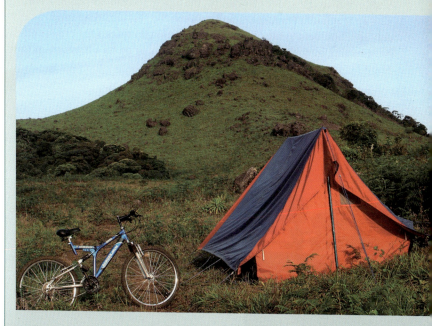

Top Highlights

1 Hampi & Anegundi

The erstwhile Vijayanagara Kingdom, Hampi (p180), and its relatively unknown neighbour, Anegundi, transport you to a world of unique relics in the form of ruined temples and buildings that are more than 700 years old. Scattered through a rocky landscape, the topography looks magnificent. The Tungabhadra River meanders between the vast jumble of sand coloured boulders, neatly cutting the area into two sides. One can spend hours sitting by the river admiring the boulders or go on a monument trail.

2 Plantation life, Chikmagalur

Vintage styled bungalows, cottages and plantation homes in Chikmagalur (p112) give visitors a chance to experience plantation life at close quarters. The small coffee town offers a soothing holiday replete with nature walks, coffee orientation with planters, mild hikes or a getaway with absolutely no agenda. Staying at a plantation bungalow also means that you get to taste the traditional Malnad food of the region.

3 Adventure activities, Coorg

An opulence of wild terrains, high mountain peaks and ferocious river makes the Western Ghats of Karnataka an adventure zone, placing Coorg (p106) on the map for outdoor enthusiasts. Rafting down the Barapole or Kaveri rivers is popular, along with treks like Tadiyandamol and Brahmagiri. Travellers can also camp on the fringes of the Harangi Reservoir or whet their canoeing skills in the calm parts of the Kaveri. Relatively new sports like micro light flying are also catching up fast.

4 Badami, Pattadakal & Aihole

The Chalukyan expertise in transforming sand coloured boulders and caves into masterpieces of architecture can still mesmerise travellers. The monument trail of the three towns (p170) offers an inimitable experience of 7th and 8th century temples built in Dravidian styles, with an infusion of north Indian architectural nuances. Of these, the four Badami caves merging into a hilly cliff are the most popular. The exquisite carvings, murals, sculptures and even inscriptions in old Kannada script, which are still intact in the hollows of the caves, bear testimony to the architectural skills of an earlier age.

Bengaluru

This city scores high with the discerning traveller who is ready to soak in its cosmopolitan identity and is equally thrilled to explore the remnants of its Hindu, Mughal and colonial ties. Revel in its lively pub culture, art scene and ever-pleasant weather. Bengaluru is also a perfect base to explore other Deccan destinations of India.

Trip Planner

GETTING THERE

The Bengaluru International Airport has daily flights to all metros and other major cities. The city is an important node on the South Indian Railways and Indian Railways sector. The main trains from the metros are Udyan Express (6529) from Mumbai, Karnataka Express (2628) from New Delhi and Shatabdi Express (12007) from Chennai.

SUGGESTED ITINERARY (5 DAYS)

Given that Bengaluru is not too large, it is easy to explore its key sights in five days. Keep a day to orient yourself to the city's vibe with a guided walk, followed by a stroll down the arterial MG Road. The major sightseeing options can easily be covered in a couple of days. Keep the fourth day for shopping and meandering through markets in the old city, followed by a daylong trip to the outskirts. Keep all your evenings to experience the effervescent pub culture and restaurants here.

BEST TIME TO GO

J F M A **M J J A S O N** D

GREAT FOR

Top 5 highlights

- Rangoli Metro Art Center (p58)
- National Gallery of Modern Art (p58)
- Bangalore Palace (p58)
- Tipu Sultan's Palace (p60)
- Parks of Bengaluru (p61)

Urbane Medley

Skyline of Bengaluru at dusk

Most people refer to the city by its former name 'Bangalore' possibly because it exudes a sense of nostalgia and belonging, even to those who come here for a short while. It must be the city's deep-rooted tradition of amicability and acceptance, which has given **Bengaluru** its cosmopolitan vibe. Today, this IT hub of India is a melange of energetic youthfulness in its love for music, food, pubs, art, culture and tradition. It has a pulsating ambience and the pleasant weather only adds to its many attractions.

In the mid 17th century the waning hold of the city's founder Kempe Gowda resulted in its transfer into the hands of the rulers of Mysore, namely father-son duo Hyder Ali and Tipu Sultan, and eventually to the British in late 18th century. Till date, religious and holy structures are scattered around the city, but this just makes its cultural tapestry more vibrant.

Highlights

1. Rangoli Metro Art Center (Bangalore Boulevard)
2. National Gallery of Modern Art
3. Bangalore Palace
4. ISKCON Temple
5. Dodda Basavanaguddi (Bull Temple) & Ganesha Temple
6. Tipu Sultan's Palace
7. Venkatappa Art Gallery & Government Museum
8. Temple Street, Malleshwaram
9. Jawaharlal Nehru Planetarium
10. The Heritage Centre & Aerospace Musuem

❶ RANGOLI METRO ART CENTER (BANGALORE BOULEVARD)

In May 2013, the much-awaited, restored boulevard of MG Road which had been disfigured by the metro construction, was opened. Now we have a much better version of the older hang-out spot: a two tiered pathway with a gallery, shops, children's play area, artisan's hub and even a friendship band-tying corner all along the 500m stretch below the metro. Afternoon is the best time to visit.

www.rmac.bmrc.co.in; Boulevard MG Rd; 10am–7pm

❷ NATIONAL GALLERY OF MODERN ART

The venue of this gallery is a 100-year-old restored heritage building, dotted with gigantic shady trees, fountains and gardens. It hosts exhibitions by eminent artists, workshops, film screenings, talks and events centred on music, theatre and dance. Book yourself for the free walks, 'Introduction to the language of visual art' (Wednesday, 3pm) and 'Introduction to Modern Indian Art' (Saturday, 10.30am).

www.ngmaindia.gov.in; 49 Palace Rd, Vasanthanagar; adult/child/foreigner ₹10/1/150; 10am–5pm; Mon closed

❸ BANGALORE PALACE

The private residence of the royal Wodeyar family, the ivy-clad Bangalore Palace, constructed by Rev. Garrett, is considered a replica of the Windsor Castle in London. Now owned by the Mysore royal family, its lavish interiors

✓ Top Tip: Getting around the city

The metro rail covers only six stops, so autorickshaws (minimum fare is ₹20) are the best way to get around, though you should be prepared to haggle. Cabs cost ₹1200 for 8 hr/80km.

preserve a slice of royal life. Take the well-organised audio tour of the ballroom on the ground floor and the elaborate Durbar Hall on the first, packed with paintings, artefacts, mounted animal heads and more. A horse carriage ride around the palace grounds in an old buggy is also available.
☏ 080 23360818; 1 Palace Rd, Vasanthanagar; Indian/foreigner/camera/mobile photography ₹225/450/675/280; 10am–5.30pm

> Bangalore Palace is said to be a replica of Windsor Castle in London

❹ ISKCON TEMPLE

The International Society for Krishna Consciousness (ISKCON) temple is a massive complex lavishly decorated in a mix of ultra-contemporary and traditional styles. It accommodates hundreds of visitors and devotees each day. Meticulously run, the complex has ten temples and an eatery (7.30am–2pm, 4.30–9pm). Strains of 'Hare Rama, Hare Krishna' provide a constant backdrop to your visit.
☏ 080 23471956; www.iskconbangalore.org; West Chord Rd, Hare Krishna Hall, 1st Block Rajaji Nagar; 4.15–5 am, 7.15 am–1pm, 4.15–8.30pm

❺ DODDA BASAVANAGUDDI (BULL TEMPLE) & GANESHA TEMPLE

Built in 1537, this temple is dedicated to Shiva's vehicle, Nandi. A large rocky outcrop, known as Bugle Rock,

Tipu Sultan's palace dates back to the 18th century

straddles the temple compound as you walk towards the right from the adjacent Ganesha Temple. The towering 15ft high Nandi statue is said to be one of the biggest in India.
Basavanagudi; 7.30am–8.30pm

❻ TIPU SULTAN'S PALACE
Enter through a well-manicured garden to the deceptively double storeyed, rather inornate palace of Tipu Sultan (1781) located in a crowded city market. Incongruous with the development all around it, the palace sits like an oasis in between modern buildings. The palace is notable for its Indo-Islamic architectural features. Besides that, wooden pillars and the unexpectedly cool flooring on the ground floor are the highlights.
📞 080 26706836; Albert Victor Rd, Chamrajpet; Indian/foreigner/video ₹5/100/25; 8.30am–5.30pm

❼ VENKATAPPA ART GALLERY & GOVERNMENT MUSEUM
An assortment of artefacts, weathered utility objects, weapons, musical instruments and paintings (following no clear trajectory) are spread over the double-storeyed halls of the museum. However, there are only a few references to the

16th-century king, Tipu Sultan. The attached Venkatappa Gallery has a collection of well-displayed sculptures dating back to 2nd century AD. It preserves several works and personal memorabilia of K. Venkatappa, the court painter to the Wodeyar royal family.
☎ 080 22864483; Kasturba Rd; adult/child ₹4/2; 10am–5pm

❽ TEMPLE STREET, MALLESHWARAM
See the four magnificent temples in the decidedly Hindu part of town, Malleshwaram – **Kadu Malleshwara, Nandeeshwara, Lakshmi Narsimha** and **Gangamma Devi Temple**. The grandest of the four is the Kadu Malleshwara Temple. True to its name, the Shiva temple lies in a thicket of greens – 'kadu' means forest in Kannada. Its tranquil environment is an alluring backdrop for meditation and yoga. On the opposite side of the road, Nandeeshwara's legacy goes back 7000 years; the temple was excavated much later from beneath layers of soil. Gangamma Devi and Lakshmi Narsimha Temple lie adjacent to Kadu Malleshwara, and are usually packed with morning worshippers.
Basavanagudi; 7.30am–noon, 5pm–8.30pm

> ## 📷 *Snapshot: Kempe Gowda's legacy*
>
> To mark the city boundaries, founder Kempe Gowda built four cardinal towers in 1537. History lovers can give it a whirl by visiting all four. One of the towers lies atop a hillock in Lal Bagh, the second at the edge of Ulsoor Lake, a hidden one near Kempambudhi Lake, close to the Bandi Mahakali temple at Hanumanthanagar and the last one stands near the Mekhri circle underpass in a park.

If You Like: Parks

- **Lal Bagh Botanical Gardens** (Lal Bagh, Mavalli; adult/parking ₹10/10; 6am–7pm): Spread over 240 acres, Lal Bagh has one of the largest collections of rare botanical gems. The highlights of the park, which spreads around one of the four towers erected by the city's founder, Kempe Gowda, include a glasshouse, and a hillock made up of 3000 million-year-old peninsular gneissic rock.
- **Cubbon Park:** Statues of Queen Victoria and King Edward, gazebos, thickets of bamboo, grassy stretches, a tennis academy, a children's park and rocky outcrops are encompassed inside the 300 acres of Cubbon Park. It also houses three monuments: Seshadri Iyer Memorial Library, State Archeological Museum and Attara Kacheri (court).

The Jawaharlal Nehru Planetarium is a hit with kids

🟠 JAWAHARLAL NEHRU PLANETARIUM

Established in 1989, the planetarium and science park is a great place if you are travelling with kids. There are 30 science exhibits and 45-minute shows that are regularly held in the spacious campus located in the heart of the city. A recently launched show that the kids might like, 'Dawn of the Space Age', starts at 1.30pm.

📞 080 22379725; www.taralaya.org; Sri T. Chowdaiah Rd, High Grounds; adult/child ₹35/20; show timings in English 12.30pm, 1.30pm, 4.30pm; Mon and second Tues closed

🟠 HERITAGE CENTRE & AEROSPACE MUSEUM

Six decades of India's aviation history is depicted in neat, meticulously placed exhibits and photographs at the HAL Museum. It also has models of early planes and helicopters used by the Indian aviation industry. Interesting exhibits include the infamous MIG-21, homegrown models such as the Marut and Kiran, and a vintage Canberra bomber. One can also climb to the Heritage Centre's Air Traffic Control Tower to view the runway of the old airport.

www.hal-india.com; Old Airport Rd; entry/camera ₹30/50; 9am–5pm

Detour: Day-trips around Bengaluru

Bengaluru is the hub to explore the rest of the Deccan destinations and many can be done in a daylong trip.

- **Banerghatta National Park** (☏080 22352828; entry ₹50, safari and zoo ₹210, butterfly park ₹20, camera/video ₹25/110; 9am–5pm, Grand safari 11am–4pm; Tues closed): Make your way to this national park, 22km from Bengaluru to enjoy a day in the wild. The canter safari takes you through a small section of this sprawling park and if you are lucky, you can spot the bison, bears and deer. The tigers don't roam around freely and are usually caged. Banerghatta National Park is home to a zoo and a butterfly park as well.

- **Nrityagram** (☏080 28466314; www.nrityagram.org; entry ₹50; children below 12 years and senior citizens free; 10am–2pm, dance classes 10.30am–1pm; Mon closed): The serene campus of Nrityagram Dance School, 35km from Bengaluru, started by Odissi exponent, late Protima Bedi, makes for a refreshing weekend getaway. Here you can learn about a unique Gurukul system amid a scenic backdrop, where architect Gerard De Cunha's nature-inspired architecture merges perfectly with the rural setting.

- **Nandi Hills and Bhoganandeeswara Temple:** Located 57km off the city, Nandi Hills is popular for its scenic views complemented by hot tea and noodles. There are a few attractions here like Tipu Drop and the Veer Bhadra Swamy Temple. At the foothills, lies the thousands of years old Shiva temple, Bhoganandeeswara. Sit by the Kalyani River and admire the 9th-century architecture of this beautiful temple.

At Nrityagram you can learn about traditional forms of dance

Accommodation

ITC Gardenia   Hotel ₹₹₹
📞 080 40580444; www.itchotels.in; No. 1, Residency Rd; d from ₹12,000–3,75,000 (incl of breakfast) Suffused in green, ITC's latest addition to Bengaluru's five-star accommodation scene is the eco-inclined Gardenia. With uniquely themed rooms, a helipad, pool, spa and six dining options, this makes for a great stay option. Cubbon Pavilion, the multi-cuisine fine dining restaurant is open round the clock.

The Leela Palace   Hotel ₹₹₹
📞 080 25211234; www.theleela.com; 23 Old Airport Rd, Kodihalli, d from ₹14,500–27,000 (incl of breakfast) Enjoy the high-end facilities, aesthetic Indian interiors and rich ambience of one of the poshest addresses in town. The hotel's dull pink architecture has been inspired by the royal splendour of Mysore and a theme of 'Indian opulence' runs through it. It has three restaurants, two bars, a swimming pool, spa, and a shopping arcade.

The LaLiT Ashok   Hotel ₹₹₹
📞 080 30527777; www.thelalit.com; Kumara Krupa High Grounds; d from ₹9000 (incl of breakfast) Overlooking the world's fifth oldest golf course, Bangalore Golf Club, the hotel's pleasingly green ambience makes you instantly forget the city's traffic woes. Its five-star amenities are in top shape, especially the spa, Rejuve. The cuisines at the restaurants range from Pan Asian to north Indian. Access to the golf course is an additional facility.

Purple Lotus   Boutique Hotel ₹₹₹
📞 080 40056300; www.purplelotus.in; 46, 6th Cross, Lavelle Rd; d from ₹9000–9500, ste ₹9950 (incl of breakfast) Just off St. Marks Road, this boutique hotel is sprinkled with lotus ponds and lotus themed stone art. The hotel's glass and dark wood decor is minimalistic, with plants adding some green to the rooms. It also has a yoga studio and spa. The hotel was once home to freedom fighter M.V Krishnappa.

Taj Vivanta   Hotel ₹₹₹
📞 080 66604444; www.vivantabytaj.com; 41/3 MG Rd; d from ₹10,000–13,000 (incl of breakfast) At the end of the arterial high street of Bengaluru, MG Road, Vivanta by the Taj group offers its signature five-star luxury in the contemporary decor of the rooms, great hospitality and amenities like a swimming pool and restaurants. The highlights or 'motifs' as the hotel calls it, are guided heritage walks of Bengaluru, Sous Vide Culinary Art (a style of cooking at Graze, the in-house restaurant) and pampering your senses with customised gourmet fare.

Jüsta Hotels   Boutique Hotel ₹₹
📞 080 41135555; www.justahotels.com; No.21/14, Craig Park Layout, MG Rd; d from ₹5000–5500, ste

₹9000 (incl of breakfast) If gorgeous art from Tagore's Shantiniketan in the lobby doesn't impress you, the cosy and aesthetic rooms definitely will. This 18-room boutique hotel has a multi-cuisine restaurant and the service is prompt.

Escape   Hotel ₹₹
080 42415555; www.escapehotels.in; #770, 100 Ft Rd, Indiranagar; d from ₹5500–6000 (incl of breakfast) Inspired by the world's most stylish cities (New York, London and Tokyo), the 30-room boutique hotel has contemporary interiors, immaculate personalised service and amenities like a rooftop pool, spa and gymnasium. Centrally located, it is close to the city's favourite shopping destinations and business centres. Dig into an elaborate Parsi menu along with other Indian and continental cuisines at the dreamily white, partially open-air restobar, Bricklane Grill.

Jayamahal Palace   Heritage Hotel ₹₹
080 40580444; www.jayamahalpalace.in; 1, Jayamahal Rd; d from ₹4500, ste ₹7000–8000 (incl of breakfast) Wooden floors thumping below carpets, high ceilings and the sprawling rooms of Jayamahal Palace are testimony to the century-old colonial architecture of this 19-acre property of the Raja of Gondal. Facilities include a pool, multi-cuisine restaurants and a bar. If you want an economical option, the standard rooms in the hotel's non-heritage wing are comfortable.

Casa Cottage   Heritage Hotel ₹₹
080 22990337; www.casacottage.com; 2 Clapham Rd, Richmond Town, behind Richmond Town Post Office; d from ₹3600–4500 (incl of breakfast) A peaceful retreat, Casa Cottage's

> ## TOP CHOICE *Places to stay*
> - **ITC Gardenia** (p64) An eco hotel with six dining options and a helipad.
> - **Escape** (p65) Central location, contemporary interiors and a multi-cuisine restaurant.
> - **Villa Pottipati** (p66) A heritage hotel with an old-world charm.
> - **Villa Camelot** (p66) A charming Bed & Breakfast option.

Rooms at Casa Cottage are done up with period furniture and overlook a lush grassy patch

legacy of over 95 years is intact in its vintage look, period furniture and soothing ambience. Opt for the more spacious rooms on the first floor, which have great private sit-outs overlooking a grassy patch. The cafe by the garden serves only breakfast. Casa Cottage is great for travellers looking for a heritage experience and personalised service in the heart of this city.

Villa Pottipati   **Heritage Hotel ₹₹**
📞 080 23360777; www.neemranahotels.com; 142, 8th Cross, 4th Main, Malleshwaram; s/d from ₹3000–5500 (incl of breakfast)
One of Bengaluru's best-kept secrets, Villa Pottipati draws you into its classic, old city charm with black and white pictures, antiques and dated furniture. Named after the village of the Reddy family that owned it, the five rooms and three suites of the ochre walled garden home are named after traditional south Indian saris.

Villa Camelot   **Bed & Breakfast ₹₹**
📞 080 32723965; www.villa-camelot.com; 94/95, 4th Cross, ECC Rd, Prithvi Layout, Whitefield; d from ₹3000–3700 (incl of breakfast & snacks)
Expect an unforgettable time with hosts Raghu and Yamini, as you share stories over delicious north Indian food, enjoy their hospitality, the open spaces of the modern house and the couple's love for movies, music and Bengaluru. With Indian themes, all the rooms are aesthetically pleasant. The 'Mogra' set of rooms on the ground floor is suitable for large families.

Thyme the Transit   **Service Apartments ₹**
📞 080 25254303; 20 NGEF lane, parallel to CMH Rd, next to Indiranagar metro station, Indiranagar 1st Stage; s/d from ₹1600–1900 (incl of breakfast)
Thyme hits the nail on the head with an apt tariff, proximity to the metro station, clean though spartan rooms, a dining space and good spread for breakfast.

Eating

The cultural amalgam of Bengaluru is reflected in its variety of delicious food that the city

| Dig into the delicious wood-fired thin crust duck pizza at Like That Only

offers. A vast choice of high-end speciality restaurants, friendly cafes and nostalgic outlets make the gastronomic journey through Bengaluru truly delightful.

100 ft. — Boutique Bar & Restaurant ₹₹₹

080 25277752; www.100ft.in; 777/I, 100ft Rd, HAL 2nd Stage, Indiranagar; mains ₹750–1000; 11am–11pm Bengaluru's first boutique restaurant, namesake to the city's most popular high street, has a soothing white and blue ambience – the perfect Mediterranean feel and an equally delicious menu. Simple yet brilliantly cooked and delicious food with excellent service makes 100 ft one of those places with which you can never go wrong.

Like That Only — Continental ₹₹₹

080 65475610; www.likethatonly.in; 14/31A Hagadur Rd, Whitefield; mains ₹740–1000; 11.30am–3pm, 6.30–11pm Making a trip all the way to Whitefield is worth your while for a slice of this self proclaimed, 'irreverent' restaurant, dishing out creative continental concoctions. You will not be disappointed with anything you pick at this warmly lit, partially open-air place.

Sunny's — Continental ₹₹₹

080 41329391; www.sunnysbangalore.in; No 34, Embassy Diamante, Vittal Mallya Rd, opp Canara Bank; mains above ₹1000; noon–3.30pm and 7–11pm Named after a golden retriever, this place is a great pick for the choicest gourmet Italian and European cuisine. If you get confused and are not sure what to order, just go for their wood-fired, thin crust pizzas!

> **TOP CHOICE** *Places to eat*
>
> • **Koshy's** (p69) A favourite with locals, it is famous for a range of dishes, especially appam and stew.
> • **Peppa Zzing** (p71) It offers the biggest burgers in the city.
> • **Corner House** (p71) This place serves delicious ice cream combos.
> • **Mavalli Tiffin Room** (p72) The best place for south Indian food in the city.

Secret Garden — Continental ₹₹

080 41131365; Bldg No. 7/1, Edward Rd, off Queens Rd; mains ₹500–750; 12.30pm–4pm; Sun closed Tucked away in an elusive rooftop, this is a good choice for a hearty lunch of home-made salads, soups and sinful desserts. The menu scribbled on a blackboard and an open kitchen add to the intimacy of this restaurant.

Monkey Bar — Gastropub ₹₹₹

080 41116878; www.mobar.in; 14/1 Krishna Manere, Wood St, Ashok Nagar; mains ₹500–750; noon–11.30pm The 'tongue in cheek' and easy vibe of Monkey Bar

Full of quirky posters, Monkey Bar's decor is funky and colourful

immediately knocks one into a good mood! A vintage Lambretta scooter, quirky posters and an equally fun menu makes this a favourite. Given the bar's young ambience, it is no surprise that dishes like Butterfly Chicken Gangnam Style have found their way into the menu.

Imli Vegetarian ₹₹₹
080 40949464; www.imli.co.in; 204, 5th Main, 7thCross, Indiranagar 1st Stage; mains ₹500–750; 11am–11pm With airy seating on the first floor, this bright yellow cheerful place fills the lacuna of home cooked north Indian vegetarian food. Imli is a perfect place to enjoy Bengaluru's evenings over a lazy cup of tea, some crispy chaat, vada pao and a host of board games. They make certain dishes such as khichdi aur baingan bhaaja, maa ki dal and moong dal cheela transport you to the comfort of your mother's kitchen.

Konark Vegetarian ₹₹
080 41248812; 50, Field Marshall Cariappa Rd, Residency Rd; mains ₹250–500; 8am–10.30pm A delight for vegetarians, Konark's central location, splendid food, family appropriate ambience and prompt service has helped it stay on top of the list for many years.

Empire Multi-Cuisine ₹₹
080 40414041; www.hotelempire.in; No. 36 Church St Rd; mains ₹250–500; 12.30pm–midnight Post drinking hunger pangs bring hoards to one of the 14 Empire restaurants in and around the city (the flagship one being on Church Street) after the pubs close down. Prepare to pounce on the first seat you get and order from the most popular coin parotta, ghee rice, chicken kebab and other Indian and Chinese dishes.

Olive Bar & Kitchen — Mediterranean ₹₹₹
☎ 080 41128400; www.olivebarandkitchen.com; 16, Wood St, Ashok Nagar; mains above ₹1000; noon–11.30pm Decidedly Mediterranean in its white-blue ambience and menu, enjoy the elegant aura of Olive Bar & Kitchen and the delicately prepared dishes they offer. Go there with a generous wallet to enjoy the extensive variety of drinks and food.

Koshy's — Multi-Cuisine ₹₹₹
☎ 080 22213793; No. 39, St. Marks Rd; mains ₹500–750; 9am–11pm Get consumed by the intellectual buzz at this hang-out for authors, artistes and actors (Jawaharlal Nehru and the Queen of England have also eaten here). Uniformed waiters flit around busily with steel trays, balancing favourites like appam and stew, mutton cutlets, potato smileys, tea, baked beans, and caramel custard.

Ebony — Multi-Cuisine ₹₹₹
☎ 080 41783344; www.ebonywithaview.com; Hotel Ivory Tower, The Penthouse Floor, Barton Centre, 84, MG Rd; mains ₹750–1000; 12.30–3pm, 7.30–11pm A spectacular panoramic view of the cityscape from the 13th floor is what Ebony offers along with a substantial multi-cuisine menu. The service can be painfully long – but it enables you to linger over the view.

Mangalore Pearl — Coastal Karnataka ₹₹₹
☎ 080 25578855; www.mangalorepearl.com; #3 Coles Rd, above K.C Das Sweets, Frazer Town; mains ₹500–750; noon–2.45pm, 7.30–10.30pm Seafood aficionados will love this one! Coastal Karnataka cuisine is plated with traditional themed graffiti on all walls by famous cartoonist, Prakash Shetty. Sol Kadi and prawns of Mangalore Pearl are highly recommended.

Mahesh Lunch Room — Seafood ₹₹₹
☎ 080 41311101; opp Bengaluru Club, before Chancery Pavilion, Residency Rd; mains ₹500–750; noon–3.30pm, 7–11.30pm Bengaluru is no more seafood starved! In comes Mahesh Lunch Room, latest addition to 'must try' food joints. Quick service, value for money and seafood expertise makes this cosy joint buzz with customers.

Vidyarthi Bhavan — South Indian ₹
☎ 080 26677588; #32, Gandhi Bazaar Main Rd, Basavanagudi; mains below ₹200; Mon–Thurs 6.30am–11.30am, 2pm–8pm and Sat/Sun/Govt. Holidays 6.30am–noon, 2.30pm–8pm; Fri closed Dishing out south Indian tiffin items and meals since 1943, Vidyarthi Bhavan is a time-tested Bengaluru landmark for old-world ambience and crisp dosas. Clad in traditional dhotis, the waiters flit busily trying to

accommodate long queues at prime breakfast and lunch hours.

Halli Mane — South Indian ₹₹
☎ 080 65611222; www.hallimane.com; 3rd Cross, Sampige Rd, Malleshwaram; mains ₹250–500; 6am–11.30pm The mud plastered walls and hand painted traditional designs, south Indian music and traditionally dressed waiters are in sync with the typical south Indian rural fare (think ragi mudde, kundapura pathrode and akki rotti) served here.

Sri Krishna Cafe — South Indian ₹₹
☎ 080 41104345; 143, KHB Colony, 1st Floor, 60 Feet Rd, 5th Block, Koramangala; mains ₹250–500; 7:30am–11am, noon–3.30pm, 5.30pm–10.30pm For a hearty Tamil style lunch, there is nothing more worthwhile than Sri Krishna Cafe. Do not expect great ambience.

> Imli offers a range of vegetarian delicacies including chaat and vada pao

Just concentrate on ordering from a variety of idlis, pooris, vadas, meals, uthappams, idiyappams etc.

Coorg — Coorgi ₹₹₹
☎ 9845493688; 477 Krishna Temple Rd, 1st Stage, Indiranagar; mains ₹500–750; Fri 8pm–11pm and Sat & Sun noon–3.30pm, 8pm–11pm A 'weekend only' special, Priya and KC Aiyappa ensure that you keep dreaming the whole week for their authentic home-made Coorgi food! Traditional techniques and fresh spices are used in the food. The rooftop buffet area is abuzz with chatter as regulars book ahead for the weekend lunch here.

Daddy's Deli — Parsi ₹₹₹
☎ 080 41154372; www.daddysdeli.in; No: 594, 12th Main Rd, HAL 2nd Stage, Indiranagar; mains ₹500–750; 9am–10.30pm Authentic Parsi delights like dhansak, chicken farcha and laganu custard never disappoint at Daddy's Deli. If you want to hang around here the entire day, Red Fork, the cafe wing is open for waffles, breakfast and even wine.

Thindi Beedi — Street Food ₹
VV Puram; mains less than ₹200; 6.30–11.30pm Old Market Road or Eat Street starts stirring with activity at 6.30pm. Soon, the area bustles with masses of people hollering for their chaat orders, local snacks, juice, paper dosas and sweets. The crowd really

BENGALURU

If You Like: Cafes

A medley of nostalgia, organic goodies, rich coffee and experimental food comes alive in the many cafes of Bengaluru.

- **Cafe Max** (080 41200469; www.cafe-max.in): For authentic German and European cuisine, try the rooftop with green vines drooping from planters, large open windows and cheerful ambience.
- **India Coffee House** (080 25587088; 19, Ground Floor, Church St, Brigade Gardens): Owing to its legendary visitors, namely artistes, freedom fighters and jhola wielding intellectuals, this is a nostalgia soaked stop. Turbaned waiters push the menu and rush you through the meal with frosty hospitality.
- **Lake View** (080 25582161; www.lakeviewmilkbar.com): Make a quick stop at Lake View, one of the oldest establishments (since 1930) on MG Road for the legendary black forest cake.

---

swells after 8pm and buzzes with foodies until 11pm. Try local Kannadiga favourites like milk-dipping chirotti.

Peppa Zzing   Street Food ₹
080 41232843; G-18, Kedia Arcade, 92 Infantry Rd; mains ₹250–500; 11am–11pm Peppa Zzing has definitely notched up the game of burgers with their Whammy and Monster options – the biggest burgers of Bengaluru! A ridiculously big, super thick and juicy burger with 700gm of meat is a great challenge – if you are up for it.

Spoonful of Sugar   Desserts ₹₹₹
080 25255534; 421g, 1st Main, 3rd Cross, 1st Stage, Indiranagar; mains ₹500–750; 9.30am–9.30pm This cosy cafe packs in scrumptious desserts with large helpings that could be an entire meal by themselves. Their Banoffee pie and blueberry cheesecake, are particularly fast to fly off the shelf. Get some insider tips at a baking workshop held by the mother-daughter duo who own this blissful sweet-treat.

Corner House   Desserts ₹₹
080 25583262; www.cornerhouse.in; 45/3 Gopalkrishna Complex near Mayo Hall, Residency Rd; mains ₹250–500; 11am–11.30pm A landmark dessert haunt, Corner House has been dishing out delicious ice cream combos for the last 25 years. The popularity of favourites like 'Death by Chocolate', seasonal fruit and ice cream combos and the classic hot chocolate fudge prompted the chain to open 15 outlets in Bengaluru and around. The ice cream combos are a bit expensive but the size of their serving will fill your tummy for sure.

Airlines   Breakfast ₹
080 22273783; No.4 Madras Bank Rd, off Lavelle Rd; mains less

than ₹200; 7am–10pm Mostly early morning joggers and students bunking college make up the coterie under the two large Banyan trees at Airlines. Do not expect prompt service, but look out for delicious south Indian 'tiffin' items. Enjoy a lazy breakfast of shivage bhath, idlis and dosas, washed down with brilliant coffee! There is a drive-in service as well.

Mavalli Tiffin Room (MTR) Breakfast ₹₹

080 22230471; No. 14 Lal Bagh Rd; mains ₹250–500; 6:30am–11pm, 12.30–2pm, 3.30–8.30pm; dinner on Sat & Sun 7:45–9pm; Mon closed Veer towards MTR for authentic south Indian food with a touch of old Bengaluru nostalgia. The pure veg delights are served in silver plates if you are going with Bengaluru Walks. If on your own, you might need to jostle for space and share the table with strangers. Nevertheless, the experience is enriching.

The Hole in the Wall Breakfast ₹₹

9845464784; No.4, 8th Main, Koramangala 4th Block; mains ₹250–500; Tue–Fri 8am–3pm, 5.30pm–8.30pm, Sat & Sun 8am–3pm; Mon closed The best hangover remedies camouflaged in juicy sausages, veggies and eggs complimented by fresh juices, this is one breakfast place that you don't want to miss.

 Nightlife

For years Bengaluru has been the beer bastion of the country with more than 70 bars and pubs around MG Road. Despite the ban on dancing implemented in 2008, and the time cap of 11pm (often stretched till 11.30pm), the city has held onto its legacy and reinvented its nightlife around breweries and pubs. You will never have a dull evening in this city!

Toit Brew Pub & Eatery

080 25201460; www.toit.in; 298, 100ft Rd, Metro Pillar 62, Indiranagar; 11am–11pm Toit single-handedly redeemed Bengaluru's waning pub culture in 2010, with a much-needed fun and large, wooden floored brewery, which can fit more than 360 happy beer drinkers. Try the Toit Weiss white beer and team it with grilled fish.

Arbor Brewing Company Brew Pub & Eatery

080 50144477; www.arborbrewing.in; Magrath Rd; noon–11.30pm Get more brew savvy with your beer at Arbor Brewing Company. Seven special brews (more to come) are the highlight of this American styled spacious minimalistic brewery! The menu suggests the best pubfare that goes with different ales along with a short history of how it came to be!

BENGALURU

Bl!mey — Pub & Eatery
☏ 080 22086777; Level 05, 1 MG Rd Mall, ½ Swamy Vivekananda Rd, Trinity Circle; 11am–11pm An Irish-English eatery and pub on the 5th floor of 1 MG Mall, with a splendid view (especially at night) promises to become the next big thing in Bengaluru! Its large spread of pub fare like pork ribs is best teamed with Irish themed cocktails. The double tiered and partially open-air space is done up in warm colours with Irish bric-a-brac on the walls. The upper floor has a more lounge-like feel to it. It's the perfect place to spend an afternoon playing board games (Air hockey, Bingo and more) and sipping beer.

Mother Cluckers Bar — Gastropub
☏ 9845096332; 957, 12th Main, Indiranagar; noon–11.30pm The latest addition from the Plan B camp, the snug American pub with industrial interiors and quirky pop Art & advertising posters, Mother Cluckers is great to spend the evening listening to familiar rock music and downing a couple of beers.

Windmills Craftworks — Brew Pub & Eatery
☏ 080 25692012; www.windmillscraftworks.com; #331, Rd 5B, EPIP Zone, Whitefield; 12.30–3pm, 7–11.30pm The book-lined walls, perfect acoustics of a small stage for live gigs and the open-air wooden deck of Windmills is reason enough

MTR is one of the best options in the city for a typical south Indian meal

to splurge on six in-house brews and largely American cuisine, ordered innovatively on a tablet. Since it is on the 5th floor, this place is specially recommended on a breezy evening.

Opus — Gastropub
☏ 9844030198; www.myopus.in; #4, 1st Main, Chakravarthy Layout, Palace Cross Rd; 11.30am–11.30pm This Goan themed watering hole and live-gigs venue, with an octopus as a mascot, is a favourite with karaoke singers (Wednesday and Sunday). Visit the place for an easy-going vibe, Goan cuisine and of course singing.

⭐ Entertainment

The BFlat Bar — Live Music
☏ 080 25278361; 776, 100 Feet Rd, Indiranagar; noon–3.30pm and 7–11.30pm Make your way to BFlat for live gigs by eclectic musicians and performers who come to perform

here from across the world. This cosy bar has an intimate set up, perfect acoustics and offers good cocktails.

Counter Culture — Live Music
☏ 080 41400793; www.counterculture.co.in; #2D2, Whitefield Rd, 4th Cross, Dyavasandra Industrial Area, Mahadevpura; 12.30–3.30pm, 7–11.30pm open **Fri–Sun** Enter through the big, yellow door of Counter Culture to enjoy live performances in music, dance, theatre and comedy. A weekend only alternative space that encourages experiencing rather than just seeing, the wide open spaces here are also a venue for larger festivals.

Ranga Shankara — Theatre
☏ 080 26493982; www.rangashankara.org; No.36/2, 8th Cross, 2nd Phase, next to post office, J P Nagar A world-class theatre space was the brainchild of Bengaluru based, late director, Shankar Nag. His wife and actress, Arundhati realised this dream by building Ranga Shankara, which stages more than 300 plays in different languages each year. Stay updated on their listings through their website.

 ## Activities
Bengaluru's pleasant weather and proximity to outdoor sites throws up some great activities and adventure options.

Thousands of people gather at Vishalakshi Mantap, at the Art of Living centre

Cycling
Art of Bicycle Trips ☏ 9538973506; www.artofbicycletrips.com See Bengaluru's countryside and destinations like Nandi Hills and Nrityagram at close quarters with Art of Bicycle Trips. If you are in the city for long, you can also contact 'atcag' (☏ 7760790038; www.atcag.in), a bicycle sharing system, which will issue you a smartcard; pick your bike from any of the nine docking stations in the city and leave it at another as per your convenience.

Holistic Healing
Home to the world famous spiritual centre, **Art of Living** (www.artofliving.org), Bengaluru also has excellent rejuvenation and healing retreats like **Soukya** (☏ 080 28017000), **Shreyas Yoga Retreat** (☏ 080 27737016) and **Our Native Village** (☏ 080 41140909). Most of these establishments prefer

long stay options, but they offer basic rejuvenation packages for a single day as well.

Heritage Walks
Bangalore Walks ☎ 9845523660; www.bangalorewalks.com It is impossible to understand the tapestry of a city with such vast history and cultural influences in just a few days. Bangalore Walks offers 'easy on the legs' walking tours of the city. The Victorian Bengaluru Walk is particularly popular. It takes you down the small stretch from Trinity Church, covering East Parade Church, landmark buildings and monuments like Mayo Hall, Utility Building and Kittel's statue on MG Road, ending in breakfast at the Barton Centre. The walk is peppered with numerous anecdotes. This is also a good way to see Lal Bagh, Basavanagudi and the old city areas.

Shopping

Levitate Boho Clothing & Accessories
☎ 080 64528190; Mezzanine Floor, 100 Ft Boutique Restaurant, 777/1, 100 Ft Rd, Indiranagar; 11am–9.30pm Biker and an aficionado of all things handcrafted, Meghna Khanna has steered Bengaluru's taste into vibrant boho apparel, kitschy knick-knacks, muted silver and costume jewellery and much more, at this shop inside 100 ft. restaurant.

UB City Mall
www.ubcitybangalore.in; No. 24, Vittal Mallaya Rd; 11am–11.30pm Whether it is browsing through brands like Louis Vuitton, Canali, Ermenegildo Zegna or indulging in the culinary delights at the city's top restaurants, UB City is hard to miss. Multiple restaurants like Fava, Cafe Noir and Toscano serve continental fare while City Bar or Skyee Lounge are great places for a couple of drinks. A central floor fountain, amphitheatre and a shopping arcade adds to the festive feel of the place.

Rain Tree Clothing & Accessories
☎ 080 32723251; No. 4 Sankey Rd, High Grounds; 10am–7pm Hand picked collection of chic hi-end jewellery, designer clothing, antiques, furniture and artefacts can be found in Rain Tree, an old colonial style house converted into a boutique store.

> *If You Like: Books*
>
> For an unusual experience, follow the bookshop trail on MG Road, Brigade Road and Church Street. Nine prominent stores and many pavement shops make for an interesting walk. Don't let the glossy exteriors of shops like **Variety Book House and Magazines** (that also has five resident cats for company) make you miss the history that shaped the reading culture of the city. Pick second hand books at **Book Worm**, **Select** and **Blossoms**.

Ants — Crafts

☎ 080 41715639; www.theantstore.com; #2286, 1st Cross, 14th A Main, HAL II Stage, Indiranagar; 10.30am–8pm Here you can find a range of clothes in Bodo tribal weaves, bamboo baskets, black pottery, footwear, jewellery and more, largely from craftsmen of North Eastern states. A cafe on the first floor offers continental breakfast options (9.30am-8.30pm).

The Orange Bicycle — Clothing & Accessories

☎ 080 41255242; www.theorangebicycle.in; House No. 3353, 5th Cross, 12th A Main, HAL II Stage, Indiranagar; 11am–7.30pm If nothing else, the colourful milieu of shoes, bags, pillows, clothes, clocks, jewellery make a visual treat here. Sourced from over 100 vendors across India, this assortment of pieces is exclusive.

Cauvery Arts & Craft Emporium — Crafts

☎ 080 25581118; www.cauverycrafts.com; 49 MG Rd; 10am–8.30pm Chances are that you will not leave Cauvery without buying something! It has a wide range of prices in products like silver jewellery, inlay work, clothes, toys, bags, brass and sandalwood curios, elaborate furniture and shawls.

aPaulogy Curious Illustration — Art

☎ 8105436700; www.paulfernandes.in; 15 Clarke Rd, Richards Park Entrance, Richards Park; 11am–7pm Sun noon–7pm Explore the laid-back life and times of Bengaluru with cartoonist Paul Fernandes' depiction of the city at a time when riding a cycle in the dark, minus a kerosene oil lamp, was a serious crime. Pick up original prints (₹1300–2500) or bookmarks.

Commercial Street — Market

10.30am–9pm Test your bargaining skills at Commercial Street where there is everything from branded clothes, jewellery, furnishings, shoes to trinkets. Our recommendations include **The Silver Shop** (☎ 9845128759, 28 Commercial Street), **Asiatic Arts & Crafts** (☎ 080 41517915, 133/2 Commercial Street) for antiques and the famous sari haven, **Mysore Sari Udyog**. The shop is plastered with silk, cotton, Kanchipuram and Banarasi goodies.

Chickpet and Avenue Road — Market

11am–8pm Get anything under the sun in this 400-year-old market, right from antiques to crafts. Our picks include the famous Balaji Antiques and some popular sari shops. At **Balaji's** (☎ 9342410288; 64 Balaji Silk Complex, 1st Floor, Avenue Rd) get lost in a jumble of weathered antiques; you can find anything from a few hundreds to lakhs. To get embellished silks and cottons, step into the 90-year-old **Rukmini Hall** (☎ 080 22254938; 711-712, Chickpet) or the even older **Shankari Mahalakshmi Hall** (☎ 080 41242926; No.218 Chickpet).

Expert Recommendation
Best books on Bengaluru

Bengaluru based author of the book *I'll Do It My Way* **Christina Daniels** talks about the best books to read about this incredible city.

Bangalore is a city of many well-kept secrets and hidden layers. And this is perhaps the reason that good writing chronicling the city is rare.

Peter Colaco's **Bangalore** is written in a conversational, anecdotal style, and illustrated by the artist Paul Fernandes. The book strings together a century of tales from the cantonment and the city. While steeped in stories from yesterday, the book takes you straight to the unseen soul of today's Bengaluru.

In more recent times, **Bengaluru, Bangalore, Bengaluru: Imaginations and their Times**, compiled by editors Narendar Pani, Sindhu Radhakrishna and Kishor G Bhat, infuse historical writing on the city with contemporary relevance.

As a city that historically prided itself on its trees, gardens and old-world elegance, Bengaluru has many coffee table books that have tried to capture the city's flowering trees and its visual appeal. My favourite attempt is TP Issar's **The City Beautiful**. Another interesting project was late photographer Raghav Shreyas' work at capturing prominent Bangaloreans at Koshy's in Bangalore. This book **Table By The Window** takes you to the people that give this city its unique flavour.

Finally, in **Multiple City: Writings on Bangalore**, editor Aditi De brings together some of Bangalore's most important thinkers, writers and creative voices to reflect the contradictions of this city torn between its roots and aspirations for the future.

The busy streets of Bengaluru are packed with shopping options

Mysore

Visiting Mysore is a heritage-rich experience. Savour its art and architecture or simply ride up to the Chamundeshwari Temple for some great views. Keep the kids busy for hours at the Mysore Zoo, and drive out to Srirangapatnam for some Tipu Sultan lore. Visit the Ranganathittu Bird Sanctuary if you are into birding.

Trip Planner

GETTING THERE

Mysore airport is 12km from the city, but connectivity is limited with daily flights to just Bengaluru. The other option is Bengaluru airport (150km) which is better connected to the rest of the country with daily flights to major cities and metros. Mysore Junction is connected to Bengaluru and Chennai via the Shatabdi Express (12007). There are daily Volvos from Bengaluru.

SUGGESTED ITINERARY (4 DAYS)

Three days is ideal time to spend in Mysore. Keep a morning to explore the stunning Mysore Palace followed by a visit to Jayachamarajendra Art Gallery in Jaganmohan Palace. Next day go to Chamundeshwari Temple located atop the Chamundi Hill and then the Mysore Zoo. Keep the third morning for a visit to St Philomena's Cathedral and then go to Brindavan Gardens for the fountain show. After this visit Srirangapatnam and Ranganathittu Bird Sanctuary where you can spend a day.

BEST TIME TO GO

J F M A M J J A **S O N D**

GREAT FOR

Top 5 highlights

- **Mysore Palace** (p79)
- **Chamundeshwari Temple** (p79)
- **Mysore Zoo** (p80)
- **Srirangapatnam** (p81)
- **Ranganathittu Bird Sanctuary** (p81)

Historical Extravaganza

Mysore, the second largest city in Karnataka, is known for its royal heritage, bustling markets, magnificent monuments and cosmopolitan culture. It was the capital of the Wodeyar Dynasty till 1947. Patrons of art and culture, the rulers built many grand palaces, and also encouraged traditional crafts such as weaving and painting. Saris in silk and gold (zari) threads are a Mysore trademark. The Mysore style of painting, with its distinctive gold foil work, goes back to the turn of the 17th century. The festival of Dasera is the hallmark of Mysore's traditional heritage.

❶ MYSORE PALACE

The domed, three-storey structure in grey granite, surrounded by large gardens, is a fine example of late 19th century Indo-Saracenic architecture. Also known as Amba Vilas, the palace is the official residence of the erstwhile royal family, and is beautifully illuminated every Sunday and on public holidays, between 7pm and 8pm. Photography is prohibited; visitors are required to remove their shoes.

> ### Highlights
> ❶ Mysore Palace
> ❷ Chamundeshwari Temple
> ❸ Mysore Zoo
> ❹ Sri Jayachamarajendra Art Gallery
> ❺ St Philomena's Cathedral
> ❻ Brindavan Gardens

📞 0821 2421051; www.mysorepalace.gov.in; adults ₹40, entry free for children under 10 years; 10am–5.30pm

❷ CHAMUNDESHWARI TEMPLE

Located atop the Chamundi Hill, this temple is dedicated to the reigning goddess of the royal family of Mysore. Legend states that she slayed the demon Mahishasura (after whom the city is named) in a fierce fight; the Dravidian-style temple honours her feat. A 1000-step approach to the temple is popular with both devotees and fitness enthusiasts. For the less adventurous, there is a motorable road too.

📞 0821 2590027; www.mysorechamunditemple.com; entry ₹20, ₹100 (fast-track queue for those short on time); 7.30am–2pm, 3.30–6pm, 7.30–9pm

The Mysore Zoo is more than a century old

❸ MYSORE ZOO

This zoo was established under royal patronage in 1892. Starting out as a 10-acre park, it is today spread over 250 acres comprising large enclosures, a bandstand and an artificial island for birds amidst the Karanji Tank. Besides elephants, the zoo houses rhinos, gorillas, bison, zebras and also a white tiger.
📞0821 2520302, 2440752; Indira Nagar; adult/child (5 to 12 years)/camera/video ₹40/20/20/150; 8.30am–5.30pm; Tues closed

❹ SRI JAYACHAMARAJENDRA ART GALLERY

Housed in the Jaganmohan Palace, this museum is an art lover's dream: three floors of paintings (including those by Roerich and Ravi Varma), portraits, furniture, ceramics and musical instruments.
Jaganmohan Palace; ₹20; 8.30am–5.30pm

❺ ST PHILOMENA'S CATHEDRAL

Drawing inspiration from the Cologne Cathedral in Germany, this neo-Gothic church with its twin spires, stained glass and buttresses is a distinctive landmark of Mysore. Built by the Maharaja in 1933, it is dedicated to a Greek saint.
Ashoka Rd; 8am–5pm

❻ BRINDAVAN GARDENS

Envisaged along the lines of the Shalimar Gardens in Srinagar, it's a popular tourist spot 20km outside Mysore. The illuminated musical fountain show is a big crowd puller.
Adult/child (below 7 years)/camera ₹15/5/40 (video cameras prohibited); 6.30am–9pm, fountain show timings Jan–Sep (Mon–Fri) 7–7.55pm (Sat–Sun) 6.30–7.30pm; Oct–Dec (Mon–Fri) 6.30–7.30 pm (Sat–Sun) 6.30–8.30pm; Dasera 6.30–9.30pm

Detour: Srirangapatnam & Ranganathittu Bird Sanctuary

• **Srirangapatnam** (adult ₹5, free entry for children under 15 years; photography prohibited; 9am–5pm): Situated 19km north of Mysore on the Bengaluru highway, this town derives its name from the ancient **Ranganathaswamy Temple**, an important Vaishnavite shrine. In recent history, it has been associated with Tipu Sultan's short (albeit heady) reign of Mysore. It is home to the **Dariya Daulat**, his fresco-filled summer palace set amidst sprawling grounds. Built largely out of wood, the palace is notable for the lavish decoration covering every inch of its interiors. The ceilings are embellished with floral designs, while the walls bear murals depicting courtly life and Tipu's campaigns against the British. There's a small museum within, which houses several artefacts including a portrait of Tipu Sultan aged 30, painted by European artist John Zoffany in 1780. Nearby is the Gumbaz complex housing the tombs of Tipu and his parents; this is open to visitors free of charge from 8am to 6.30pm.

• **Ranganathittu Bird Sanctuary** (adult/child ₹50/25; parking ₹30; boat tour (shared) adult/child ₹50/25, boat tour (for two) ₹1000; 9am–6pm. Check for student concessions): This small sanctuary, comprising six islets in the Kaveri River, is located a stone's throw away from Srirangapatna town. With their riverine reed beds, these isles are the favoured nesting places of painted openbill and woolly-necked storks, common spoonbills and blackheaded ibis, amongst others.

The trees are home to colonies of flying fox, while the odd marsh crocodile is routinely spotted. The best season for sighting water birds is June to November, while in December, you can spot migratory birds.

Srirangapatnam got its name from the ancient Ranganathaswamy Temple

Accommodation

Royal Orchid Metropole   Heritage Hotel ₹₹₹
☏ 0821 4255566; www.royalorchidhotels.com; 5 Jhansi Lakshmibai Rd; d from ₹6000–12,000 A colonial-era heritage hotel in the heart of the city, it comes with a central courtyard and al fresco dining. The lavish rooms are of varying sizes and can get noisy, given their location. The ones at the back, while pool-facing, are somewhat uncomfortably walled-in. But the food at their evening-only BBQ restaurant, Shikari, makes up for the negatives.

Hotel Regaalis   Hotel ₹₹₹
☏ 0821 2426426; www.ushalexushotels.com; 13–14 Vinoba Rd; d from ₹6500–11,000 Located in the heart of the city, the gracious Hotel Regaalis is set amidst four acres of verdant landscape. It has well-maintained, spacious and clean rooms, a well-stocked pastry shop, and good food – the kebabs at Charcoals, the hotel's wonderful poolside restaurant, are a must-try.

Lalitha Mahal Hotel   Luxury Hotel ₹₹₹
☏ 0821 2526100; www.lalithamahalpalace.in; Lalitha Mahal Rd; d from ₹6000–50,000 This elegant building, perched on a ridge near the Chamundi Hills, is another of Mysore's striking landmarks. It was built by the Maharaja in 1927 for the exclusive use of the Viceroy. It is today an elite heritage hotel of the government-managed Ashok Group. The palace wing, with its original furnishings and fittings, gives the hotel a sense of history and splendour.

The Green Hotel   Heritage Hotel ₹₹
☏ 0821 2512536, 4255000, 4255001; Chittaranjan Palace, 2270 Vinoba Rd, Jayalakshmipuram; d from ₹3250–6750 This large old mansion, with expansive grounds and al fresco seating, has a quaint feel to it. Rooms in the main building, though small, have retained their old-world charm, as have the spaces leading to them. The spacious new wing comes with basic but modern amenities. For meals, stick to Indian preparations.

Royal Orchid Metropole has lavish rooms of various sizes

Windflower Spa & Resorts   Spa Resort ₹₹
☏0821 2522500; www.thewindflower.com; Maharanapratap Simhaji Rd, Nazarbad; d from ₹5100–9900 One of the earlier Windflower properties, its sheen has begun to fade. Yet the location, along with well-priced and well-appointed (and reasonably plush) rooms, work for this hotel. The popular spa therapies here range from ₹700–5000, depending on the duration.

Jasmine Apartment Suites   Service Apartments ₹
☏0821 2415505, 2415504, 4242632; www.jasminesuites.com; 83, 2nd 'B' Cross, 2nd Main, Vijaynagar 1st Stage; d from ₹2000 Conveniently located in a quiet residential area, these suites are comfortable, clean and come equipped with a kitchenette. Tariff includes breakfast (basic English or south Indian). Cutlery, crockery and toiletries are provided on request.

Eating

RRR Hotel   Andhra ₹
☏0821 2442878; 2721/1-2, Sri Harsha Rd; 11.45am–3.45pm, 6.45pm–11pm RRR Hotel is the place to go if you're craving for Andhra food. Devoid of all frills, this restaurant prepares the most delectable chicken and mutton biryanis, as well as vegetarian thalis. Hearty food is served quickly at this larger and newer of the two outlets in close proximity to Mysore Palace.

Green Leaf Food Court   Vegetarian Fast Food
☏0821 6550857, 9731939208; 2813 Kalidasa Rd, VV Mohalla; 7.30am–10.30pm A popular hang-out for students, it serves both north and south Indian meals (best to stick to the latter). A great place for breakfast and wake-me-up filter coffee. It tends to get busy given its popularity and location, but the food is well worth it.

Down Town   Fast Food ₹
☏0821 2513942; Chandra Complex, 42 Kalidasa Rd, VV Mohalla; ₹250 for two; 11am–2.30pm, 5.30pm–10pm This youthful hang-out takes you back to the pre-burger-chain era. For over two decades, owners Sagari and Roy have been dishing out comfort fast food to Mysore residents. Their home-style non-vegetarian burgers, rolls and hotdogs score over the vegetarian items any day.

Malgudi Cafe   Coffee Shop ₹
☏0821 2512536, 4255000, 4255001; Chittaranjan Palace, 2270 Vinoba Rd, Jayalakshmipuram; 9.30am–7pm This quaintly named coffee shop is located in The Green Hotel, a former palace for royal princesses. Managed by a UK charity, this cafe dishes out the most awesome filter coffee and cakes, prepared by a local women's self-help group.

Caffe Pascucci — Italian ₹₹₹
📞 0821 2511125; www.pascucci.in; 2713/1, New D3, Adipampa Rd, Jayalakshmipuram; 9am–11pm Part of a chain, this recently opened cafe has a decent Italian selection. While pizzas remain the fast-moving choice, give the salads, piadinas and pastas a chance too. Desserts are fine – notably the apple cinnamon pie – and the coffees, many.

La Gardenia — Multi-Cuisine ₹₹₹
📞 0821 2426426, 2427427; 13–14 Vinoba Rd; 6.30am–11pm This multi-cuisine restaurant at the Regaalis boasts a sumptuous buffet and a la carte selection. Spacious and sophisticated, the staff here is efficient and knowledgeable. It's just the place to treat yourself to a leisurely meal.

Activities

Silk Weaving Factory
📞 0821 2481803; KSIC (Karnataka Silk Industries Corporation) Factory, Manandavadi Rd; 9am–11.15am, 12.15pm–3pm, Sun and public holidays closed Visitors are welcome to stroll through the different sections of this factory, located behind the showroom on Manandavadi Road. Learn how the bobbins and the tremendously loud looms assist a single, almost invisible thread of pure silk to metamorphose into the beautiful Mysore sari. Entry is free; deposit cameras and collect passes at the office adjacent to the factory gate.

Swaasthya Ayurveda Centre
📞 0821 6557557, 9845913471; www.swaasthya.com; 726/B, 6th Cross, opposite Yoganarasimhaswamy Temple, Vijaynagar 1st Stage A consultation and treatment centre, it offers a wide range of wellness and curative therapies. The place is pocket-friendly, fuss-free, and the therapists skilled and efficient. Allow yourself a relaxing Abhyanga, Swedna or Shirodhara treatment under the guidance of Dr Sujatha JR, chief physician. Remember to call ahead for an appointment.

Shopping

N Kauvery

Handicrafts Emporium — Handicrafts
📞 0821 4262849, 4262759; www.nikauvery.com; 3149, Dawood Khan St, Five Light Circle, Lashkar Mohalla; 9am–9pm Mysore is synonymous with silk, paintings, sandalwood oil (and its many by-products) and rosewood carvings, most of which can be purchased at this Karnataka Silk Import Export Corporation-run (KSIEC) emporium, near St Philomena's Cathedral.

Devaraj Urs Road — Market
A kilometre-long stretch flanked on both sides by traditional shops, branded stores and trendy outlets. Scour the narrow alleys leading off for more. Take a break at Bombay Tiffanys Annexe and try the sinfully sweet Mysore pak, a local delicacy.

Expert Recommendation
Karnataka's cultural calendar

Vani Ganapathy, Bharatanatyam performer and cultural exponent is based in Bengaluru.

- **Bengaluru Habba** (www.bengaluruhabba.co.in): The week-long youthful fest brings a medley of performing arts at venues across the city in January after Sankaranti.
- **Chitrasanthe** (www.karnatakachitrakalaparishath.com): They host an annual one-day art and sculpture festival in late January.
- **Hampi Utsava** (www.thehampi.com): Classical music and dance, folk arts and crafts come alive before the temples and archaeological site of Hampi in November.
- **Karavali Utsava:** Witness the best of Carnatic and Hindustani music and dance. It is held in Karvar and Mangalore each winter.
- **Ramanavami Music Festival:** The Garden City's classical music fest held at Fort School grounds at Chamrajapet over a month, beginning April. For the connoisseur.
- **Lakkundi Utsav** (May–Jun): In Gadag, the festival hosts classical performances and folk arts.
- **Nagamandala** (Dec–Apr): This ritual performance to appease the spirit of a serpent is unique to Dakshina Kannada and coastal districts of Udupi.
- **Rangashankara Fest** (Nov–Dec; www.rangashankara.org): Karnataka's theatre gurus Girish Karnad and Arundathi Nag host the annual theatre festival.
- **Yakshagana Festival:** Yakshagana is a native folk art form of Karnataka that involves dance, music, pantomime, with elaborate costumes. Yakshagana festivals are held in venues across Karnataka.

> Vani Ganapathy is among the most famous Bharatanatyam dancers in the country

Bandipur & Around

Bandipur, along with the Kabini reservoir and Nagarhole National Park, offers a great experience for wildlife enthusiasts and has the country's largest population of Asiatic elephants. Other wildlife destinations around – BRT Wildlife Sanctuary, and Masinagudi – also offer a chance to unwind and spot plenty of animals.

Trip Planner

GETTING THERE

Bandipur: Mysore (90km) is the closest airport and railway station but very few flights operate on this sector. Instead, Bengaluru (235km) has daily flights and trains to all parts of the country. For other places see inside.

SUGGESTED ITINERARY (8 DAYS)

To do complete justice to this wildlife circuit spend two days at each place. Start with a visit to Bandipur National Park. The safaris into the jungle can be done only twice in the day, so two whole days gives you a chance for four trips into the jungle. After this make your way to Masinagudi (20km) that offers a refreshing break from city life. Next in line is Kabini (100km) that is home to an amazing variety of wildlife, has stunning landscape and lush forests. The last destination is BRT Wildlife Sanctuary (125km) where you can spot abundant wildlife. Of course, you need not visit all four places on one trip.

BEST TIME TO GO

J F M A M J J A S **O N D**

GREAT FOR

Top 5 highlights

- Jeep safari, Bandipur (p88)
- Mangala Village Walk, Bandipur (p89)
- Road safari, Masinagudi (p90)
- Nagarhole National Park, Kabini (p91)
- Biligiri Rangaswamy Temple, BRT Wildlife Sanctuary (p92)

Wildlife Trails

A herd of chital at Bandipur

The closest spot to Bengaluru for a wildlife fix, **Bandipur** contributes to nearly a quarter of the Nilgiris Biosphere and shares its borders with the other zones of Nagarhole National Park, Mudumalai Sanctuary and Wayanad Wildlife Sanctuary. It was one of the first reserve forests chosen under 'Project Tiger' in 1974. Elephants, deer and wild boar are often seen crossing the road. Deeper into the forest you can spot Asiatic elephants, tigers, leopards, gaurs (Indian bison), hyenas and sloth bears. Amongst birds, there are Indian silver bill, munia, purple-rumped sunbird and the jungle babbler.

Often overlooked as a weekend getaway from Bengaluru, **Masinagudi** is the perfect place to soak in the lovely countryside in comfortable stays, furnished with rustic authenticity to blend with the jungle. Here, in the backdrop of the Mudumalai Forest you can enjoy the company of wildlife veterans who run resorts and homestays in the area. Private safaris are not allowed, but you can spot elephants, bison, gaur, sambar and deer at the side of the highway.

About 110km from here lies Kabini Lake, a giant forest-lined reservoir formed by the damming of Kabini River. This separates the rich tropical forests of Bandipur Tiger Reserve from those of the Rajiv Gandhi National Park at **Nagarhole**. Once the exclusive hunting ground of the erstwhile maharajas of Mysore, Nagarhole is today counted as one of India's best wildlife parks.

Covering almost 540sq km of densely forested hills, the **Biligiri Rangaswamy Temple (BRT) Wildlife Sanctuary** stretches across the confluence of the Eastern and Western Ghats, showcasing the biodiversity of both ranges. Famous for its wildlife, the sanctuary is also home to the semi-nomadic Soliga tribe, experts in jungle medicine and preservers of a truly diverse range of plants. The sanctuary also presents birdwatchers an astonishing variety of species. Jungle guides here are knowledgeable and sincere and they must accompany you since BRT has approximately 39 tigers, not to mention herds of elephants and bison.

You can see tigers this close at Bandipur

Highlights
1. Jungle Jeep Safari
2. Mangala Village Walk
3. Himavad Gopalaswamy Betta
4. Birdwatching

Bandipur

1 JUNGLE JEEP SAFARI
With less strict rules than bordering Mudumalai Sanctuary, one can take jeep safaris into Bandipur. These are operated solely by the government enterprise Jungle Lodges and Resorts. Only 22 vehicles can enter the forest per day and routes have been limited; this is a boon for the animals, but a disappointment for tourists. Groups are packed in a large vehicle, and little can be done to control the combined din.
📞0821 2480902; Bandipur Forest Information Centre; ₹300 (45min), ₹1250 (2½ hr); video camera ₹1000; to book with your resort prepare to pay a convenience charge of ₹250; 6am–9am, 4pm–6pm

BANDIPUR & AROUND

> ✓ **Top Tip: Exclusive safari**
>
> The monopoly on jeep safaris lies with **Jungle Lodges and Resorts** (☏08229 233001, 9449599754). Contact them prior to your visit if you are looking to hire a smaller vehicle for a group. This facility is available to those who are staying at JLR properties.

❷ MANGALA VILLAGE WALK

The Bandipur region was home to the Kuruba shepherd tribe, who were also honey collectors. Tourism and outside influences, however, led to the slow decimation of the fragile habitat, and today only a few households of the Kurubas remain in Mangala village. Take a walk with a local guide and get to know more about their lifestyle. This activity is included in most resort packages.

Mangala village gives a peek into the culture of Kuruba shepherd tribe

❸ HIMAVAD GOPALASWAMY BETTA

Get a stunning bird's-eye view of the forest from the hilltop Krishna temple. At 4774ft, this is the highest point in the Bandipur hills. It is a 21km drive from the Bandipur checkpost on your way back from the sanctuary. Take a left from Hangala village.
8.30am–4pm

❹ BIRDWATCHING

Most of the properties in Bandipur are spread over acres of uncultivated land where you can spot many birds. Take guidance from the resident naturalist at your resort. You can enjoy some great birdwatching within the sanctuary too.

> ℹ **Quick Facts**
>
> - **Wildlife:** Indian bison, Asiatic elephant, tiger, deer, boar, dhole (wild dog), leopard and a variety of bird species.
> - **Area:** 880 sq km
> - **Entry fees:** Jeep Safari ₹300 (45min), ₹1250 (2½ hr)
> - **Park timings:** 6am–9am, 4pm–6pm

Masinagudi

❶ ROAD SAFARI
Ever since private safaris were stopped by the Karnataka government, resorts and homestays have introduced jeep rides on the highway. There are fair chances of spotting wildlife on these trips, as animals tend to come up to the fringes of the forest rather frequently.
This activity is included in the package in most resorts.

❷ BIRDWATCHING
Fortunately this is one activity that remains personalised since naturalists at resorts can take you on permissible trails around the properties. In this region you can spot the rare black and orange flycatcher, Malabar trogon, rufous-bellied hawk eagle, and more. There are over 320 species in the region.
This activity is included in the package in most resorts.

❸ NATURE TRAILS
Again, the forest limits are out of bounds but properties on large areas organise nature trails with naturalists. The walks are quite educational and give you a good perspective on the flora of the region.
This activity is included in the package in most resorts.

Highlights
❶ Road Safari
❷ Birdwatching
❸ Nature Trails

The lush forest at Masinagudi

ℹ️ Quick Facts

- **Best time to visit:** October–July
- **Getting there:** The closest airport to Masinagudi is in Mysore (110km), but very few flights operate on this sector. Instead, Bangalore (255km) has many other options from all parts of the country and multiple carriers. From Bandipur follow the forest road for 20km till you hit Masinagudi.

Kabini–Nagarhole

Highlights
1. Kabini Dam
2. Nagarhole National Park

❶ KABINI DAM
Following the construction of the Kabini Dam in 1974, the bamboo-rich fringes have become fantastic wildlife sighting spots, especially for herds of Asiatic elephants. This unspoilt wilderness is also home to predators like tigers, leopards, sloth bears, wild dogs and hyenas. Access is via HD Kote town, 14km from the dam.
Between Beechanahalli and Biddarahalli villages, Mysore-Manathavady Rd

❷ NAGARHOLE NATIONAL PARK
The gentle slopes and shallow valleys of Nagarhole are home to the spotted deer, barking deer, sambar, wild boar and the gaur. The deciduous forest cover is also an ideal habitat for avian life, with over 250 species. You can experience

Rare birds can be spotted at Kabini reservoir

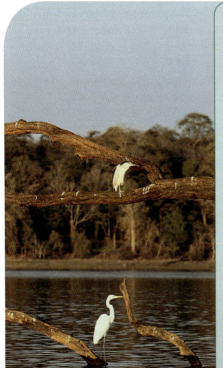

ⓘ *Quick Facts*
- **Best time to visit:** July–April
- **Getting there:** Mysore airport (100km) is the closest. From here take the SH33 for Mananthavady and follow the road signage. A KSRTC super deluxe bus departs from the Central bus stand at 7.30am daily. From Masinagudi it is about 110km.
- **Area:** Nagarhole National Park 643 sq km
- **Wildlife:** Asiatic elephants, tiger and leopard, spotted deer, barking deer, sambar, wild boar, the gaur and over 250 species of birds.
- **Entry fees:** ₹50
- **Park timings:** 6am–6pm
- **Safari timings:** 6am–9am, 3pm–5pm

> ### ✓ Top Tip: Photography
> Kabini's many moods are a shutterbug's delight. Incredible sunsets, exquisite moonrises, tranquil backwaters, a habitat teeming with animals and sundry forest life – all just a click and frame away. Do carry all the needful lenses.

the wildlife with Karnataka Tourism's 'Jeep & Boat Safaris'. Though private vehicles are permitted inside during specified hours, it would be advisable to sign up for the excursions. Most resorts at Kabini have a limited number of seats in the safaris. Therefore, confirm your seat early.

6am–6pm (park timings), 6am–9am, 3pm–5pm (safari timings)

BRT Wildlife Sanctuary

❶ BILIGIRI RANGASWAMY TEMPLE
Although the Soliga tribals are primarily nature worshippers, they also revere Lord Venkatesh, called 'Biligiri Ranganatha' locally, who gives his name to the land and the hills. The temple is the site of the annual spring festival. But something to be relished all year round is the view of the dense, green hills, unfolding up to the horizon. An hour's walk away from the camp, the climb up to the temple is quite steep.

❷ DODDA SAMPIGE MARA
Estimated to be almost 1500-years old, the Dodda Sampige Mara – or 'Big Champak Tree' – is truly enormous: over 30.5m tall with a trunk approximately 18m wide. The tree is sacred to the Soliga tribe. Hundreds of stones (meant to be Shiva lingams) surround the base. The 80-minute long trek from the camp is worth it.

❸ JEEP SAFARIS
The K Gudi Wilderness Camp (p96) has two jeep safaris every day: in the morning at 6.30am, and in the afternoon at 4.30pm. The morning safari holds higher promise of viewing

Highlights
❶ Biligiri Rangaswamy Temple
❷ Dodda Sampige Mara
❸ Jeep Safaris
❹ Jungle Treks

BANDIPUR & AROUND

🛈 Quick Facts

- **Best time to visit:** July–Novemember
- **Getting there:** The closest airport and railway station is in Mysore (82km).
- **Area:** 540 sq km
- **Wildlife:** Deer, bison, elephant, sloth bear, leopard, tiger and an array of birds.
- **Entry fees:** Free

a tiger but usually, you can spot elephants, herds of deer, and the white-socked bison. Sightings of animals during the rainy season are rare.

BR Hills span over Western and Eastern Ghats

❹ JUNGLE TREKS

The sanctuary has a number of well-marked forest trails open to trekkers, though one should be careful not to stray away from these paths. This is, after all, the natural habitat of a number of fairly territorial animals. That said, the trek offers some extraordinary terrain to walk through under large, broad-leafed plants and a host of flowering trees.

Top Tip: Be prepared

The BRT Wildlife Sanctuary is far from shops, restaurants and pharmacies, and one ought to travel prepared. Some items recommended are:

- **Flashlight** for the night, particularly for when there is no electricity.
- **Mosquito repellent cream**.
- **Snacks**, should one get peckish between meals (though beware of the monkeys).
- **First-aid kit**, including band-aids, antiseptic cream and anti-allergens (and prescribed medication for those with pre-existing conditions).
- **Warm clothing**, depending on the season, and for early morning and night.
- **Binoculars** for wildlife watching.

Accommodation

BANDIPUR

Dhole's Den Luxury Homestay ₹₹₹
08229 236062; www.dholesden.com; Kaniyinapura village, Bandipur National Park, Gundlupet Taluk, Chamrajnagar Distt; d ₹10,000 (incl of full board) A set of luxury units with wide airy balconies come alive with bright animal-themed art and lively furnishings. The food spread is elaborate and delicious. And with its rainwater harvesting and electricity generated through wind turbines, this is a homestay that cares for the environment.

The Windflower Tusker Trails Resort ₹₹₹
08229 236055; www.thewindflower.com; 125 Mangala village, Chamrajnagar Distt; studio ₹8400, ste 10,500 (incl of full board) Though the facade of the erstwhile Tusker Trails is intact, the refurbished studio rooms and suites, camouflaged by a dense grove, come with all the features associated with a high-end resort. But this unfenced, rustic property also advocates cutting oneself off from television, internet and phone.

The Serai Bandipur Resort ₹₹₹
08229 236075; www.theserai.in; Kaniyanapura village, Chamrajnagar Distt; d ₹17,915–₹25,000 (incl of full board); check season/weekend packages Opened last year in May, this 36-acre property provides a lavish stay in rustic environs. The courtyard, cabin and residence cottages have white walls and thatched roofs, and have been built using traditional stonework. To blend in with the surroundings, 17 acres have been left uncultivated.

Bandipur Safari Lodge Resort ₹₹₹
08229 233001; www.junglelodges.com; Mysore–Ooty Rd, Melukamanahalli, Angala Post, Gundlupet Taluk, Chamrajnagar Distt; cottages from ₹10,000 (incl of full board) The landmark Jungle Lodges and Resorts property houses 22 adequately finished 'value for money' cottages amidst 9.5-acres. The only visual standouts are wildlife artist Sunita Dhairyam's paintings on the walls of five of the rooms. The Gol Ghar (common gazebo) restaurant and the bonfire area teem with families, leaving little privacy.

The Serai Bandipur is surrounded by the lush Nilgiri biosphere

MASINAGUDI

Jungle Hut — Resort ₹₹₹
📞 0423 2526240; www.junglehut.in; Bokkapuram, Nilgiri Distt; d ₹6900 (incl of full board) A combination of luxury tents, enclosed camping site and deluxe rooms, the Jungle Hut is suitable for large and small groups alike. If you are not admiring the regular pack of deer in the courtyard area, you will find yourself lounging by the swimming pool.

Jungle Retreat — Family-Run Resort ₹₹
📞 0423 2526469; www.jungleretreat.com; Nilgiri Distt; d ₹5939–15,940 (incl of full board) One of the oldest family-run resorts in the area, Jungle Retreat is also one of the best. Owner Rohan Mathias and his knowledgeable team offer a host of nature based activities, for ecologically-conscious leisure travellers and wildlife enthusiasts. You might spend much time at the pool.

Forest Hills — Resort ₹₹
📞 0423 2526216; www.foresthillsindia.com; Bokkapuram, Nilgiri Distt; d ₹3890–5240 (incl of full board) Forest Hills lies at the end of Bokkapuram Road, with a vantage point next to the jungle limits. With its well-spaced cottages, Forest Hills is ideal for groups both large and small; opt for the 'Machan' for an exclusive view. Multi-cuisine veg and non-veg food is served in a common area as per buffet timings.

Bamboo Banks — Resort ₹₹
📞 9443373201; www.bamboobanks.in; Nilgiri Distt; d ₹6140 (incl of full board) Almost four decades old, Bamboo Bank is the veteran among resorts in the area. Soak in the hunting stories of Mr Kothavala, the owner, and admire his collection of memorabilia. A garden pool and the Parsi food at the multi-cuisine restaurant will make your stay worthwhile.

The Wilds at Northern Hay — Resort ₹₹
📞 9843149490; www.serendipityo.com; Singara Post, Nilgiri Distt; d ₹5835–6547 (incl of full board) This century-old, luxuriously furnished bungalow blends perfectly with the coffee plantation and forest area around it. The 98-acre expanse allows one to enjoy a more personalised sighting experience. And even when safely ensconced in your cottage, you'll keep hearing sounds coming from the jungle.

Wild Haven — Nature Stay ₹
📞 0423 2526490; www.wildhaven.in; Chadapatti village, Mavanalla Post; d ₹2500–3000 (incl of breakfast) Nature lovers are sure to be lured by this neighbour of the jungle. Wild Haven is extremely popular in the wildlife circuit for its offbeat location in the middle of the forest. Lose yourself in the green cover as you bask in the comfort of aesthetically-styled rooms.

KABINI–NAGAROLE

Waterwoods — Eco-Lodge ₹₹₹
📞08228 264421; www.waterwoods.in; 19 Karapura, N Belthur Post Office, HD Kote Taluk, Mysore Distt; d ₹7000–13,500 (incl of full board) This boutique eco-lodge is located on the Kabini river front, affording one an uninterrupted slide show of nature's beauty. The five well-appointed rooms in the converted country home are ideal for small groups seeking privacy.

The Serai — Luxury Resort ₹₹₹
📞08228 264444, 9731396221; www.theserai.in; Karapura village, Mysore Distt; d ₹17,500–25,000 (incl of full board) Stretched along the river bank, every suite and plush villa at this luxury resort boasts spectacular views of the landscape – come sunrise or sunset. A row of hammocks out front, under coconut palms, can quickly become your favourite spot here.

Orange County Luxury Resort — Luxury Resort ₹₹₹
📞08228 269100; www.orangecounty.in; Bheeramballi village & Post, HD Kote Taluk, Mysore Distt; d ₹26,000–33,000 (incl of full board, coracle ride and guided nature walk) Do not be taken in by the tribal look and feel of the place; this resort is the very embodiment of luxury. The cottages, the reading lounge, Ayurvedic spa and infinity pool, have been designed to provide guests with a holistic experience in the wild.

BRT WILDLIFE SANCTUARY

K Gudi Wilderness Camp — Camp ₹₹
📞080 25597944, 25584111; www.junglelodges.com; Kyathadevara Gudi, Chamrajnagar, Yelandur; log hut/tented cottage/family room ₹5500/4500/4000 (charges include forest entry fees, food and lodging, jeep safaris, nature walk and elephant ride) This settlement of tents and lodges is the only place to stay within the BRT Wildlife Sanctuary. K Gudi Wilderness Camp is a serene and secluded getaway and it maintains the presence of the forest within the camp. The tents, log cabins and rooms are clean and well kept. The camp provides guests with lanterns at night as electricity is in short supply. The food is basic but nourishing, and the staff are happy to cater to the needs of children. The camp also has a bar at the Maharaja's Hunting Lodge, open during the evenings for guests to relax and unwind. The camp offers guides for trekking, conducts safaris into the sanctuary, and screens films during the evenings for guests to learn more about the terrain that surrounds them.

Eating

BANDIPUR

Pugmark Restaurant – Bandipur Safari Lodge — Multi-Cuisine ₹
📞08229 233001; www.junglelodges.com; Mysore–Ooty Rd, Melukamanahalli, Angala Post, Gundlupet Taluk, Chamrajnagar

Distt; 1.30pm–3.30pm, 7pm–8.30pm
Most of the resorts in Bandipur have their own restaurants and do not allow guests who aren't checked in. Pugmark is the only decent eatery open to the public. Largely a one-man show, the service here is slow, and it can whip up only the most basic of Indian and some Chinese dishes.

MASINAGUDI
Casa Deep Woods Multi-Cuisine ₹₹₹
☏ 0423 2526335; www.zestbreaks.com; Bokkapuram village, Nilgiri Distt; breakfast 8am–10am, lunch 1pm–3pm, dinner 8pm–10pm Casa Deep Woods is the only resort in Masinagudi which allows non checked-in guests for a la carte and buffet meals. A reasonable spread is served here, but you are unlikely to visit if you are staying in one of the resorts.

Popeye's Chicken Multi-Cuisine ₹₹
☏ 9886261454; 8/70 Ooty-Mysore Rd, Masinagudi, Nilgiri Distt; 9.15am–10pm A clean and cheerful option for western snacks and meals in Masinagudi town, Popeye serves delicious chicken delights. For visitors, this is the only reasonable restaurant in town.

 Activities

BANDIPUR
Film Screenings
Wildlife documentaries are screened in the evenings at most resorts. The

Dhole's Den offers the opportunity for camping

practice is standard at Dhole's Den, where it is taken seriously by most guests. All the resorts also have wildlife literature in common areas for guests to scan through.

Shopping

BANDIPUR
The Souvenir Shop
☏ 9449818796 (Indra Kumar); www.templetreedesigns.com; Mariamma Temple Rd, Mangala village, Gundlupet Taluk, Chamrajnagar Distt; 7am–7pm Bandipur is evidently no shopping hot spot but a few souvenirs here are worth picking up: tees, coasters etc, are available in wildlife themes. It's run under the patronage of Temple Tree Designs – the brainchild of Sunita Dhairyam, who has gotten the locals involved in the shop – and the Mariamma charitable trust, which runs health and education programmes in the area.

Coorg

Nestled amid ageless hills that line the eastern edge of the Western Ghats is Coorg (Kodagu) district. The diverse topography of mountains, coffee plantations, thick forests, paddy fields and rivers are a suitable backdrop for a number of adventure activities. Madikeri, the chief town and transport hub of Coorg has many interesting sights and places which give ample reason to visit this area.

Trip Planner

GETTING THERE

The closest airport and railhead to Coorg lies in Mysore (118km), but few flights operate on this sector. Instead, Mangalore (140km) and Bengaluru (248km) have better connectivity to all parts of the country. Taxis from Mangalore and Bengaluru to Madikeri cost ₹3000 and ₹5000 onwards.

SUGGESTED ITINERARY (4 DAYS)

Coorg has the option of a relaxed holiday or an adventure-packed weekend. To do both spend at least four days. Make Madikeri your base and spend a couple of days visiting places like Abbi Falls, Raja's Seat, Madikeri Fort and roam around the plantations. You are never more than 1½ hours away from any attraction. Keep the next two days for adventure sports like rafting, trekking, quad biking or kayaking.

BEST TIME TO GO

J F M A M J J A S **O N D**

GREAT FOR

Top 5 highlights

- **Raja's Seat** (p100)
- **Madikeri Fort & Palace** (p100)
- **Abbi Falls** (p101)
- **Adventure Sports** (p106)
- **Plantation homestays** (p108)

Nature's Bounty

Bird's-eye view of Coorg's lush landscape from Brahmagiri Peak

Gifted with emerald landscapes and acres of plantations, Coorg is a major centre for coffee and spice production. The region's chief town and transport hub is **Madikeri**, once the seat of the Kodava rulers and named after Mudduraja.

The region is home to the unique Kodava race, believed to have descended from migrating Persians and Kurds, or perhaps Greeks left behind from Alexander the Great's armies. Coorg was a state in its own right until 1956, when it merged with the state of Karnataka.

This hill station has pleasant weather all year round (only interrupted by heavy monsoon downpours from July to September). Consequently, the town and its surrounds have been bestowed with a rich canopy of teak forests and acres of coffee and spice plantations. For an authentic **Coorg** experience, you have to venture into the plantations. Avoid weekends, when places can quickly get filled up by visitors from Bengaluru.

KARNATAKA

Highlights
1. Raja's Seat
2. Madikeri Fort & Palace
3. Omkareshwar Temple
4. Abbi Falls
5. Royal Tombs
6. Igguthappa Temple
7. Nalnad Palace
8. Golden Temple
9. Dubare Elephant Camp

❶ RAJA'S SEAT
A well-maintained garden used by the Kodava rulers, it offers stunning views of the Coorg Valley below. Visit in the evening to see the sun descend behind rolling hills; after sunset, the musical fountains are switched on. Easy to find, Raja's Seat is located at the western end of Madikeri.

₹10; fountain show 7pm Mon–Fri, 6.45pm and 7.30pm Sat, Sun and festivals

❷ MADIKERI FORT & PALACE
The original mud fort here was replaced by the present one built by Tipu Sultan. The stone ramparts enclose the palace of the Kodagu rulers, which now houses the offices of the deputy commissioner. Within the sprawling complex is a former church doubling as a museum and a temple. Two large elephant statues stand alongside the double-storeyed colonial palace. Though the fort and palace aren't as impressive as they sound, a visit is a good way to kill time.

Museum 10am–5pm; photography not allowed

Omkareshwar Temple, dedicated to Lord Shiva

> ## ✓ *Top Tip: Where to stay in Coorg*
>
> Spread over 4100sq km, it is impossible to cover the entire Coorg region in a short duration. Base yourself at any one of the regional hubs listed below according to your choice of activity:
>
> • **Madikeri:** This is the administrative headquarters of Coorg district. Stay at a homestay and from here visit the town and the scattered sights around it. Whether it's Abbi Falls, the Buddhist settlement at Bylakuppe, the Igguthappa Temple in Kakkabe, or the elephant camp at Dubare, you are never more than 1½ hours away from any attraction.
>
> • **Kutta:** Serves well as base camp if you want to climb the Brahmagiri Peak, tumble down the white waters of the Upper Barapole River in a raft, or experience flying in a microlight.
>
> • **Kakkabe:** Tadiandamol, the highest peak in Coorg, is just next door from here. You can also indulge in kayaking or canoeing on the Kakkabe River, or go for half-day adventure activities like quad biking and the jungle gym with Now or Neverland (p107).
>
> • **Kushalnagar:** Pitch tents by the Harangi Dam and go kayaking in the still waters of the reservoir. You can also climb the Kotta Betta (the third-highest peak in Coorg).

❸ OMKARESHWAR TEMPLE

This temple was built by King Lingarajendra in 1820, as penance for killing a brahmin. It is dedicated to Lord Shiva (the Shiva lingam was reportedly brought from Kashi). Located in the heart of Madikeri, the complex encloses a large water tank which lies across from the steps that lead to the main shrine of the temple.

6.30am–12pm, 5pm–8pm; photography not allowed

❹ ABBI FALLS

An 8km drive beyond Madikeri, through cardamom and coffee plantations, will bring you to a point little short of the falls. A brief walk down a paved path from here takes you to a hanging bridge opposite the wide cascade of water. Visit in the mornings and afternoons to avoid crowds. Swimming is dangerous and best avoided, and the place is infested with leeches during monsoon season.

8km from Madikeri

Royal Tombs are a prime attraction in Madikeri

5 ROYAL TOMBS

Also called Gadduge, these early 19th-century mausoleums of the Kodava rulers are located just short of the Abbi Falls. Built in the Indo-Saracenic style, the domes and minarets of these structures tower over the town of Madikeri. The caretaker lives just outside the premises, and may be requested to show you around.
9am–5pm

6 IGGUTHAPPA TEMPLE

Dedicated to the main deity of the Kodavas, this temple, the warrior race's holiest shrine, is located in Kakkabe, a small village about 40km from Madikeri (said to be southern Asia's largest producer of forest honey). Every March, during

📷 Snapshot: Talakaveri

Located 50km from Madikeri, on the Brahmagiri Hill near Bhagamandala, Talakaveri is the origin of Kaveri, southern India's most sacred river. While there is no visible source of water, a perennial spring is said to swell the water in the holy tank at the temple here, before emerging as the river some distance away. Come mid-October, on the day of Tulasankramana, thousands of pilgrims converge to witness the gush of water from the spring. Talakaveri is a longish, yet doable, day-trip from Madikeri. Combine your visit with a walk or drive up to the Brahmagiri peak, 8km away, for awesome vistas of the Western Ghats.

the Kaliyarchi festival, the temple idol is taken around in a procession before being reinstalled in the shrine of this remarkable and holy temple.
📞 08272 238400; 5.30am–12.30pm, 6.30pm–7pm

❼ NALNAD PALACE
This former hunting lodge and summer home of the Kodava kings is also in Kakkabe, at the base of Tadiyandamol, Coorg's highest peak. The low-slung double-storey structure, built in 1792, is embellished with intricate wooden friezes and frescoes, while a pavilion crowned by Nandi adorns the garden. A caretaker will let you into the palace for free.
9am–5pm; near Palace Estate, Kakkabe

❽ GOLDEN TEMPLE
This Buddhist temple is located in Bylakuppe, the largest Tibetan settlement in South India, some 30-odd km from Madikeri. It gets its name from the three magnificent gilded statues of Buddha, Padmasambhava and Amitayus in the cavernous prayer hall. Nearby, two monasteries, Namdroling

> ### ✓ Top Tip: Rain alert
> If you're planning on visiting Madikeri during its stunning monsoon, be well-equipped; for it doesn't just rain here, it pours. Light and quick-dry raingear should include hooded jackets and pants, hiking boots (ankle high, if not higher) and plenty of socks. You can also throw into your daypack an all-encompassing poncho for those emergencies.

Gilded statue of Buddha at Golden Temple

A short boat ride on the Kaveri takes you to Dubare Elephant Camp

and Tashilunpo, stand cheek-by-jowl with Sera, an educational monastic institution where thousands of monks and nuns receive instruction.
7am–8pm

❾ DUBARE ELEPHANT CAMP
This unique facility, managed by Jungle Lodges and Resorts, is located on an island in the Kaveri River. Providing visitors with an intimate interface, trained naturalists help you observe, learn and participate in numerous elephant-centric activities. A short boat ride takes you across to the camp, where you can watch the pachyderms being bathed, groomed and fed; this is followed by an elephant ride. Extremely touristy, it will earn you brownie points with the kids.
8.30am–12pm; ₹300 onwards (depending on choice of activities); 14km from Kushalnagar, 40km from Madikeri

---

₹ *Value for Money: Food blessed by gods*

If you find yourself at the Igguthappa Temple in the forenoon, with time to spare, wait around for the clock to strike one, when a simple yet scrumptious lunch is offered free of cost to visitors daily.

Expert Recommendation
Coorgi cuisine

Priya and **KC Aiyappa**, owners of the exclusive 'weekends only' restaurant, Coorg, in Bengaluru mention the specialities and nuances of Coorgi cuisine.

- **History of Coorgi cuisine:** Coorg is a warrior tribe from the southwestern part of India and their cuisine is predominantly non-vegetarian. Pork (from wild boar), jungle mangoes, jackfruit, kembh leaves (edible colocasia) and rice are the prime ingredients of their cuisine.

- **Interesting facts about Coorgi food:** Kachampuli provides the sauce base for most Coorgi dishes, especially non-vegetarian ones. The thick, black pasty sauce is a product of the concentrated juice of the namesake fruit. In fact, most households have this ready to use, as it acts like a preservative for chicken, mutton and pork. The use of green chillies is more prevalent than red chillies. None of the meats cooked use any additional source of oil, except for the fat. Wheat is a recent addition and lentils are rarely used.

- **Coorgi specialities:** Rice forms the base for Coorgi dishes. **Nooputtu** (string hoppers), **otti** (baked pieces of rice flour), pulao and **kadumbuttu** (rice-flour balls) are staples in every household. Amongst the meats, pork is usually prepared dry, while chicken and mutton are cooked in a curry. Seasonal vegetables like bamboo shoot (May–August), jungle mango (April–June) or jackfruit (September–December) will be served depending on which time of the year one is visiting. **Koovaleputtu** is a savoury item made from ripe jackfruit or banana, steamed in banana leaves. **Kajaya** is a sweet that one will often find in Coorgi kitchens. Made from jaggery and rice flour, these deep-fried donuts are delicious.

A typical Coorgi meal, that mostly consists of non-vegetarian dishes, is a must-try

If You Like: Adventure sports

Coorgs' adventure activities are spread across the district with Kutta as the hub for rafting and trekking on the Brahmagiri range. Tadiyandamol can be accessed from the centre of the district and Kushalnagar forms the base for activities like kayaking and camping. Depending on which activity you want to cover, two days is enough. Guides are available for hire and can arrange food, transport and accommodation. The best time for adventure activities is October to May.

RAFTING (OFF KUTTA)

Manoeuvre the rapids (1–4 class) of the Upper Barapole (Kithu-Kakkatu River) with Coorg Whitewater Rafting. The camp, located in Ponya Devarakad Estate is well organised where guests are oriented and trained before setting out. You have to sign an indemnity bond before your start. Enjoy the 2.8km stretch where you bounce across rapids of varying difficulty.

✆9481883745; www.coorgwhitewaterrafting.com; Ponya Estate (off T Shettigeri); ₹1200 per head (3–4 hours, including jeep pick-up, gear, tea, use of base camp)

MICROLIGHT FLYING (OFF KUTTA/ GONIKOPPA)

Experience a 'wind in your face' adventure with Muthanna of Coorg Sky Adventures, in a two-seater open plane which takes you to a height of 3500 feet. You have to sign an indemnity form – and arrive at 7.30am or 3.30pm in sturdy footwear, to cross the paddy-field runway. Not for the faint-hearted.

✆9448954384; www.coorgskyadventures.com; Ponnampet (off Gonikoppa); ₹2250 per head (10min), ₹5000 per head (30min, 50 km), ₹8000 per head (60min, 100 km)

BRAHMAGIRI TREK (OFF KUTTA)

The forested Brahmagiri range is a challenging trek that varies from moderate to difficult. The trek

Rafting is one of the most popular adventure sports in Coorg

Try microlight flying and experience verdant Coorg from a thrilling height

involves an overnight stay and offers an excellent opportunity to see wild animals and Coorg's impressive biodiversity.

KAYAKING & CANOEING (OFF KAKKABE)

Enjoy the more tranquil side of Kaveri River with Jungle Mount Adventures at their 7-acre campsite. Experience, with the aid of instructors, a ride on a kayak (3-man) or a canoe (2-man) on this 20ft deep stretch of the river at the edge of the camp.

📞 9845831675; www.junglemountadventures.com; Kakkabe village, Yavakapady Post; d incl full board ₹3200

TADIANDAMOL TREK (OFF KAKKABE)

The highest peak in Coorg offers a short but demanding trek of 5km. It can be covered in a day, and is suitable for trekkers of intermediate level, although physically fit beginners may take a shot at it too.

QUAD BIKING & MORE (OFF KAKKABE)

Indo-British company Now or Neverland presents a host of activities, including quad biking, jungle gym, paintball and mountain biking. The most exciting of these is taking a 250cc quad bike off road through forests and slushy tracks on a 1km circuit. Supervised by instructors and with top-notch safety equipment, this makes for a safe family outing.

📞 08274 323023; www.noworneverland.com

CAMPING & KAYAKING BY THE HARANGI (OFF KUSHALNAGAR)

Camps by the backwaters of the Harangi Dam are organised by Eco Habitat Homestay (14km from this spot). A coffee estate and bamboo stands skirt the property. Few places in Coorg allow camping and this is a popular one. Kayaking and canoeing are also available here (under supervision). Food and bonfire can be arranged at an additional cost.

📞 9448127245; www.ecohabitat.in; Narkur village; ₹500 per tent; ₹1500 for group of 4 for barbeque

HIKE TO MANANGERI (OFF MADIKERI)

Hire a jeep from Madikeri (₹1000 one way) and take the Madikeri–Mangalore Road, 10km off the toll junction, to the small village of Manangeri. Then hike up to the Manangeri ridge (2km). This beautiful trail is not on the tourist map and the view from the ridge is gorgeous. If you have time, you can hike up the entire 7km.

Accommodation

MADIKERI

Gowri Nivas — Homestay ₹₹
☏ 9448493833, 9448193822; www.gowrinivas.com; New Extension; d ₹3800 (children under 12 years/above 12 years ₹500/1000) This tastefully done up modern Kodava house set in a lush garden offers an independent two-room cottage and one room in the main family unit. Hospitable and helpful, the owners are mostly at hand to provide insightful information about all things Coorgi. They also serve delicious home-cooked meals. To get here, ask for the New Extension autorickshaw stand.

Jade Hills — Homestay ₹₹
☏ 9916618829; Kaloor Rd, Galibeedu village; d ₹3000 Located on a hilltop, this privately owned cottage of recent vintage is accessed through verdant forest slopes. The gazebo out front reveals the most stunning views of the valley beyond. The homestay is quiet, clean and comfortable.

> ✓ **Top Tip: Roads**
>
> Be conservative about covering distances in Coorg. Roads from one location to another can be quite bumpy and do not, in any case, match the regular time-distance ratio. A small stretch of 20km could well take an hour given the road conditions.

Berry Lane — Plantation Homestay ₹₹
☏ 8274252978, 9448721460, 9343631236; Ontiangadi Rd, Ammathi; d ₹2500–3500 If relaxing in wooded coffee and spice-rich environs is foremost on your mind, head for this private estate. Located in the plantation-rich region south of Kaveri River, it has a large verandah that opens onto a dense verdure of pepper-vines, papayas and plantains. Take a walk around the plantation.

Silver Brooks — Homestay ₹₹
☏ 8272200107; www.silverbrookestate.com ; Kadagadal village; d ₹3300 (incl of breakfast) The wide verandah, spacious rooms, handpicked collection of wooden furniture and small library of Silver Brooks make it a delight to stay in. A small, winding road leads to this pleasant homestay with an alluring garden and wide, sunny sit-outs. The stone pillar bases are designed as board game.

Sayuri — Heritage Homestay ₹
☏ 8272225107, 9448190990; Munishwera Temple Rd; d ₹2000 This 100-year-old Kodava house may well be that proverbial home away from home. Quaint, comfortable and lived-in, the resident help (speaking only the local language) understands and takes care of your every need. We highly recommend the traditional breakfast (included in the tariff) of rice-flour roti and curried beans.

Palace Estate Plantation Homestay ₹
☏ 8272238446, 9880447702;
www.palaceestate.co.in; Kakkabe;
d ₹2000–2500 Overlooking Nalnad Palace, this plantation home has astonishing views of densely forested mountains. Set at the base of Tadiyandamol peak, the 50-acre coffee and spice estate is a solitude seeker's haven. The ride to Palace Estate is uncomfortable in stretches but the destination makes the journey worth your while.

Victorian Verandaz Homestay ₹
☏ 9448059850; www.livingcoorg.com; Modur Estate, Kadagadal Post; d ₹2500 (incl of breakfast) The two rooms and a dining area here are neatly kept and personal – perfect for a family unit. This homestay offers a view of the valley below, a jeep drive through the thick coffee plantation and delicious homely food. It is just off Madikeri, and conveniently central for reaching other parts of Coorg for adventure activities.

KUTTA

Culmaney Homestay ₹₹
☏ 9448469659; Faith Cinchona Estate, Kutta; d ₹4000 (incl full board) Stay at Prabhu and Maya's estate house for a complete orientation on Coorgi history and culture. You won't be leaving the dining table in a hurry (after having finished your meal), for conversations here lead from one topic to another.

An elegant room at the Gowri Nivas, a comfortable homestay

Culmaney's hosts truly represent Coorgi hospitality, and most guests leave as friends of the couple.

Bison Manor Nature Retreat ₹₹
☏ 8105118877; www.bisonmanor.com; New Grand Estate, Kutta; d ₹3900 (incl full board) You'll enjoy spending time at Bison Manor, run by Hugh and Vivian. The ambience of this old Coorgi home has been kept intact by preserving the paintings of the original owner. The nine spacious rooms, aesthetically done up in warm hues, overlook the Brahmagiri range (the view from the upper-floor rooms is the best). Nature trails within the estate, friendly dogs on the property and a serene backdrop make Bison Manor a wonderful choice.

Machaan Resort ₹₹
☏ 9900437002; www.machaan.com; Churikad, K Bagada village, Kutta; d ₹3500 (incl full board) Tucked away on a coffee plantation, Machaan is one

of the few luxury options to stay in Kutta. Comfortable wooden cottages, enthusiastic staff and in-house activities for guests make this a good choice for families.

The Jade — Heritage Homestay ₹
☏8274244396; www.thejadecoorg.com; Manchalli, Kutta; d ₹2700 (incl of breakfast and dinner) Experience an exclusive stay in this old Coorgi-style house with low wooden doors, after crossing a bright green patch of paddy fields. The Brahmagiri Peak base camp is just 2km away, making The Jade a convenient choice for trekkers.

Narikadi — Homestay ₹
☏9972232400; www.narikadihomestay.com; Narikadi Estate, Kutta; d ₹2600–3000 (incl of full board) Choose between the newly-built four rooms overlooking the coffee-drying yard, or the two snug rooms, over 100-years old, attached to the house. The splendid view of paddy fields here will keep you enthralled.

KUSHALNAGAR

Bel Home — Plantation Stay ₹₹
☏9880908135; www.belhome.co.in; Bellarimotte Estate, Madapura Post; d ₹4200 (incl of full board) The breezy sit-out areas of this 1928 cottage, access to the faraway coffee plantation crossing the Madapura River and proximity to Kotta Betta (the third-highest peak in Coorg) make Bel Home a very attractive choice. Get a real taste of Coorg here, with a 'bean to cup' coffee experience, local food and a spot of birdwatching. Families seeking less strenuous adventure activities, like an easy hike to Kotta Betta or a picnic by the placid stream (Madapura) close to the property, should stay here.

Eco Habitat — Homestay ₹₹
☏9448127245; www.ecohabitat.in; Chikbettagere village, Guddehosur Post, Kushalnagar; d ₹5000 (incl of full board; lunch and dinner ₹250 per meal per head) Eco Habitat has two exclusive cottages, with personal 'splash' pools attached. Immaculately furnished, the cottages are spacious enough for extra beds. Stay here for Chethana's delicious lemon-grass tea and food along with Som's engaging penchant for taking guests to unexplored parts of Coorg. Eco Habitat offers privacy as well as the hosts' fantastic company.

Cardamom and other spices are widely available in the old market of Madikeri

Eating

MADIKERI

Pause, The Unwind Cafe — Cafe ₹
☎9343076006, 9341380456; Shop No. 4, Kodava Samaj Building, Main Rd; 11am–8pm On offer here is a limited-item food menu, yet enough to appease hunger on the go. Popular for coffee and cakes on order, as well as quick bites which are tasty here. The star attraction is the home-style chicken biryani which is delicious.

Neel Sagar — Vegetarian ₹
☎8272220477, 9141226975; Kodava Samaj Building, near Police Station; 7am–10pm A pure vegetarian restaurant, Neel Sagar offers north and south Indian meals and snacks, and also Jain food. It's spacious, with utilitarian interiors, and it can get rather noisy. But if you are looking for well-prepared vegetarian fare, you don't have to look any further. However, it is not for those who are seeking a leisurely experience.

Coorg Cuisinette — Coorgi ₹₹
☎9448127358, 9449699864, 9480208933; Yelakki Krupa Building, opp Head Post Office, Main Rd; 12.30pm–4.30pm, 7.30pm–9.30pm Drop by for traditional Kodava dishes (mainly non-vegetarian) if you are not in a rush; it takes 20–30 minutes for your meal to arrive. Sip on their fresh passion-fruit juice with honey, it's a great way to bide your time. Located on the first floor, it is easily missed; keep a sharp lookout.

Raintree — Multi-Cuisine ₹₹
☎8272220301; www.raintree.in; 13/14 Pension Lane, behind Town Hall; 11am–3pm, 6pm–10.30pm Mon–Thurs, 11am–11pm Fri–Sun A multi-cuisine fine-dining restaurant, Raintree occupies the many spaces of a former house. Their exhaustive menu features generous helpings of delicious, well-prepared seafood, tandoori, Mughlai and Coorgi cuisines. Try the ghee roast items, especially the prawns (a must try).

If You Like: Tea over coffee

It's no blasphemy to want a hot cup of tea in the land of coffee! **KT Tea** in **Hotel Green Land** (☎08278 224820; Near IB, Mangalore Road; ₹15 per glass), at the toll junction in Madikeri, should not be missed.

Shopping

MADIKERI

A browse around the old market in the heart of Madikeri will yield almost anything produced in Coorg. Coffee, honey, cardamom, pepper, cinnamon, cloves, vanilla, ginger, nutmeg, cashews, areca nut, are all up for grabs. They come in packets of different sizes and make for great souviners as well.

Chikmagalur & Sakleshpur

Besides its historic links with coffee, Chikmagalur is a scenic getaway with a plethora of destinations. There are options for nature and adventure lovers, as well as for the spiritually inclined. A lesser-known coffee destination, under-the-radar Sakleshpur makes for a welcome change from the regular stops on the plantation trail.

Trip Planner

GETTING THERE

Chikmagalur: The closest airport is in Bengaluru (245km), which has daily flights to all the major cities. Taxis from Bengaluru cost ₹5000 onwards. Kadur (40km) is the nearest railhead but train connectivity is better from Bengaluru.

Sakleshpur: The nearest airport is in Bengaluru (226km). The railhead is connected to Mangalore and Bengaluru.

SUGGESTED ITINERARY (5 DAYS)

Chikmagalur is spread over a vast area and you need at least three days here. On the first day do the big mountain loop of Mullayangiri and Baba Budangiri and next day make your way to Kemmanagundi, Hebbe Falls and Kalhatti Falls. Keep the last day at Chikmagalur for Coffee Yatra and Horanadu Temple. After this go to Sakleshpur (63km), an unexplored coffee destination with wild and unmanicured landscape and spend two days exploring the highlights.

BEST TIME TO GO

J F **M A M** J J A S **O N D**

GREAT FOR

Top 5 highlights

- **The Big Mountain Loop, Chikmagalur** (p114)
- **Kemmanagundi & Hebbe Falls, Chikmagalur** (p114)
- **Coffee Yatra, Chikmagalur** (p116)
- **Manjarabad Fort, Sakleshpur** (p118)
- **Plantation Visit, Sakleshpur** (p118)

Coffee Culture

Imagine the difficulties faced while smuggling coffee beans across borders in the 17th century. India owes its coffee lineage to Baba Budan, a Sufi pilgrim who managed to bring in seven beans from his trip to Mecca. He found that **Chikmagalur** had the perfect altitude for planting this crop. You can actually wake up and smell the coffee here!

Chikmagalur is a large area, so it's best to divide your trip into parts, depending on the experience you are looking for. Choose between the big mountain loop of Mullayangiri, Baba Budangiri and Kemmanagundi, or the section that comprises Kudremukh, Horanadu and the Bhadra River. Be ready to do a lot of exploring on foot as the region demands walking through coffee estates and covering easy hiking trails. Chikmagalur is a popular trekking area.

Cross the bridge over the Hemavathi River at the entrance of **Sakleshpur**, a small but busy town and turn into any of the two arterial roads. The dramatically wild and unmanicured landscape, quite typical of coffee plantations, unfolds

You're never too far away from coffee in Chikmagalur

around you. Home to the second highest peak in Karnataka, **Jenukal Gudda**, Sakleshpur offers scenic mountain views from everywhere. Unfortunately, trekking to this peak has recently been stopped by authorities. Bear in mind that the interior roads are difficult to negotiate; a four-wheel drive is recommended, especially during the monsoon, as the roads change very quickly from paved to muddy.

Sakleshpur's history goes back to the 6th century, when it was ruled by the ancient Chalukya dynasty; during the medieval period, the Hoysalas held sway here. However, it was British rulers who recognised its potential as a fertile coffee location, with the pleasant weather adding to its appeal. Colonial touches can still be seen in the plantation life that revolves around old bungalows and the club culture.

Chikmagalur

❶ THE BIG MOUNTAIN LOOP

Go past city traffic towards Kaimara and start in the foothills and head straight to Sheethalagiri, a 1000-year-old Mallikarjuna temple. Duck below the low door into this intriguing shrine to receive your share of 'prasadam', a fistful of water from a natural pool inside. It is better to arrive early in the morning, when the tourist rush is less. Next on the 'loop' is the mist-covered **Baba Budangiri Hill** (or Dattagiri Hill Range). Here, a small temple perched at 6217ft offers breathtaking views of the valley below. Finally there is **Mullayangiri**, Karnataka's highest peak (6332ft), which affords another great view (it can get windy and cold, so be sure to carry a jacket). If you're lucky, you might catch the Kurinji flower in bloom.

Highlights
❶ The Big Mountain Loop
❷ Kemmanagundi & Hebbe Falls
❸ Kalhatti Falls
❹ Coffee Yatra
❺ Horanadu Temple
❻ Belavadi
❼ Ayyanakere

❷ KEMMANAGUNDI & HEBBE FALLS

The hill station of Kemmanagundi provides an access point to the picturesque Hebbe

CHIKMAGALUR & SAKLESHPUR

View from Mullayanagiri hill, Karnataka's highest peak

Falls. Though hugely popular with tourists, Kemmanagundi itself does not have much to offer apart from an unimpressive rock garden, a government-run children's park and a badly-managed restaurant. Getting to Hebbe Falls involves an adventurous off-road journey. Rickety jeeps are available on hire (₹300 per person in a shared vehicle) for a round trip. You will reach the falls after a short walk on foot. There are a couple of points where you'll need to hop across a shallow but rocky stream (take off your shoes and wade across the stream). Be wary of leeches in the rainy season. The effort, however, is absolutely worth it for you'll get to see a 551ft drop from below the gushing water.
₹10; parking ₹50; 8am–4pm

❸ KALHATTI FALLS

From Kemmanagundi, the drive is only 10km to Kalhatti where the main point of interest is a Lord Veerabhadra (Shiva) temple. The temple gets its share of zealous pilgrims in the months of March and April for a three-day festival to commemorate the god. Kalhatti Falls are at their prettiest just after the monsoons. If you are driving down from the Kemmanagundi loop, the falls are just off the main road and make for a very short stop. If you have to choose between the two, Hebbe Falls is a better bet.

Reaching Hebbe Falls is an adventurous off-road journey, but worth the effort

❹ COFFEE YATRA

A Coffee Board of India initiative, the Coffee Yatra is a thematic and well thought-out museum display on the origin of coffee (including the different types of coffee) and its subsequent evolution in the country. The touch-screen displays are disappointing as they are perpetually not working, but the rest of the exhibits are informative and creatively showcased. There is also a laboratory where one can watch a demonstration of how coffee is processed. Unfortunately, a tasting experience is missing.

Coffee Centre, Behind ZP Office, Kadur Rd; ₹20; 10am–1pm and 2pm–5.30pm, closed on Sat, Sun and general holidays

❺ HORANADU TEMPLE

Horanadu is an important pilgrimage centre in Chikmagalur and is famous for the deity of Annapurneshwari – a goddess who feeds one and all – which was installed by Adi Shankaracharya. Queue up in a long but fast-moving visitors' line to get a quick glimpse of the goddess. Do not miss out on the simple but tasteful prasadam, served every day. Thousands sit in neat rows on the floor while Malnad-style food is served by priests in a hurried but orderly manner. An elaborate menu of the offerings can be obtained at the information counter.

Lunch noon–2.30pm, dinner 8pm–9.45pm

❻ BELAVADI

A pleasant break from the overtly touristy places in Chikmagalur and around, the 13th-century Belavadi Temple is a haven of peace and quiet. More than 100 soapstone pillars greet you in the main hall before your eyes latch on to the three shrines of Lord Vishnu: Narayana, Venugopala and Yoganarsimha. If you are lucky, you'll bump into the temple's

CHIKMAGALUR & SAKLESHPUR

young English-speaking priest, who will be only too happy to share details with the trickle of visitors who come here. The temple, dating back to the Hoysala Empire which ruled Karnataka between the 10th and 14th centuries, is also mentioned in the Mahabharata as the location where the demon, Bakasura, was slain.

29km from Chikmagalur; dawn to dusk

❼ AYYANAKERE

Located just 26km from Chikmagalur, Ayyanakere is yet another picturesque spot and makes for a good drive. The tank here is said to have been built by Rukmangada Raya, a chieftain of Sakrepatna (a small town in Chikmagalur). Its history can be traced from 1156, after the Hoysala rulers renovated it. The lake, built to provide irrigation to the nearby village fields, is now a picnic spot.

26km from Chikmagalur; dawn to dusk

>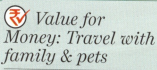
> ## Value for Money: Travel with family & pets
>
> Hunkal Woods (p120) encourages travelling with the family. If you are accompanied by family members who are above 60 years, it will cost only ₹1500 per head. Those above 70 years can stay free of cost. And pets are important to the Gowdas too; you can get 70% off on your stay if you bring a pet along (discuss details before booking).

The main hall of Belavadi Temple has more than 100 soapstone pillars

Saklespur

Highlights
1. Manjarabad Fort
2. Manjehalli Falls
3. Plantation Visit
4. Betta Byreshwara
5. Bisle Reserve Forest

❶ MANJARABAD FORT
Trek up a stairway (unfortunately littered with plastic) to this weathered fort, built by Tipu Sultan as a strategic defence location. The effort of dragging yourself up the steep hill is certainly rewarding, for you'll get to experience a wonderful bird's-eye view of the surrounding area. The view apart, the fort has little to recommend it; Manjarabad is, in fact, rather unimpressive due to lack of upkeep. The information provided about the site is also inadequate.

Bengaluru-Mangalore Highway, 7km beyond Sakleshpur

❷ MANJEHALLI FALLS
A certain amount of nimbleness is required to reach the 20ft-high falls, as you manoeuvre your way down to a good spot near the water. A great place for a picnic close to Sakleshpur, Manjehalli Falls is particularly beautiful after the monsoon season.

❸ PLANTATION VISIT
Almost all homestays and hotels are flanked by coffee plantations. A walk through any of these is a leisurely

Acres of green plantations at Sakleshpur

📷 Snapshot: *The Green Route, or Sakleshpur railway trek*

Green Route was the name given to a verdant stretch of a non-functional railway track from Sakleshpur to Kukke Subrahmanya, on the Mangalore–Bengaluru sector, many decades ago. It has become popular on the trekking circuit. People hiked from Donigal to Edkumeri railway station via the Gondiya Pass, crossing tunnels, waterfalls and deep gorges, since the track was closed down in 1996 (to change the gauge from metre to broad). Before passenger trains again started plying on this route in 2008, trekkers could enjoy a long, arduous trek of 56km, crossing 58 tunnels and 109 bridges on foot. For those who have heard fabulous stories about this route, note that the trek is no longer possible. Even though a lot of trekking groups might urge you to join in, locals will suggest that you steer clear of this as it's illegal and unsafe.

experience, with opportunities to indulge in some birdwatching. The coffee-picking season, which is in December is particularly fun as there is a lot of activity at that time. Coffee beans are picked before being spread and left to dry in almost all courtyards. If you are visiting during March or April, you may chance upon the small window of three days when the coffee flowers are in bloom and entire hillsides turn white.

④ BETTA BYRESHWARA

This temple, located a short distance from Sakleshpur, is over 600 years old. Not much can be gauged about the history of the structure, but it definitely offers a great view from atop the hill it stands on. Some people opt to climb the steep steps instead of trekking to the top.

⑤ BISLE RESERVE FOREST

The rainforest cover that spills onto Sakleshpur, is a joy for nature lovers with its many bird and animal species. The drive through the Bisle Ghats is full of verdant views. However, permission granted at the entry gate to enter the forest is sporadic.

◆ Detour: *Belur–Halebidu circuit*

Sakleshpur is an excellent base for exploring Belur and Halebidu (p124). At a maximum distance of 55km (an hour's drive), the temple towns can be easily covered in a day, yet you won't stray far from the lush green plantations of this region.

Accommodation

CHIKMAGALUR

The Serai — Resort ₹₹₹
8262224903; www.theserai.in; KM Rd, Mugthihalli Post; d ₹22,000–69,000 (incl of full board) Luxury accommodation was first introduced here by The Serai (a holding of Coffee Day). The folks here arrange visits to the plantations, where you can learn about the processes of coffee making, and also get to taste coffee (only for checked-in guests). The Serai also offers an OMA Spa and personal pool (or Jacuzzi) in every villa.

Flameback Lodges — Resort ₹₹₹
8263215170; www.flameback.in; Billur Post, Pattadur village, Mudigere Taluk; paddy cottages ₹12,000, ste/luxury villas ₹15,000 onwards (incl of full board) Private villas, suites, and cottages with wide sunny decks and personal Jacuzzis are the attractions at this exclusive boutique resort. The lodge offers views of a lake, waterfall and paddy fields, making for a welcome break from the coffee topography. Flameback has only eight rooms, ensuring privacy.

Villa Urvinkhan — Luxury Homestay ₹₹₹
9449651400; www.villaurvinkhan.com; Niduvale, Mudigere; d ₹10,000 (incl of full board) Perched atop a hill, this luxury homestay with five cottages is located in the middle of a 400-acre coffee estate that has been around since the 1800s. The five cottages, spread across a small area, come with private verandahs and complete privacy. Most guests tend to spend a lot of time in the pool. Breakfast time is abuzz with everyone sharing their travel experiences.

Woodway — Ayurveda Resort ₹₹
9663071775; www.woodwayhomestay.com; Jakkanhalli Post; d ₹6000 (incl of full board) Sushmita and Shreedev have run Woodway for over 10 years. You can look forward to some great company, knowledgeable plantation walks and delicious local food. The highlight for most guests is the walk in the coffee plantations led by Browny, the old family dog. Woodway is tastefully furnished and very comfortable.

Villa Urvinkhan, offers five cottages and is located in the middle of a lush coffee estate

CHIKMAGALUR & SAKLESHPUR

Coffee Village Retreat Heritage ₹₹
☎ 8262229599; www.coffeevillageretreat.com; Kimmane Plantation, Billur Post, Mudigere; d ₹5000–7000 (incl of full board) Choose between a 150-year-old colonial plantation bungalow and a unit that oozes modern luxury at this unique set-up on a 300-acre coffee estate. You can also join activities like indoor games, cycling, birdwatching, trekking, boating and fishing – or just relax by the bonfire.

Hunkal Woods Homestay ₹₹
☎ 9886000788; www.hunkalwoods.com; Thogarihunkal Group Estates; d ₹4400 (incl of full board) Offering both comfort and serving as a starting point for treks, Hunkal Woods is ideal for family getaways and adventure groups. The Gowda family have put together some interesting trails, including a graveyard walk and sambar track (and one for birdwatching too). The property was built in 1875 and still retains an old-world charm.

SAKLESHPUR

The Hills Resort ₹₹₹
☎ 080 41158187; www.thehills.in; Kuntahalli village, Devaladakere Post, Sakleshpur Taluk, Hassan Distt; d ₹7000–8000 (incl of full board) The only luxury option in the area, The Hills is a combination of Indonesian-style wooden cottages and lavish tents. While the rooms are well equipped, the standard of service unfortunately leaves much to be desired.

Some of the villas at Flameback Lodges overlook a lake

The Planters Bungalow Homestay ₹₹
☎ 9481925930; Kadamane Checkpost, Hassan Distt; d ₹4851 (incl of full board) This century-old, English-styled house comes with typical high ceilings, sprawling verandahs and a marvellous view of tea plantations. Expect some great food, treks on the property, tea tasting and elephant sighting (they are regular visitors to the property). The massive 7500-acre Kadamane Tea Estate, on which the Planters Bungalow is located, has had illustrious owners like the Earl of Warwick and tea conglomerate Brooke Bond.

Jenukallu Valley Retreat Resort ₹₹
☎ 9241611610; www.jenukallu.com; Athibeedu, Devaladakere Post, Sakleshpur Taluk, Hassan Distt; d ₹6000 (incl of full board) The wide expanse of a bare hill dotted with four cottages is a pleasant relief to the eyes after the thick coffee copses. Opt for

the cottage right at the edge of the hill for a better view.

Tusk And Dawn — Nature Stay ₹₹
☏9845503354; www.tuskanddawn.com; Agani Post, Hanbal; dorm per head/d ₹1800/4200 (incl of full board) Enjoy a camp like ambience (without any real roughing out) with three comfortable twin cottages and a log house 8-bedded dormitory. There is an open pavilion for meals, hiking trails off the property and a small water body.

Eating

CHIKMAGALUR

Town Canteen — South Indian ₹₹
☏8262222325; RG Rd; 11.30am–2.30pm, 6.30pm–8.30pm Mon–Sun, after 1pm Sat Get your dosa fix at the 52-year-old Town Canteen. Though the unassuming ambience of weathered wooden benches is far from glamorous, the food is definitely something to write home about.

Food Palace — Multi-Cuisine ₹₹
☏8262228116; RG Rd; 7am–9.30pm A quick stop for south Indian snack food or slightly more elaborate Indianised Chinese. There is not much to recommend about the fare here, but the service is efficient.

SAKLESHPUR

The Ossoor — Vegetarian ₹₹
☏08173 318072; BM Rd; 7am–11am The Ossoor, just out of town, is an offshoot of the estate by the same name. It is the best place for a quick vegetarian meal on the highway.

Mythri Restaurant — Vegetarian ₹₹
☏08173 245244; Puspagiri Comforts, BM Rd; 7am–11am One among the few choices to eat out in Sakleshpur, Mythri is nothing out of the ordinary, but is nonetheless a decent stop for vegetarian food.

Surabhi's Nxt — North & South Indian ₹₹
☏9008271807; BM Rd; 6am–10am A branch of the famous Surabhi restaurant, this new eatery has more seating and plenty of parking space. Ask to be seated on the first floor to enjoy the view of the lush countryside.

Activities

CHIKMAGALUR

Trek to Kemmanagundi and Mullayangiri

Private groups can trek to the Kemmanagundi and Mullayangiri ranges with local guides. But camping is strictly prohibited in these areas (though it is advertised by many adventure groups in Bengaluru).

Chikmagalur Golf Club

☏8262656500; PB No 154, MG Rd, Karadihalli; 6.30am–6.30pm This well-maintained nine-hole golf course is a fantastic setting for those looking

CHIKMAGALUR & SAKLESHPUR

to play on their holiday. Members of affiliate clubs like Bangalore Golf Club and the KGA (Bengaluru) are allowed entry. But even if you're not a member, many homestay owners are, and they can get you in as a guest. A caddy (₹70 for nine holes) and golf set (₹200 per hour) are available on hire.

SAKLESHPUR

Jenkal Gudda — Trekking

Also known as the 'honey stone mountain', one can see this high peak from many points in the area. An erstwhile favourite with trekkers and camping enthusiasts, to climb Jenkal Gudda you need permission (which is now sporadically given). A medium-level hike to the windy summit is recommended only if you are in good shape, and are accompanied by locals.

 Shopping

CHIKMAGALUR

Hunkal Heights — Coffee

☎ 8262230472; KM Rd; 10am–5.30pm Watch how coffee is ground here, and pick up a pack of fresh and authentic Chikmagalur coffee.

Panduranga Coffee Works — Coffee

☎ 8262235345; PB No 150, MG Rd; 9am–9.30pm Though coffee is best consumed fresh, if you must carry a souvenir back, try the well-known Panduranga shop on MG Road, a one-stop shop for locally branded coffee. Not big on service, though.

> ✓ **Top Tip:**
> *Get clear directions*
>
> Ensure that you're given proper directions to the place you are staying in, as resorts and homestays are far apart and set among scattered villages with very few passers-by. Non-Kannada speakers are bound to find it even more difficult to get directions.

Kamadhenu Provision Store — Spices

☎ 8262237823; MG Rd; 8am–10pm MG Road is lined with small traders and you are bound to find options for spices and honey. Among these is the Kamadhenu store, which has a reasonable selection of pepper, cardamom and other local spices.

SAKLESHPUR

Salish Tea — Tea

☎ 08173 319353; BM Rd, Kollahally; 9.30am–10pm The shop stocks locally procured tea, coffee, pepper and honey. Though many small shops dot the main Bengaluru-Mangalore Road, what makes Salish Tea a pleasant choice is its polite staff.

The Bee Keepers Co-operative Society Limited — Honey

☎ 08173 344075; near bus stand, Sakleshpur; 10am–5.30pm Sakleshpur is famous for its fresh honey. The Bee Keepers Co-operative is the best place to buy some delicious local honey.

Belur & Halebidu

The Hoysala temples at Belur and Halebidu are the apex of one of the most artistically exuberant periods of Hindu cultural development. The towns of Belur and Halebidu are usually spoken of together since they are located close to each other. These magnificent shrines are a delight for architecture and history buffs. If you are neither, you can always enjoy the beautiful countryside.

Trip Planner

GETTING THERE

Hassan: Keeping Hassan as the base to explore the Hoysala trail, Bengaluru airport (182 km) is closest. Cabs from here cost ₹3800 onwards. Though Hassan has a railway station, which is connected to Bengaluru and Mangalore with a weekly train from Mumbai and New Delhi, the closest station with multiple options is Bengaluru.

SUGGESTED ITINERARY (3 DAYS)

Not only Belur and Halebidu, but many other Hoysala temples also lie in this region. The Hoysala temples at Belur and Halebidu are South India's answer to Khajuraho and Konark, and represent a high point in ancient Hindu architecture. One needs three days to cover these. Shravanbelagola, a Jain pilgrim centre, can also be visited en-route to Bengaluru.

BEST TIME TO GO

J F M A M J J A S **O N D**

GREAT FOR

Top 5 highlights

- **Chennakesava Temple, Belur** (p126)
- **Hoysaleswara Temple, Halebidu** (p126)
- **Shettihalli Church, Hassan** (p126)
- **Gorur Dam, Hassan** (p127)
- **Shravanabelagola** (p127)

Divine Relics

The hook for this circuit is the two famous temples of **Belur** and **Halebidu**, built during the Hoysala empire, between the 11th and 13th centuries. These temples signify one of the most artistically creative periods in medieval Hindu culture.

> The Chennakesava Temple has lovely carvings in slate stone

Of the 1500 temples built during the period, 92 temples remain. Out of these, the ones in Somanathapura, Belur and Halebidu are the more elaborate and boast of exquisite carvings. The ones in the **Chennakesava Temple** (Belur) and **Hoysaleswara Temple** (Halebidu) are the most intricate. Keep an eye out for sculptural details ranging from meticulously carved monkey teeth to bangles that still rotate around the wrists, and the depiction of see-through clothing on dancers. Besides scenes from the Ramayana and Mahabharata, the sculptures also throw light on life all those centuries ago. The best way to cover the Belur–Halebidu circuit is by following the trail of the Hoysala-specific sites sprinkled around these two towns. There's little to see in Hassan but the town is a perfect base for exploring the area.

Highlights
1. Chennakesava Temple
2. Hoysaleswara Temple
3. Shettihalli Church
4. Gorur Dam
5. Mosale

❶ CHENNAKESAVA TEMPLE
This star-shaped shrine, typical of the Hoysala style, is the main temple in Belur and is dedicated to Lord Vishnu. It was commissioned in 1116 to commemorate the Hoysalas' victory over the neighbouring Cholas and it took 103 years to complete the superb carvings – 4000 in all – in slate stone. Hoysala emblems, statues of dancing ladies and stories of epics unfold in this black stone. Apart from the awe-inspiring sculptures, there's also a monolithic 15m lamp tower in front of the temple, which stands fascinatingly without a foundation; one can see the gap between the foot of the lamp and its base.

Temple Rd, Belur; shoes ₹2, light inside ₹20; 7.30am–1pm, 3–7.30pm

❷ HOYSALESWARA TEMPLE
Aesthetically, the Hoysaleswara Temple in Halebidu is similar to the one in Belur but it also has a number of distinct features, such as the depiction of the mythological 'seven-in-one' animal, Makara, and tales from the Ramayana and Mahabharata. Hire a guide to take you through this Shiva temple, with its manicured lawns; spare at least an hour for a rehearsed but informative guided tour.

Temple Rd, Halebidu; shoes ₹2; sunrise to sunset (best to visit between 8am and 5pm)

Shettihalli Church dates back to the 19th century

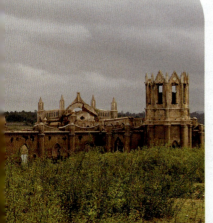

❸ SHETTIHALLI CHURCH
The remains of Shettihalli Church, 18km from Hassan, look almost fairy tale-like against the backdrop of the Gorur Dam catchment area. Though marred by graffiti, the church stands grandly on the banks while fishermen row their coracles to the middle of the water body. It is said to have been submerged in the waters of the Hemavathi Dam at one point of time. Built by French missionaries in the

Detour: Shravanabelagola

The massive statue of Bahubali, looking over the town of Shravanabelagola, is often seen in brochures of the Hassan-Belur-Halebidu circuit. It is certainly intriguing enough to merit a detour. Though the town has no connect with the Hoysala temple trail, it can be conveniently clubbed on the same route. A centre for Jain pilgrimage, Shravanabelagola deserves a couple of hours.

Climb the two temple hills of Chandragiri and Vindhyagiri. The monolithic statue of Lord Gomateshwara (Bahubali), 57ft tall, dwarfs anyone who ascends the steep rock steps of Vindhyagiri. Reach in time for the early morning prayers (8am), when devotees gather to chant. Look out for the Mahamastakabhisheka, a festival celebrated every 12 years. On this day, the statue is bathed in consecrated water, milk, sugarcane juice and saffron paste. The next big day will be in 2018. Chandragiri, which houses an older set of Jain temples, is shorter and easier to climb; it has fewer tourists, so it is relatively peaceful.

Apart from the Jain Association guesthouses, the 40-year old Hotel Raghu is the only place where one can put up for a night. And you'll find a number of 'Jain food only' joints here. Shravanabelagola is 50km from Hassan and 158km from Bengaluru.

19th century, it is a good change from an otherwise temple-dominated trip.
Banks of the Gorur village and Hemavathi River

❹ GORUR DAM
The Gorur Dam makes for a good drive from Hassan. The dam gates are opened after the monsoon, which is the best time to visit the spot. After a long walk to the dam area, one can get pretty close to the gushing water below.
10am–5pm

❺ MOSALE
About 12km from Hassan, the village of Mosale houses two temples dedicated to Nageshwara and Chennakesava. One passes through a village with bright doors to reach these shrines. They too belong to the Hoysala period but are less intricate. If they are locked, you can invariably ask someone to find the key custodian, who lives in Mosale, to open them.
8am–5pm

Accommodation

HASSAN

Hoysala Village Resort — Resort ₹₹₹
☏ 08172 256764; www.hoysalavillageresorts.in; Belur Rd; d ₹8100–9100 (incl of full board)
Set up in 1992, this is the only luxury resort in the region. It gets a steady stream of guests through the year, so book ahead. The kolam (flour patterns made on the ground), Indian motifs and names of the rooms add to the Indian theme in this 34-room property. The cottages and suites are spacious, and come with all the trappings of a good resort. The resort also has a restaurant, a spa (6am–9pm only for checked-in guests) and indoor games.

The Ashok Hassan — Hotel ₹₹
☏ 08172 268731; www.hassanashok.com; Post Box No 121, BM Rd; d ₹4856–7892 (incl of full board)
Boasting great ambience and service,

Hoysala Village Resort offers well-appointed and spacious cottages and suites

The Ashok also has multiple plush rooms. Its green environs make for a pleasant change from the bland options in town. There's also a 24-hour cafe and a bar.

Southern Star — Hotel ₹₹
☏ 08172 251816; www.hotelsouthernstar.com; BM Rd; d ₹4776–5941 (incl of full board) The spacious reception and polite staff immediately make you feel welcome and relaxed. Rooms are predictably clean and well equipped; some of the bathrooms even have a bath-tub. The property also has a spa (timings 8am–8pm; book in advance).

Suvarna Regency — Hotel ₹
☏ 08172 264006; d ₹1760 Newly refurbished, the hotel is in the heart of the city, which makes it a very convenient option. You might wish you were in a quieter place, but the rooms are spacious and clean. But do not expect any fringe advantages. Also, don't choose the non-AC double rooms – these are too stuffy and small.

BELUR

Hotel Mayura Velapuri — Hotel ₹
☏ 08177 222209; Temple Rd; d ₹950–1800 (incl of full board)
Surprisingly clean and well equipped, ideal if you're looking to make Belur a base. But very few people choose this Karnataka State Tourism Department Corporation (KSTDC) hotel, considering Hassan has more options.

Eating

HASSAN

Suvarna (Suvarna Regency) South Indian ₹₹
📞 08172 264006; www.suvarnaregencyhotel.com; 7am–10pm The largely south Indian fare is prepared quickly to service the milling crowds. Not high on ambience or decor, but it is a decent place to catch a wholesome breakfast.

Karwar (Southern Star) Multi-Cuisine ₹₹₹
📞 08172 251816; www.hotelsouthernstar.com; BM Rd; 12.30pm–10pm Courteous staff, quick service and superb Indian food – Karwar is a great place to unwind after a hectic day's sightseeing. The perfect restaurant for a hearty meal.

Ashok Hassan Multi-Cuisine ₹₹₹
📞 08172 268731; www.hassanashok.com; Post Box No 121, BM Rd; 12.30pm–10pm One of the better restaurants in town, the Ashok Hassan is one place where you can order non-Indian cuisine without worrying. It also has a decent bar.

HALEBIDU

Hotel Mayura Shanthala Multi-Cuisine ₹₹
📞 08177 273224; University Rd, opp Hoyslala Aishwarya Temple, Halebidu; 8.30am–9pm A KSTDC unit, this is the only reasonable place in Halebidu where you can have a meal. Located just opposite the temple, it gets quite crowded at lunch time during the season. The restaurant is basic but clean. Both vegetarian and non-vegetarian dishes are served.

BELUR

Hotel Mayura Velapuri Multi-Cuisine ₹₹
📞 08177 222209; Temple Rd; 10am–8pm Also run by the KSTDC, this is a fairly new establishment. The restaurant serves basic food (vegetarian and non-vegetarian) in a clean environment. Its proximity to the temple makes it easier to cover Belur in a short span of time.

Vishnu Regency Multi-Cuisine ₹₹
📞 08177 222209; Temple Rd; 10am–8pm There are not too many eating options in Belur, but this restaurant dishes out vegetarian fare in a hygienic environment. Don't, however, go with high expectations – the elaborate menu may not live up to them.

Shopping

BELUR–HALEBIDU

Slate Stone Curios
The only worthy place to pick up a souvenir is from outside Halebidu Temple. A row of women use the same stone as the one which went into building the shrine to make curios like Ganeshas, Buddha busts and more. Make sure you bargain well.

Mangalore, Udupi & Around

The relatively undiscovered and raw landscape of coastal Karnataka, mainly the beaches around Mangalore and Udupi, offer a heady concoction of spiritual bliss with numerous temples, water adventures like surfing and a chance to unearth a whole new destination, waiting to be pegged on the travel map of the country.

Trip Planner

GETTING THERE

Mangalore: The airport here is connected to all major cities. The railway station lies on the Konkan Railway belt and has several trains. Overnight private and KSRTC buses are a good option from Bengaluru (354km).

Udupi : Mangalore airport is 54km. The Udupi railway station is also on the Konkan Railway belt.

SUGGESTED ITINERARY (5 DAYS)

It's best to explore this stretch by car. Arrive in Mangalore and use the day to see some of the famous temples. You can stay an extra day if travelling with children, in which case, a trip to Pilikula Nisargadhama is recommended. During the next three days, make Udupi your base and explore the coastline upto Murudeshwar. A day should be kept aside at Netrani Island for scuba diving.

BEST TIME TO GO

J F M A M J J A S **O N D**

GREAT FOR

Top 5 highlights

- Pilikula Nisargadhama, Mangalore (p132)
- Beaches, Mangalore (p136)
- Sri Krishna Temple, Udupi (p137)
- Coin Museum, Udupi (p137)
- Agumbe & Around (p141)

Discovering Tulu Nadu

The quiet Murudeshwar Beach is home to a temple of the same name

Tinged with weathered red tiles, characteristic of homes in **Mangalore**, **Udupi** and places around here (also known as Tulu Nadu), the landscape of the region also offers vivid shades of green with its lush forests and a dash of pale brown along the beaches. The area is a beautiful mix of ancient temples and sun-kissed sandy stretches with water sports luring travellers for an adventure-packed holiday.

Start your journey in Mangalore, a city on the verge of turning into a fast paced business centre, yet tacitly holding on to its easy paced coastal life. You will find scenic spots, old temples and beaches merging seamlessly with malls and shopping areas in this erstwhile 'beedi' capital of the country. Udupi, on the other hand, is still destined to be a religious destination for Hindu pilgrims, who visit the famous Sri Krishna Mutt. Discerning travellers can enhance their travel experiences in this busy town by stretching the itinerary to other coastal towns, which extend right upto Murudeshwar. With surfing and other water sports catching up as exciting activities, the region is not too far from exploding into a top destination for travellers. Till then, it remains a surprisingly exotic, untouched stretch on the west coast of the country.

Mangalore

Highlights
1. Pilikula Nisargadhama
2. Someshwar Beach & Temple
3. Temples of Mangalore
4. Cathedrals & Churches
5. Mosques
6. Sultan Bathery
7. Seemanthi Bai Government Museum
8. Beaches

1 PILIKULA NISARGADHAMA

Less than 11km from the city, a visit to Pilikula Nisargadhama, a theme park, can take up an entire day if you are travelling with children. Start with the **Biological Park**, moving onto the **Artisan's Village**, a medicinal garden, **Manasa Amusement Park** and the **Lake Garden**. Spread amidst thick tropical forests, the Biological Park houses many animals in enclosures emulating their natural habitat. This is the main highlight of the entire cluster of sights and is likely to take most of your time. Stroll through the artisan's village, where you can watch potters, cane and bamboo workers at their craft. The Manasa Amusement Park has water specific rides (carry an extra pair of clothes and towels). The best part of this complex is the Lake Garden and Pilikula (Tiger's) Lake, where self-pedalled boats are available.

☎0824 2263565; www.pilikula.com; Mudushedde; Biological Park adult/child (6–12 years)/camera/video camera ₹30/15/25/100; 9.30am–5.30pm; Manasa Park adult/child/seniors/camera/video camera ₹250/170/150/25/100; 10.30am–5.30pm; Pilikula Lake adult/child /camera/video camera ₹10/5/25/100; pedal boat 2/4 seater ₹100/120, motor boat ₹30

2 SOMESHWAR BEACH & TEMPLE

The waves at Someshwar Beach slap against a huge rocky hill, on which a Shiva temple of the same name is built. This falls about 9km from Mangalore at the cusp of the Netravati River and the Arabian Sea, in **Ullal**. The temple was built during the regime of Rani Abbakka Devi, one of the first freedom fighters who resisted Portuguese rule in the coastal region. Arrive here in the evening for a dramatic view of the sunset. **6am–1pm, 3–8pm**

❸ TEMPLES OF MANGALORE

The streets of Mangalore are dotted with a number of temples nestled amidst modern buildings and residential complexes that have propped up around them. Most of them are not architecturally grand but are well-known amongst those religiously inclined. You can spend an entire day on a temple trail, covering the most important ones. The 9th-century **Mangaladevi Temple** is famous. Though not particularly ornate, it has a strong following, especially during Navaratri when devotees pray to all the avatars of the goddess. **Sharavu Ganapathi Temple's** grey, ornate exterior steers one into the dark 800-year-old sanctum where there is a revered Shiva deity. Urwa Marigudi lies incongruously in the middle of a residential complex but includes the important **Mariyamma Temple**. **Venkataramana Temple** is a mid-17th century shrine built for Lord Veera Venkatesha Swamy.

The massive **Kadri Manjunatheswara Temple** dates back to 1068. It contains an unusual six-armed statue of Lokeshwara

The century-old Kudroli Gokarnanatha is one of the main temples in Mangalore

📷 Snapshot: Red hued town

Mangalore is bathed in a deep red, with almost every old construction having used the famous 'Mangalore tiles' on their roof. These eco-friendly tiles are now hugely popular across all of south India, especially the coastal regions. Plebot, a German missionary set up the first tile factory here in the mid-19th century. To see one of the oldest factories of the region (1868), contact **Albuquerque & Sons** (📞0824 2425079, Hoige Bazaar, Bolar; 9am–5.30pm, Sun closed).

in the sanctum. The elaborate **Kudroli Gokarnanatha** is one of the most visited temples here. It's just a century old and was built by the Kerala-based saint, Sri Narayana Guru. The immense patronage he received is evident in the grand structure with elaborate carvings. Slot mornings and evenings for temple sightseeing as all of them close for about four hours in the afternoon.

Mangala Devi Temple www.mangaladevitemple.com; Bolara; 6am–1pm, 4–8.30pm; Sharavu Ganapathi Temple, Hampankatta; 6am–12.45pm, 4.15–8.45pm; Urwa Marigudi, Bolar Rd; 6am–2pm, 4–8.30pm; Venkataramana Temple, Car St; 6.15am–1pm, 6–8pm; Kadri Manjunatheswara Temple, near Kadri Hill; 5am–1pm, 4–8pm; Kudroli Gokarnanatha Kudroli; 6am–2pm, 4.30am–9pm

The imposing white structure of Rosario Cathedral

❹ CATHEDRALS & CHURCHES

A unique infusion of Christianity in this region through Goan Catholics has resulted in a healthy and interesting religious composition in Mangalore and is manifested in two important structures: **Rosario (Portuguese) Cathedral**, and **Milagres Church**. The 1568 Portuguese Cathedral has an elaborate dome and a cross which looks lovely when lit up at night. Milagres, on the other hand, was built a century later in 1680 by the Roman Catholic bishop Thomas de Castro. Besides these, you can visit **St Aloysius Chapel** atop Lighthouse Hill built by Italian missionaries, who played an important role

MANGALORE, UDUPI & AROUND

The striking Seyyid Muhammad Shareeful Madani Dargah in Ullal

in the development of the Mangalorean Catholic community. You can see marvellous paintings on its walls.
Rosario (Portuguese) Cathedral, Hampankatta; 9am–noon, 3–7pm; Milagres Church www.milagreschurchmangalore.com; Hampankatta; 6am–7pm; St Aloysius Chapel Lighthouse Hill; 9.30am–6pm; Sun 8.30am–6pm

❺ MOSQUES

There are two significant mosques in Mangalore: **Seyyid Muhammad Shareeful Madani Dargah** in Ullal and **Kudroli Jamia Masjid.** Ullal Dargah commemorates saint Seyyid Muhammad who arrived here over 500 years ago, supposedly on a floating chador (prayer mat) that carried him across from Medina. The Urs festival is held here every five years with much aplomb. The Kudroli Masjid is linked to the time of Tipu Sultan, as remnants of his rule in the form of a battery (watchtower) lie close to this spot. Both mosques allow women inside.
Seyyid Muhammad Shareeful Madani Dargah; Ullal; 5am–10pm; Jamia Masjid 0824 2493133; www.kudrolijamiamasjid.com; Karbala Rd, Kudroli; 5am–8.15pm

❻ SULTAN BATHERY

Though the Sultan Bathery in Mangalore is not a very glamorous monument, it's a mark of Tipu Sultan who

constructed this watchtower in 1784 to look out for British ships coming in through the Gurupura River behind it. Climb up to the small fortress for great views.
4km from city centre; 6am–8.15pm

❼ SEEMANTHI BAI GOVERNMENT MUSEUM
Also known as the Bejai Museum, it houses coins, sculptures, remnants of the British East India Company and paintings in neat exhibits in a few halls. Do make a visit if you have time at hand.
Bejai Main Rd; ₹2; 10am–5pm, Mon closed

❽ BEACHES
Many of the breezy beaches along the coast are just fishing villages with no infrastructure for tourists. The three worth a visit are: **Tannir Bavi** (8km), **Panambur** (10km) and **Suratkal** (14km). Of these, the first has a huge parking area (₹20 for cars) and stone benches to relax as well as a few shops selling tea and snacks. Panambur, on the other hand, is action packed with plenty of snack shops, lifeguards, horse and camel rides and even some water sports facilities from October to February. Suratkal is famous for its imposing NITK lighthouse, however this is off limits during the monsoon months.
Lighthouse entry adult/child/foreigner/camera/video ₹10/3/25/20/25; 4–5.30pm

Panambur Beach is popular for water sports

MANGALORE, UDUPI & AROUND

Detour: Moodbidri and Karkala

The towns of **Moodbidri** (33km) and **Karkala** (50km) on NH13 make for a day-long detour from Mangalore. The epithet 'Jain Kashi' is attached to Moodbidri, a small town packed with Jain shrines. There are 18 important Jain temples in this seat of Digambara culture, of which the Thousand Pillar Basadi (7am–6.30pm) is the most important. Over 600 years old, its architectural features are a fascinating mix of oriental, Nepalese and Hoysala influences. The other two temples worth visiting are Guru Basadi and Vikarama Shetty Basadi. In Karkala (18km) visit two important monuments on this Jain temple trail. The statue of Thyagaveera Bhagwan Shree Bahubali Swami (9am–6pm) is on a low granite hill. From here you can see the beautiful Jain Chaturmukh Temple (9am–6pm) on the opposite hill. It has 108 intricately carved pillars.

Udupi

❶ SRI KRISHNA TEMPLE

The 13th-century Sri Krishna Temple is a key highlight of Udupi, with thousands of pilgrims (Hindus only) meandering in a slow long line along the temple kalyani to pay homage to the Lord Krishna for a brief moment, before they are hastily ushered away. The temple is packed with devotees, especially during Janamashtami festival. Men have to be bare-chested to enter. An elephant is one of the key attractions here. He blesses devotees with a pat on the head with his trunk after accepting coins and bananas. There are a number of temples nearby dating back 1500 years. The spacious Car Street stands parallel to the temple and is the entry point for the eight mutts that surround the temple.
Parking ₹10; 5am–9.30pm

❷ COIN MUSEUM

Trace the evolution of Indian coins right from their inception to the latest launch in this museum. Housed in founder Khan Bahadur Haji Abdullah Haji Kasim Saheb Bahadur's house, two large rooms have coin and rupee note exhibits as old as 2400 years ago, through

Highlights

❶ Sri Krishna Temple
❷ Coin Museum
❸ Temples around Udupi
❹ Museum of Anatomy & Pathology
❺ Jomlu Teertha Falls
❻ Beaches
❼ St Mary's Island

The Sri Krishna Mutt is Udupi's key religious centre

various dynasties, colonial rule and independent India. MK Krishnayya guides visitors with enthusiasm, pointing out the details and enriching one's knowledge in numismatics!
☎ 0820 2530955; **PB 15, Corporation Bank Building;** 10am–5pm

❸ TEMPLES AROUND UDUPI

On the coastal stretch from Udupi to Murudeshwar, there are plenty of temples worth a visit. The **Kunjarugiri Sri Durga Devi Temple**, believed to have been established by Lord Parasurama thousands of years ago, lies south of the city on a low hill, overlooking the lush countryside. Moving north 30km from Udupi the **Annegudde Sri Vinayaka Temple**, **Mookambika Devi Temple** and **Murudeshwar Temple** are the most important ones. Mookambika Temple lies on the banks of the Souparnika River; it is held in great reverence because 1200 years ago, Adi Shankara himself installed the idol here.

The 20-storeyed gopuram (ornate tower) of Murudeshwar Temple at the beachside town of the same name emerges as soon as you approach the Kanduka Hill. Surrounded by the Arabian Sea on three sides, you will find it packed with tourists. Make your way through a gate flanked by two life-sized elephant sculptures to the sanctum on an elevated hillock on the left. You can also go up the lift to the 18th floor of the gopuram for a spectacular view of the coastal stretch.

MANGALORE, UDUPI & AROUND

In a park behind the temple, a 123ft statue of Shiva overlooks the surrounding areas.
Kunjarugiri Sri Durga Devi Temple 0820 2559444; www.kunjarugiri.in; 7am–7.30pm; **Annegudde Sri Vinayaka Temple, Kumbhasi;** 6.30am–8.30pm; **Mookambika Devi Temple, Kollur;** 75km from Udupi; 6am–1pm, 3–8.30pm; **Murudeshwar Temple,** 102km from Udupi ; 6am–1pm, 3–8.30pm; Park 7am–7pm, Sat & Sun 7am–9pm

> ### ✓ Top Tip: Exploring the coastline
> The drive along the Karnataka Coast from Udupi upto Murudeshwar and beyond is extremely scenic passing through a landscape still raw in its beauty. It is best to explore this in a car so you can make stops to admire the picturesque coastline or halt at various temples and resorts on the way.

❹ MUSUEM OF ANATOMY & PATHOLOGY
Renovated in 2011, this museum is more than 40-years old. It contains hundreds of specimens of human and animal anatomy. In tune with the fine reputation of Manipal University's medical college, the museum is well maintained. Stroll through galleries of pickled human and animal organs, taking your time to understand and process the bizarre biological exhibits.
Manipal; adult/child ₹10/5; 8am–5pm

❺ JOMLU TEERTHA FALLS
Drive through a shady forest path flanked by cashew trees and thick undergrowth to reach Jomlu Teertha waterfall. The 20ft falls on the Sita River are a local hot spot, so avoid weekends. Though the area is lush and beautiful in the rainy season, the water levels are alarmingly high. For closer access to the falls, it's best to go in the non-monsoon months.
30km from Udupi

❻ BEACHES
Innumerable fishing villages and small towns line the coastal stretch from Udupi to **Murudeshwar**. Many of the beaches are not developed for tourism and retain their laid-back fishing culture. They are worth

The Coin Museum has exhibits as old as 2400 years

Bird's-eye view of Kaup Beach

a visit, but are unsafe for swimming. Close to Udupi, **Kaup** (15km), locally called Kapu is popular with tourists. Besides the pristine, silver stretch of sand, a towering lighthouse with a panoramic view is its key attraction. **Mattu Beach** (8.5km) is more elusive, because access to it lies through a small bridge across the backwaters. It makes a scenic drive and is not plagued by a surge of tourists. **Malpe Beach** (8km) is an energetic, local tourist spot with horse and camel rides, food stalls and even water sports in non-monsoon months.

Another stop by the highway is **Maravanthe Beach** (53km), flanked on the other side by the Souparnika River. You can also halt here at the Turtle Bay Resort. The **Baindur Beach** (70km) has a dramatic rocky outcrop as a backdrop; you can follow the hillside along the beach and get a better viewing spot from the top. Murudeshwar's popular tourist beach has the RNS Residency, where you can stop. It commands a vantage point by the sea and is a stone's throw away from Murudeshwar temple.

Kaup Beach lighthouse entry ₹10; 4–6pm, closed in monsoon; Malpe Beach water sports ☏7411559953; www.karavaliadventures.com; parasailing ₹500 per head; Turtle Bay Resort www.turtlebayeco.com; RNS Residency: ☏08365 268901; www.naveenhotels.com

❼ ST MARY'S ISLAND

Off the Malpe coast, during the non-monsoon months you can take a short 3km excursion into the sea, where you can visit a cluster of islands, namely Dari Bahadur Garh, Coconut Island, South Island and North Island. Together, these are called St Mary's Islands and were formed by basaltic lava. The best time to visit is between December and March.

☏9740981755; ₹100–150 to visit one island; pay more to visit all; 8am–5pm

Detour: Agumbe & around

Agumbe, a 650m high rainforest plateau, lies 55km northeast of Udupi, through a breathtaking forested path and countryside full of jasmine plants. This World Heritage Site is one of the wettest parts of the Western Ghats, and also known as 'Cherrapunji of the south' and specifically known for its King Cobra population and other rare amphibians and reptiles.

Renowned herpetologist P Gowri Shankar runs a camp and workshops, about 7km from Agumbe where you can learn more about snakes (✆9986291641; d tent incl food and activities ₹2000; 3-day Herp Camp ₹2500 per day/ person).

The government run **Seethanadi Nature Camp** (✆9480807650; Hebri Village; d tent incl food ₹1500) alongside the River Sita offers tented accommodation and nature trails

A safer haven is Kastur Akka's home, **Dodda Mane** (✆08181 233075) in Agumbe, where two episodes of the legendary TV serial *Malgudi Days* were shot in 1985. The resident family is happy to host guests and feed them at no cost. Voluntary offerings are recommended.

Agumbe is a base for several picturesque waterfalls like **Jogi Gundi**, **Onake Abbi**, **Barkana**, **Kundadri** and **Kudlu Theertha**. You may have to walk upto 6km to reach these. Avoid going in the monsoons when the paths are ridden with leeches.

The famous **Dakshinamnaya Sri Sharada Peetham** (✆08265 250123; www.sringerisharadapeetham.org; 6am–2pm, 4–9pm; meals 12.15–2.30pm, 7.15–8.30pm) at Sringeri, established by Sri Adi Shankara, 12 centuries ago, lies 28km from Agumbe. It was a seat of learning for the Sanatana Dharma. Free meals are offered at the temple.

Reaching Kudlu Theertha waterfall around Agumbe requires a long walk

 Accommodation

MANGALORE

Goldfinch — Boutique Hotel ₹₹₹
0824 4245678; www.goldfinchhotels.com; Bunts Hostel Rd; d ₹3950–5950, ste ₹8500–15000 (incl of breakfast) Your best bet for a stylish boutique hotel in town, Goldfinch's shiny interiors with modern facilities and impeccable service, will make your stay pleasant. However, the double occupancy, superior rooms are a bit small to accommodate an extra bed.

The Ocean Pearl — Hotel ₹₹₹
0824 2413800; www.theoceanpearl.in; Navabharath Circle, Kodialbail; d ₹5500, ste ₹8500 (incl of breakfast) With a busy check-in counter, buzzing travel desk and guests milling in and out of the three in-house restaurants, you can be sure that you are in the most popular hotel of Mangalore. Black and white photographs of the coastal region adorn its walls. The rooms are well lit and spacious with clean bathrooms. The hotel has a gym, 24-hour coffee shop and a lounge bar.

Pilikula Nisarghadhama — Boutique Hotel ₹₹
0824 2263565; www.junglelodges.com; Nisargadhama; d ₹5000–6400 (incl of full board & entry fee to all Pilikula activities) The tawdry looking building owned by Jungle Lodges has, however, the most magnificent view of the Gurupura River and the lush valley around. The accommodation is close to the Manasa Amusement Park and the Pilikula Nisargadhama complex which has a zoo, artisans' village and other interesting spots. Ask for a river-facing room.

Hotel Deepa Comforts — Hotel ₹₹
0824 2497101; www.hoteldeepacomforts.com; MG Rd; d ₹2950–3750, ste ₹4750 (incl of breakfast) The advantage of staying here is that you will be in the centre of town and walking distance from the main shopping district. The rooms are reasonably comfortable and have flat screen televisions and other modern facilities. There is also an in-house Indian restaurant.

Ginger — Hotel ₹₹
0824 6663333; www.gingerhotels.com; Kottara Chowki Junction, Kuloor Ferry Rd, Kottara; d ₹3999

A self-catering home, Blue Matsya at Kaup Beach, is ideal for families

(incl of breakfast) The self-sufficient business hotel is a bright and clean option if you want to stay on the outskirts of the city. The hotel has all the usual modern amenities like an in-house restaurant, gym, and in-room dining. It is not over-the-top, but service is quick and efficient and your stay will be hassle-free.

Hotel Prestige — Hotel ₹
☏ 0824 2410601; www.hotelprestige.in; near Collectors Gate, Balmatta Junction; d ₹2395–3795 (incl of breakfast) Don't go by the run-down, dull exteriors of the hotel. It's actually great value for money and the newly refurbished rooms on the 4th floor are a good option. They are spacious, well-lit and clean with modern facilities.

The Saffron — Boutique Hotel ₹
☏ 0824 4255542; www.thesaffron.in; GHS Rd, Hampankatta; d ₹2999, ste ₹4999 (incl of breakfast) Though The Saffron provides decent value for money, the rooms leave much to be desired in terms of being clean and bright. However, the pro is that you will be close to the two main temples of the town – Venkataramana Temple and Kudroli Gokarnanatha.

UDUPI

In this small town, accommodation options are around the Sri Krishna Temple. To enjoy the best of its coastline and verdant green cover, as well as proximity to town, you can choose to stay in Malpe, Kaup, Yermal and Manipal, which are close to Udupi.

Fortune Inn Valley View — Hotel ₹₹₹
☏ 0820 2571101; www.fortunehotels.in; PB No 174, Manipal; d ₹6000–7000, ste ₹9000–11000 (incl of breakfast) One of the best options in both Manipal and Udupi, the Fortune Hotel provides in-house dining and well-decorated, comfortable rooms. It lies in the middle of Manipal city.

Blue Matsya — Self Catering Beach House ₹₹
☏ 9820770427; www.thebluematsya.com; Lighthouse Rd, Kaup Beach; d ₹3800-5000 (minimum 2 nights) A pleasant respite for travellers who just want to kick off their shoes and immerse themselves in the windy environs of coastal Udupi, Blue Matsya lies just off the lighthouse at Kaup Beach. A stylishly furbished self-catering home, it offers ample privacy, but you also have help close at hand; Ramanna the caretaker lives next door. A well thought out instruction guide by the owner, Swati, equips you sufficiently to have a great time while you are here.

Paradise Isle — Beach Resort ₹₹
☏ 0820 2538666; www.theparadiseisle.com; Malpe; d ₹3500–5000, ste ₹5500–8500, (incl of breakfast) One of the oldest hotels in the area, Paradise Isle is a

good choice mainly for its proximity to Malpe Beach and excellent service. Both salvage the experience of its simple rooms and unimpressive breakfast spread. The resort also offers houseboat options for you to explore the backwaters around Udupi.

Sai Radha Heritage — Beach Resort ₹₹
☏9243350458; www.sairadhaheritage.com; behind Muloor Panchayath, Bikriguthu Rd, Muloor; d ₹3000–5000 (incl of breakfast) A cosy unit of four rooms in a traditional house, a beach facing three-roomed complex and a single room make up the cathartic Sai Radha Heritage. Aimed at Ayurveda enthusiasts you will find the hotel full of long-stay guests; you must book ahead to ensure that you get a room of your choice.

Palm Grove Beach — Beach Resort ₹
☏9008444891; Fisheries Rd, Yermalbada; d ₹2500 (incl of breakfast) If you want a secluded spot on the beach, Yermal's Palm Grove is a simple but tasteful option. There are 10 AC and 18 non-AC rooms, which are spartan in decor, but comfortable. Guests can order both vegetarian and non-vegetarian food in the resort, but give the staff prior notice about your meal plans. It's a super spot for a close encounter with the fishermen of the region, as the resort lies next to a small fishing colony. Watching the catch arrive in the morning is the most exciting activity here.

Diana — Hotel ₹
☏0820 2520505; near Big Bazar, Jodukatte, Ajjarjad; d ₹2000–2200 (incl of breakfast) Everyone in Udupi will tell you to visit Diana restaurant, a time-tested establishment for south Indian snacks at a reasonable price (also try an ice cream called 'gadbad'). The new address of the restaurant also has a spanking new set of rooms; which are clean and spacious.

Summer Park — Hotel ₹
☏0820 2535904; www.hotelsummerpark.com; Vidyasamudra Rd, Badagupet; d ₹1200–1500, ste ₹2000 (incl of breakfast) Though Summer Park is not in the most scenic part of town, it is clean and provides value for money. All the rooms have a TV and are divided into double, deluxe and suites and non-AC options are also available.

Hotel Century Executive — Hotel ₹
☏ 0820 2593333; www.centurycomforts.com; Aroor Arcade, near Swarna Jewellers; d ₹1299 The newly constructed Century Executive does not promise an atmospheric stay, but clean rooms, proximity to the Krishna Math and wi-fi in every room makes this small establishment of 18 rooms a good choice for the money you pay.

Eating

The region is replete with multi-cuisine options but what you will really want to dig your teeth in, is the coastal cuisine. Don't leave without trying the iconic sol kadi, a popular beverage.

MANGALORE

Woodlands   North/South Indian ₹
☏ 0824 2443751; Bunts Hostel Rd; mains below ₹200; 6am–9.45pm
Forget the ambience, and enjoy the quickly served delicious meal at the iconic 52-year-old Woodlands Hotel. Prepare to share tables with strangers and be served on banana leaves.

New Tajmahal Cafe   South Indian Snacks ₹
☏ 0824 4269335; near Sankai Gudda Rd; mains below ₹200; 6am–10pm A babble of conversation hits you as you enter this bustling snack joint, with regulars catching up over snacks and coffee.

Pallkhi   Multi-Cuisine ₹₹
☏ 0824 2444929; www.pallkhi.com; Tej Towers, 3rd floor, opp Jyothi Cinema, Balmatta Rd; mains ₹250–500; noon–3pm, 7–11.15pm
Do not go by the exteriors of Pallkhi. Even though the building is weathered, the restaurant itself is a cosy, family-friendly option for multi-cuisine dishes. We recommend that you stick to the tasty Indian fare, especially the assortment of fish curries.

Pallkhi is a good option for those who want to try an assortment of fish curries

Coral & Sagar Ratna   Multi-Cuisine ₹₹
☏ 0824 2413800; Navabharath Circle, Kodialbail; mains ₹250–500; 11am–3.30pm, 6.30–11.30pm The Ocean Pearl Hotel is home to two interesting restaurants; the spacious fine-dining restaurant Coral, that offers largely seafood delicacies and north Indian fare and Sagar Ratna (7am–11pm), where you can have a south Indian meal. Both restaurants are local favourites so prepare to queue up for a place at meal times.

Sanadige   Multi-Cuisine ₹₹
☏ 0824 4245678; www.goldfinchhotels.com; Bunts Hostel Rd, near Jyoti Circle; mains ₹250–500; noon–3.15pm, 7–11.15pm For a bite of typical Mangalorean cuisine, head straight to Sanadige at Goldfinch Hotel. If you are looking for a grill spread, Kabab Studio at the same hotel is also a good option.

UDUPI

Woodlands — Vegetarian ₹
📞 0820 2522807; Dr UR Rao Complex, near Sri Krishna Math, Thenkapet; mains below ₹200; 8.30am–3.30pm, 5.30–10.30pm One of the oldest establishments in town, you are likely to get the most authentic Udupi dosa here, along with a reasonable spread of north and south Indian dishes. The dingy basement restaurant is packed during lunchtime.

Thonsepar — Snacks ₹
📞 9902009595; Malpe Beach; mains below ₹200; 10am–8pm Malpe's only claim to a beachside shack, this small and neat cafe near the parking section is a relaxing spot for an evening coffee or sandwiches. The cafe also has a few rooms right at the beachfront (₹1500–2500).

Food Court — Multi-Cuisine ₹
Food Court, Manipal; mains below ₹200; 8.30am–10.30pm A buzz of conversation hits you as soon as you enter the Food Court of Manipal. This is after all the eating hub for students of the multiple colleges that Manipal is famous for. You can get a wide variety of options here: oriental, north Indian, south Indian, fast food and more. It's a convenient, quick and cheap stop.

Thaamboolam — Vegetarian ₹₹
📞 0820 4296418; opp Kalpana Theatre, Comfort Tower; mains ₹250–500; 10.30am–3.30pm,

The Food Court of Manipal offers a range of cuisines including thalis

6.30–11.30pm The owners have put in an insurmountable effort in its ethnic decor, which includes a bullock cart, indigenous wall designs and more. On top of that the brilliant food (especially the fish) ensures a fulfilling experience.

Mitra Samaj — South Indian ₹₹
📞 0820 2520502; Car St; mains ₹250–500; 5.30am–9.30pm, Wed closed A symbol of Udupi's famous south Indian cuisine, Mitra Samaj is another busy place in town with waiters making their way through packed tables with crisp dosas. It is next to the Krishna Temple.

Sarovar — Vegetarian ₹₹
📞 0820 2529145; Karvali Bypass; mains ₹250–500; 7.30am–9pm For veg multi-cuisine fare, you won't be disappointed with Sarovar, which lies between the middle of the city and Malpe. The restaurant is spacious and has a separate AC section.

MANGALORE, UDUPI & AROUND

Activities

Water sports are slowly catching up on the coastal stretch of Karnataka. Barring the monsoon months of June, July and August, there are plenty of exciting options during the high season from October to February.

ALONG THE COAST
Surfing
Ashram Surf Retreat, Mulki; 9880659130; www.surfingindia.net; Mulki; d ₹3500 (incl of full board, yoga, day activities and wi-fi); surf equipment and lessons ₹2000 per person If you have caught the surfing bug, there is no better place to test your skills other than the Ashram Surf Retreat in Mulki, 22km from Mangalore. Tucked away in the inconspicuous coastal village, this is complemented by the Mantra Surf Club that was established with a view to soak in yoga, meditation, simple veg food and, of course, riding the waves. Four rooms ensure that the group is intimate and the learning experience exclusive. Experts Jack Hebner and Rick Perry lead the team to help you manoeuvre surf breaks like Baba's Left and Swami and try in kayaking, body boarding, wake boarding, and more.

Water Sports
Mani, Udupi; 9916773834 Try your hand at different aqua activities like banana boat rides (₹200), water scooter rides (₹300) and a trip to New Clean Island, 8km into the sea, off Udupi. On this trip you may also watch dolphins (₹500)

If You Like: Art forms & festivals

Coastal Karnataka is rife with ancient traditions and festivals. Betting on cockfights and Pulikkali (tiger dance) are also common. You have to depend on hearsay, posters and local newspaper announcements to find out the venues of performances.

- **Bhuta Kola:** This ancient ritualistic dance form can be seen in coastal villages from November to May, most frequently December to January. The overnight dances are held to solicit blessings from the spirits.

- **Yakshagana:** Ritualistic folk theatre transports you to the world of the Ramayana and Mahabharata (best seen December–January, though performed November–May). Temples like Kateel Durga Parameshwari, 43 km from Udupi and Mandarthi Sri Durgaparmeshwari, 27km from Udupi are famous for Yakshagana.

- **Kambala Buffalo Race:** Over 1000 years old, the tradition of racing buffaloes in swampy tracks was originally a farmer's sport, but was later patronised by kings. Over 45 kambalas are held from November to March. Kadri Kambala in Mangalore is the most famous, but the ones in villages are less commercial and give you a more authentic insight into this sporting tradition. There is no fixed calendar for these events.

Mangalore is famous for cashews that are available at many shops in the city

Parasailing
Karavali Adventure; www.karavaliadventures.com On Malpe Beach you can try guided parasailing (₹500). Weekends and holidays are packed with locals.

Snorkelling and Scuba Diving
Dreamz Diving; 9740752480, 9326151300; www.dreamzdiving.com; beginners (discover) ₹4500 onwards; min age 10 yrs; 8.30am–4pm Start from Murudeshwar, 20km to Netrani Islands, for a day of instructed scuba diving. You will be given training and then made to dive with an instructor up to 18m deep. The underwater world of tropical sea creatures is dazzling. Try and avoid the weekends and public holidays.

Rafting
Adreno Rafting; 94481 66970; www.adreno.org; 57, 2nd Cross, 7th C Main, RPC Layout, Vijayanagar 2nd Stage, Bengaluru; packages from ₹1750–4250 Between 15 June to 30 September, ride the rapids of Seethanadi River. You can experience up to class 3 plus rapids here on stretches starting from 10km to 38km. You can choose to stay for a few hours or opt for an overnight stay.

🔒 Shopping

There aren't too many souvenirs that one can pick up from the region. Mangalore's badam and banana halwa and cashews, which grow abundantly in the region, are popular.

MANGALORE
Taj Mahal — Halwa
0824 2421751; Hampankatta; 7am–9.30pm This sweet shop in the heart of the city sells sticky sweet banana halwa and toffee-like wrapped blobs of the delicious badam halwa.

Phalguni Cashew Centre — Cashew
0824 6566011; Shop No 4, Hotel Roopa Bldg, Balmatta Rd; 8.30am–9.30pm, Sun 9.30am–1.30pm An assortment of dry fruits is displayed temptingly at the town's best cashew stop (₹600/kg onwards).

UDUPI
Airody — Handicrafts
0820 2520957; Car St; 8am–1pm, 3–8pm, Sun closed Udupi Metal statues, incense stick holders and metal pots, are available at Airody Radhakrishna Pai & Sons.

Expert Recommendation
Beachside behaviour

Actor **Gul Panag** is a regular visitor to the Konkan Coast and is involved in conservation work with The Energy and Resources Institute (TERI).

TOSS THAT TRASH

- Stop littering. Leaving trash on the beach – be it leftover food, tetra juice box or rubbish – is not just bad manners but pollution.

- Don't leave behind bottles of beer on the sand. Broken glass on beach dunes is harmful.

- Dispose of plastic waste responsibly. Don't let polybags fly on the beach. They are known to choke marine animals.

- Reduce, recycle and reuse. Pack a traditional picnic in a basket. If it's a beach with no waste bins, take your trash back home to dispose it.

- The beach is neither an open public lavatory nor a garbage yard.

VISITING RIGHTS

- The crabs are at home on the beach. Don't swipe at creatures because you need to sunbathe.

- Avoid walking beyond tidal lines. Hiking on marshes or seagrass beds can lead to beach erosion.

- Enjoy your beach holiday but don't forget to be sensitive to local fishing or tribal communities on the shore.

- Picking pieces of coral off the waters can seriously alter the delicate marine environment. Avoid this.

- Stay clear of oil-spilling, fume-spouting water boats that pollute the delicate balance of the ocean.

SHOW A LITTLE CARE

- It's a nice gesture to give back during your travels. Try offering your service for even an hour or support local NGOs in places like the Andaman that are assisting people to piece their lives after the tsunami.

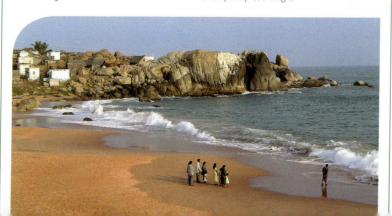

Not littering a beach is a one of the key steps in preserving it

Gokarna, Karwar & Dandeli

At Gokarna wild cliffs break out into rocky beaches dotted with shacks, making for a dramatic getaway. Karwar on the other hand is getting popular for its islands, dense hills that are alive with adventure, besides spectacular beaches. Dandeli is best for a rafting trip down River Kali as you experience the Anshi Dandeli Tiger Reserve, making a perfect setting for adventure activities.

Trip Planner

GETTING THERE

Gokarna: The closest airport is in Goa (154km). Gokarna is connected by rail from Ankola (20km), Kumta (35km) and Margao (140km), and various trains stop at these stations.

Karwar: Goa (95km) is the nearest airport. Karwar railway station falls on the Konkan Railway line and has trains to important cities and towns.

Dandeli: Hubli (80km) is the closest airport, but has limited flight connections, while Goa (142km) has daily flights to all metros. The closest railway station is in Alnavar (36km).

SUGGESTED ITINERARY (7 DAYS)

A week's time is enough to explore the region starting at Gokarna, heading up to Karwar and then veering off inland to Dandeli. Keep an extra day to drive or trek upto Castle Rock.

BEST TIME TO GO

J F M **A** M J J A S **O N D**

GREAT FOR

Top 5 highlights

- Gokarna Beach (p152)
- Yana Rocks, Gokarna (p155)
- Karwar Beach (p157)
- Rafting, Dandeli (p168)
- Syntheri Rock, Dandeli (p159)

In the Land of River Kali

Fertility idols under a tree at Gokarna

At first glance, the tattooed tribe of backpackers and sun worshippers may appear to be hedonists, but as you see ash-smeared dreadlocked sadhus, posters for yoga sessions and shacks called Om and Nirvana, you will sense that running through the air in **Gokarna** is a desperate search for spirituality. For people who say they truly love the beach, the sand and the sea, wild and gritty Gokarna is the ultimate touchstone.

While **Karwar** has been given a tentative foothold on the tourist map of the country for its spectacular beaches, its other natural bounties often go ignored. With islands that are studies in solitude and dense hills alive with adventure, Karwar, tired of being overshadowed by the flashier Goa, is finally coming into its own. Here you see an immense river against the backdrop of rugged hills, furiously emptying itself into the sea. This fusion of river, sea and mountain makes for a heady draw.

A visit to **Dandeli** can be broken down in two parts: for rafting and non-rafting. Unlike other destinations known for the sport, here the water in the Kali River is a result of the dam gates opening to clear the excess drain-off. October to May is the best season to visit. Having said that, the monsoon months are equally enthralling, as the entire area is covered in copious amounts of green with umpteen waterfalls pummelling down deep valleys with ferocity. The dark forested area of the **Anshi Dandeli Tiger Reserve**, the paddy fields and areca trees all add to the greenery.

Gokarna

Highlights
1. Gokarna Beach
2. Om Beach
3. One Tree Point
4. Kudle Beach
5. Half Moon Beach
6. Paradise Beach
7. Mahabaleshwar Temple
8. Mirjan Fort
9. Yana Rocks

1 GOKARNA BEACH
Once perhaps used for evening strolls and to soak in the sunset by its residents, Gokarna Beach now performs the function of a temple as well. Devotees entering the Mahabaleshwar Temple cleanse themselves here before entering its sacred portals. As a result, the beach is not secluded any more. Large Tata Sumos loaded with devotees leaving a long trail of puja flowers are the ones who usually come here. It is worth a visit if you're planning a trip to the temple or the numerous lunch homes.

The Om symbol shapes Gokarna's shoreline

2 OM BEACH
Let it be said right away that Om Beach won't win any Best Beach awards. The two semi-circular coves joined in the middle that give this beach its name don't have pristine

> ## Top Tip: *Carry your own essentials*
>
> The simple rule to follow while going to Gokarna is 'carry everything'. This includes not only travel essentials like creams, repellents, liquor or trekking shoes, but also things like towels, soaps and torches. A couple of bed sheets or beach mats may not be a bad idea too.

sand or blue waters, but as you descend the steps at the end of the road, you can tell you've come to some special place. The peaceful hillocks surrounding the beach, the simple shacks dotting the stretch and the yoga sessions on its rocky outcrops at sunrise give this strip of sand a more contemplative than playful vibe that lives up to its name.
4km from main Gokarna town; autorickshaw ₹250

❸ ONE TREE POINT
Walk up the dirt track towards the cliff from Dolphin Shanti cafe at the end of Om Beach and you will find the path that goes towards Half Moon Beach. As you pass through a rocky divide, casuarina trees and wild thorn bushes and climb higher, the sea views get more spectacular. Ten minutes into the hike, you will find one lone tree defiantly standing on the cliff that juts into the sea. Stand here to see the holy shape of Om and feel connected to the cosmos.
20min trek from Om Beach

❹ KUDLE BEACH
Kudle Beach is like a fiercely guarded bastion of privacy. It is easily a 20-minute trek on a treacherous footpath from Om Beach. Kudle gets a smaller share of the random beach crowd and is populated more by people who live long-term in its numerous guesthouses and shacks. This clean, one kilometre stretch with a generous length of sand is lively with volleyball players, sunbathers and shacks jostling with each other for space. Frequented mostly by foreigners, Kudle is the perfect place for a sundowner and, if you're lucky, the residents will whip out their guitars to lend the right background score to a glorious sunset.
20min trek from Om to Kudle Beach; autorickshaw ₹80

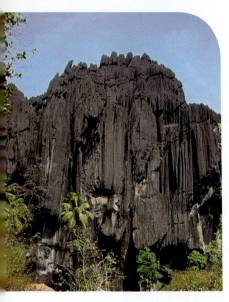

Yana rocks are located in the middle of a lush forest

❺ HALF MOON BEACH

More of a cove than a beach, Half Moon is somewhat of a hideout with an illicit, 'away from it all' vibe. It's a beach where you can enjoy the starlit sky and noisy waves without gawking tourists. After you finish the long trek here from Om Beach you may be disappointed by the sight of this small strip of rocky sand flanked by hillocks on both sides, with just two shacks and five foreigners periodically dunking themselves in the sea between reading their books.

Boats to Half Moon Beach ₹300 per passenger

❻ PARADISE BEACH

Once believed to be a nudist beach and the party capital of the hippies, the plug was rudely pulled on it in December 2012. With construction and commerce led by the government leaving only debris in its wake, the beach now wears a forlorn and abandoned look, earning itself the title of 'Paradise Lost'. Come this side only if you are overcome by a strong desire to be totally alone. The fresh fruit vendor who trawls this beach might be the only person you see while you're there.

Paradise Beach can be reached by foot, but the trek is arduous – do not attempt in the evening; by boat ₹300

❼ MAHABALESHWAR TEMPLE

Very few spiritualists can resist visiting this temple, designated as one of the seven muktisthals (soul-liberating temples). This ancient shrine, with its twisted Shiva Lingam, makes Gokarna the mother lode of divine blessings. Expect large crowds, long queues and pushy priests, but they are a small price to pay for eternal salvation.

6am–12.30pm, 5–8pm; foreigners not allowed; men allowed in if bare chested

GOKARNA, KARWAR & DANDELI

8 MIRJAN FORT

Less than an hour away from Gokarna lies what is perhaps one of the best-preserved forts in India. Mirjan was an important port for the trade of spices, mostly pepper, which earned its Queen – Chennabhairavi Devi Gersoppa – the moniker of Pepper Queen. Built in the 1600s under both Portuguese and Islamic influences, the fort had living quarters, an audience hall, functioning kitchens and elaborate waterworks, most of which still stand strong and make history come alive effortlessly.

11km from Gokarna on the main highway; sunrise to sunset

9 YANA ROCKS

It's worth keeping a full day aside for the extraordinary sight of gigantic black rock formations shooting out from the middle of a dense forest an hour's drive from Gokarna. From the car park, walk for over an hour in the silent, cool forest and resist the urge to turn back when you see signs that warn you about the leopard. At the end of this hike, and about 250 steps away, you will be rewarded by the sight of Bhairaveshwara Shikara and Mohini Shikara, two black limestone beauties that house secret temples in their caves. Dawn and dusk are the best time to enjoy this spot.

40km from Gokarna on Sirsi Rd

Kudle is a lively beach, popular with foreigners

Detour: Jog Falls

Jog Falls (also known as Gerusoppa Falls) is 113 km from Gokarna. A monsoon special (Jun–Sep), the suite of Raja, Rani, Roarer and Rocket waterfalls plunges down from a height of 830ft. Part of the Sharavathi River, the falls create a magical haze of spray for those who brave proximity to them.

There are two ways to see Jog Falls: one from **Shimoga** district (adult/child/two-wheeler/cars ₹5/5/10/30; 7am–7pm) and the other from **Karwar** just a few kilometres ahead (not ticketed). While the more popular Shimoga side is the point from where you see all four waterfalls, the Karwar side has the closest access. You have to walk down 1500 steps (there are proper railings) to the base of the falls from the main side and can get as close as 30 meters from the base of the falls to enjoy the spray.

The **temple trail** around Jog Falls with Ikkeri, Keldai, Gerusoppa and Kalasi is also worth your while. The **Gudavi Bird Sanctuary** (Indian/foreigner ₹50/300; 9am–6.30pm) is yet another highlight that could be part of the itinerary.

If planning on staying for a night, **Gundi Mane Homestay** (✆9900956760; www.gundimane.com; Gundimane Aralgodu; d ₹1700, meals separate) and the **KSTDC accommodations** (✆0818 6244732; www.karnatakaholidays.net; Jog Falls; Sharavathi Block; d non AC ₹1800, AC ₹2200, Tunga Block non AC ₹800, 10-bed dorm ₹1800) just by the falls are highly recommended.

The gushing Jog Falls plunge from a height of 830ft

GOKARNA, KARWAR & DANDELI   157

Karwar

Highlights
1. **Karwar Beach**
2. **Lighthouse Island**
3. **Kurumgad Island**
4. **Devbagh Beach**
5. **Majali Beach**

1. KARWAR BEACH

The town of Karwar lives by its beach. Evening walks, kiddie play dates, navy fetes and fun fairs all come together here in a fusion of colour and chaos. This isn't a beach where you can soak up the sun with a chilled beer. Instead, this is the beach to take a long walk with the kids and stop at its myriad attractions en route – the fantastic Warship Museum with its life-sized replica of the INS Chapal, or the aquarium, and top it off with the most surreal experience of them all – a twinkling musical fountain set to Kannadiga beats!

Warship Museum is on the main beach road; ₹15; 10am–7.30pm, musical fountain plays 7–7.30pm every evening

2. LIGHTHOUSE ISLAND

'In the middle of a vast ocean there is a lighthouse with an old lighthouse-keeper as its only resident.' It may sound like fiction, but this is what you see when you step off the boat at the 1679 Oyster Rock lighthouse that stands in splendid isolation on an island. With its polished brass fittings, teakwood cabinets and wrought- iron railings, this relic of a bygone era stands frozen in time, struggling to stay relevant in a contemporary world that's moved on to terribly efficient and unromantic things like Global Positioning Systems.

8km off the coast of Karwar; boats cost ₹1500 for a return trip

 If You Like: Trekking

Karwar is not a land of easy charms. You have to climb a mountain – literally – to see the primal beauty of this land. It's only at the top that it will reveal its best secrets. Lace up your hiking boots and get ready to hit Gudahalli Peak – one of the most outstanding viewpoints in the region. This 6–8km trek takes you through springs, temples, friendly villages till finally you view all of Karwar's bounty – the sea, river, islands and the ghats.

Karavali Boating and Adventure Centre; 9880953626; ₹500 per guide for the trek

Devbagh Beach's raw beauty is its chief attraction

❸ KURUMGAD ISLAND

The 45-minute boat ride to Kurumgad Island is worth your time if you manage to wake up early. It's only in the morning, before the sun has had a chance to turn the island into an overheated rock in the middle of the ocean that it teems with birds and abounds in flora and fauna which you will discover during your nature walk. You can end up at the beach or creek or at the most stunning viewpoint. This serene hideout in the middle of the ocean makes you feel like Tom Hanks in *Castaway*, except here you can order tea instead of having to make your own.

☎ 08382 594574; Great Outdoors' nature walk ₹500 (incl of pick-up & drop), 8am

❹ DEVBAGH BEACH

Devbagh Beach is not easy to get to. Caught in the confusion between an island and a beach, it can be accessed only by boat with a fixed time schedule that charges a pretty penny per head. This makes you wonder why you shouldn't skip it, but when you get there you realise it's this elusiveness that makes it one of the best beaches in the area. Bereft of crowds, backed by a thick tree cover and decorated with sun decks and hammocks, Devbagh is what we would get if we started preserving our beaches instead of plundering them.

☎ 08382 226596; Jungle Lodges boat service to Devbagh Beach all through the day; ₹200 per head

GOKARNA, KARWAR & DANDELI

❺ MAJALI BEACH

The fishing village of Majali carries on with its business of trading and transporting fish along a 5km sliver of road that runs next to the beach, indifferent to the fact that it lies on one of the most scenic roads in the county. The windswept and little frequented Majali Beach doesn't have the privacy or tree cover of Devbagh, but it does have an incredible stretch of beach-facing road that demands a bicycle ride down it, and a fantastic outcrop of jagged rock that beckons to be climbed.

Devbagh–Majali 5km stretch runs parallel to NH17

Dandeli

❶ SYNTHERI ROCKS

Finding your way down more than 250 steps from the parking lot is certainly worth your while to see the mammoth near-vertical monolithic 300ft tall granite rock with the Kaneri River splashing at its bottom. Bleached by the sun and weathered by the ferocious water corroding its base, the rockscape has myriad colours and unique cave-like formations. Before you arrive here there is a long drive on a forest road, flanked by bamboo clusters. The swollen river during the monsoon is at its ravenous best, but take care, the path down is very slippery. When the water level is low, you can go right upto the edge of the river.

Adult/child/two-wheeler/car ₹10/5/10/20; 8.30am–5pm

❷ BACKWATERS OF SUPA DAM

The Supa Dam on the Kali River is seen as soon as you enter Ganesh Gudi from Dandeli. Its reservoir is a massive expanse of calm water, the third biggest catchment area in the country. This is best viewed from a road bridge 10km from Ganesh Gudi.

Highlights

1. Syntheri Rocks
2. Backwaters of Supa Dam
3. Dandeli Wildlife Sanctuary
4. Anshi National Park
5. Dudh Gadi View Point
6. Vajra Waterfall
7. Kavala Caves
8. Ulavi Channa Basaveshvar Temple

❸ DANDELI WILDLIFE SANCTUARY

The best way to see wildlife at Dandeli is on a safari from the Pansoli gate of the Wildlife Sanctuary. Arrive early or ask your hotel to book ahead as only 16 jeeps are allowed per day. You can only access the buffer zone of the total 845sq km park, but are likely to spot deer, elephants, gaur, bison and a host of other mammals. The same stretch of the forest extends into Anshi, making the two regions part of the Anshi Dandeli Tiger Reserve. The reptile and avian life here is also fascinating. Though the months of April and May are the best for sighting, the park is open through the year.

Pansoli; adult/child/foreigner/foreigner child ₹400/200/1200/600; 6–8am, 4–6pm; trek ₹275 per head, ₹500 for guide/group

❹ ANSHI NATIONAL PARK

Part of the Tiger Reserve, this protected forest area lies 52km from the Dandeli Wildlife Sanctuary's gate and is less visited due to the distance. But, the road leading to the region is as breathtaking as the jungle itself. The safaris here are not operational, but trekking is possible, giving an intimate option to see the forest cover. The Indian bison, gaur, wild boar, barking deer and many other mammals inhabit this region along with a fair population of reptiles and birds, including different varieties of hornbill.

♥ *If You Like: Untreaded paths*

To access some of the secret spots around Dandeli, it's best that you connect with a local. Since this is a forested area, the check posts maintain limited access. Dandeli is also a hydropower station with four dams in close vicinity, making some areas accessible only by permission:

- **Sykes Point:** You can get here only with a letter from a government body in Dandeli (wildlife or forest divisions). The viewpoint, named after a British collector who was posted here, reveals the spectacular sight of the snaking Kali River through a deep valley. Photography not allowed.

- **Kaneri River Dam:** A detour on the Dandeli-Anshi road leads to the Kaneri River Dam, which has a fantastic view of the River Kaneri making its way through a rocky river bed.

❺ DUDH GADI VIEW POINT
This viewpoint lies before Anshi National Park if you are driving from Dandeli. A pavilion with seating is the perfect spot to gaze at the bubbly river plunging down a valley.

❻ VAJRA WATERFALL
If you are going all the way to Anshi, an additional 3km ride does not hurt to see the thundering Vajra Waterfall just by the road. It's in its full glory during the rains.

❼ KAVALA CAVES
Inaccessible during the rains, Kavala Caves are a set of beautiful limestone stalagmite formations at the base of a cave. The spot is 25km from Dandeli and you have to climb 375 steps down and further crawl into a narrow cave to see a natural Shiva lingam formation.

❽ ULAVI CHANNA BASAVESHVAR TEMPLE
Ulavi lies 63km from Dandeli town but at the end of the drive is an important pilgrimage centre for the Lingayat community of north Karnataka. The pink and orange gopuram of the temple can be seen from a distance. The sculptures depict common life rather than gods and goddesses. Inside lies the samadhi of saint Channabasavanna.
6am–8pm

> It is easy to spot elephants at Dandeli Wildlife Sanctuary

Accommodation

GOKARNA

JJK Resort — Resort ₹₹
☎9620884136; Kudle Beach; d ₹3000 The fancy building may look like it doesn't belong in this hippie world, but when you go there, and sink into its king-sized bed and switch on the 32-inch plasma TV with the Arabian Sea laid out like a carpet in front, you realise that big structures may not be such a bad thing after all.

Om Beach Resort — Resort ₹₹
☎08386 257052; www.ombeachresorts.com; Om Beach Rd; d ₹6000 (incl of full board) One of the only 'resort' options in Gokarna, Om Beach Resort sits at a civilised distance from the mad chaos of the beach. The rooms are simply furnished in relaxing shades of green and white, but are big and come with balconies. It makes for a great family holiday destination.

Namaste Cafe & Namaste Yoga Farm — Guesthouse ₹
☎08386 257141; Om Beach; d ₹900–1500 This famous guesthouse in the midst of Om Beach offers the quintessential Gokarna experience with everything you could possibly need, from a convenience store, a tattoo studio and internet services to Ayurvedic massages. If you're more into yoga, head to the Namaste Yoga Farm on a hillock above Kudle Beach.

Nirvana Cafe — Beach Shack ₹
☎9742466481; Om Beach; d ₹500 The pretty little huts with colourful kitschy artwork, scattered in a small grove, are in high demand, as is its big, clean, beach-front cafe. It is the liveliest place in the evenings and offers a glorious sunset.

Khushi Village — Resort ₹
☎08386 257903; www.khushivillageresorts.com; Om Beach Rd, Niralla; d ₹1200 The first thing that bowls you over about this place is its location. Nestled in a grove in the middle of a forest, with a restaurant, it's suited more to the rugged nature lover who is not squeamish about snakes. Nevertheless, Khushi Village is a great option for a night under the stars with your buddies.

Gokarna International — Resort ₹
☎8884741005; Kudle Beach; d ₹2000 When in Gokarna, you usually have to make a choice – whether to live in a proper room with an attached bathroom, or stay by the sea. But at Gokarna International, you get both. This hotel offers the joys of indoor plumbing, as well as a great view of the sea, and has kept true to its Gokarna roots by offering a shack as its restaurant.

Arya Ayurveda Panchakarma Centre — Hotel ₹
☎9341254771; www.ayurvedainindien.com; Kudle Beach;

Om Shanti Cafe — Restaurant ₹
Om Beach; 8am–11pm Om Shanti is a big, clean shack with the most jaw-dropping wall art and a menu card that spells correctly, giving you the confidence to place an order of spinach mushroom pasta (₹75) or calamari macaroni (₹85) and not regret it.

Dragon Cafe — Pizzeria ₹
Kudle Beach; 8am–11pm This shack is rumoured to be the new avatar of an old pizzeria and carries the legacy of great wood-fired oven pizzas. There are at least 20 different varieties here, from the delicious seafood pizza (₹180) to the dubious cheese egg pizza (₹140), all served fresh and hot.

Jazzmin Cafe — Continental ₹
Kudle Beach; 8am–11pm Open all day, this funky place with just six lovely cane chairs and a vivid Shiva mural on its main wall, prides itself on its homemade bread and does a fantastic breakfast. Opt for their cinnamon rolls (₹50) and delicately flavoured ginger honey lime tea (₹20) for a breakfast that's light on the tummy and the pocket as well.

Prema Restaurant — South Indian/Vegetarian ₹
Main Beach; 8am–9pm Located right next to Gokarna Beach, Prema is where sadhus, hippies, tourists and winos sit side by side working through their meals. Operating on a strict 'pay first and eat fast' basis, Prema is cramped and is not that pretty, but none of the visitors really care about this. Most are just busy digging into their delicious south Indian vegetarian thali, (₹60) accompanied by a fresh fruit juice (₹80).

Pai Restaurant — Indian/Chinese ₹
08386 256755; Main Rd; 8am–9pm Not to be confused with the Pai Hotel next door, Pai Restaurant rivals the fame of Prema. This dingy little place in the middle of the market is also known for its south Indian

---

Snapshot: Havyaka food

This is traditional vegetarian cuisine made in Brahmin households of northern Karnataka. Easy on the stomach, with minimal spices, the focus is more on the nutrition and natural taste. The dishes in this cuisine use locally found roots, leaves and herbs. Common ingredients include jonibella, a jaggery liquid used in most Havyaka sweets. This is eaten with a dosa-like dish called 'tellevu'. Look out for the 'mavina hannushira', a mango tinged halwa, 'nugge soppina tambli', a buttermilk dish with drumstick leaves, the delicious 'appehuli' – mango rasam – the green gourd peel chutney, 'hirekai soppina' chutney and a steady accomplice at all meals, 'huleelu' – a cucumber, raw banana or banana 'pithraita'. Even the arrangement of food on the banana leaf is done in a specific manner.

also check into a small five-roomed property called Old Magazine House by the same group, for a place with more character.

Nature's Nest — Homestay ₹
☏9740751666; Village Ilava; d from ₹1200 per head (incl of all meals)
The six basic, though clean and spacious rooms of Nature's Nest give you a unique setting that's a pleasant change from the riverside lure. The house lies right in front of a paddy field, bordered by areca trees. A small pavilion outside is the common food area and there's no TV or even mobile signal to distract you.

Shikra Jungle Resort — Resort ₹
☏9663885492; Gobral Dandeli; d from ₹1500, tents ₹2000, treehouse ₹2500 (incl of all meals) Located 6km from Dandeli, this is a large green property, perfect for families travelling with children. You can choose between tents and treehouses. A play area, a resident pony, shooting targets, tree climbing apparatus and a small water body at the back keeps the kids busy, while elders can enjoy the natural beauty around, especially as the resort lies on the fringes of the Dandeli forest.

Kulgi Nature Camp — Camps ₹
☏08284 231585; Kulgi; tents ₹2000–2400, dorms ₹125 per head (incl of all meals) The oldest campsite and accomodation in the Dandeli region is still in pristine condition. It lies close to Dandeli Wildlife Sanctuary and the tented options can be locked and have attached bathrooms. Food is served in a common pavilion. A free interpretation centre and exhibits of local life lie right next to the campsite.

Eating

GOKARNA

Namaste Cafe — Multi-Cuisine ₹
☏08386 257141; Om Beach; 8am–11pm You know that you are in Gokarna when the menu offers fully loaded breakfast options from five different countries (₹110 each) and hardly anything on the menu crosses ₹200. At Namaste Cafe, you can spot people lounging around all day long over really tasty, if slightly inauthentic food. The big sellers here hail from Europe (chicken schnitzel ₹85) and China (veg fried rice ₹50).

Dolphin Bay Cafe — Cafe ₹
Om Beach; 8am–11pm If you come across a board with 'Hello to the King, Hello to the Queen, Bhagsu with ice cream' at the Dolphin Bay Cafe, don't mistake it for a feverish rhyme from a crazy mind. It's actually a menu of the Dolphin specials. Located right in the middle of the beach, across the rocky outcrop which gives Om Beach its shape, Dolphin Bay Cafe is hard to miss. 'Hello to the King' (₹115), a uniquely Gokarna concoction made of ice cream, cake and Parle biscuits is definately a must-try.

Tarang Resort — Resort ₹

📞 08382 655850; www.tarangresorts.com; Maldarwada, Devbagh; d ₹2100 Tarang offers large, spotlessly clean rooms dominated by intricately carved furniture, overlooking green lawns and swaying palms, vaguely reminiscent of Goa. It has a restaurant and children's play area – good for a family holiday.

DANDELI AND AROUND

Resorts, camps and homestays are spread across the area and not just in Dandeli town. They are often far from each other, so one never feels the weight of a busy season because of packed hotels.

Hornbill River Resort — Resort ₹₹

📞 9880683323; www.hornbillriverresort.in; Village Ambeli; d from ₹4500 (incl of all meals & activities), treehouse ₹7000

| Besides regular rooms Hornbill River Resort offers tree houses as well

(rates vary per season) Two comfy tree houses and a deck at the edge of Kali River are the highlights of Hornbill. Unlike most tree houses, these have large stable steps and well maintained interiors, including a tub in the bathroom. The accomodation is spread over 6.5 acres of land by the river. The Hornbill rafting experts are one of the two operators in the town.

Bison River Resort — Resort ₹₹

📞 08383 256539; www.indianadventures.com; Village Ambeli; d from ₹5000 (incl of breakfast; rates vary per season) One of the oldest resorts on the banks of River Kali, Bison has good access, view of the river, hospitable staff and spacious rooms. The first rapid of the Kali rafting stretch can be seen from here. Make sure you book the cottages closest to the river. It's the most popular resort for water-based and adventure activities.

Jungle Lodges Resort — Resort ₹₹

📞 9449599795; www.junglelodges.com; Dandeli; tents ₹3200, r ₹3500–4000 per head (incl of all meals) Book ahead to stay at the riverside property of Jungle Lodges, with option of sleeping in tented cottages or rooms. If it's a room, ask for the first floor options from where you can see the River Kali. Indoor games, rafting, safari in the jungle and nature walks with a naturalist are the activities offered by the resort. You can

GOKARNA, KARWAR & DANDELI

d ₹1200 This Ayurveda-inspired place, that includes an organic cafe, panchakarma massage centre and lodging, stands apart from other beach shacks on this strip. Their all-white rooms, with verandahs overlooking a pretty little courtyard with flowering bougainvillea, are high in demand and cheap for the price.

KARWAR

Devbagh Beach Resort — Resort ₹₹
☏ 08021 2444444; www.devbaghbeachresort.com; Devbagh Beach, Kodibagh; d ₹4000 (incl of all meals) One of the most popular resorts in the area, Devbagh stands alone on an incredible stretch of sand. The resort has log cabins and cottages that are large, but minus the frills. The prices are high. The restaurant has buffet meals and the resort offers water sports.

Some rooms at Emerald Bay in Karwar overlook the Kali River

Emerald Bay — Hotel ₹₹
☏ 08382 266602; www.sterlingholidays.com; NH17; d ₹4500 (incl of breakfast) The closest Karwar has come to luxury is with this highway hotel that overlooks the Kali River. Emerald Bay shines in comparison to the other more rugged options in the area, since it comes equipped with a concierge, restaurant, play area and offers room service.

Great Outdoors — Island Resort ₹₹
☏ 0824 4279152, 9844042152; www.thegreatoutdoorsindia.com; Kurumgad Island; d ₹3000 (incl of all meals) This resort commands an entire island, blessed with fantastic ocean views. Yet they've managed to offer rooms without a view. The restaurant makes up for what the tents don't deliver and the private beach is a great place for water sports.

Majali Beach Village — Resort ₹₹
☏ 08382 266891; www.majaliresorts.com; Devbagh, Majali Beach Rd; d ₹3300 (incl of breakfast) You may cross Majali Beach Village a couple of times before you actually find it. In a strange streak of shyness, the property refuses to announce itself and would rather that you do the chase. This is a simple unassuming resort with spartan rooms and a restaurant. The rooms don't face the sea but before you get disappointed, come out of the back door to the sit-out that overlooks a quiet lake.

GOKARNA, KARWAR & DANDELI

veg thali (₹50). While it does have a Chinese and north Indian menu as well, you are better off sticking with the south Indian staples.

KARWAR

Hotel Amrut — Seafood ₹
☎ 08382 226609; Main Rd; noon–3pm, 7–11pm Famous enough to have people driving over from Goa, Amrut, in their own words is 'the sea food specialist' in Karwar and even after 34 years, it has not settled into complacency. The waiter will ply you with suggestions like the excellent Karwar-style fried prawns (₹150) and squid chilli (₹120), and serve beer as you enjoy the spicy meal.

Shweta Lunch Home — Restaurant ₹
☎ 9986675726; Green St; 11.30am–3.30pm, 6.30–10.30pm This tiny eatery is nothing to look at, but it puts all its energy into serving freshly made home-style seafood. Offering every variety of fish in the sea, Shweta Lunch Home does a spicy and authentic fish

> Dragon Cafe offers at least 20 varieties of fresh wood-fired oven pizzas

thali (₹90) which must be paired with their garlic flavoured sol kadhi (₹15).

DANDELI

Most accommodations offer packages with meals included, as there are few eating options in the town. The other option is to rely on the roadside dhabas.

Tiger Heritage — Multi-Cuisine ₹
☎ 9448336233; mains ₹120–500; 11am–11pm Though Tiger Heritage is a homestay, the farm-like ambience with paddy fields across a gushing stream, geese, ducks and turkeys running around and organically produced veggies around the house, makes this a great stop for a meal as well. The owner, Wilson, is happy to have guests only for meals (book prior to arrival) and enjoy the farm life. Children will love this place. You can also take a swim in the shallow river pool within the property.

Activities

GOKARNA

Trekking

A world dominated by cliffs and the sea makes for a trekking paradise. In addition to the beach treks, which come highly recommended even for amateurs, there are a host of others to be done. While hard core trekkers swear by the Kumta–Gokarna trek (22km), it's the Ramanagram–Gokarna circuit (11km), passing through the lovely beaches of Barkha, Sangam and Belikhana, that is more popular.

Water Sports

Om Water Sports; 9632332651; **Om Beach** The good news about water sports here is that you'll probably be the one doing them, since the nirvana seeking foreigners aren't interested in being dragged across the sea. The bad news is that there isn't too much variety. The bumper boat ride (₹300) is by far the most fun, followed by the water scooter (₹300).

KARWAR

Water Sports

Karavali Boating and Adventure Centre; 9880953626; **Karavali, Aligadda, Baithkol** Whichever beach you choose at Karwar for your day of aqua sports, you will be assured of bright shining sands, blue water and gentle waves. If you're not staying at the Devbagh Resort, Adigadda Beach (end of main beach) will be your playground, where you can take a kayak (₹300) to Karwar Port, among other activities.

DANDELI

Rafting

Wild Raft Adventures; 9880131762; www.indiarafts.org; **Dandeli;** ₹1400 per trip (incl of pick and drop if coming from Jungle Lodges Resort or Old Magazine), equipment and instruction; age/weight limit 15–60yrs/below 100 kg White-water rafting on River Kali is what draws people to Dandeli. Unlike other rafting destinations which are active in the monsoons, Dandeli's season begins after the rains. You can experience upto grade 3 plus rapids here on the 9.5km stretch from Ganesh Gudi to Maulangi. Choose between two slots: 9.30am and 2.30pm, and after the preliminary orientation it's a two-hour journey, interjected by eight rapids. Trained instructors accompany you.

Adventure Sports

Flycatcher Adventures; 9481050954; treks ₹1000 per head (incl of forest entry charges, food, transport & guide) Dandeli is a hot spot for activities like trekking, river crossing, kayaking, zorbing, tree climbing, canoeing, rappelling and crossing rivers on a Burma Bridge. There are four major routes ranging from small hikes of 5km to longer treks of 11km. The easiest one is the Kali and Maulangi hike which takes you along the Supa Dam reservoir. The Nagjeri Valley trek is the most challenging one; for this permission from the forest department is required. The 4km-long Dudhsagar Waterfalls trek can start from villages Diggi and Qureshi, which are jeep rides away from Dandeli.

Water Activities
Adventurers; ☏9448485508; 2-day programme ₹3000 per head Adventurers runs a water-based activities programme in the backwaters of Sharavathi at Honnemaradu. Since this is 21km away from any habitation, they need advance intimation of your arrival. They offer coracle rides, boating, canoeing and island visits. Facilities are very basic so it's advisable to bring your own sleeping bags. This is an eco senstive zone so the group is careful about the admission of people.

🛍 Shopping
DANDELI
Kaadumane   **Handicrafts**
☏**9480085707; Potoli Village; 9am–1.30pm, 2.30–8pm** Dandeli is not a big shopping destination, but Kaadumane brings the best of local crafts to visitors in a small shop in Potoli Village. Women from 15 households produce masks made from lavancha grass, key chains and other knick-knacks that are sold here. Warli paintings are a favourite around villages here and you can see them come alive on small mud pots and key chains. You can also find locally sourced squashes and honey here. Try the tropical speciality cocum.

Gokarna is a popular spot for water sports

Badami, Pattadakal & Aihole

History enthusiasts will love this mystical sandstone trio of architectural wonders from the 6th century onwards, largely the work of the Chalukyan Empire. The rock-cut caves of Badami and the temple complex of Pattadakal and Aihole strewn with over 120 temples make for a three day-long immersion in Deccan India's most captivating temple architecture.

Trip Planner

GETTING THERE

Badami: Hubli is the closest airport (106km). It's better to pre-book a taxi through your hotel at Badami. A car will cost ₹2000–3000. Badami has a railhead and Hubli bound trains from Bengaluru stop here. KSRTC and private operators have overnight buses from Bengaluru (512km).

Pattadakal and Aihole: Pattadakal is 22km and Aihole is 35km from Badami. It's best to hire a car as local buses take longer routes. Hiring a taxi will cost ₹1500–2000 per day.

SUGGESTED ITINERARY (3 DAYS)

Use Badami as the base and start your sightseeing with the caves and monuments on the first day. The next morning, climb up to the Shiva shrines on the South Fort area. Move on to Pattadakal on the evening of the second day. Explore Aihole on the third day.

BEST TIME TO GO

J F **M A** M J J A S **O N D**

GREAT FOR

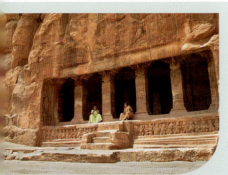

Top 5 highlights

- **Cave Temples, Badami** (p172)
- **Agastya Lake, Badami** (p173)
- **North Fort, Badami** (p174)
- **Temple Complex, Pattadakal** (p175)
- **Durga Temple Complex, Aihole** (p176)

Chronicles in Sandstone

View of Badami from the rocky caves

The architectural masterpieces of ancient **Badami**, earlier known as Vatapi, and nearby towns of **Pattadakal** and **Aihole**, were conceived by the Chalukyas and further influenced by a succession of dynasties including the Pallavas and Rashtrakutas, and later the rulers of the Vijayanagara Empire, Adil Shah, Tipu Sultan and finally Aurangzeb. Today, only the buildings of five dynasties and rulers still exist.

The techniques and creativity of the early Chalukyas between the 6th and 8th centuries resulted in a complete metamorphosis of the jagged sandstone cliffs that mark this little town. The result was an outstanding cluster of sculpted caves and temples that overshadow everything else in this little settlement.

The deep ravines and mammoth sandstone hills of the Malprabha Valley in the region became the breeding ground for a profusion of styles (both North and South) in temple architecture, as seen in the nearby towns of Pattadakal and

Aihole. These temples also served as a social melting point and veritable examples of secular rule, with Jain and Buddhist monuments finding a place here too. Apart from the temples and village homes, you are not going to find any restaurants; perhaps some small shacks selling water, cold drinks etc.

This trinity of temple towns is a paradise for history enthusiasts and students of architecture. It is advisable to hire a guide for the entire trip to fully imbibe the historical and artistic experience while visiting them.

Badami

❶ CAVE TEMPLES

Idol of Lord Vishnu at Cave 3

These beautiful cave temples just can't be missed. However, you have to climb up to the four cave temples of Badami from the foot of South Fort. Chiselled from deep red sandstone, the temples lie along a stepped pathway and are heavily 'patrolled' by monkeys. Cave 1 is a Shiva temple. Cave 2 and 3 are dedicated to Lord Vishnu, where you can see the eight-armed icon of Vishnu seated on Adisesha and the fierce lion-headed Narasimha. Besides the main sculptures, if you crane your neck upwards, you will see intricate carvings on the ceilings. Cave 4 is dedicated to the widely worshipped Jain tirthankara, Mahavira.

Looking down from the caves, it's hard to miss a domed tomb near the car park. This is a 17th-century monument built by Malik Abdul Aziz, a governor in Adil Shah's time. The South Fort above the cave temples was Tipu Sultan's citadel, from where a cannon still peeps down but entry to this is now closed. The fort wall and the cannon are visible from the North Fort.

Indian/foreigner/video camera/car parking ₹5/100/25/5; 6am–6pm

Highlights

❶ Cave Temples
❷ Agastya Lake
❸ Museum
❹ Bhutnatha Temples
❺ North Fort
❻ Silidaphadi

Bhutnatha Temple is at the edge of Agastya Lake

② AGASTYA LAKE

This green oasis offsets the encircling pale brown Badami monuments. This man-made stepped water body keeps excessive rain water in check because of its efficient drainage system. Besides its cooling properties, the water of the lake is also said to have healing powers. Smaller temples like Yellama, Virupaksha and Jambulinga lie near the lake. You can visit them on your way to the museum.

③ MUSEUM

Badami's archaeological museum displays a collection of sculptures from these three towns and includes prehistoric exhibits found near Badami. A Pallava inscription can also be seen on a large boulder here. The museum falls on your route to the Bhutnatha temples and is good for a quick stop.
₹5; 10am–5pm, Fri closed

④ BHUTNATHA TEMPLES

At the eastern edge of Agastya Lake, two temples face the tank, one built in the 6th century and the other in the 12th. The older temple is a Shiva shrine, though you will be surprised to find a sculpture of sleeping Vishnu in one of the smaller caves behind the temple. These are dry stone structures, a common style seen across the towns.
6am–6pm

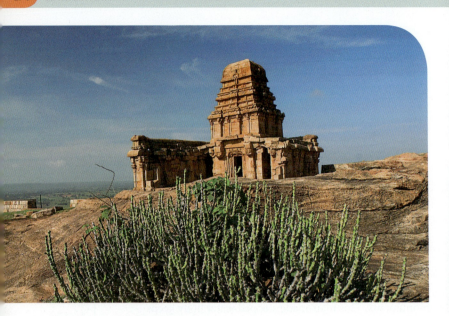

The Upper Shivalaya Temple at North Fort

❺ NORTH FORT

A steep climb of 200m above the lake area along a stepped path leads you to the North Fort. A short distance from the arched entrance near the museum are the open mandapas, and further on are the Lower and Upper Shivalayas. The climb is worth it for the panoramic view of the city with the caves on the opposite side. Right at the top of the North Fort lies a ruined complex with the Upper Shivalaya. A dargah dedicated to Sayyid Hazrat Badshah Pir has been built here. This walk can take a long time, so ensure that you come here in the morning. Another interesting monument is the Malegietti Shivalaya, which is perched precariously on a massive boulder.

6am–6pm

❻ SILIDAPHADI

A 3km long walk starting near the Badami bus stand leads to a natural rock shelter, which spans over 28m. Muted traces of prehistoric paintings can be seen here. Two other prehistoric sites are Ranganathgudda and Aralitirtha, which can also be reached only on foot and are not recommended for elders and children.

Pattadakal

Highlights
1. Temple Complex
2. Papanatha Temple
3. Jain Temple

1 TEMPLE COMPLEX
A number of Shiva shrines are located in this sprawling temple complex. The three major temples are **Sangmeshwara**, **Virupaksha** and **Mallikarjuna**. Of these, the Virupaksha shrine is still an active temple. Others that stand here are **Jambulinga**, **Galaganatha**, **Kashivishvanatha** and Kadasiddheshvara. The temples house fascinating sculptures inspired by episodes from Mahabharata and Ramayana.
Indian/foreigner/video camera ₹10/250/25; 6am–6pm

2 PAPANATHA TEMPLE
A small path runs along the river-facing side of the main complex to the Papanatha Temple, where you can see an interesting mix of the northern and southern styles of architecture. The walls are carved with stories from the Ramayana and its entrance is flanked by elephant sculptures.
6am–6pm

3 JAIN TEMPLE
The Jain temple, just half a kilometre away from the main complex, mostly exhibits the style of the Rashtrakuta dynasty, with large elephant torsos sculpted in the walls.
6am–6pm

The temple complex at Pattadakal is home to several Shiva shrines

Aihole

Highlights
1. Meguti Hill
2. Durga Temple Complex
3. Ladkhan Temple
4. Ravanaphadi

❶ MEGUTI HILL
Start the trip to Aihole from Meguti Hill early in the morning to get an idea of the town spread below. A short climb leads you to the only Buddhist temple in Aihole, a double-storeyed structure marked by a headless statue of the Buddha on its facade. At the top of the hill is the spacious 7th-century Jain temple, with ancient burial tombstones and dolmens. As you begin the journey down, you can visit the Mallikarjuna complex which has a simple shrine, below which is a Jain cave temple.
6am–6pm

❷ DURGA TEMPLE COMPLEX
Aihole's star attraction is the Durga Temple, which is a blend of Hindu and Buddhist styles. The name is deceptive, as the temple is actually dedicated to Surya. A masterpiece of Chalukyan architectural skills, this 8th-century temple has carvings of stories from the Ramayana inside. Look out for the dramatic sculptures of Shiva with Nandi, the lion-headed Narasimha, Vishnu on Garuda and many more icons from

Ladkhan Temple's columns are heavily carved

BADAMI, PATTADAKAL & AIHOLE

Detour: Mahakuta & Banashankari

There are two short detours on this route, which make for interesting stops on this temple trail.

- **Mahakuta:** As it is located 14km from Badami, many visitors give this spectacular site a miss. Mahakuta is connected to Badami by a secret eucalyptus lined 3km pathway, the gateway of which is flanked by skeletal figures of Kala and Kali. The main attraction of this walled complex is the Mahakuteshvar Temple, the surrounding 7th-century shrines and the large tank fed by a natural spring.

- **Banashankari:** Situated just 5km from Badami, Banashankari Temple does not date back to the rest of the temples of the region, but holds great importance for pilgrims. The structure has used some of the late Chalukyan columns, but the most awe-inspiring and beautiful feature is its lamp-studded tower, which is lit only on special occasions.

mythology. There is also a museum with artefacts dating back to the 12th century.
Indian/foreigner/camera/video camera ₹5/100/25/25; 6am–6pm, museum Fri closed

❸ LADKHAN TEMPLE

This 8th-century temple has a sloping roof and from a distance it looks as if it's been made from wooden panels. The temple columns inside are embellished with carvings and decorative motifs. It also has a mysterious name – Ladkhan, believed to have been the name of the person who inhabited it.
6am–6pm

❹ RAVANAPHADI

Ravanaphadi dates back to the 6th century and it has large sculptures of Ardhanarishvara, a ten-armed Shiva, and a collage of elaborate carvings. Do notice the sculpted gatekeepers at the entrance, unusually wearing Iranian dresses, which are believed by some to have been inspired from the many foreign travels of the ruler of the time.
6am–6pm

✓ Top Tip: Guide for the temple trail

ASI guides are available in all major sites (₹1000 for a group of four). From October onwards guides charge ₹1200 for a group of five and ₹1600 for a group of 6 to 14. Chandru, who has been part of INTACH (Indian National Trust for Art and Cultural Heritage), and also taught at a small college in Badami, is well versed in English, and can modify his style based on your time and inclination to see the temples. 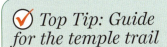9448823161

Accommodation

Make Badami your base and travel to Pattadakal and Aihole.

BADAMI

Hotel Badami Court — Hotel ₹₹
📞 08357 220230; 173 Station Rd; d ₹3750–4200, ste ₹5200–5600 (incl of breakfast) Badami Court is one of the oldest hotels in town. The rooms are snug and old fashioned (in some cases musty smelling). The triple bed options, however, are spacious and airy. Ask for the first floor rooms overlooking the central garden.

Krishna Heritage — Hotel ₹₹
📞 08357 221300; www.krishnaheritagebadami.com; Ramdurg Rd; d ₹3500 (incl of breakfast) The most luxurious address in town, Krishna Heritage offers lavish cottages with modern amenities. The hotel can help with sightseeing tours.

| The Heritage Resort has rooms that overlook the rocky outcrop

The Heritage Resort — Hotel ₹
📞 08357 220250; www.theheritage.co.in; Station Rd; d ₹2900–3900 (incl of breakfast and taxes) This is a suitable place to enjoy the wonderful view of the almond coloured, large rocky outcrop in front of you. Cottages have sit-outs, nicely furnished interiors, clean bathrooms and there is also an in-house restaurant.

Hotel Mayura Chalukya — Hotel ₹
📞 08357 220046; www.karnatakaholydays.net; Ramdurg Rd, PWD Compound; d ₹1850–2200 (incl of breakfast) If you do opt to stay at the Mayura, choose from the eight rooms of the newly built wing. These are spacious enough for three beds to fit in comfortably and all have a flat screen TV, AC and a large clean bathroom. This state tourism-run hotel is great value for money.

Eating

There are not too many options for eating out in Badami but there are a handful of places that you might want to try out.

BADAMI

Krishna Bhavan Lingayat Khanavali ₹
📞 9845277748; Main Rd; mains less than ₹200; 10am–10pm If you're up for a local veg meal of jowar rotis, rice and spicy local curries, make your way to Krishna Bhawan, a small dingy joint with a bright purple door.

Hotel Mayura Chalukya   Multi-Cuisine ₹
☎ 08357 220046; www.karnatakaholydays.net; Ramdurg Rd, PWD Compound; mains ₹200 This is the best place for speedy service and south Indian meals. Ensure that you get here early, though, as the place is packed with visitors at lunchtime, especially during the peak season.

Banashri Hotel   Multi-Cuisine ₹₹
☎ 9916259676; opp KSRTC Bus Stop, Main Rd; mains ₹250–500; 6.30am–10.30pm A busy restaurant, which serves both north and south Indian food, though you may have to jostle for seating space. Banashri is a viable option for a no-frills, quick meal.

Krishna Heritage   Multi-Cuisine ₹₹
☎ 08357 221300; www.krishnaheritagebadami.com; Ramdurg Rd; mains ₹200–500; noon–3pm, 7–11pm The spacious and breezy restaurant of Krishna Heritage has a brilliant ambience and a decent choice of multi-cuisine fare. It's always safe to order simple dishes and ensure that you give specific instructions for spice levels in the food.

Badami Court   Multi-Cuisine ₹₹
☎ 08357 220230; 173 Station Rd; mains ₹200–500; noon–3pm, 7–11pm Badami Court has an in-house restaurant, with multi-cuisine dishes on the menu. It's best to stick with north Indian or south Indian fare.

Activities

BADAMI

Rock Climbing   Adventure
☎ 9886664666; www.marsadventures.in; No 5 Kamakshi Nilaya, RM Nagar Main Rd, Dodda Banaswadi, Bengaluru; weekend trip ₹2500–3000 per head Bengaluru based Mars Adventures organise weekend trips (stay, food, equipment, instructions included) for beginners and pros to climb heights from 40-70ft with top ropes. The routes are first inspected by instructors before participants can climb. With route names like 'Top Rope Gorge', 'Fire or Retire', 'French Disaster', 'Hungry Climber' and more, adventure seekers should be raring to go!

Shopping

Located 60km from Badami, Ilkal is famous for its hand-woven saris.

BADAMI

Shri Shiddalingeshwara Javali & Cloth Stores   Saris
☎ 9480535310; Main Rd; 9.30am–9pm, Sun 10.30am–2.30pm Selling saris directly from their own looms since the last 40 years, the weavers of Ilkal offer a great option to choose from a large variety of Ilkal specials ranging from ₹300–4500. Varied designs of the iconic 'pallus', options in silk and cotton and a chance to see the weavers at work (30km from Badami) are reason enough to visit this shop.

Hampi

The magnificent capital of the Vijayanagar Empire is an architecture buff's dream. Declared a Unesco World Heritage Site, the ruins of over 20 elaborate temples, and many other smaller structures bear testimony of a flourishing empire in the medieval era. In addition, the boulder-strewn topography, dissected by the Tungabhadra River, provides a stunning backdrop to your experience.

Trip Planner

GETTING THERE

Hubli, the closest airport is 162km from Hampi. Taxis from the airport cost ₹3000. Since Hubli does not have frequent flights from major cities, most travellers prefer coming to Bengaluru and catching the overnight train to Hospet (13km) as it is the closest rail junction from Hampi and is well connected to Bengaluru. The Hampi Express (16592) departs at 10pm and reaches Hospet at 7.42am.

SUGGESTED ITINERARY (3 DAYS)

Three days are plenty to explore the ruins of Hampi and the adjoining village of Anegundi. Arrive in Hospet, transfer to Hampi and check into a riverside accommodation. Start your tryst with the boulder-strewn city with one end of Hampi, moving along the ASI marked trail.

BEST TIME TO GO

J F **M A M J J A S** O N D

GREAT FOR

Top 5 highlights

- Virupaksha Temple (p182)
- Matanga Paravath (p182)
- Queens' Bath (p184)
- Vijaya Vittala Temple (p184)
- Hanuman Temple (p185)

Past Glory

The Virupaksha Temple rises above Hampi's landscape

Hampi and its neighbouring areas find mention in the Hindu epic Ramayana as Kishkinda, the realm of the monkey gods. In 1336, Telugu prince Harihararaya chose Hampi as the site for his new capital Vijayanagar, which over the next couple of centuries grew into one of the largest Hindu empires in Indian history.

Hampi today has three themes running parallel to each other: a strong religious attachment to Lord Hanuman; the historical perspective of the ruins of an ancient kingdom; a Bohemian and hippie-like vibe (thanks to the influence of the many backpackers from the West who converge here).

Across the Tungabhadra, about 5km northeast of Hampi Bazaar, sits **Anegundi**, an ancient fortified village that's part of the Hampi World Heritage Site but predates Hampi by way of human habitation. Gifted with a landscape similar to Hampi, Anegundi is quainter and has been spared the blight of commercialisation. It thus continues to preserve the local atmosphere minus the touristy vibe.

KARNATAKA

Highlights
1. Virupaksha Temple
2. Matanga Paravath
3. Mahanavami Dibba
4. Lotus Mahal & Elephant Stables
5. Queens' Bath
6. Vijaya Vittala Temple
7. Achyutaraya Temple
8. Hanuman Temple, Anegundi

❶ VIRUPAKSHA TEMPLE

This Shiva temple is synonymous with the image of Hampi – the town is practically spread around it. A long 'bazaar' street stretches out in front of the shrine, ending in a large monolithic Nandi Bull facing it. The main gopuram, almost 50m high, was built in 1442, with a smaller one added in 1510. The main shrine is dedicated to Virupaksha, an incarnation of Shiva. Virupaksha is an active temple with plenty of devotees coming here to worship. After manoeuvring through a monkey-infested path, admire the intricate paintings on the ceiling, and look out for an interesting pin-hole camera image of the tower inside the temple complex.

Hampi Bazaar; ₹2; 6am–8pm

❷ MATANGA PARAVATH

The Matanga Paravath stands directly opposite the Virupaksha Temple at the far end of the street. Irregular steps lead up to the top, from where you can get an incredible

The intricately carved Virupaksha Temple depicts scenes from Hindu mythology

view of the shrine, the bazaar, the Achyutaraya Temple in front, and other ruins. On the hilltop is the small and simple Veerabhuvneshwara Temple. The trek up takes about 30 minutes. The sunrise view is highly recommended (for that you will have to stay this side of the river, closer to the spot).

❸ MAHANAVAMI DIBBA
For relief from the temple trails, visit the Mahanavami Dibba, which was a monument built to commemorate King Krishnadevaraya's victory over the Kingdom of Kalinga. The 22ft tall plateau has a 1600sq ft-wide platform on top. The walls are embellished with carvings of hunting scenes and elephant processions. The complex also has a geometrically-designed 'kalyani' (bathing pool).
8am–5.30pm

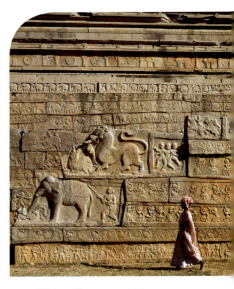

The walls of Mahanavami Dibba. have elephant carvings

❹ LOTUS MAHAL & ELEPHANT STABLES
The distinctive look of this monument is apparent in its blend of Hindu and Muslim architectural styles. The Lotus Mahal is flanked by lush and well-maintained gardens; it was probably a rest house for royalty. Further on from the gate stand eleven dome-shaped stables; these were constructed for the royal elephants.
Hampi Bazaar; ₹10; 6am–8pm

ℹ️ *Quick Facts: Hampi lowdown*

The three key points to explore here are the main street leading from Virupaksha Temple; the Virupapur Gaddi; and the village of Anegundi. Hampi Bazaar and the village of Kamalapuram are the two main points of entry to the ruins. The ruins are divided into two areas: the Sacred Centre, around Hampi Bazaar; and the Royal Centre, towards Kamalapuram. To the northeast across the Tungabhadra River is the Virupapur Gaddi, and the historic village of Anegundi further beyond.

The hammam or Queens' Bath

❺ QUEENS' BATH

The Queens' Bath is deceptively plain on the outside but amazing within. It is one of the more detailed structures here, there is no doubt that the bath or hammam, with its special aesthetics, was built for the many queens that Krishnadevaraya married. Beautiful windows hang over a central bathing pool, hinting at a life of extravagance.
8am–5.30pm

❻ VIJAYA VITTALA TEMPLE

The undisputed highlight of the Hampi ruins, this temple built in 1513, is dedicated to Lord Vishnu and is considered an architectural marvel for its extraordinary workmanship and its musical pillars, which emit musical tones when tapped. However, due to heavy wear and tear, the Archeological Survey of India (ASI) has now banned guides from showing visitors how the pillars sounded when struck. The iconic chariot, inspired by the one in Konark, was functional till it was cemented in by authorities. The long pathway

> ### ✓ Top Tip: River crossing
>
> Hampi street and Virupapur Gaddi are separated by the Tungabhadra River, across which two boats ferry people every day between 7am and 6pm (₹15 per ride). Take care of the timings, as getting stuck on either side would mean a ride of 40km by auto on a different route.

Detour: Daroji Sloth Bear Sanctuary

Just 17km from Hampi, the immaculately clean and well maintained **Daroji Bear Sanctuary** (Kamlapura; adult/child ₹50/25; camera ₹300; 1.30–6pm) is home to (amongst other animals) 120 sloth bears; they can be seen roaming a wide gorge from a watch tower. The bears are given their food at 2pm, so it's best to get here an hour later, when you can watch them from relatively closer. You can drive up to the watch tower.

---

to the temple can now be crossed in battery-operated vehicles (₹20 per ride). Retain your ticket for same-day admission into the Zenana Enclosure and Elephant Stables in the Royal Centre, and the archaeological museum in Kamalapuram.
Hampi Bazaar; ₹10; 6am–8pm

❼ ACHYUTARAYA TEMPLE

The deserted Achyutaraya Temple is an important Vishnu temple marked by its pillared walkway, which can be distinctly seen from the Mathanga Paravath. The pillars have carvings depicting episodes from the Mahabharata and Ramayana (as do the other large shrines here). It has a wide 'bazaar' street in front, indicating that the Vijayanagar Kingdom had flourishing trade. Like many other temples from that era, it also has a kalyana mandapa (marriage hall), like many other such temples from the era.
8am–5.30pm

❽ HANUMAN TEMPLE, ANEGUNDI

Accessible by a 570-step climb up the Anjanadri hill, this temple has fine views of the rugged terrain around. Many believe this is the birthplace of the Hindu monkey god Hanuman. On the pleasant hike up, you'll be courted by impish monkeys, and within the temple you'll find a horde of chillum-puffing resident sadhus.

The Hanuman Temple is located on Anjanadri Hill

Accommodation

Hospet (the rail and bus hub closest to Hampi) is 13km away, and is suitable for those travelling with families. Hampi provides mostly backpacking stay options.

HOSPET

Royal Orchid Central Hotel ₹₹₹
☎ 08394 300100; www.royalorchidhotels.com; Station Rd, Hospet; d ₹8359 (incl of breakfast) This is undoubtedly the best luxury option in Hospet and has all the expected amenities, though they are not in top condition. A pool, spa and gym make up for what is otherwise a modest place to stay.

Sri Krishna Inn Hotel ₹₹
☎ 08394 294300; www.krishnapalacehotel.com; Station Rd, Hospet; d ₹4770–5500 (incl of breakfast) The first thing that strikes you about this four-year-old establishment is the extremely

Royal Orchid Central is one of the best luxury stay options in town

courteous and accommodating staff. They extend a warm welcome even if you arrive at an ungodly hour. Rooms are clean and well equipped (though slightly musty-smelling).

HAMPI

Boulders Hotel ₹₹₹
☎ 9242641551; www.hampisboulders.com; Narayanpet, Bandi Harlapura Munirabad, Koppal District; d ₹9000–11,000 (incl of breakfast and dinner) The only non-backpacking option in Hampi, Boulders is for those seeking a plush holiday. Spacious sit-outs and exclusive rooms promise undisturbed views of the River Tungabhadra, flowing right beside the property. The hotel offers a nature trail where you can view stunning rock formations from a rickety wooden walk-bridge and a vantage deck set up on a cave.

Shanthi Guest House Guesthouse ₹
☎ 08394 325352; www.shanthihampi.com; Virupapur Gaddi, Hampi; d ₹800–1500 (incl of full board; depending on season) In terms of aesthetics and amenities, Shanthi has led the way since 1992. It has basic, clean rooms (thatched or concrete) and a swing outside. The in-house travel desk can arrange for sightseeing with local guides.

Mowgli Guest House Guesthouse ₹
☎ 9448003606; www.mowglihampi.com; Virupapur Gaddi, Hampi;

d ₹990–1200 (incl of full board; depending on season) The basic rooms at Mowgli either face lush paddy fields or the courtyard. A mosquito net is the only additional necessity provided. The lounge area has Hampi-style floor seating, great food and some lazing farm animals in the vicinity to add to the ambience of an easy-paced holiday.

Eating

Mango Tree — Multi-Cuisine ₹₹
☎ 9448765213; Riverside Drive, Hampi; 7.30am–9.30pm An inconspicuous gate into a banana plantation lead you to Hampi's most popular haunt. You are greeted by a dozen cats and dogs, and a stepped, amphitheatre-like area with 'barefoot' seating. The egg curry and roti combo, downed with a mango lassi, is the perfect start to a lazy afternoon here.

Activities

Coracle Rides
There are two points in Hampi from where coracles operate; near the Kodanda Rama Temple and Talwarkatta in Anegundi. Immensely popular with tourists, apart from the novelty of the ride, it also gives an opportunity to see rock formations on the banks. If you are starting from the Kodanda Rama side, ask to see the thousand lingas and sleeping Vishnu sculptures on the rocks. Depending on the duration of the ride, it can cost between ₹150 and ₹250 per head.

Kishkinda Trust — Cultural programs, outdoor adventure
☎ 08533 267777; www.thekishkindatrust.org This NGO promotes sustainable tourism in Anegundi, organises soft adventure activities such as rock climbing, camping, trekking and boating around the village. Equipment and trained instructors are provided. A slew of cultural programs, including performing arts sessions and classical and folk music concerts are also conducted periodically.

Shopping

Clothes & Jewellery
In tune with its Bohemian status, Hampi is sprinkled with small shack-like shops selling clothes and jewellery. You can find flowing harem pants, string tops and such on the other side of the river. These shops were earlier lined adjacent to the Virupaksha Temple in the main Hampi Bazaar, but have been shifted to Virupapur Gaddi.

Gali Music Shop — Instrument
☎ 9449982586; Virupapur Gaddi; 10am–7pm Meet the music wizard, Gali, at his shop on the Virupapur Gaddi. A multitude of Vietnamese and African instruments line his tiny but interesting shop; you can learn to play – and buy – some of the instruments. Gali picked up the technique from visiting foreigners but now plays regularly at some of the guesthouses in the evenings.

Kerala

Why Go?

Expect to be mesmerised by Kerala's idyllic environs, laid-back pace and pulsating cultural vibe. Visually, Kerala is undoubtedly one of the most scenic destinations in the country. The famous backwaters of **Alappuzha**, **Kumarakom**, **Kollam**, the azure sea and sun-kissed beaches at **Thiruvanthapuram**, **Kovalam** and **Varkala**, the verdant spice and tea plantations in hilly **Munnar**, coffee-clad Wayanad, the wild elephants and the odd tiger at **Periyar Tiger Reserve** make you realise that the phrase 'God's own country' is not an exaggeration.

Locals take great pride in their traditional roots, and this imbues every aspect of life – be it lip-smacking cuisine, carefully-preserved architecture, language or art forms. And just a flight away from Kochi is the scenic Union Territory of **Lakshadweep** – a string of palm-covered coral islands which are a magnet for travellers and divers alike.

Getting There & Away

Air: Thiruvanthapuram (Trivandrum), Kozhikode (Calicut) and Kochi (Cochin) are Kerala's three international airports. They are connected via daily flights to all metros and major cities in the country. Agatti Island in Lakshadweep is connected via air to Kochi.

Train: The main cities in Kerala are well connected to all the Indian metros. The state has 13 major rail routes. The key railheads are at Ernakulam, Thiruvanthapuram, Alappuzha and Kozhikode. Visit the official railway website www.irctc.co.in for more information.

The lighthouse is a towering landmark at Kovalam Beach

Kerala Map

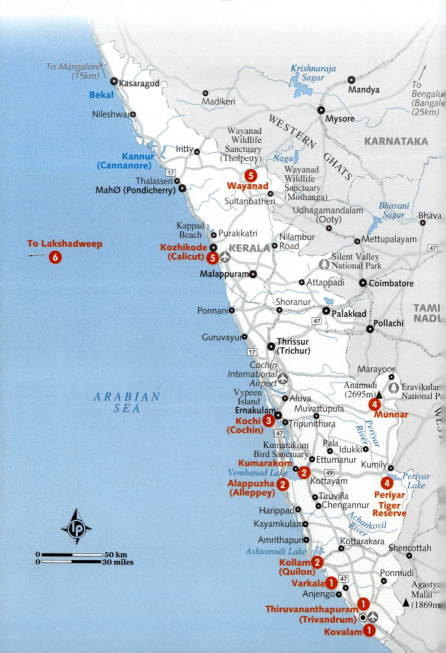

⭐ 6 Best Trips

❶ Thiruvananthapuram, Varkala & Kovalam (p194) While the capital city is ideal for visiting a variety of museums, Kovalam and Varkala, with their white beaches and rustling palm trees, are a visual treat.

❷ Alappuzha, Kumarakom & Kollam (p216) Take a houseboat cruise on the palm-fringed network of rivers, lagoons and canals that pass fishing villages, green paddy fields and coconut groves.

❸ Kochi & Around (p234) Combine a beach sojourn with a sense of history at Kochi. It is packed with historical hot spots and is also a culinary centre.

❹ Munnar & Periyar Tiger Reserve (p256) Stay in a beautiful remote resort, trek through the tea plantations around Munnar and discover stunning mountain scenery. At Periyar try spotting a tiger.

❺ Kozhikode & Wayanad (p270) The lush coffee-clad plantations at Wayanad, surrounded with forests and the virgin coastline of Kozhikode provide contrasting experiences.

❻ Lakshadweep (p282) This cluster of islands has blue waters and silver sands. Whether you swim or dive, the incandescent water will be the undisputed star of this story.

Theyyam, Kerala's most popular ritualistic art form

Top Highlights

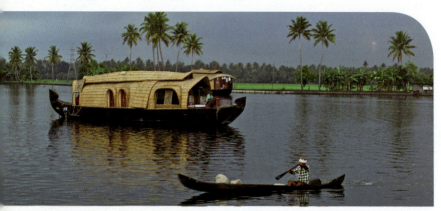

1 Houseboat Cruises, Vembanad Lake

Houseboats are without doubt the best way to experience the lusciously green landscape of the backwaters of Vembanad Lake (p218) in Alappuzha. The longest lake of the country, Vembanad accommodates over a thousand of these floating structures that glide lethargically past the equally laid-back countryside, with scenes of houses, schools, shops and temples passing by along the canals. With a cook on board dishing out scrumptious local fare, a TV and cosy, well-furnished rooms (depending on the size of the boat), you are equipped to cruise for as long as you wish.

2 Chinese Fishing Nets, Fort Kochi

The captivating sight of local fishermen heaving and tugging at the Chinese fishing nets (p242) is the perfect way to start your day at Fort Kochi. These enormous, spiderlike contraptions – a legacy of Mongolian traders from AD 1400 – scoop up kilos of sea creatures, but need some brawn to get the job done. At least four people are required to operate their counterweights at high tide.

3 Planters' Bungalows, Munnar

In Munnar you'll be engulfed in a sea of a thousand shades of green. The rolling hills all around are covered by a sculptural carpet of tea plantations, and the mountain scenery is magnificent – you're often up above the clouds, watching veils of mist cling below the mountaintops. A stay at one of the many planters' bungalows (p264) here ensures you experience all this and more at close quarters. Look forward to classic colonial-style features – wooden floors, dusty libraries, high ceilings and weathered furniture – in these graceful bungalows.

4 Bamboo Raft Cruise, Periyar Tiger Reserve

The best way to experience South India's most popular wildlife sanctuary (p261) is by drifting languidly in the namesake lake on a bamboo raft. These day-long trips can be arranged by the Ecotourism Centre, run by the Forest Department. The massive sanctuary encompasses 925 sq km and has a 26 sq km artificial lake created by the British in 1895. The vast reserve is home to bison, sambar, wild boar, langur, elephants and tigers.

Thiruvananthapuram, Kovalam & Varkala

Uncharacteristic of a capital city, Thiruvananthapuram is easy going. It is a haven for history lovers with its museums and traditional architecture. On the other hand Varkala and Kovalam are known for their sandy stretches to soak in the sun and sea. Laterite cliffs and remnants of hippie life in Varkala are a stark contrast to the premier resorts in Kovalam.

Trip Planner

GETTING THERE

Thiruvananthapuram: Thiruvananthapuram International Airport has direct flights from all metros. It is 8km from the city centre. Taxis and autos are easily available and cost ₹200 and ₹150 respectively. Thiruvananthapuram Central is the main railway station that is well linked by trains from across the country.

Varkala: Thiruvananthapuram's airport is 50km away. Varakala Sivagiri railway station has trains to Mumbai, Delhi and Bengaluru.

Kovalam: Thiruvananthapuram's airport (15km) and railway station (10km) are the closest. Pre-paid taxis are easily available.

SUGGESTED ITINERARY (8 DAYS)

Arrive at Thiruvananthapuram and spend three days visiting various museums and sites. After this travel north to Varkala for a bohemian aura reminiscent of the 60s and spend the next two days here. Next in line is Kovalam, further south, where you can spend three days. You will be spoilt for choice with an array of budget and luxury places to stay and eat.

BEST TIME TO GO

J F M A M J J A S **O N D**

GREAT FOR

Top 5 highlights

- Sree Padmanabhaswamy Temple, Thiruvananthapuram (p197)
- Zoological Gardens & Museums, Thiruvananthapuram (p196)
- Ayurveda, Varkala (p201)
- Anjengo Fort, Varkala (p201)
- Beaches, Kovalam (p202)

Serenity at Sea

The 60km coastal stretch of **Varkala**, **Thiruvananthapuram** and **Kovalam** constitutes an interesting trajectory where a beach holiday merges effortlessly with the fascinating historic overtones of the region. The unassuming capital of Kerala, Thiruvananthapuram, is steeped in centuries of art and history. Home to a number of famous poets and artists, the city's cultural and intellectual ambience is hard to miss. Though it is transforming into a technology hub, it has managed to retain its old-world charm.

Further north from Thiruvananthapuram is Varkala. The unusual coastal topography consisting of red laterite cliffs dropping down to clean patches of sand will enthrall you at this small seaside town. The unique blend of a strong Hindu religious influence and a vibrant bohemian beach culture makes Varkala an intriguing destination to explore. You can indulge in Ayurvedic treatments and tuck into fresh seafood.

Down south is Kovalam, the serene, seaside getaway that has emerged as one of the top beach destinations with its mix of palm-fringed beaches and a plethora of cafes, resorts and sightseeing options. Kovalam also promises a holiday filled with the healing touches of a range of Ayurveda treatments.

> Kovalam Beach is lined with sun decks to enjoy this peaceful bay

Thiruvananthapuram

Highlights

1. Zoological Gardens & Museums
2. Keralam, Museum of History & Heritage
3. Kerala State Science & Technology Museum & Priyadarsini Planetarium
4. Sree Padmanabhaswamy Temple
5. Puthe Maliga Palace Museum
6. Margi Kathakali
7. Shankhumugham Beach
8. Veli Tourist Village

❶ ZOOLOGICAL GARDENS & MUSEUMS

Head to the heart of the city and spend the day visiting museums and the city zoo. Over 55-acres of well-manicured land are dotted with interesting establishments: the Natural History Museum, KCS Panicker's Gallery, Sree Chitra Enclave, Napier Museum, Sree Chitra Art Gallery and the Zoo. Even though the complex is buzzing with visitors, school groups and locals, you will have ample breathing room to absorb the offerings of each place.

❷ KERALAM, MUSEUM OF HISTORY & HERITAGE

A recent addition to Thiruvananthapuram's list of museums, this well-organised, bright white repository of history and heritage is a pleasure to visit. Situated outside Zoological Gardens & Museums, it elucidates the history of the state with exhibits ranging from the Neolithic age to more recent temple architecture. Intricate palm leaves depicting Vedic scriptures in Tamil and Malayalam are fascinating.
📞9567019037; Park View; adult/camera ₹20/25; 10am–5.30pm, Mon/public holidays closed

❸ KERALA STATE SCIENCE & TECHNOLOGY MUSEUM & PRIYADARSINI PLANETARIUM

This expansive complex has six sections to explore. When it all gets too serious, a 3D movie or a break at the planetarium

---

📷 *Snapshot: The secret chamber*

Sree Padmanabhaswamy Temple is believed to be the world's richest temple with an undisclosed treasure trove worth ₹90,000 crore. A secret chamber hoarding this wealth has evoked much debate and speculation within political circles on its rightful ownership. Despite this, the spiritual footfalls have not decreased.

Snapshot: Raja Ravi Varma

The 19th-century painter, Raja Ravi Varma successfully fused European art techniques with themes from the *Mahabharata* and *Ramayana* to produce an exquisite collection of paintings that won him many accolades, both in India and internationally. Prepare to get familiar with his works as people here proudly display prints of them at hotels, restaurants and even their homes. The sheer number of imitations of Raja Ravi Varma's oleographs that are available in the market in Kerala is evidence of how popular he remains.

will lighten the experience. The simulation of the night sky, both from the past and projected for the future, is one of the best shows to catch here.
☏ 0471 2306024; www.kstmuseum.com; Vikasbhavan PO; adult/child ₹15/10 (separate charges for all sections); 10am–5pm

❹ SREE PADMANABHASWAMY TEMPLE

References to it in the epics suggest that this temple is thousands of years old. It is the spiritual heart of the city ('Thiru' 'Anantha' 'Puram' means sacred abode of Lord Anantha Padmanabha). Expect long queues for a darshan of the sleeping deity which can be seen only in parts through three doors. Seven yellow, tiered gopurams tower around the complex. If you strain your neck you can see the Methan Mani clock high on the temple's outer wall, which rings hourly as metallic goats swing into a demon-faced man's cheeks.

Sree Padmanabhaswamy Temple draws thousands of pilgrims daily

Detour: Balaramapuram

Just 14km south of Thiruvananthapuram, Balaramapuram is a congested bustling town, the lanes of which resonate with the constant rhythm of weaving looms. The traditional weavers, Shaliyars, have settled here on four main streets; Single Street, Double Street, Vinayagar Street and New Street. If you are walking down any of these, you are sure to be invited into houses to see the weaving process. You can also buy the typical white-and-gold combination of saris and mundus at a much lower cost than in town.

We recommend **SS Handloom Centre** (0471 2400261; New St; 9.30am–7.30pm), **Kannan** (9895612361; Double St; 10am–10pm) and **R Paramasivan** (0471 2407293; Double St; 10am–6pm).

0471 2464606; www.sreepadmanabhaswamytemple.org; West Nada, Fort; 3.30–4.45am, 6.30–7am, 8.30–10am, 10.30–11.10am, 11.45am–12pm, 5–6.15pm, 6.45–7.20pm

❺ PUTHE MALIGA PALACE MUSEUM

Walk through a small banana plantation to reach the 200-year-old museum next to the Padmanabhaswamy Temple. The erstwhile palace of the Maharaja of Travancore sports carved wooden ceilings, marble sculptures and even imported Belgian glass. The palace is also called Kuthira Malika (Palace of Horses) after the 122 horse figures in the brackets of the walls. A scheduled guide takes small groups around regaling them with anecdotes and pointing out the highlights. The annual classical music festival is held from 6–12 January; entry is free.
Museum; Indian/foreigner/photography outside/video outside ₹15/50/30/250; 8.30am–12.45pm, 3–4.45pm, Mon closed

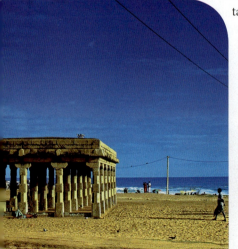

Stunning stone pavilion at Shankhumugham Beach

❻ MARGI KATHAKALI

Barely 200m west of Fort School lies this inconspicuous building housing the Margi Kathakali institution. Visitors can peek at informal

Wooden horses at Puthe Maliga Palace Museum

practice sessions of the dramatic dance form in the main hall every day for two hours.
☎0471 2478804; near Fort School; 10am–noon Mon–Fri,

❼ SHANKHUMUGHAM BEACH
Watch the fishermen tug at the boats late morning as they bring the catch in, and then enjoy a variety of snacks at the seafront shacks on Shankhumugham Beach. The sandy stretch is not fit for swimming and has lifeguards at short intervals to ensure your protection.

❽ VELI TOURIST VILLAGE
The 12km ride to the Veli Tourist Village is worth while if you are travelling with children. A Kerala Tourist Development Corporation (KTDC) establishment, the park has swings, boating, enormous and slightly overbearing sculptures and a floating restaurant at the cusp of the sea and Veli Lake.
☎0471 2500785; Veli Tourist Park; adult/child ₹5; boating ₹100–1000; 8am–630pm

KERALA

Highlights
1. Janardhana Swamy Temple
2. Beaches
3. Anjengo Fort
4. Ayurveda

A bird's-eye-view of Varkala Beach

Varkala

1 JANARDHANA SWAMY TEMPLE
This 2000-year-old Vishnu temple stands in stark contrast to the bikini-clad visitors sprawled on beaches just a kilometre away. The temple overlooks a kalyani (pond) which is mostly occupied by youngsters splashing about. It allows non-Hindus, as long as they remain on the temple grounds, and do not enter the sanctum. During the annual festival in March, the temple is decorated with palm fronds as an elephant procession ambles by.
Temple Beach Rd; 4am–noon, 5–8pm

2 BEACHES
Bright beach umbrellas, reclining chairs and baked sunbathers are a permanent fixture in the strand of golden beaches that nuzzle Varkala's cliff edge. **Papanasam** lies at the far end and is mainly known for its religious connect with Hindus. You can see small ceremonies for ancestors being

---

 ## Top Tip: Torrid waters

Do note that the beaches at Varkala have strong currents; even experienced swimmers have been swept away. This is one of the most dangerous beaches in Kerala, so be careful and swim between the flags or ask the lifeguards to point out the safest place to swim.

performed under beach umbrellas. Walk south towards **Black Beach**, **Odayam** and **Manthara** for a typical beach ambience.

❸ ANJENGO FORT
History buffs will love the immaculate and well-preserved Anjengo Fort built in 1695, 12km from Varkala. The seaside ride takes you through colourful fishing villages and small townships. The fort lies in a village called Anchuthengu, from which it derives its name. This unassuming village was an early trade settlement of the East India Company and the fort was an important signalling station for ships coming in from England. Do climb up the windy lighthouse nearby for a bird's-eye view of the surrounding areas.
10am–5pm

❹ AYURVEDA
It seems as if everybody has an Ayurveda-related product or treatment to sell, although many aren't qualified practitioners. Ask for recommendations before you go to get herbalised. **Kadaltheeram Ayurvedic Beach Resort** (www.kadaltheeram.org) has an intensive programme that lasts for a minimum of 14 days. A simpler rejuvenation package is also available at **Absolute Ayurveda Spa** (www.absoluteayur.com) on Temple Road.

> Varkala is an apt place to try an Ayurveda massage

Kovalam

Highlights
1. Beaches
2. Sri Parasurama Temple, Thiruvallam
3. Vizhinjam Harbour
4. Poovar Backwaters
5. Chowara Beach

❶ BEACHES
The stretch of beach is divided by a blurred line between **Lighthouse**, **Hawa**, **Eve** and **Grow** beaches, of which Lighthouse is the most crowded. Though there are no organised water sports at Kovalam, surf boards can be rented (₹50–100, depending on the season). Else, you can hire a beach lounger for a few hours (₹100–200). Further down the beach is the lighthouse, a towering landmark at Kovalam. If you want to take in the beauty of the horizon and landscape, climb the lighthouse in the evenings, the sight is worth it.

Lighthouse visit; adult/child/camera/video ₹10/3/20/25; 3–5pm

❷ SRI PARASURAMA TEMPLE, THIRUVALLAM
The Sri Parasurama Temple lies about 6km from Kovalam towards Thiruvananthapuram, on the banks of Karamana River. A small dusty compound next to the main Thiruvallam junction is the site of this 2000-year-old temple, the only one in Kerala which is dedicated to the creator of the state.

4–11am, 5–8pm

The relatively secluded Chowara Beach

THIRUVANANTHAPURAM, KOVALAM & VARKALA

📷 Snapshot: Of myths & legends

The myth behind Kerala's creation is based on the story of Parasurama (Rama with the axe), the sixth incarnation of Vishnu. He is believed to have freed the region from the oppressive Kshatriyas. After killing all the male Kshatriyas, Parasurama meditated near Gokarna and then Kanyakumari, to repent for his sins. From here, he threw his axe towards the ocean, forming the landmass that is now Kerala where it landed.

❸ VIZHINJAM HARBOUR

Vizhinjam Harbour comes to life as early as 7am as the fishing boats arrive with the late night catch. The place is bustling with frenzied activity of selecting and sorting fish and makes for a great photo opportunity. Across the harbour lies an imposing long pier that juts into the sea.

❹ POOVAR BACKWATERS

Though Kovalam is not on the typical backwater sector of Kerala, a handful of operators provide the leisurely experience at Neyyar River close to Poovar junction (17km). Hop onto a small country/speed boat for a cruise through the mangroves down the narrow water canals that eventually open out into the sea. The backwaters and the Arabian Sea are bifurcated by a small stretch of sand, the **Golden Beach**. You can stop at any of the floating restaurants at the cusp of the Arabian Sea and the backwaters for a meal.
📞9349756521; Leela Backwater Craze; Bridge Rd, cruise per person 1hr/2hr ₹1500/2000

❺ CHOWARA BEACH

If you are not a fan of the umbrella-crammed beaches of Kovalam, head to Chowara (6km from Kovolam) for a comparatively secluded experience. If you are not a guest at one of the resorts here, you may have to carry your own paraphernalia like an umbrella, towels and snacks. It's worth the trouble as you can find a quiet spot for yourself and not be part of the mass experience.

✓ Top Tip: Swim safely

There are strong rip currents at both ends of Lighthouse Beach that carry away several swimmers every year. Swim only between the flags in the area patrolled by lifeguards – green flags show the area is safe, red flags warn of danger zones.

Accommodation

THIRUVANANTHAPURAM

Amruthum Ayurvedic Village Resort — Ayurveda Resort ₹₹₹
☎ 0471 2484600; www.amruthum.in; RKN Rd, Panangodu, Venganoor PO; d ₹7000–8000 (incl of full board) The fact that no signboards are brandished on the highway makes the yoga-and Ayurveda-inspired Amruthum a little secret in the village of Panangodu. Densely green, it has seven rooms and a swimming pool. You can enjoy meals on the roof deck or just laze in the sunny garden between yoga and massage schedules. You can stay here even if you don't require any Ayurveda treatment.

Taj Vivanta — Hotel ₹₹₹
☎ 0471 6612345; www.vivantabytaj.com; C V Raman Pillai Rd, Thycaud; d ₹9500–12,000, ste ₹20,000–30,000 (incl of breakfast) The never disappointing chain of Taj hotels has a conveniently located property in Thiruvananthapuram as well. In classic Taj style, the rooms are slick and well-furnished. The usual features such as an in-house restaurant, gymnasium, swimming pool and wi-fi complement the warm hospitality of its professional staff.

SP Grand Days — Hotel ₹₹
☎ 0471 2333344; www.spgranddays.com; Panavila Junction; d ₹4000–5000, ste ₹7000 (incl of breakfast) Choose from a selection of four types of rooms at the comfortable SP Grand Days. Though centrally located, it is still pleasantly away from the busy city area. Apart from the rather bare and unused swimming pool area, the rest of the hotel is rife with action with an in-house restaurant and coffee shop. Do not hesitate to crack a better deal on the tariff if you are booking a room for more than one day.

Maurya Rajadhani — Hotel ₹₹
☎ 0471 2469469; www.mauryarajadhani.com; Statue-GH Rd; d ₹3500–4000, ste ₹6000–7000 (incl of breakfast) This hotel is located just off the main MG Road making it easy to step out for meals or just walk around the main street. The cosy rooms are clean, bright and spacious. Do not opt for the fourth floor as muffled sounds of a live band from the restaurant reach the rooms on the same floor.

A well-manicured garden at Amruthum Ayurvedic Village Resort

The Residency Tower — Hotel ₹₹
☎ 0471 2331661; www.residencytower.com; Press Rd; d ₹4500–5000, ste ₹7000 (incl of breakfast) The flexi rates policy at Residency Tower can get you a great deal if occupancy is low or the peak season has not set in. Rooms are clean, comfortable and the decor is reasonable. There is also a fitness centre, curio shop, a pool, wi-fi facility and an in-house restaurant.

The South Park — Hotel ₹₹
☎ 0471 2333333; www.thesouthpark.com; MG Rd; d ₹5000–5500, ste ₹6500–9200 (incl of breakfast) Stay at The South Park for its proximity to MG Road and for its spacious rooms which can be made family friendly by adding an extra bed. There is a coffee shop, terrace garden, pub and a restaurant, and an incongruous gold embossed bright lift in this over 20-year-old hotel.

Mascot Hotel — Hotel ₹₹
☎ 0471 2316736; www.ktdc.com; Mascot Square; d ₹5000–7000, ste ₹9000–15,000 (incl of breakfast) Period touches, massive hallways and an imposing reception lend an old-world charm to this KSTDC establishment. Rooms are extremely spacious though minimalistic in decor. Some overlook the enormous pool. The hotel is also known for its Ayurvedic Centre and a refreshing garden cafe, Sahyana (5–10pm).

Beach and Lake Resort — Beachside Resort ₹₹
☎ 0471 2382086; www.beachandlakeresort.com; Pozhikara Beach, Pachalloor PO; d ₹5915–9165 (incl of full board) As the name suggests, Beach and Lake Resort gives you the experience of staying both by the sea and a lake. The property lies at the edge of the ocean and is fragmented by a backwater canal which divides the rooms from the restaurant and the yoga house. The in-house canoe is a fun way to get across to these sections. Though the resort is focused on long-stay, Ayurveda inclined guests, rejuvenation massages are available to weekend visitors also. Choose the first floor rooms for a fabulous view of the sea from large, breezy balconies. Facilities include wi-fi and a reasonably sized swimming pool.

Varikatt Heritage — Homestay ₹₹
☎ 0471 2336057; www.varikattheritage.com; Punnen Rd; d ₹5500, ste ₹6500 (incl of full board) Be sure to read the historical docket put together by Colonel Roy, the owner, to truly enjoy your stay at this 18th-century, British built villa. The home has been tastefully refurbished to include all modern amenities. It has three suites and two double rooms, all of which are spacious and aesthetically done up. The villa is just behind the central MG Road; which is a convenient location.

Windsor Rajdhani   Hotel ₹₹
☏0471 25477755; www.windsorrajdhani.com; Kowdiar; d ₹4500, ste ₹8000–16,000 (incl of breakfast) Choose Windsor Rajdhani for elegantly furnished and comfortable rooms, as well as easy access to the city's sightseeing options. If you are travelling with family, choose the well-appointed suite as it can accommodate an extra bed.

Riverside Eco Homestay   Home to Hire ₹₹
☏9847062392; VP XIII 764, Shankaramukham, Vellanad; full house $100 (quoted rate in $ but they also accept Indian rupee equivalent) The exquisite Riverside Eco Homestay, overlooking the Karamana River, lies just beyond the Aruvikara dam (15km from Thiruvananthapuram). Located behind a rubber plantation, it is set against a lush, sloping garden leading down to the river, crossed by a 90-year-old bridge. Suitable for those who would like to take the entire house for a holiday, guests will have to bring their own food supplies for use in the kitchenette as food is not provided and there are no restaurants close by.

The Lakewood Retreat   Homestay ₹
☏0471 2134053; www.shalimarlakewoods.in; NH Rd, Thiruvallam; d ₹1200–1600 (incl of breakfast) Lakewood Retreat offers an escape to the soothing suburbs of Thiruvananthapuram, where the water from the Karamana River splashes against the front porch. The two guest rooms and a bamboo cottage suite face the idyllic setting of backwaters. Lakewood Retreat is just 5km from Thiruvananthapuram.

VARKALA

The prices of hotels increase by 30–40% between mid December and first week of January for the holiday season. Some close down for two to three months in summer.

The Gateway Hotel   Hotel ₹₹
☏0470 6673300; www.thegatewayhotels.com; Janardhanapuram Varkala; d ₹6600–7600, ste ₹8600 (incl of breakfast) Rebranded, revamped, refurbished, the Gateway hotel is looking hot – especially the new rooms, with beds

---

📷 Snapshot: Kalaripayattu

Kalaripayattu is an ancient tradition of martial training and discipline still taught throughout Kerala. Some believe it is the forerunner of all martial arts, with roots tracing back to the 12th-century skirmishes among Kerala's feudal principalities. Masters of Kalaripayattu, called Gurukkal, teach their craft inside a special arena called a kalari. Kalaripayattu movements can be traced in Kerala's performing arts, such as Kathakali and kootiattam, and in ritual arts such as theyyam.

covered in gleaming linen and mocha cushions, and with glass shower cubicles in the bathrooms, complete with electric blinds. There's a pool also.

Villa Jacaranda   Bed & Breakfast ₹₹
0470 2610296; www.villa-jacaranda.biz; Temple Rd West; d ₹5175 (incl of breakfast) Away from the North Cliff clutter, Villa Jacaranda is tucked on the comparatively peaceful Temple Road. A hand-painted signboard ushers you into this relaxing retreat with just a handful of huge, bright rooms, each with a balcony and decorated with a chic blend of minimalist modern and period touches. The breakfast is served on your verandah.

Hindustan Beach Retreat   Hotel ₹₹
0470 2604254; www.hindustanbeachretreat.com; Papanasam Beach; d ₹4500–5000, ste ₹5500 (incl of breakfast) Feast your eyes on the blue sea across the Papanasam Beach from the pool area or any of the sea-facing rooms here. Hindustan Beach Retreat has spacious comfy rooms, with a balcony. The in-house Ayurvedic spa, Turtle Bay, has an impressive menu of massages.

Thanal   Hotel ₹₹
0470 2604342; www.thanalbeachresort.com; North Cliff; d ₹3500 A pleasant relief from the predictable resort ambience, Thanal is

Hindustan Beach Retreat is a good stay option close to the sea

a new property with four rooms, right in the middle of the North Cliff. The rooms are clean though there are no extra services other than wi-fi. They don't have an in-house restaurant but there are plenty just outside.

Palm Tree Heritage   Beach Resort ₹₹
9946055036; www.palmtreeheritage.com; Odayam Beach; d ₹4000–4500, ste ₹6000 (incl of breakfast) Pleasantly away from the packed North Cliff area, Palm Tree lies at Odayam Beach. Exemplary service, Kerala themed cottages, an in-house restaurant, an Ayurveda spa and proximity to the swimming area of the beach keeps regulars coming back. The resort also has an annexe with slightly less atmospheric but comfortable rooms.

Woodhouse Beach Resort   Resort ₹
9562454757; www.woodhousebeachresort.com; Thiruvambady; d ₹2200, cottage

₹2800 Sea-facing cottages and a fabulous sunset view make Woodhouse an undisputed option. Situated on the right edge of the North Cliff, the hotel seems slightly cluttered, but is neat and good value for money.

Clafouti Beach Resort — Resort ₹
0470 2601414; www.clafoutiresort.com; North Cliff; d from ₹1750 This seaside resort offers a medley of options to stay. You can pick from Kerala-styled wooden cottages overlooking a bright green garden, bamboo huts or standard rooms. With a clean Ayurveda spa as part of the property, you do not have to walk far for a massage.

La Exotica — Homestay ₹
0470 2608866; www.laexotica.in; Helipad; d ₹2500–3500 (incl of breakfast) The only homestay option in Varkala, La Exotica lies just behind the helipad, an earshot away from the sea. Centrally located, it offers basic but clean rooms and a hammock in the garden to relax in. Select a room on the 1st floor for a view of the sea.

KOVALAM

Kovalam is chock-a-block with resorts, but budget places cost more than usual and are difficult to find. Look out for smaller places tucked away in the labyrinth of paths which lie behind the beach amid palm groves and rice paddies; they are much better value.

Vivanta by Taj — Hotel ₹₹₹
0471 6613000; www.vivantabytaj.com; GV Raja Vattappara Rd; d ₹8500 Located on a quiet extension of Kovalam, this Taj property has 59 stone and wood cottages placed at different levels in a tropical garden. All have balconies and sit-outs, and the better placed ones look on to the ocean. The all-day dining space overlooks the newly renovated pool. There is also an Indian restaurant and seafood beach side restaurant, Bait, where you can while away the evening.

The Leela — Hotel ₹₹₹
0471 3051234; www.theleela.com/locations/kovalam; d ₹12,500–18,500 One of India's first 5-star hotels, designed by Charles Correa, the Leela is a sprawling property perched on a cliff with breathtaking views. Retaining its classic Correa touches, it has now opened a swank and modernistic Club Section. The beach view and garden view rooms are the older ones, the latter being a good bargain. The three pools and greenery are the property's plus point, and the cuisine is top class, especially the Malayali fare.

Turtle On The Beach — Resort ₹₹₹
0471 2514000; www.turtleonthebeach.com; VPI/439 ITDC Rd; d ₹10,000–11,000, ste ₹13,000–27,000 (incl of breakfast) This resort, with large artistic wooden sculptures strewn across the property, lies at the bend of Lighthouse Beach. It

has a lovely wooden deck overlooking the sea, a lush garden, sea view rooms, a pool and offers free yoga classes (5.30–6.30pm). Though the rates change weekly as per occupancy, the flexi tariff policy could land you an excellent deal in the low season.

Manaltheeram, Chowara — Resort ₹₹₹
0471 2268610; www.manaltheeram.com; near Chowara PO Vizhinjam Poovar Rd; d ₹6329–15,173 (incl of breakfast and taxes) Location wise, Manaltheeram is a dream! This Ayurveda specific resort sits on the edge of the cliff with steps leading down to the beach below. The garden cottages, with a small personal grassy patch in front, are the most economical. It's a good place to have an Ayurvedic treatment, relax by the pool and get pampered by the excellent staff. You can spend your time at the outdoor restaurant which is the most popular haunt here.

Niraamaya Retreats, Chowara — Resort ₹₹₹
0471 2267333; www.niraamaya.in; Pulinkudi, Mullur Post; d ₹18,000–35,000 (incl of breakfast) Recently re-christened, Niraamaya (earlier Surya Samudra) is draped with an air of extravagance. Built in the shadow of large banyan trees, Niraamaya, one of the finest resorts in the area, has two restaurants, an infinity pool, Kerala-style cottages, yoga pavilions, a gym, wi-fi facility and a spa.

Karikkathi Beach House — Guesthouse ₹₹₹
0471 2720238; www.karikkathibeachhouse.com; via Nagar Bhagavathi Temple, Mullur, Vizhinjam; d ₹9665 (incl of breakfast) Escape from the ubiquitous resorts and predictable guesthouses to this double-bedroom unit off the Chowara Beach in Mullur. Enter through a red door and drift into the lazy cliff-top beach house with only the sound of the waves to keep you company. You are unlikely to bump into other guests.

Isola Di Cocco, Poovar — Resort ₹₹₹
0471 2210800; Poovar; d ₹6000–10,000 (incl of breakfast) This is a terrific option for the family despite its faraway feel. Sandwiched between swampy, coconut plantations and the Arabian Sea, it has multiple categories of accommodation (the Kerala styled

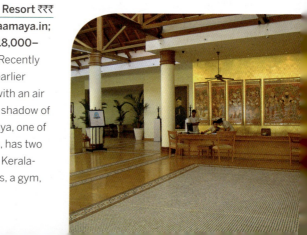

The sprawling Leela lobby designed by Charles Correa

lake-view one being the best), a pool, wi-fi facility, a children's play area, an Ayurveda clinic, free transfer to the Golden Sands Beach in front of it and a courteous staff that you will love.

Marina Guest House — Guesthouse ₹
☏0471 2488220; Lighthouse Beach; d ₹1600–2800 Situated just behind Beatles restaurant, the 10 sparkling clean rooms of Marina Guest House are real value for money, apart from its welcoming atmosphere and distance from the beach.

Varma Cottages, Kovalam — Cottages ₹
☏9847498007; www.calangutebeach.com; Howah Beach; d ₹2500–3000 The charming picket-fenced cottages at the edge of the beach offer wonderfully comfortable rooms. Though it's tempting to take the rooms which are right beside the sea, we recommend that you opt for those that are a little behind the grassy patch for more privacy and peace of mind; every beach sauntering chap seems to enjoy peeking inside from the pavement which may not appeal to you.

Adam Beach Resort — Guesthouse ₹
☏9387813908; www.adambeachresort.com; near Lighthouse Beach; d ₹2200 The real luxury in Kovalam is if you're close to the sand or have a sea view. These standards are unquestionably met by Adam Beach Resort right on the Lighthouse Beach, even though the interiors are austere. Ask for the ocean facing upper floor room, which is spacious enough for at least four people and has a balcony. The place is a real steal.

Eating

THIRUVANANTHAPURAM

Villa Maya — Multi-Cuisine ₹₹₹
☏0471 2578901; Airport Rd; mains ₹1000–1500; 11am–11pm Frangipani trees in the courtyard, water spewing fountains, lotus ponds, dim lighting and the music notes of classical instruments give a chic ambiance to the newly opened Kerala-themed Villa Maya. 'The Fabled Kitchen' as the name translates, serves a fusion cuisines which includes a range of authentic Kerala dishes, Indian grills and continental food. Start with their signature pineapple shikanji.

The lush courtyard at Villa Maya, a Kerala-themed restaurant

Snapshot: The Indian Coffee House story

The Indian Coffee House is a place stuck in a time warp. Its India-wide branches feature old India prices and waiters dressed in starched white with peacock-style headdresses. It was started by the Coffee Board in the early 1940s, during the British rule, but in the 1950s the Board began to close down cafes across India. At this point, communist leader Ayillyath Kuttiari Gopalan Nambiar began to support the workers and founded with them the India Coffee Board Worker's Co-operative Society. The intention was to provide them with better opportunities and promote the sale of coffee. The Coffee House has remained ever since, always atmospheric, and always offering bargain snacks and drinks such as Indian filter coffee, rose milk and idlis. It's still run by its employees, all of whom share ownership.

Azad Indian ₹₹
☎ 0471 3070601; www.azadhotels.com; mains ₹200–500; 7.30am–9.30pm Manoeuvre past waiters balancing heaped biryani plates and asking to make way in this legendary, hectic joint. Having branched out into six restaurants since its inception in 1940, Azad is hugely popular for its efficient service and delicious biryani. Visit the Overbridge branch and get a seat in the basement for a nostalgic ambience amidst old-style low doors and windows.

Indian Coffee House, Maveli Cafe Coffee Shop ₹
☎ 0471 2333517; Thampanoor; mains ₹100–200; 6.30am–10pm Heave yourself up a steep spiral, red tower to this one-of-a-kind India Coffee House. Maveli Cafe brings back the nostalgia of uniformed waiters, and the familiar coffee shop menu – with a slightly unique touch of its own.

Sree Arul Jyothi Vegetarian ₹
☎ 0471 2470240; TC 26/143, opp Secretariat, MG Rd; mains ₹100–200; 7am–10pm Arul Jyothi has been dishing out both south Indian snacks and Kerala specials for years. One of the most famous vegetarian joints, you will find it packed in the evenings. Piping hot coffee and masala dosas are perfect for an evening snack here.

Ambrosia Coffee Shop ₹₹
☎ 9497442211; www.theambrosia.com; Bakery Junction; mains ₹200–500; 10.30am–10pm Look out for one of the four branches of Ambrosia for the best baked goodies in town. You can settle down for a quick snack of yummy biscuits and cakes in the brightly lit cafe or grab a roll to go.

Suprabhatham South Indian ₹
☎ 0471 2471723; MG Rd; mains ₹100–200; 7am–9.30pm This is one of the viable options for vegetarians out of the many similar joints on MG

Road. Decent south Indian fare like thalis and dosas are speedily served in this eatery.

Annapoorna — South Indian ₹
Pazhavangadi, MG Rd; mains ₹100–200; 5.30am–11.30pm The clean and brightly lit Annapoorna serves the regular south Indian food (idlis, dosas and uthappams) and also local delights like puttu. Since it opens early, you can get breakfast while visiting the Padmanabhaswamy Temple.

Ayswariya — Indian ₹₹
0471 3082000; www.aswariya.in; Overbridge, MG Rd; mains ₹250–500; 11am–10pm Tired of dawdling around MG Road? Hop into the spic and span Ayswariya restaurant for a quick bite of south Indian specialities and some fresh juice.

VARKALA

Hotel Suprabhatham — South Indian ₹
0470 2606697; NH Rd, Mythanam; mains 100–200; 7am–9.30pm The narrow entrance to Suprabhatham opens into a world of delicious south Indian fare – idlis, uthappams and filter coffee – a relief from the overwhelming foreign cuisines on offer near the beach.

Trattorias — Multi-Cuisine ₹₹
9746983917; North Cliff; mains from ₹250; 7am–10.30pm Chat with the friendly waiters at the upper deck of Trattorias where they constantly

Filter coffee is popular not just in Kerala, but across South India

play 80s pop music. Yummy fresh juices, goodies from the German bakery and a large multi-cuisine spread can keep you here for a while.

Cafe Italiano — Italian ₹₹₹
8129751097; North Cliff; mains ₹500–750; 7.30am–11pm The wooden floor and woody Cafe Italiano deserves appreciation for its aesthetic ingenuity; droopy vines hang lazily on a central tree adding to the languorous ambience. Sit on the upper deck for a better view of the sea and choose from the Italian fare.

Hungry Eye — Multi-Cuisine ₹₹₹
9633253591; Middle Cliff; mains ₹500–750; 7.30am–11pm This atmospheric restaurant with tiered seating and candle-lit tables offers a massive Thai-inclined menu to choose from. It's a good place to relax and

watch the fishing boats come in after a long day at sea.

Clafouti Restaurant — Multi-Cuisine ₹₹₹
Middle Cliff, Papanasam; mains ₹500–750; 7am–11pm Clearly the most popular hang-out, Clafouti seems to have a sizeable fan-base for its fresh salads and pizzas. The place is buzzing with guests from 7.30pm onwards till post 11pm. Take a seat close to the street.

Milestone Cafe — Multi-Cuisine ₹₹₹
☎9995920651; North Cliff; mains ₹500–750; 7am–11pm Watch the sunset as you gorge on juicy grills and momos at the Milestone Cafe. The lengthy menu offers a variety of cuisines you can choose from.

KOVALAM

Mini House (Sea Pearl Cafe) — Multi-Cuisine ₹₹
☎9947480969; www.minihousekovalam.com; Lighthouse Beach; mains ₹250–500; 10am–11pm A short walk away from the restaurant hub, Mini House is right behind the Lighthouse at the edge of the sea. The decor and menu might be frugal, but the ambience is brilliant.

Santana — Multi-Cuisine ₹₹₹
☎0471 2481599; Lighthouse Beach; mains ₹500–750; 7.30am–11pm Plastic chairs covered with towels (if you have just emerged from the sea) are perfect to settle for an 'ocean view' meal at Santana. Order from the fresh catch of the day or regulars from the exhaustive menu.

Jeevan — Multi-Cuisine ₹₹₹
☎0471 2483062; www.jeevanresort.net; Lighthouse Beach; mains ₹500–750; 10.30am–11pm For those who are hoping to hear the latest Bollywood tunes and enjoy fresh grills, visit Jeevan – one of the few to have an alcohol license among the many beachside cafes.

Rock Café — Seafood ₹₹
☎0471 2480411; Bend at Lighthouse Beach; mains ₹250–500; 10.30am–11pm Visit Rock Cafe and watch fishermen bringing the catch home and packing up for the day as you tuck into utterly delicious fresh fried and grilled seafood.

Beatles — Multi-Cuisine ₹₹₹
☎9387801942; www.beatlesrestaurant.com; Lighthouse Beach; mains ₹500–750; 9.30am–11pm Beatles provides an exclusive

---

✓ Top Tip: Liquor & beer availability

Only a few restaurants like Jeevan have license to serve alcohol. Beer is available at every eating joint, but only in 650ml bottles. Beer is not served in pint glasses but in coffee mugs or newspaper wrapped bottles.

atmosphere, well thought-out menu and a 1st floor view of the sea from its wooden floored and thatched roof deck. The rock music puts you in a good mood, but the music can sometimes stray into the 90s Hindi pop variety – a request will have them play the original jiving tracks.

🛍 Shopping

THIRUVANANTHAPURAM

Pothys — Clothing
☎ 0471 2574133; www.pothys.com; MG Rd, near Ayurveda College Junction; 9.30am–10.30pm An extravaganza of colour unfolds in this massive shop just off MG Road. Even though Pothys is always spilling over with eager shoppers, well categorised sections make it easy to locate saris.

Sarwaa — Souvenirs
☎ 0471 3022220; www.sarwaa.com; Shankar Rd, Sasthamangalam; 9.30am–8pm Get your kitsch fix at Sarwaa, with its large collection of bright bags, curios and an assortment of jewellery and lingerie. Expect a contemporary selection of souvenirs instead of Kerala themed articles.

SMSM Institute — Handicrafts
☎ 0471 2330298; Puthenchanthai; 9am–8pm, Sun closed An elaborate collection of handicrafts, brass curios, coir products and paintings makes this a good stop to pick up souvenirs. Since the establishment is a Kerala government undertaking, you can rely on the quality and pricing.

Khadi Gramodyog Bhavan — Souvenirs
☎ 0471 2331627; Gramodaya, MG Rd; 10am–7.30pm Sun closed Centrally located, Khadi Gramodyog on MG Road is great for Kerala themed souvenirs, especially cheap copies of Raja Ravi Varma paintings.

Chalai Market — Market
10am–8pm Fruits, clothes, jewellery, spices, utensils and plenty of local vibe can be found in this busy market. If you are planning on going there on a Sunday, expect it to be slightly lean as compared to other livelier days.

Antique Shop — Antiques
☎ 9447464161; MG Rd; Sun closed A motley of antiques and distressed curios sit packed in the slimmest shop on MG Road. The bric-a-brac is not necessarily Kerala themed, but still makes for memorable takeaways.

Spices are a popular pick at Thiruvanathapuram's Chalai Market

Connemara Market — Market
MG Rd; 8am–8pm For an authentic local Kerala market experience, wander around Connemara Market amidst a sea of vendors. Established in 1888, the market is more of a historic landmark rather than an essential shopping venue.

VARKALA

Karnataka Shop — Clothing
North Cliff; 7am–10pm There is a large collection of harem pants, cotton kurtis, spaghetti tops, slippers and jewellery. It will be difficult to leave without spending money here.

Balaji Handicrafts — Handicrafts
North Cliff; 7am–10pm The assertive and convincing owner of the shop will let you leave only after you have gone though the entire collection of Kashmiris shawls, jewellery, tees, tops and footwear.

KOVALAM

Anugraha Galleria — Souvenirs
0471 2485968; I/1483, near Orion Hotel, Lighthouse; 9.30am–8pm Though a little pricey, you may want to indulge in some non-essential bric a brac – there are some unusual antiques and handmade paper diaries at Anugraha.

Tibetan Handicraft Shop — Souvenirs
0471 2483540; Near Lighthouse; 10am–10pm Earthy Tibetan scrolls, silver jewellery and brass figures are laid out temptingly at Sangmo's handicrafts shop. Women are likely to spend more time here as the silver is quite irresistible.

Hastkala — Souvenirs
0471 2487694; Kovalam Beach Rd; 9am–9pm It has a larger collection of artefacts, paintings, rugs, shawls and a spattering of Kerala wooden curios. They also have a small collection of framed photographs of original Ravi Varma paintings.

Cottage Industries Exposition Ltd — Souvenirs
0471 2485840; Beach Rd; 9am–9pm The CIE showroom gives a feeling of credibility as compared to the numerous shops by the beach. Its vast collection of carpets, brass items, candles, wood crafted souvenirs can keep you engaged for long.

Chowara Lanes — Lifestyle
Chowara Beach Rd; 10am–10pm The narrow lanes have curio shops that sell the same kind of bohemian clothes (try Shiva Textiles) and jewellery, so one does not have to make the 6km trek to Lighthouse Beach.

Chandrakantha Arts — Handicrafts
9633609801; Lighthouse Beach; 9am–10.30pm A sanctuary for painted copies of Dali, Jimi Hendrix, Bob Marley and the Joker are worth a look. You can also get customised T-shirts with similar themes.

Alappuzha, Kumarakom & Kollam

The quintessential Kerala experience lies in the backwaters of Alappuzha, Kumarakom and Kollam. While the channels of Alappuzha and Kumarakom open out into Vembanad Lake, the Kollam water bodies congregate at Ashtamudi Lake. You will be able to glimpse vignettes of village life along the banks from your houseboat.

Trip Planner

GETTING THERE

Alappuzha: The closest airport is in Kochi (84km) with daily flights to all metros. The railway station has trains to main south India cities and Mumbai, New Delhi, Bengaluru and Chennai.

Kumarakom: The nearest airport is in Kochi (73km) and Kottayam (14km) is the closest railway station, with trains to New Delhi, Mumbai, Bengaluru and Chennai.

Kollam: Thiruvananthapuram is the closest airport (69km). Trains to Kanyakumari stop here. There are regular, daily trains that ply between Alappuzha and Kollam. Government ferries connect Alappuzha and Kollam. It takes eight hours and costs ₹300 per person.

SUGGESTED ITINERARY (8 DAYS)

To experience the alluring backwaters, kick off your journey at Alappuzha. Spend three days here and then make your way to Kumarakom. It offers a range of resorts at the edge of Vembanad Lake. After luxuriating here for three days head to Kollam for a couple of days. It offers a glimpse of local life from the banks of Ashtamudi Lake. The green paddy fields (Kuttanad) are unique as they lie two metres below sea level.

BEST TIME TO GO

J F M A M J J A S **O N D**

GREAT FOR

Top 5 highlights

- Backwaters Cruise, Alappuzha (p218)
- Pathiramanal Island, Alappuzha (p219)
- Sri Krishna Temple, Ambalappuzha (p218)
- Kumarakom Bird Sanctuary, Kumarakom (p221)
- Ashtamudi Lake, Kollam (p224)

Water-bound Beauty

The lush endless backwaters of Alappuzha

Alappuzha, the gateway to Kerala's famed backwater region, largely spreads across three districts. The magical green topography of the town derives from an endless carpet of water hyacinths that flourish in its network of narrow canals. As you manoeuvre your way past watery highways, which eventually meet the **Vembanad Lake** on one side of the town, you realise why Alappuzha is also called 'Venice of the East'.

Kerala's other popular backwater gem, **Kumarakom,** 16km west of Kottayam, lies on the shore of the Vembanad Lake. Despite its popularity on the travel map, Kumarakom's peaceful environs make it an extremely relaxing destination. A number of upscale resorts dot the landscape and the exotic location works like a charm.

Of all the spice trade junctions on the southwestern coast, **Kollam** (Quilon) was exalted by ancient travellers like Marco Polo and Ibn Batuta. The Arabs, Chinese and later Portuguese, Dutch and British made a beeline to tap the cashew resources. Traces of a bustling seaport can still be seen, with an active industry focused on fishing, coir making and, lately, tourism.

Highlights

1. Backwaters Cruise
2. RKK Memorial Museum
3. Sri Krishna Temple, Ambalappuzha
4. Pathiramanal Island
5. Beach Area & Vijay Park
6. Sea View Park
7. Jain Temple

Alappuzha

1 BACKWATERS CRUISE

The presence of over 1000 houseboats in Alappuzha alone bears testimony to the popularity of the cruise experience. Indeed, it is difficult to have your fill of gliding in the placid waters. Besides, with all the comforts close at hand, it's the ultimate form of relaxation. An overnight stay (22-hour cruise) is the best way to enjoy the experience. Day cruises last 4–6 hours. For information on houseboat operators, see p223.

2 RKK MEMORIAL MUSEUM

Embark on an international odyssey of artefacts, murals and paintings: porcelain from China, a 1948 Buick, sculptures from Africa, curios from Belgium, South America, Japan, Italy and Turkey, among other places. The RKK Museum is the private collection of Mrs Betty, wife of deceased coir magnate, Revi Karuna Karan. Her worldwide acquisitions consist of a large private collection of ivory and Swarovskis. The museum is organised and well-kept.

📞 0477 2242923; www.rkkmuseum.com; Shree Karunakaran Charitable Trust, Shanthi Bhavan; Indian/foreigner ₹100/250; 9am–5pm, Mon closed

3 SRI KRISHNA TEMPLE, AMBALAPPUZHA

One of the most revered temples in Kerala, it lies only 14km south of Alappuzha in a small town called Ambalappuzha.

📷 *Snapshot: Eco-friendly cruises*

Pollution and land reclamation threaten the habitat of the waterways and it's estimated that water levels have dropped by two-thirds since the mid-19th century. Opt for an eco-friendly cruise and choose houseboat owners who have a 'Green Palm Certificate'. This means they have installed solar panels and sanitary tanks. It's also better to avoid using ACs.

ALAPPUZHA, KUMARAKOM & KOLLAM

Built in AD 790, the temple is famous for its prasadam (payasam), which is prepared every day for hundreds of devotees. You can walk around the beautiful lamp-lined walls of the sanctum, where a black granite idol of Krishna sits in a unique pose, holding a whip and a conch. A large weighing scale is placed outside the sanctum – it's a common practice to match the weight of rice or oil to the person making offerings to the deity.
3am–noon, 5–8pm

> ## 📷 Snapshot: Vembanad Lake
>
> All the water channels of the town converge at Vembanad Lake, India's longest lake. Spread over 2033sq km, it is flanked by three districts – Alappuzha, Kottayam and Ernakulum – and is known for its variety of fish and migratory waterfowl. Vembanad's wetland system also supports other traditions like lime shell collection, coir netting and fishing.

❹ PATHIRAMANAL ISLAND

Eloquently translated to 'midnight sands' this pastoral island in the middle of the Vembanad Lake is only accessible by boat. Migratory birds are partial to this location, given its green surroundings of 10-acres. Visitors can walk around a 2km path inside. Even the hour-and-a-half motor boat ride (speed boats take only 30min) offers spectacular sights of cormorants diving for fish from their secret hideaways in water hyacinths, as fishermen set up their nets.
📞 0474 22244599; boats ply only until 6pm; motor boat/speedboat ₹600 (10 persons)/1500 (4 persons)

Sri Krishna Temple, Ambalappuzha has traditonal Kerala architecture

Alappuzha Beach is a great spot for sunsets

❺ BEACH AREA & VIJAY PARK

You can enjoy a breezy evening on the busy Alappuzha Beach. It's a local hot spot where impromptu football games are held while vendors sell hot bhaji. There is no entry into the old lighthouse across the beach. A section of the beach has been converted into a children's park.

Vijay Park; Beach Rd; ₹5; 3–8pm

❻ SEA VIEW PARK

Another way to enjoy the seafront is to visit the Sea View Park across Alappuzha Beach, which has a few options for boat rides in an adjoining backwater canal.

Beach Rd; row boat/pedal boat/photography/video ₹20/25/10/50

📷 Snapshot: Snake boat races

Kerala's snake boat races on the backwaters are a marvellous display of sinew and sportsmanship. The honour of an entire village hinges on the annual 'Vallam Kalli'. Between July and September, 15 such races are held. The four most popular are: Nehru Boat Race in Punnamada Lake of Alappuzha, Champakkulam Moolam, Payippad Jalotsavam on Payippad Lake and the Aranmula Race. The 100-seater narrow boats, steered by six to seven team members or oarsmen on either side, are 80–100 feet long. Two to three team members clap and sing to encourage the rowers. The Nehru Boat Race is held on the second Saturday of August.

❼ JAIN TEMPLE

A fair number of traders from the western state of Gujarat settled here many years ago. A narrow street named after them houses a white marble temple built by the community, which is open to visitors. Enter through the small blue gate of the ashram on the left and a dark passage full of paintings will lead you into the temple.

Gujarati St; 7am–5pm

Kumarakom

❶ KUMARAKOM BIRD SANCTUARY

This well-maintained KTDC (Kerala Tourism Development Corporation) sanctuary draws a number of birds such as night herons, paradise fly-catchers, golden backed woodpeckers and more. You can spot these during a walk through the 2km trail, which leads up to three watchtowers at the edge of the lake. Though most visitors choose to walk, there is a provision of a boat (₹550 per hour) to cruise. The best time to visit is from January to June.

www.ktdc.com; Kumarakom North; Indian/foreigner/guide ₹30/100/300; 6am–5pm

❷ BAY ISLAND DRIFTWOOD MUSEUM

Spend some time with the intrepid Raji Punnoose and her collection of driftwood, acquired from the shores of the faraway Andaman Islands. A trip through her meticulously arranged wooden collection requires ample ingenuity to

Spot a variety of birds at Kumarakom Bird Sanctuary

Highlights

❶ Kumarakom Bird Sanctuary
❷ Bay Island Driftwood Museum
❸ Backwaters
❹ Vaikom Mahadev Temple

Vaikom Mahadev Temple is a good day trip from Kumarakom

decipher the shapes of various animals. Of course, Raji is constantly at hand to nudge you in the right direction.
☎9447464296; www.bayislandmuseum.com; Chakranpady; ₹50; 10am–5pm, Sun 11.30am–5pm

❸ BACKWATERS

Veer off the route and take your boat behind Windsor towards the Lighthouse. Most cruise boats tend to take you straight to the C Block and R Block islands, where, typical of the Kuttanad region, the paddy is grown 2m below sea level. The other route is more scenic and refreshingly secluded.

❹ VAIKOM MAHADEV TEMPLE

Those interested in history and spiritual pursuits will find the 29km trip to the Shiva temple at Vaikom worth their while. Unusual to Hindu religious practice, this temple attracts both Shaivite and Vaishnavite devotees. If you happen to be in the region in the months of November or December, look out for the annual Vaikkath Asthami festival. Caparisoned elephants and grand celebrations are held the entire day. Arrive in the evening at 7pm to see the evening aarti.
www.vaikomtemple.org; Vaikom; 4am–noon, 4.30–8.30pm

If You Like: Backwater tours

Kettuvalams or houseboats are an architectural marvel and one can find basic to ultra-lavish accommodation. Peak season rates can be up to 25–30% higher. Here are some of the top operators (incl of full board):

ALAPPUZHA

- **River & Country Tours** (☎0477 2253581; www.riverandcountry.com; No 13, Municipal Library Shopping Centre, opposite boat jetty; d from ₹6000): With a small but reliable fleet of five houseboats, the company is well regarded in the area.

- **Pulickattil Tourism Group** (☎0477 2264558; www.pulikattilbackwaters.com; Nehru Trophy Finishing Point; d from ₹6000): One of the top houseboat groups, Pulickattil has a troupe of one to six bedroom houseboats.

- **Rainbow Cruises Backwaterworld** (☎0477 2261375; www.backwaterkerala.com; Green Shore Holidays & Resorts (P) Ltd, VCNB Rd, opposite boat jetty; d from ₹9000): Over 12 years of experience, 25 kinds of houseboats plus classy aesthetics makes it a good option.

- **Marvel Cruise** (☎0477 264341; www.keralahotel.com; Mullakkal; d from ₹6000): Marvel has eight comfortable houseboats with eco-friendly features.

- **Evergreen Tours** (☎0477 2763385; www.evergreen-kerala.com; Room No 709, St Thomas Church Building, Pallathuruthy; d ₹7500–13,000): Years of cruising and 14 houseboats makes Evergreen a fitting choice. The interiors are neat and the staff well versed with the region.

KUMARAKOM

- **Eco Trails Kerala** (☎0481 2526201; www.ecotourskerala.com; Tharavadu Heritage Home; d from ₹6000): Eco Trails is definitely off-beat and Kence Georgey (owner) can chalk out a unique experience of the backwaters.

- **St Crispin Heritage Houseboat** (☎0481 2524314; www.kodianthara.com; Kodianthara; d ₹6000–12,000): All three boats are cheerfully furnished and comfortable.

Tourists enjoying a ride on the backwaters

Highlights

1. Ashtamudi Lake
2. Kollam Beach & Mahatma Gandhi Park
3. Thangaserry Fishing Village & Lighthouse
4. Neendakara Fishing Harbour
5. Thirumullavaram Beach
6. Oachira Parabrahma Temple
7. Amritapuri
8. Sasthamkotta Lake & Temple

Kollam

1 ASHTAMUDI LAKE

Compared to the backwaters of Alappuzha and Kumarakom, these are virtually untouched as there is little houseboat traffic here. There are 10 islands in the lake, of which Munroe is the most famous. The district tourism department has convenient day-and night-long tours of the lake, which one can board from the District Tourism Promotion Council (DTPC jetty).

0474 2745625; www.dtpckollam.com; near KSRTC bus stand; Munroe cruise ₹400 per person; 9am–1.30pm, 2–6.30pm

2 KOLLAM BEACH & MAHATMA GANDHI PARK

Kollam Beach is good to drive by or take a walk in the evening to see the sunset, but it's not awfully clean. The beach remains alive late into the evening with a children's park at one edge. Swimming here is not recommended.
Beach Rd; ₹5; 9am–9pm

3 THANGASERRY FISHING VILLAGE & LIGHTHOUSE

Colourful fishing boats line the sandy banks of this village stretch, ending in the Thangaserry Fort. The 18th-century fort now stands crumbling at the end of the beach. Slightly further down is the 144ft-high lighthouse.
Thangaserry Point Lighthouse; Indian/foreigner/camera/video ₹10/25/20/25; 3–5pm

4 NEENDAKARA FISHING HARBOUR

Arrive here at 7am to watch the frantic activity of fishing boats coming in. It might be an olfactory challenge but the harbour makes for great photo opportunities.
Neendakara Fishing Harbour; suggested visiting hrs 7–8.30am; parking ₹20

❺ THIRUMULLAVARAM BEACH

A quiet but small stretch of sand, this beach is perfect to escape the crowd. It is just 6km from the town and has a kalyani (pool) behind it, usually full of local children.

❻ OACHIRA PARABRAHMA TEMPLE

Thirty two kilometres from Kollam, Oachira may at first seem like a small dusty town but the unique idol-and structure-less temple here is sure to amaze you. A large ground ends in two trees around which devotees pray with a small wooden doll in hand (dosh doll), which apparently is said to help you atone for your sins.
Oachira village; open 24 hrs

❼ AMRITAPURI

You'll be greeted with a warm hug from spiritual guru, Mata Amritanandamayi Devi when you visit her seaside ashram, 33km away. Amma, as she is fondly known, is engaged in charitable work. Queue up before 9am for the famous hug.
0476 2897578; www.amritapuri.org; Amritapuri

❽ SASTHAMKOTTA LAKE & TEMPLE

This largest freshwater lake in Kerala, is 29km away. It's the main source of drinking water here, owing to the presence of a unique larva called chaoborus in it that destroys bacteria. At the edge of the lake is the ancient Sasthamkotta Temple dedicated to Lord Ayyappa.
Sasthamkotta; 4am–8pm

The calm waters of Ashtamudi Lake

Accommodation

ALAPPUZHA

Citrus Retreats Resort ₹₹₹
☎0477 2288611; www.citrushotels.in; 8/504A-504N, Karimba Valavu, Punnapra North; d ₹7500–18,000 (incl of breakfast) Flanked by paddy fields of Kuttanad and the Pallathuruthy River, Citrus offers a refreshing stay by the river. It has lavish, well-equipped rooms, a restaurant with an organic menu, pool, Ayurveda services – all with touches of earthy Kerala aesthetics. The water-facing rooms offer scenic views.

Vembanad House Boutique Homestay ₹₹₹
☎0478 2868696; www.vembanadhouse.com; Puthankayal, Muhamma; d ₹10,500 (incl of breakfast) The property, an erstwhile coconut farm, is just a stone's throw away from Pathiramanal Island. The hosts can arrange for a small boat to take you across to it. The family-run homestay offers authentic home-cooked meals and has a garden which opens out from the main house towards the water. There is reasonably good wi-fi connectivity.

Lake Palace Resort ₹₹₹
☎0477 2239701; www.lakepalaceresort.com; d ₹13,000–25,000 (incl of breakfast) A boat at the Alappuzha ferry junction brings you straight to the resort. The excitement of this special entry via the backwaters follows right through, even after you check in at the rooms overlooking a central manmade lake. There is a large central pool on an elevation, an in-house restaurant, wi-fi and a range of activities.

Lemon Tree Vembanad Lake Resort Resort ₹₹₹
☎0478 2861970; www.lemontreehotels.com; Jana Sakthi Rd, Kayippuram, Muhamma; d ₹9500–14,375, ste ₹16,675–29,325 (incl of breakfast) Lemon Tree has all the trappings of a resort with its list of engaging activities, well-furnished rooms and well-trained staff, making it a good choice for a family vacation. If not interested in the activities planned by the resort, you can simply relax by the pool. All but four rooms face the

Vembanad House is surrounded by a lush garden

> **If You Like: Toddy**
>
> Toddy, also known as 'kallu' is a white, frothy and potent alcoholic beverage that is best consumed fresh. Toddy shops are announced by a classic black and white sign and their frequency increases in the backwater regions. Most of them are dingy and besides locals hardly anyone (especially women) frequents these shops. Toddy is usually served with beef fry, meen (fish) and tapioca. To see what it's all about, visit **Tharavadu Family Restaurant** (p232), a toddy shop converted into an 'all permitted' restaurant in Kumarakom.

backwater expanse, so ensure that you book right. There is wi-fi facility.

Emerald Isle — Homestay ₹₹
0477 2703899; www.emeraldislekerala.com; Kanjooparambil, Manimalathara, Chathurthyakary; d ₹5700–7300 (incl of breakfast) Leading the heritage experience in homestays is the much awarded Emerald Isle, a 150-year-old house owned by Mr Vijo. Portions of the old house, like the granary, have been converted into beautiful rooms. Situated at the edge of the Pampa River and the paddy fields of the Kuttanad region, Emerald presents enviable access to the best of Alappuzha.

Punnamada Resort — Resort ₹₹
0477 2233690; www.punnamada.com; Punnamada Thondankulangara Rd; d ₹6500–8600 (incl of breakfast) A small road from the town leads to this 10.5 acre property at Vembanad Lake's periphery. Choose between lake, pool or garden facing rooms. The cottages give a true feel of Kerala architecture with materials sourced from traditional houses.

Akkarakalam Memoirs — Homestay ₹₹
0477 2762345; www.akkarakalammemoirs.com; Chennamkary; d ₹5000 (incl of breakfast) The well-preserved, 150-year-old Syrian Christian house has the Pampa River at its backyard. Period furniture, open showers, an intact ancient granary and authentic Kerala cuisine are its highlights. Activities offered include canoeing, fishing, cycling, Ayurveda massages and cycling around the nearby village.

Keraleeyam Ayurvedic Resort — Resort ₹₹
0477 2231468; www.keraleeyam.com; Thathampally; d ₹4156–5289 (incl of breakfast) This 18-year-old establishment's USP is its Ayurvedic treatments. Located on the border of the Punnamada backwater canal, Keraleeyam is mostly frequented by long-stay guests, but it also offers quick rejuvenation packages. Keraleeyam lies at the border of the Punnamada backwater canal,

where the Nehru Boat Race is held each year.

Taamara — Homestay ₹₹
9388988811; www.taamara.in; Thaneermukkam; d ₹5500 (incl of breakfast) You wouldn't want to step out of this one! A lush garden faces the four cottage units, each with personal wooden decks, at the edge of the Vembanad Lake. Most guests spend time at a semi-covered common area and attached open kitchen. The upper storey rooms offer more privacy.

Tharavad Heritage Resort — Heritage ₹
0474 22244599; www.tharavadheritageresort.com; Sea View Ward; d ₹1500–2000 (incl of breakfast) Out of the heritage accommodations in Alappuzha, Tharavad stands out with its 100-year-old architecture, terracotta tiled roof, teakwood heavy furniture and old artefacts. Its proximity to town and the beach is a big advantage.

> ### Detour: Marari Beach
> Since Marari and Alappuzha are only 15km apart, you can get the best of the beach and the backwaters if you stay at Marari Beach (between Fort Kochi and Alappuzha). Private service villas, hotels and homestays are all available here. Marari Villa (www.mararivillas.com) and CGH Earth (www.cghearth.com) are good options.

Cherukara Nest — Homestay ₹
0477 2251509; www.cherukaranest.com; IX 774, Cherukara Buildings, east of KSRTC Bus Station; d ₹1500 (incl of breakfast) This 85-year-old homestay at the edge of town is away from the touristy din. The back opens into a unique tomb-like pigeon coop in a garden, with a long rope swing and common eating area. It is reasonably priced for its facilities and location.

KUMARAKOM

Coconut Lagoon — Resort ₹₹₹
0481 2525834; www.cghearth.com; d ₹16,300–31,000 (incl of breakfast and taxes) A CGH Earth initiative, Coconut Lagoon embodies the true essence of Kerala in a lavish avatar. Traditionally dressed staff, authentically styled cottages, a kalarippayat (martial art form) rink, yoga pavilion and a maze of canals inside the property make Coconut Lagoon a great choice for those wanting to sample the nuances of local Kerala living.

Vivanta by Taj — Resort ₹₹₹
0481 2525711; www.vivantabytaj.com; 1/404 Kumarakom; d ₹12,500–24,000 (incl of breakfast) Replete with history, the 140-year-old structure is considered one of the best at Kumarakom with its inventive cottages, including one with a private pool. The 28-room resort overlooking the Vembanad Lake has a swimming

pool, in-house restaurant and offers well-planned activities.

Philipkutty's Farm — Homestay ₹₹₹
☏ 04829 276530; www.philipkuttysfarm.com; Pallivathukal, Ambika Market PO, Vechoor; d regular/peak season ₹12,500/15,000 (incl of full board) Ferry across a hyacinth-carpeted canal to six artistically styled Kerala villas at the edge of Vembanad Lake. Delicious local food, a coconut plantation and the backwaters complement the frangipani trees in a courtyard facing each cottage. The hosts of this luxury farm stay have great hospitality standards, with their attention to detail and are lovely company.

Kumarakom Lake Resort — Resort ₹₹₹
☏ 0481 2524900; www.thepaul.in; Kumarakom North; d ₹12,500–

Taamara offers scenic views of Vembanad Lake from most rooms

17,500, ste ₹48,000 (incl of breakfast) This resort offers premium services like a swimming pool, wi-fi, stylish cottages and a well-packaged 'Kerala' experience with houseboats and Ayurveda treatments at the Ayurmana Spa. Local snacks are served at the in-house street food joint, Thattukada, in the evening. You will be pampered and spoilt here by the attentive staff.

Zuri — Resort ₹₹₹
☏ 0481 2527272; www.thezurihotels.com; V235 A1 to A54, Karottukayal; d ₹7500–35,000 (incl of breakfast) Zuri's 72 rooms guarantee a high-energy ambience. To relax, head to the pool or the Maya Spa and try traditional Kerala treatments or Thai/Swedish massages.

Tharavad Heritage Home is a traditional Kerala house built in 1870

Kodianthara Heritage Farm House — Homestay ₹

☏ 0481 2524314; www.kodianthara.com; Kumarakom PO, Vechoor; d non-AC/AC ₹2000/2500 (incl of breakfast) The sunny nadumuttam (central courtyard) is encircled by cosy refurbished rooms of this 160-year-old house. The carefully preserved structure, with a granary and old portraits, is a pleasure for history lovers. Traditional food, a canal running inside the house, backwater cruise and a village setting are the highlights.

Coconut Creek — Homestay ₹

☏ 0481 2524203; www.coconutcreek.co.in; near Nazareth Church; d non-AC/AC ₹1750/2250 (incl of breakfast) Only three rooms of this heritage house are let out for guests, ensuring privacy. The lakefront is just a five-minute walk.

Tharavad Heritage Home — Resort ₹

☏ 0481 2525230; www.tharavaduheritage.com; near Boat Jetty; d ₹950–2500 (incl of breakfast) The fact that one gets to stay in a house built in 1870 at a moderate price is reason enough to ignore the slightly dowdy but cheerful service. Identified as a landmark in town, it's conveniently located near the government boat jetty.

KOLLAM

Raviz — Resort ₹₹₹

☏ 0474 2751111; www.theraviz.com; Thevally, Mathilil PO; d ₹11,000–22,000, ste ₹30,000 (incl of breakfast) The latest addition to the handful of five-star properties in Kollam, Raviz is a lavish Kerala-themed hotel at the edge of Ashtamudi Lake. The grand facade has Kathakali dancing statues and there is a snake boat replica in the lobby. Plush rooms overlooking the backwaters,

> ### Snapshot: Erstwhile cashew country
>
> The moniker 'cashew country' seems inappropriate for Kollam as its cashew plantations and processing units are fast disappearing, largely due to soaring land and labour prices. But you can still buy processed cashew at **Vijayalaxmi Cashew Company** (☏ 0474 2741391) and the Kochupilammoodu area in town.

Top Tip: Bite of nostalgia on Main Street

Restaurants established from the 1940s are the highlight in Kollam market. Set up in the 1960s, vegetarian establishments **Padma** and **Guruprasad** (0474 2741359, 7am–9.30pm), retain the old charm with blue walls and wooden furniture. **Hotel Azad** (1940), near Guruprasad, serves both vegetarian and non-vegetarian food. **Indian Coffee House** (1965, 8am–9.30pm), on the opposite side of the street, has a classic, nostalgic feel and is great to visit.

a pool and a restaurant make it one of the best ranked hotels here. Don't hesitate to ask for discounts, as the rates vary according to the season and you may be lucky enough to get a good deal.

Club Mahindra, Backwater Retreat Ashtamudi Resort ₹₹₹
0476 2884000; www.clubmahindra.com; Chavara South; d ₹7000–15,000 (incl of breakfast) In typical Mahindra style, the Backwater Retreat experience is chock-a-block with activities for children, making it an excellent choice for families. If you are feeling especially indulgent, book a floating cottage for your family. A multitude of cruise, boating and sightseeing day trips are listed in the games room and can be arranged by the management.

The Quilon Beach Hotel ₹₹
0472 2769999; www.thequilonbeachhotel.com; on the beach; d ₹6450–7450, ste ₹9450–18,950 (incl of breakfast) All the rooms offer a fabulous view of the Arabian Sea. Apart from the musty carpets in the hallway, the rooms, lobby, restaurant and 24-hour coffee shop are decent. The staff is extremely helpful in arranging day trips to nearby sightseeing destinations. There is a swimming pool as well.

Nani Hotel ₹
0474 2751141; www.hotelnani.com; opp Clock Tower, Chinnakada; d ₹1850–3250 (incl of breakfast) This boutique business hotel comes as a surprise in Kollam's busy centre, and is exceptionally good value. Built by a cashew magnate, it is gorgeously designed and mixes traditional Kerala elements with modern lines for an appealing look. The in-house restaurant serves reasonable multi-cuisine food.

Eating

ALAPPUZHA

Indian Coffee House Coffee Shop ₹
18004251125; www.indiancoffeehouse.com; Mullakkal outlet: 8am–9pm, mains below ₹200; Beachside outlet: noon–8pm, mains below ₹200 The nostalgic air and turbaned waiters of the oldest

national coffee establishment has attracted both locals and visitors for the last 52 years. Apart from the near-perfect coffee, try the rose milk, mutton cutlets and bread-butter-jam combos. The cafe also serves beef fry which can be teamed with dosa. Don't forget to pick up a sweet milk peda while paying at the counter.

Hotel Royale Park — Multi-cuisine ₹₹
0477 2237828; www.hotelroyalepark.com; YM A Rd; 7am–10.30pm This is your best bet in town for a 'Kerala meal'. It gives a choice of white or brown husk rice. Choose the latter with a combination of fish curry for an appetising lunch. Vegetarian food is also available.

Kream Korner Restaurant — Multi-cuisine ₹₹
9847007087; www.kreamkornerartcafe.com; Mullakkal; 9am–10pm; mains ₹200–500 Kream Korner is an art gallery and restaurant rolled into one bright, spacious art cafe. A steady stream of travellers keeps the cafe buzzing, many dropping by to see paintings based on local Kerala themes.

Sisir Palace — Multi-cuisine ₹₹
0477 2254100; www.sisirpalace.com; north of boat jetty; 8.30am–10pm; mains ₹200–500 The newly constructed Sisir Palace serves both elaborate meals and snacks. Spacious and brightly lit, the cafe's decent menu attracts many tourists. It is a good idea to stick to Kerala specialities.

Alleppey Prince Hotel — Multi-cuisine ₹₹
0477 2243752; www.alleppeyprincehotel.com; AS Rd; 6.30am–10.30pm; mains ₹200–500 Grab a beer with your food at Prince Hotel. The multi-cuisine restaurant has a two-section seating arrangement, the left one is suitable for families as it does not have a bar.

KUMARAKOM

Tharavadu Family Restaurant — Kerala Meals ₹
Kavanattinkara; 9am–9pm; mains less than ₹250 A local toddy shop that has been converted to a family restaurant. However, it has few takers (among families), but still this is an interesting concept where the entrepreneur has tried to elevate the

Traditional Kerala food is served on a banana leaf

local beverage to a legitimate status for families.

Dubai Hotel — Kerala Meals ₹₹
📞0481 2525821; Anna Centre; 9am–9pm; mains ₹250–500 You cannot miss the big red signs of 'Dubai Hotel' as you enter Kumarakom. It is without doubt the best place to grab a local Kerala meal, though options for vegetarians are limited.

KTDC Waterscapes Multi-cuisine ₹₹₹
📞0481 2525861; www.waterescapeskumarakom.com; Kumarakom North; 7.30am–9.30pm; mains ₹500–700 The view of Vembanad Lake from this glass and wood restaurant will make you want to stretch your lunch for hours. Built on stilts, the structure overlooks the hyacinth-clad calm waters. A range of reasonable vegetarian and non-vegetarian multi-cuisine dishes are served here.

🛍 Shopping

ALAPPUZHA

Pulickattil Handicrafts Souvenirs
📞0477 2264558; www.pulickattil.com; boat jetty; 8am–8.30pm Alappuzha is far from being a shopper's paradise – there are very few options to pick up souvenirs and this one tops the sparse list. Find a plethora of wooden boat replicas, elephant heads, key chains and the much talked about Aranmula mirrors.

Wooden artefacts are popular souvenirs across the state

These can range from ₹800–12,000 and are rarely stocked by shops.

Collections Souvenirs
📞0477 2261434; Mullakkal; 9.30am–8pm A reasonable collection of brass, wooden and coir bric-a-brac awaits you at Collections. Since the mementos here are not expensive, much of your time might be spent on deciding and picking up small trinkets for gifting friends and family.

KUMARAKOM

Old Curiosity Shop Souvenirs
📞0481 2526160; Tourist Complex, Cheepumkal; 9am–6pm Pick up small bric-a-brac or more elaborate antiques from Liji's shop, just off the main Kumarakom road. You will find old lamps, wooden artefacts, period furniture and spices.

Kochi & Around

Serene Kochi (Ernakulam, Fort Kochi and a knot of tiny islands) has been drawing traders and explorers to its shores for over 600 years. The historical towns of Fort Kochi and Mattancherry remain redolent with the past. Nowhere in India could you find such an interesting cultural mix.

Trip Planner

GETTING THERE

Cochin International Airport, the most convenient air node for the region, is well connected to all main cities of the country via daily flights. Ernakulam has two railway stations – Ernakulam Town and the Ernakulam Junction – both linking it to several major cities. The Kerala Express (12626) from New Delhi, Kanyakumari Express (16381) from Mumbai and the Ernakulam Express (12677) from Bengaluru run daily. For overnight rides from Bengaluru, Mangalore, and Chennai to the region, book Volvo buses from private operators.

SUGGESTED ITINERARY (5 DAYS)

Start your vacation at Kochi which is a combination of a cluster of islands and mainland Ernakulam. Spend a couple of days in Ernakulam, the cosmopolitan hub of Kochi. For a dose of culture, make your way to the islands of Fort Kochi and Mattancherry (the tourist hub) that are redolent of the past and spend three days here.

BEST TIME TO GO

J F **M A** M J J A S **O N D**

GREAT FOR

Top 5 highlights

- **Kerala Folklore Museum, Ernakulam** (p236)
- **Durbar Hall, Ernakulam** (p237)
- **Chinese Fishing Nets, Fort Kochi** (p242)
- **Dutch Palace, Mattancherry** (p244)
- **Pardesi Synagogue, Mattancherry** (p244)

Cultural Tryst

Chinese Fishing Nets, a landmark at Fort Kochi

You need some orientation to the cluster of islands that make **Kochi** (formerly Cochin) before you start the trip. **Ernakulam**, the district, and also the urban centre on the mainland, is chock-a-block with residential areas and narrow roads bursting with prosperous businesses. This hectic transport and cosmopolitan hub serves as a good stopover for shopping and a quick dose of culture.

Lying close to the mainland, but joined by bridges are the small islands of **Willington** (mostly government offices), **Fort Kochi** and **Mattancherry**, **Bolgatty** and **Vypeen**. The most captivating of Kochi's pack of islands, Fort Kochi and Mattancherry are a heady mix of well-preserved colonial history, a lively art scene, boutique hotels, exceptional seafood and elements that are still reminiscent of Kerala's indigenous culture. An influx of Western travellers over the years has moulded the harbour town into a haven of English-speaking, perfect-pasta-serving inhabitants, and antiques oozing from every shop. This has served well for Indian tourists as well; it's safe, clean, and language is not a problem at all. Equip yourself with comfortable walking shoes and a map and discover the narrow streets.

Highlights

1. Kerala Folklore Museum
2. Hill Palace Museum
3. Sri Poornathrayeesha Temple
4. Durbar Hall Art Centre
5. Ernakulam Shiva Temple (Ernakulathappan Temple)
6. Marine Drive
7. Edappally Church
8. Museum of Kerala History
9. Wonder La
10. Cherai Beach
11. Kodnad Elephant Camp

Ernakulam

1 KERALA FOLKLORE MUSEUM

Here lies an incredible private collection of traditional masks, theatrical costumes, artefacts, sculptures and art, packed into three storeys. The museum has more than 5000 artefacts and covers three architectural styles: Malabar, Kochi and Travancore. A visit here is time well spent. Check for classical dance performances at the beautiful wood-lined theatre; these take place sporadically, depending on daily bookings.

✆ 0484 2665452; www.keralafolkloremuseum.org; Thevara; ₹100; 9.30am–7pm

2 HILL PALACE MUSEUM

Located 16km southeast of Ernakulam, this museum was formerly the residence of the Kochi royal family, and is an impressive 49-building palace complex. Leave your slippers outside and huddle up with other visitors to hear the guide's discourse on the 14 key exhibits, which are divided into ornaments, sculptures, artefacts, coins, weapons and more.

GETTING AROUND

Bus: Plenty of local buses connect Ernakulam to Willington, Fort Kochi and Mattancherry. Budget less than ₹20 for a ride.

Taxi/Auto-rickshaw: Taking a taxi between Ernakulam and Fort Kochi is unnecessary when there are convenient buses and the ferry, but if you must, it will cost you ₹8–12 per km. Autorickshaws take between ₹150–200.

Ferry: All islands of Kochi are connected by ferry but one is likely to frequent the Ernakulam–Fort Kochi (Customs) and Mattancherry route. The service, every 20 minutes for ₹2.50 per head, starts at 6.30am and ends at 9.30pm.

Private boats: There are a few private boat operators at the Ernakulam Jetty. These take up to 12–15 people and cost ₹1000 for four hours.

KOCHI & AROUND

Avoid Sundays as it is a hot spot for locals and the queues are rather long.
Tripunithura; adult/child/camera/video ₹20/10/20/150; 9am–12.30pm, 2–4.30pm

> The Hill Palace Musuem has 14 exhibits

❸ SRI POORNATHRAYEESHA TEMPLE
Twelve kilometres from the centre of town, Sri Poornathrayeesha Temple lies close to the Hill Museum at Tripunithura. The temple is dedicated to Lord Vishnu and is popular amongst childless devotees who come here to pray for an offspring. It is also known for its small school that teaches young boys the art of playing temple percussions. If visiting around 4pm, you will hear the synchronised beating of wooden blocks with sticks during the practice session.
4am–noon, 4–8.30pm

❹ DURBAR HALL ART CENTRE
Art lovers will appreciate the local and international exhibitions at the Durbar Hall. Once owned by the Maharaja of Kochi, the hall is a highly regarded venue for art shows. Local sports and cultural events are held at the field outside.
Durbar Hall Rd; ₹50; 10am–6pm

Marine Drive is a popular hang-out for locals

❺ ERNAKULAM SHIVA TEMPLE (ERNAKULATHAPPAN TEMPLE)

Do visit the deity that looks after the city of Ernakulam in this temple, conveniently located within the Durbar Hall compound (the Durbar Hall was where the King would hold formal and informal meetings). Dedicated to Shiva, it was built in 1846 and patronised by the royal family. The large complex also accommodates a Hanuman and Murugan Temple, so one can see a daily congregation of devotees in the area.

Durbar Hall Rd; 3–11.30am, 4–8pm

❻ MARINE DRIVE

Running parallel to Shanmugham Road (behind Bay Pride Mall), Marine Drive is perfect for a sunset stroll. As in every seaside town, local food carts, balloon vendors and couples cosying up behind black umbrellas are an integral part of the topography. Having undergone extensive refurbishment, the clean seafront benches now invite you for some harbour gazing – especially in the evenings as vessels become mere twinkling jewels in the distance.

❼ EDAPPALLY CHURCH

It's official name is St George's Syro-Malabar Catholic Forane Church. Built in 594 it is one of the oldest in Kerala. Make a quick stop to see the intricate facade and detailed architecture. The church is famous for a visit made by Mother Teresa in 1994. The current church bell was installed to commemorate her visit; it is now a big tourist attraction.
Edappally; 4am–5pm

❽ MUSEUM OF KERALA HISTORY

The dome-shaped stone building at Edappally stores a well maintained repository of information on Kerala's history, depicted in miniatures that are lit up as one walks around barefoot during a sound and light show. The museum also has a small display of dolls, a shop and a gallery. A wonderful effort has been made in the overall and detailed presentation by the Madhavan Nayar Foundation; even the tickets are aesthetically designed in the form of old palm leaves.
☏0484 2558296; www.artandkeralahistory.org; adult/child ₹100/30; 10am–5pm, Mon closed; no photography

❾ WONDER LA

The kids are going to love this amusement park. It has water and dry rides with both high thrills and mild options. Be well prepared for the water park with a dress code of shorts, tees

Caparisoned elephants during a festival at the Shiva Temple

Detour: Athirappally & Vazhachal Falls

The famous Athirappally Waterfalls are a popular weekend tourist spot as they are just 64km from Ernakulam. You can choose to do a day trip here. The falls provide a dramatic entrance to the Sholayar mountain range on the Western Ghats and have acquired the moniker 'The Niagara of India'. Lying 1000ft above the Chalakudy River, they provide a refreshing break from the city.

The height of the falls is 80ft and they are at their best just after the monsoons. Visitors are allowed to walk down to a bathing spot at a distance below. Needless to say, they have been a backdrop to many Malayalam and Hindi movies.

The **Vazhachal Falls** are 5km ahead on the same road, though not as picturesque. Since they lie within the forest area, it is not uncommon to see stray wildlife on the roads. Bison, deer and sometimes elephants are found crossing into the forest on the road leading to the falls (Forest Checkpost; 8am–5pm; adult/child/foreigner/camera ₹20/2/60/10).

If you are planning on staying a night here, there is nothing better than the comfy boutique resort facing the roaring Athirappally falls. The **Rainforest** (9539078888; www.rainforest.in; Kannamkuzhy PO; d ₹10,500–18,500, tree house ₹11,500 incl of breakfast) property undoubtedly offers the best view in town (nine luxurious rooms and a tree house with a 180-degree view of the waterfalls). The in-house restaurant and the swimming pool area are located against this breathtaking backdrop. The hotel arranges a short walk within the property to the falls. If you want to stop here only for a short meal break, call before and make a booking.

The scenic Athirappally Waterfalls are a popular weekend getaway

Colourful beach parasols dot Cherai Beach

and appropriate swimwear. Students can avail discounts by showing their ID cards.
☎ 0484 2684001; www.wonderla.com; Pallikara, Kumarapuram; adult/child ₹460/360 (weekdays), ₹600/470 (weekends), ₹660/530 (peak season); 11am–6pm (weekdays), 11am–7pm (weekends)

⑩ CHERAI BEACH

A 45-minute drive from Ernakulam brings you to Cherai Beach at Vypeen Island. It's a long stretch, so you can bypass the line of snack shops and a package-tour feel to find an isolated spot. Swimming here is not recommended. The drive to the beach is marvellous, as the road is flanked by a glistening backwater lagoon.

⑪ KODNAD ELEPHANT CAMP

The 36km ride from Ernakulam to Kodnad Elephant Camp is worth it if you are travelling with children. Five adult elephants and two babies are part of this establishment that is run by the Forest Department. The highlight is the morning bath given to these elephants at the edge of the Periyar River. You can even give the mahouts a hand and click photographs (you are expected to tip). The elephants then amble back with a trail of visitors to the camp where they are fed. Arrive before 8am to witness the entire spectacle.
☎ 0484 2649052; 8am–5pm; adult/child/camera/video ₹10/5/50/250

KERALA

Highlights
1. Indo Portuguese Museum
2. Chinese Fishing Nets
3. St Francis Church (Vasco Church)
4. Dutch Cemetery
5. Santa Cruz Cathedral Basilica
6. Southern Naval Command Maritime Museum
7. Thirumala Devaswom Temple
8. Dutch Palace & Temple
9. Pardesi Synagogue

Fort Kochi & Mattancherry

❶ INDO PORTUGUESE MUSEUM
This museum preserves the heritage of one of India's earliest Catholic communities. Artefacts from different churches of the Catholic diocese from the region are on display. The museum is spread over different storeys, each denoted by a different theme: Altar, Treasures, Procession, Civil Life and Cathedral. The Portuguese-influenced collection dating as far back as the 16th century, are a rare and marvellous sight.
📞 0484 2215400; Bishop's House; 9am–1pm, 2–6pm, Mon & public holidays closed; adult/child/foreigners ₹10/5/25

❷ CHINESE FISHING NETS
At the tip of Fort Kochi sits the unofficial emblem of Kerala's backwaters: cantilevered Chinese fishing nets. The enormous ladle-like nets are permanently positioned here and it takes teams of four to five fishermen to heave the heavy nets out of the water with a pulley system. Competition is stiff with a brigade of crows close at hand. The flurry of activity starts as early as 6am and you can also take pictures for a small tip.
Vasco Square

❸ ST FRANCIS CHURCH (VASCO CHURCH)
Believed to be India's oldest European-built church, it was originally constructed in 1503 by Portuguese Franciscan friars. The edifice that stands here today was built in the mid-16th century to replace the original wooden structure. The

The striking Santa Cruz Basilica was built in 1902

highlight of the church is the dusty tombstone of explorer Vasco da Gama, who died in Cochin in 1524. He was buried here for 14 years before his remains were taken to Lisbon.
River Rd; 8.30am–5pm

❹ DUTCH CEMETERY
Another landmark colonial presence in the harbour town is the Dutch Cemetery at the end of River Road. It contains the dilapidated graves of Dutch traders and soldiers. Now locked to keep curious intruders at bay, you can just about peep over the gate and have a glimpse of the over 200-year-old graves.
River Rd

❺ SANTA CRUZ CATHEDRAL BASILICA
The imposing Catholic basilica was originally built at this site in 1506, though the current building dates to 1902. Inside you'll find artefacts from different eras in Kochi and a striking pastel-coloured interior.
☏0484 2215799; www.santacruzcathedralbasilica.org; KB Jacob Rd; 9am–6pm

❻ SOUTHERN NAVAL COMMAND MARITIME MUSEUM
If you are remotely interested in sails and seas, the spic and span Maritime Museum will keep you engrossed with exhibits on steering wheels, maps and more. It is especially enjoyable, as the upkeep of the place is excellent.
Beach Rd; Indian/foreigner/child/photography ₹25/75/15/100; 9.30am–12.30pm, 2.30–5.30pm, Mon closed

❼ THIRUMALA DEVASWOM TEMPLE
Mattancherry's vivid history begins with the Vishnu temple at Cherlai. The enormous, Hindus-only temple has a large kalyani (pond) in front of it and a huge bell that is constantly rung by someone sitting at one end of the rope. A consistent spiritual fervour is kept alive with the temple ensemble playing the panchavadyam (traditional temple instruments) during the day.
RG Pai Rd, Cherlai; 5.30am–noon, 6–9pm

Old-style chandeliers in Pardesi Synagogue

❽ DUTCH PALACE & TEMPLE

Mattancherry Palace was a gift presented to the Raja of Kochi, Veera Kerala Varma (1537–61), as a gesture of goodwill by the Portuguese in 1555. The Dutch renovated the palace in 1663, and hence it was renamed the Dutch Palace. The Kerala-style wood-floored mansion is now a museum. The complex also has the Pazhayannur Bhagvathi Temple, dedicated to the deity who was the royal guardian.

Palace Rd, Mattancherry; ₹5; 9–5pm, Fri closed

❾ PARDESI SYNAGOGUE

At the end of a narrow lane in Jew Town, the synagogue is a symbol of religious tolerance under the Kochi kings. This is the oldest active synagogue in Commonwealth countries. The synagogue was built in 1568. There is an upstairs balcony for women, who worshipped separately according to Orthodox rites. Shorts or sleeveless tops are not allowed inside.

Jew Town; ₹5; 10am–1pm, 3–5pm, Fri & Sat closed;

Value for Money: Travelling within Kochi

- **Hire a bike:** Going around in a bicycle or a bike is a good option to explore the town. Contact Arafath of Rent a Bike (📞9947478328; motorbike/cycle ₹300/100) point at the corner of Quiero's Street.

- **Tuk-Tuk Odyssey** (📞9995205828): Travel in a tuk-tuk (autorickshaw) employed brilliantly for sightseeing. A handful of rickshaw drivers are part of this scheme where they take you for a two-to-three hour speedy sightseeing tour, with the driver doubling up as a guide, along with a water bottle and newspaper.

Expert Recommendation
A nostalgic gastronomic trail

Priyadarshini Sharma, the chief sub-editor of *The Hindu* in Kochi recommends some of her favourite longstanding joints in Fort Kochi and Ernakulam.

- **Quality Bakery** (✆9995156615; Pattalam; 7am–9.30pm; mains less than ₹100): Keeping years of culinary history alive, the dingy humble bakery in Pattalam is the only place where one can taste the famous Dutch bruder bread. The sugar plum brown loaves come out of the oven regularly on Saturdays but have to be ordered through Monday to Fridays.

- **Kayees Hotel** (✆0484 2226080; New Road, Mattancherry; 5.15am–9pm; mains ₹100–200): Yet another notable gastronomic stop is this famous biryani joint, also known as Rahmatulla Hotel. Tucked away in the Kutchi Memom area of Mattancherry, it should be visited before 12.30pm, as the dish depletes at breakneck speed. You may have to strain your eyes to find a little memento (a small painting of a horse) by MF Husain on the cluttered wall, but his classic style is immediately recognisable.

- **Shantilal S Mithaiwala** (✆0484 2229860; opposite Gujarati High School, Gujarati Rd; 8.30am–9.30pm; mains less than ₹100): If you are craving for some delicious rich Gujarati snacks, visit the legendary khandvi and gatiya maker of Fort Kochi. The evenings are packed with other hungry shoppers.

- **Onasadya at Sarovaram, BTH** (✆9946103081; NH 47, Cochin Bypass, Maradu PO; noon–3pm; mains ₹500–750): For an authentic Onam banquet, visit Sarovaram's in-house restaurant in Ernakulam. If you are going at the time of the festival (Aug), ensure that you book in advance as the food here is worth the wait!

Dutch bruder bread is available at Quality Bakery, Pattalam

Accommodation

ERNAKULAM

The Taj Gateway   Hotel ₹₹₹
☏ 0484 6673300; www.tajhotels.com; Marine Drive; d ₹9500–11,500, ste ₹16,000 (incl of breakfast)
One of the older establishments in Ernakulam, The Taj Gateway offers sea view rooms, impeccable hospitality and comforts like an in-house spa, a pool and wi-fi facility. The sightseeing trips organised by the hotel are well researched and efficiently run.

Dream   Hotel ₹₹₹
☏ 0484 4129999; www.dreamcochin.com; SA Rd, Elamkulam Junction; d ₹12,000–13,000, ste ₹14,000–25,000 (incl of breakfast)
The glitzy hotel in town has garnered quite a reputation with its modern decor, luxurious rooms and friendly staff. With four in-house restaurants and comfortable lounge spaces, you needn't step out for meals. The hotel also has a pool and wi-fi facility.

Bolgatty Palace Heritage   Hotel ₹₹₹
☏ 0484 2750500; www.bolgattypalacekochi.com; Bolgatty Island, Mulavukadu; ste ₹13,300 (incl of breakfast)
The only reason to make a trip to the Bolgatty Island off Ernakulam is the Kerala Tourism Development Corporation (KTDC) run heritage hotel. This erstwhile Dutch mansion built in 1744 has an unmatched location. Golf enthusiasts will like its proximity to the Golf Club of Cochin.

Grand Hotel   Hotel ₹₹
☏ 0484 4114646; www.grandhotelkerala.com; MG Rd; d ₹3000–4200, ste ₹4500 (incl of breakfast)
A landmark on MG Road, the Grand Hotel is known for its 1960s classic construction. The in-house restaurant (The Grand Pavilion) serves excellent Kerala food and is the top choice for many travellers. Stay here to be in the city's centre and enjoy unobtrusive hospitality.

Travancore Court   Hotel ₹₹
☏ 0484 2351120; www.travancorecourt.com; Warriam Rd, opposite Lotus Club; ste ₹5000–6000 (incl of breakfast)
The plush Travancore Court promises

Old Harbour Hotel has 13 cosy rooms, a swimming pool and a sprawling garden

a comfortable stay in the heart of town, just a parallel lane away from the arterial MG Road. The supposed colonial theme of the hotel is easy to miss, but one is slightly spoilt by its polite staff and the luxurious rooms, pool and wi-fi facility.

Abad Plaza — Hotel ₹₹

0484 2381122; www.abadhotels.com; MG Rd; d ₹3500-3750, ste ₹5000 (incl of breakfast) Conveniently located on MG Road, Abad Plaza is just 2km from the railway station and close to the town's shopping hub. Other facilities include a swimming pool, an Ayurveda Spa, fitness centre, in-house restaurants and travel assistance.

Time Square — Hotel ₹

0484 2374488; www.timesquarehotel.in; Club Rd, near Collector's Camp Office; d ₹2000–2700 (incl of breakfast) Time Square is a good choice if you are looking for a clean and comfortable stop in the city's heart. The hotel is parallel to MG Road, it's peaceful and yet walking distance from the shopping hub.

Hotel Aiswarya — Hotel ₹

0484 2364454; www.aiswaryahotels.com; Warriam Rd, opposite Lotus Club; d ₹2100–2700 (incl of breakfast) Hotel Aiswarya is a good choice if you're looking for a clean budget stay near MG Road. It's walking distance from the shopping hub and good enough for a night's stay. The restaurant is, however, dingy, so you might want to hop across the road to the busy **Sree Krishna Inn** (p250) for delicious meals.

FORT KOCHI & MATTANCHERRY

Brunton Boatyard — Hotel ₹₹₹

0484 3011711; www.cghearth.com; Fort Kochi; d ₹25,600–34,000 (incl of breakfast and taxes) Brunton Boatyard has a historic Dutch ambience, complete with high ceilings, aged artefacts and decor themed after the shipping culture of Fort Kochi. All the rooms overlook the harbour, and have balconies with a refreshing sea breeze that beats AC any day.

Tea Bungalow — Heritage Hotel ₹₹₹

9388719679; www.teabungalow.in; 1/1901, Kunumpuram; d ₹10,500 (incl of breakfast) The decor of the rooms in this heritage hotel is based on ports in the Indian Ocean. Take your pick from rooms called Zanzibar, Goa, Galle and seven other ports. The classy furnishings, bright paintings and open-roofed bathrooms offer a rare luxury. It has a swimming pool and the staff is warm.

Old Harbour Hotel — Hotel ₹₹₹

0484 2218006; www.oldharbourhotel.com; 1/328, Tower Rd; d ₹9250–15,950 (incl of breakfast) Overlooking the Chinese fishing nets, Old Harbour Hotel has an intimate coterie of 13 rooms.

Its sprawling garden restaurant is a pleasant surprise and the most exquisite part of the heritage hotel.

Koder House — Hotel ₹₹
☎ 0484 2218485; www.koderhouse.com; Tower Rd; d ₹3500 (incl of breakfast) It's difficult to miss the prominent red building overlooking the Children's Park at Vasco Square. Koder House, the erstwhile home of a Jewish family is now a six-roomed luxury boutique hotel with spacious suites and a vintage aura complete with wooden floors. Its highlight is the in-house restaurant, Menorah, where you can order Jewish delicacies. Do try the pudding.

The Malabar House — Hotel ₹₹
☎ 0484 2216666; www.malabarescapes.com; Parade Rd; d ₹4000–6000 (incl of breakfast) One of the most awarded hotels in town, Malabar House draws you into its charmed world replete with touches of history, designer decor and an open courtyard cafe which serves delicious food. You can also pamper yourself with an Ayurvedic massage and laze around the poolside. All this comes with impeccable hospitality.

Eliphinstone Residency — Hotel ₹₹
☎ 0484 2218222; www.eliphinstoneresidency.com; Beach Rd; d ₹2800–4000 (incl of breakfast) If you want a personalised stay with standard hotel facilities, you will love the cheerful hosts, gleaming new rooms and sprawling garden with an old well at Elphinstone. This relatively new hotel has a combination of five rooms attached to the main house and two cottages overlooking the garden. For more privacy, choose the cottages.

Old Courtyard — Hotel ₹₹
☎ 0484 2216302; www.oldcourtyard.com; Princess St; d ₹3500–5000, ste ₹5500 (incl of breakfast) Though located on the central Princess Street, the atmospheric large garden and eight vintage rooms of Old Courtyard miraculously cut out any disturbing buzz. The 200-year-old restored building houses a multi-cuisine restaurant which hosts Indian classical musical evenings during the season.

Fort House — Hotel ₹₹
☎ 0484 2217103; www.hotelforthouse.com; 2/6A Calvathy Rd; d ₹4945 (incl of breakfast and taxes) Another inviting option, Fort House has a waterfront backyard, 16 chic rooms in soft earth and ochre colours and warm personalised service. There's a central open space filled with shady trees which houses an excellent restaurant.

Fort Muzuris — Hotel ₹
☎ 0484 2215057; www.fortmuziris.com; 1/415 Burgar St; d ₹1000–1500 (incl of breakfast) If a tariff that's easy on the pocket and a central location

Tom's Old Mansion is a 100-year-old structure converted into a heritage hotel

are prime considerations, then head straight to Fort Muzuris at the end of Burgar Street. The six AC rooms are complemented by friendly service and a hearty breakfast. The place is a little rough but great value for money.

Noah's Ark Homestay — Homestay ₹

0484 2215481; www.noahsarkcochin.com; 1/508 Fort Kochi Hospital Rd; d ₹2800–3100 (incl of breakfast) Noah's Ark truly represents the homestay culture of Kerala. Tap into the vast knowledge of your hosts, Diana and Jerry, who let out three rooms of their house. You will enjoy your stay in the modern, well-furnished rooms with wi-fi facility.

Eden Garden Heritage Homestay — Homestay ₹

9847930003; www.edengardenhomestay.com; Fort Kochi Police Quarters, Amaravathy; d ₹2500 (incl of breakfast) Mel and Judith's 250-year-old traditional Cyprian home is a pleasant change from the tourist heavy area at Fort Kochi. They have three simple rooms overlooking a small lotus pond and a lush garden, creating a veritable Eden. Besides the peaceful atmosphere, the food is scrumptious.

Tom's Old Mansion — Hotel ₹

0484 2215605; www.tomsoldmansionkochi.com; Princess St; d ₹1500–3000 (incl of breakfast) A creaking wooden floor, high ceilings and a central courtyard testify to this heritage hotel's age. A hundred years old, most of its 15 rooms are spacious and aesthetically pleasing. The central location, period feel, and a rational tariff make this a good choice.

Anns Residency — Homestay ₹

0484 2216424; www.annsresidency.com; 1/307 A, Bishop Joseph Kureethara (Rose) St; d

All rooms at Anns Residency overlook the manicured garden

₹2500–3000, ste ₹4000 (incl of breakfast) A bright white-and-gold sign at the corner of Rose Street ushers you through a traditional Kerala entrance into a comfortable, modern, nine-room homestay. Ann and Leslie are warm and informative hosts (and the fifth generation in this originally Portuguese house). All rooms overlook refreshing green patches.

Silver Weed Homestay   Homestay ₹
📞 9995205828; www.silverweedhomestay.com; 11/88 near ESI Junction; d ₹1500 (incl of breakfast) Only a few months old on the homestay circuit, Silver Weed has outdone itself with its sparkling cleanliness, warm hospitality and refreshing ambience. Potted foliage fills the spacious common balcony of the two guest rooms. The rooms have a separate entrance, ensuring privacy. The home-made food is delicious.

Eating

ERNAKULAM

Sree Krishna Inn   South Indian ₹₹
📞 0484 2366664; Warriam Rd; 8am–11pm; mains ₹250–500 No matter what time you arrive, Sree Krishna Inn is likely to be buzzing. The busy scenario is testimony to the quality of food and atmosphere of this place with a front garden and wooden furniture. Breakfast and tiffin items are favourites. Don't miss this one!

Coffee Beanz   Coffee Shop ₹₹
📞 0484 3292229; No 40/2964, opp Pioneer Tower Shanmugham Rd; 12.30–3.30pm, 7.30–10.30pm; mains ₹250–500 Step in for some delicious appam and stew or beef fry at this cheerfully bright cafe on Shanmugham Road. It is known for its reasonable prices and scrumptious mix of local and urban cuisines.

Dwaraka Restaurant Multi-Cuisine ₹₹
📞 0484 2383236; MG Rd; 7am–10.30pm; mains ₹250–500 This old, run-down joint deserves a visit purely for its nostalgic atmosphere and authentic Kerala food.

Pai Brothers   South Indian ₹
📞 0484 2374879; Pai Brothers Line, MG Rd; 9am–1.30am; mains ₹100–200 There are 187 types of the south Indian staple – the dosa, of which 36 are supposedly copyrighted by Pai Brothers. The 'Thattil Kutty'

(small) dosa is really popular. This joint is hard to miss, even though it lies in a lane off MG Road.

FORT KOCHI & MATTANCHERRY

Oceanos — Restaurant ₹₹₹
☏ 0484 2218222; www.oceanosfortkochi.com; Elphinstone Rd; 12.30–3.30pm, 7–10.30pm; mains ₹500–750 Candle-lit outdoor seating in the evenings provides the perfect atmosphere for a delicious meal of seafood specials. The absence of a needlessly long menu is welcome, and if you're looking for a safe option, the Kerala combos are flawless.

Kashi Art Café — Art Gallery & Cafe ₹₹
☏ 0484 2215769; www.kashiartgallery.com; Burgher St; 8.30am–7.30pm; mains ₹250–500 Kashi is Fort Kochi's foremost art gallery-cum-cafe, setting the tone for the many new ones springing up. It is one of the most popular joints in town, it serves delicious chocolate cake and other confectionary.

Dosas and Pancakes — Cafe ₹₹
☏ 9387542000; www.dosasandpancakes.com; 10am–10pm; mains ₹250–500 An all-day menu of local delights like puttu, appams, stew, fish curry, and even waffles can keep you here for hours. Try the Sunday Kerala special brunch if you are looking for local specialities on a lazy, unhurried morning. The cafe is attached to **Greenix Village** (p252); it can get crowded before the shows.

Loafers Corner — Café ₹₹
Princess St; 11am–9.30pm; mains ₹250–500 The cafe's name recalls the time when this spot was a local haunt for boys (loafers) hanging around on the street corner. Wooden floors and an austere setting are a refreshing break from the usual vintage decor of other cafes. The menu is delightfully tiny so you can make a quick choice and ring the bell on your table for attention.

Tea Pot Cafe — Cafe ₹₹
☏ 0484 2218035; Peter Celli St; 9am–9pm; mains ₹250–500 A large

❤ *If You Like: Vintage bars*

Apart from the high-end restaurants, try what the locals have to recommend. The harbour-facing Seagull and XL bar are often suggested for their vintage value.

- **Seagull** (Kalvatty Rd; 9am–10.30pm): The service here may be abysmal but the view of the harbour makes up for it. You can laze around on the sunny deck for hours over a couple of beers and enjoy the view.

- **XL** (Rose St; 9am–10.30pm): This old bar must be the hottest hang-out spot – judging from the stream of visitors, babble of voices and constantly squeaking wooden floors. XL has different sections for visitors and local regulars.

teapot collection and other tea-based paraphernalia unfolds in this yellow walled cafe as you enter past a modest sign on the street. It has definite character, making it an interesting place to spend an evening.

Ginger House Restaurant — Restaurant ₹₹
☎ 0484 2211145; Jew Town Rd; 9am–6.30pm; mains ₹250–500 A 100-ft-long traditional snake boat lies in the centre of the Heritage Arts antique shop, which eventually opens out to a sunny cafe overlooking the Willington Island shipyard. Multi-cuisine options are quickly served out of an open kitchen, quite contrary to the laid-back atmosphere of the place.

Dal Roti — North Indian ₹₹
Lilly St; noon–3.15pm, 6.30–10.15pm; mains ₹250–500 Arrive no later than 12.30pm to grab a table at the hugely popular Dal Roti. Though the interiors aren't great, the north Indian food will surely impress you.

★ Entertainment

FORT KOCHI & MATTANCHERRY
Cultural shows are abridged and easy to understand. These are versions of Kerala's performing arts can be seen under one roof in less than two hours. Definitely try to catch an evening of Kalaripayattu, classical dance and music here.

Greenix Village — Cultural Program
☎ 0484 2217000; www.greenix.in; Kalvathy Rd; 5.30–7.30pm; ₹450 This is a well-maintained establishment offering abridged folk performances of Kerala. Arrive at 5.30pm to see the Kathakali dancers painting their faces for the show. An hour later, you are ushered into different theatres for a dance-martial, arts-music package which lasts an hour. Greenix also has a museum, cafe and book shop.

Kerala Kathakali Centre — Cultural Program
☎ 0484 2217552; www.kathakalicentre.com; near Santa Cruz Basilica, KB Jacob Rd; ₹250; 6–7.30pm A narrow path takes you to the first floor, wooden-floored auditorium of the Kerala Kathakali Centre, where where a hour-and-half long shows pack in Kathakali, Bharatanatyam, Kuchipudi and Carnatic vocal music performances.

| Delicious red fish curry flavoured with myriad spices

KOCHI & AROUND

Activities

FORT KOCHI & MATTANCHERRY

Village Rubble — Cycling
☏9645411433; www.glhindia.com; 10/1252 KB Jacob Rd; ₹8000 for two; 14 hours For a countryside experience, hop onto the well-maintained bicycles of Village Rubble and explore the rural setting and local activities around Fort Kochi with a trip leader. You can either join a group or customise your own trip. Get acquainted with fishing techniques, coir making, crab cultivation, prawn farming, toddy tapping, and meet village women empowerment groups.

Kumbalangi — Cycling
The nearby village of Kumbalangi offers fascinating insights into the workings of prawn/crab farms, toddy tappers, coir making and local fishing methods. All this can be organized by the 70-year-old **Gramam Homestay** (☏0484 2240278; www.keralagramam.com; Neduveli House, Kumbalangi; d ₹3000, ste ₹6000 incl of breakfast), which is located just 13km from Fort Kochi. This little trip is a refreshing break to enjoy the tranquil backdrop and soak in the countryside.

Shopping

ERNAKULAM

The main MG Rd of Ernakulam is packed with gold jewellery and sari shops. If you are visiting during Onam or any shopping festival (Dec–Jan), expect heavy discounts.

Jayalakshmi — Saris
☏0484 3366699; www.jayalakshmisilks.com; MG Rd, Ernakulam; 9.30am–8.30pm One of the most renowned names for silk saris, the brand is more than 65 years old and has a large collection of not just saris, but also branded clothing.

Kalyan Silks — Saris
☏0484 4081111; www.kalyansilks.com Hospital Rd, near Maharaja's College, Ernakulam; 9am–9pm Kalyan Silks store offers a variety of silk saris and Indian branded garments. There is plenty of choice, depending on your budget.

Seematti — Saris
PB No 3651; MG Rd, Ernakulam; 10am–9pm Originally a sari shop, Seematti now offers a range of garments spread over four floors, with a coffee shop inside the premises. This is a one-stop shop for authentic Kerala saris and dress material.

Karalkada — Saris
☏0484 2352911; opposite TD Temple Gate, MG Rd; 9.30am–9pm Mon–Sat, 9.30am–8pm Sun The clean, spacious and minimal decor of this sari and clothing fabric shop is soothing after the visual assault of the regular sari and gold shops in Ernakulam. Come here for the typical

The country's largest mall, Lulu, consists of more than 300 outlets

white with gold border saris, half saris and mundus (lungi).

Kasavu Kada — Saris
☎ 0484 2372395; Church Landing Rd; 9am–8pm, Sun closed If the focus of your buying spree is only traditional Kerala saris, then head straight to Kasavu Kada for a decent variety and prices.

Joyalukkas — Gold
☎ 0484 2350512; www.joyalukkas.com; Marine Drive; 9.30am–7.30pm A household name in Kerala, Joyalukkas is one of the top names for gold jewellery. Stop by for a large assortment of contemporary and traditional designs.

Bhima — Gold
☎ 0484 2378382; MG Rd; 10am–8pm Another name to reckon with for gold shopping on MG Road. Locals will recommend this place highly.

Josco — Gold
☎ 0484 2353295; www.joscogroup.com; MG Rd; 10am–7.30pm Josco is definitely worth a visit if you want to spoil yourself silly over varieties in designs of gold jewellery and if cost is not of much concern.

Kairali — Handicrafts
☎ 0484 2354507; www.keralahandicrafts.in; MG Rd; 9am–8pm, Sun closed Do not be disappointed with the dowdy exterior of the government-run Kairali showroom – this is one of the best places for handicrafts and souvenirs. You can pick from an assortment of Ravi Varma miniature paintings (copies of course), brass bric-a-brac and range of souvenirs made from coconut husk.

Lulu Mall — Mall
☎ 0484 2727777; www.lulumall.in; 34/1000, N.H 47, Edapally; 10am-10pm Whet your shopping skills at the India's largest mall sprawled over 2.5 million sq ft of space. The mall consists of more than 300 outlets including restaurants, entertainment zones, a nine-screen multiplex as well as a large ice skating rink and a 12 lane bowling alley.

FORT KOCHI & MATTANCHERRY
Spices, antiques, Boho cotton clothes and indigenous art

encounter you at every corner. Your bargaining skills may come in handy, especially in Jew Town in Mattancherry, which has an alluring setting with its old architecture.

Jew Street and Mattancherry — Market

Antique masks, wooden chests, traditional doors and an ocean of antique artefacts are jammed together in rows of shops around the Jew Town area. The **Isidore Art Palace** (9447054369; Synagogue Lane, Jew Town; 9am–6pm) at the end of Jew Street, just before the synagogue, is less overwhelming than the others and has a decent collection for all budgets. Most shops help ship your purchase if needed.

Spices in Mattancherry — Market

The atmospheric Mattancherry area is certainly the centre of spice shops in town. The pungent aroma of an amazing variety of spices is hard to miss, even if your nostrils are jammed. You should try for a fair deal at one of the wholesale dealers **Kaycee Corporation** (0484 2225255; PB No 240, Bazaar Rd; 9am–6pm). Walk through the drying yard and inspect a large collection at massive godowns. You will be able to pay slightly less than in retail shops.

Ecoutree Boutique — Clothing & Jewellery

9961375553; Bastin St; 11am–9.30pm Ecoutree Boutique has an innovative collection of comfy cottons, bags and semi-precious jewellery.

Indian Industries — Handicrafts

0484 2216448; Indian Industries; Princess St; 9am–8pm Closer to where you are likely to stay (if opting for a central location), Indian Industries has a fair collection of old artefacts that are good souvenirs.

Idiom Book Sellers — Bookstore

0484 2217075; 1/348, Bastion St; 10am–9pm If you've run out of your travel-read supply, head to this place for a substantial collection of titles.

📷 Snapshot: Art at Fort Kochi

Fort Kochi's vivacious art scene truly exhibits the sentiments of the entire state. Influenced by its rich heritage and colonial infusion, it's easy to find a mix of poignant, dramatic and contemporary work here. The **OED Gallery** (944710811; 6/500 Bazaar Rd; 11am–7pm, Sun closed) in Mattancherry often showcases creations of Kerala based artists. And if you walk down Bazaar Road from Mattancherry to the ferry point of Fort Kochi, you will spot a number of bright contemporary murals on the walls, which have spilled onto the blocks near Princess Street.

Munnar & Periyar Tiger Reserve

A landscape of rolling hills carpeted with acres of tea and cardamom plantations, Munnar provides one of the best hill station experiences and a refreshing break from the coastal regions of Kerala. For those who want to visit for the wildlife, the notable Periyar Tiger Reserve near Kumily is close by.

Trip Planner

GETTING THERE

Munnar: The closest airport to Munnar is Cochin International Airport. It is 105km away and has daily flights to all metros and major cities. Aluva or Ernakulam (13km apart) are the nearest railway stations (110km away). Regular KSRTC buses are available for Munnar. Overnight buses by private operators cost between ₹600–1000.

Kumily/Periyar: Kumily is 155km away from Kochi, the closest airport. Aluva or Ernakulam (13km apart) are the nearest railway stations (160km away). They are connected via major trains from metros and other South Indian cities. It takes 4–5 hours by road to reach Kumily.

SUGGESTED ITINERARY (5 DAYS)

Start your holiday at Munnar, which is the tea growing heartland of Kerala and also a great place for treks. Three days will go by in the blink of an eye as you explore tea plantations and discover view points. Then make your way to Kumily, 80km away, the gateway to Periyar Tiger Reserve. Spend a couple of days here trying activities such as a day-long bamboo raft trip, jeep rides and nature walks.

BEST TIME TO GO

J F M A M J J A S **O N D**

GREAT FOR

Top 5 highlights

- **Kannan Devan Tea Museum, Munnar** (p258)
- **Eravikulam National Park, Munnar** (p258)
- **Attukal Waterfalls, Munnar** (p260)
- **Periyar Tiger Reserve** (p261)
- **Elephant Junction, Periyar** (p262)

Nature Unplugged

Covered with lush tea bushes, Munnar's hilly landscape has made it one of the state's top destinations. A pleasant change from Kerala's popular seaside destinations, **Munnar** offers delightfully green hillsides speckled with bright poinsettias. It is a classic hill station with its cool weather, verdant valleys and tea plantations as far as the eye can see. Due to Munnar's resounding popularity amongst honeymoon couples, the main bazaar is cluttered with guesthouses, hotels and resorts of all budgets. And for those yearning for tranquillity, there are some wonderful remote places to stay, just a few kilometres away from the main town.

To discover Kerala's wildlife wonder, **Periyar Tiger Reserve**, head to the small town of **Kumily** (4km from the sanctuary), on the border of Tamil Nadu and Kerala. Kumily, interchangeably used with Thekkady, is the gateway to the sanctuary. With a vibrant atmosphere, it has capitalised on selling the joys of Kerala: coffee and spices (mainly cardamom and pepper), interactions with elephants and Kalaripayattu and Kathakali shows. With massive plantations and an adjoining reserve forest area, Kumily is a relaxing break, particularly for wildlife enthusiasts.

> At Periyar you can spot Nilgiri Tahr

Highlights

1. **Kanan Devan Tea Museum**
2. **Eravikulam National Park**
3. **Top Station**
4. **Floriculture Centre**
5. **Attukal Waterfalls**
6. **Mattupetty Dam**
7. **Muniyara Dolmens**
8. **Chinnar Wildlife Sanctuary**

Guided tour of the factory at Kanan Devan Tea Museum

Munnar

1 KANAN DEVAN TEA MUSEUM

The Kanan Devan Tea Museum transports you through the trajectory of events that made Munnar a tea plantation junction since the late 1800s. The small six-room museum documents history through various artefacts and supplements the exhibits with a half-hour audio-visual show. The trip includes a guided tour of the tea factory and also tea tasting.

adult/child/camera ₹75/35/20; 10am–4pm, Mon closed

2 ERAVIKULAM NATIONAL PARK

The Kannan Devan Hills of Munnar are home to Eravikulam National Park, which aims to conserve the endangered Nilgiri tahr (a type of mountain goat). Just 16km from Munnar,

---

GETTING AROUND IN MUNNAR & PERIYAR

Due to the hilly terrain and many sightseeing options, it is best to hire a four-wheeler in Munnar. The rates range from ₹1500–3000 per day depending on the car. Kumily is spread over a very small area and you can walk anywhere with ease. If not upto walking, there are auto-rickshaws at all junctions and charge ₹20 as minimum fare. If you want to cover a lot in a day, hire a taxi.

this 97sq km park comprises large stretches of grassland with clusters of Shola forests. The park's Rajmala section (southern zone) is open to visitors except during the breeding season of the tahrs (February–April). The highest peak of the Nilgiri hills, Anamudi (2690m), lies inside the park.
04865 231587; www.eravikulam.org; adult/child/foreigner/camera/heavy vehicle/light vehicle/park bus ₹15/5/200/25 100/30/200/50/55; 8am–5pm; 31 Jan–31 Mar closed (this may change from year to year)

❸ TOP STATION
Kerala's border with Tamil Nadu affords spectacular views of the Western Ghats. Peer down the plummeting valley from a high windy point at Top Station while the mountains keep you company on all sides. En route to Top Station, stop at Echo Point, where you can shout your lungs out at a lakeside.

❹ FLORICULTURE CENTRE
The Floriculture Centre makes for a short stop on the way to Top Station. A neatly paved pathway ensures that you see the entire collection of flowers. With a stunning backdrop of dazzling colours, it's a great spot for pictures.
Top Station Rd; entry/camera/video ₹10/20/50Top Station Rd; entry/camera/video ₹10/20/50

Trekking route in Eravikulam National Park

📷 Snapshot: Neelakurinji blooms

It's still some years away, but if you decide to visit Munnar in 2018, chances are you will witness a fascinating floral phenomenon of the Nilgiris. The Neelakurinji flowers are said to bloom every 12 years in the region, when complete hillsides turn a bright purplish-blue and valleys of Shola grasslands come alive.

❺ ATTUKAL WATERFALLS

Pack some snacks and head 9km out of Munnar towards Pallivasal to the Attukal waterfalls cascading across tea plantations. Especially spectacular after the rains, these are great for a picnic. However, at the height of summer, the waterfall is barely a trickle.

❻ MATTUPETTY DAM

The tranquil green waters of the Mattupetty Dam meet you as you wend your way to Top Station. They warrant a quick picture or snack stop, with a fantastic view from the bridge that runs across it.

❼ MUNIYARA DOLMENS

On the Chinnar route, yet another wonder lies off Marayur: ancient burial grounds or dolmens. Locally known as 'muniyaras', these neolithic stone formations lie on a vast rocky platform.

❽ CHINNAR WILDLIFE SANCTUARY

Sixty kilometres from Munnar, the Chinnar Wildlife Sanctuary is a vast expanse of semi-deciduous forest. The only way to see the forest is on foot, with a guide. This is organised by **Tribal Trackers Eco Development Committee** (office at the check post). Book for a trek upfront at the Munnar office. And if you are feeling adventurous, you can stay overnight either in the Tree House or the Log House or the Hut. However, there is no electricity and no toilets in the tree house. You need to walk anywhere between 3–7km to reach the latter.

☏ 04865 231587; trek ₹100 per head for 3 hr; Tree House ₹1000 per head (extra person 250), Log House ₹1500 per head (extra person ₹300), Hut ₹2500 per head (extra person ₹500), (incl of meals and a guard); 7am–3pm

Periyar Tiger Reserve

Highlights
1. Periyar Tiger Reserve
2. Elephant Junction
3. Green Park

1 PERIYAR TIGER RESERVE

The Eco Tourism Centre run by the forest department in Thekkady organises nature walks, jungle scouting, bamboo rafting, border hiking, overnight stays and motor boat trips. Bamboo rafting is the most scenic and private. Or explore the jungle on foot with armed guards and guides for 2½–3 hour treks. For an overall feel of the place, the 1½-hour funeral-paced, motor-boat ride on large double-decker boats is ideal. It takes place four times a day. Though you are grouped with 300 others split over four boats. Book well in advance.
📞04869 224571; www.periyartigerreserve.org; Ambadi Junction, Thekkady; adult/child/foreigner/foreigners' child ₹25/15/310/110; Nature Walk/ Green walk ₹800 for 4; 7am, 10am, 2pm, 2½–3 hr; Jungle Scout ₹1500 for 2; 7pm, 10pm; Bamboo Rafting ₹3000 for 2; 8am–5pm; Border Hiking ₹4000 for 4; 8am–5pm; Tiger Trail ₹6000 for 1, overnight stay; boating ₹150 for 1, camera ₹25

The lake is the centrepiece of the Periyar Tiger Reserve

A jungle trek is the best way to spot elephants

❷ ELEPHANT JUNCTION

In typical Kerala style, 'elephant interactions' are advertised at every corner in Kumily. Elephant Junction offers the best experience and several ways to spend some pachyderm time, as you can bathe and feed them. The kids will love this one!
☏ 04869 224142; Murukkady PO; packages for half hour–full day ₹350–5000 per head

❸ GREEN PARK

The heady smell of spices lures you to Green Park, which has five acres of mixed organic spice plantation. If you're with children, this promises an hour of fun and learning, as a guide negotiates you through large leafy paths to taste, touch and be enthralled by the variety of plants, fruits and spices. You even get to climb a wooden planked hanging bridge.
☏ 9446806941; Attappallam PO; 9am–6pm; ₹100 per head/hr

✓ Top Tip: The Kumily–Thekkady confusion

Kumily, 4km from the sanctuary, is a growing strip of hotels, spice shops and Kashmiri emporiums. While Thekkady is the sanctuary-centre with the KTDC hotels and boat jetty. When people refer to the sanctuary they tend to use Kumily, Thekkady and Periyar interchangeably, which can be confusing for travellers who are unfamiliar with the area.

Expert Recommendation
The best of Periyar

Vivek Menon is founder of the Wildlife Trust of India and author of eight books on wildlife including the best-selling *Field Guide to Mammals of India*.

- **Walk or raft, don't boat:** Most people share a boat (with 60–120 people) to view wildlife from the serene 26sq km waterway. Instead, choose either the rafting trip or the several treks offered by the ecotourism programme of the Forest Department. Periyar is one of the very few tiger reserves that permit tourists to walk, so don't miss the opportunity.

- **Stay at Edapalayam or in an ecofriendly place:** You can opt to stay at the Bamboo Grove run as an eco-development measure for local communities or at Spice Village, the only eco-friendly resort. Or book into the jungle camping through the Forest Department. But if you can afford it, stay at the Lake Palace at Edapalayam.

- **Look out for birds not tigers:** People often overlook Periyar's rich bird life. It is the best place to see species endemic to the Western Ghats in one spot. In the forests look for the Malabar Grey hornbills, the Whitebellied treepie, the Malabar parakeet and the Wayanad laughing thrush. On the grasslands look for the Nilgiri pipit and the Black Eagle, and in the sholas for the White-bellied short-wing.

- **Look for endemics and rarities among mammals:** If you have to stick to animals go for the endemics and the local specialties. See the ubiquitous Nilgiri langur and the Nilgiri Tahr, both Western Ghats endemics. Search for the Jungle striped squirrel, Nilgiri Marten or the Spiny Dormouse if you trek. If not go to the river and the Periyar Lake to see large congregations of sambar.

The Nilgiri Tahr is endemic to the Western Ghats

Accommodation

MUNNAR

Ambady Plantation Estate Homestay ₹₹₹
☎ 9447662193; www.ambadyestate.com; 3rd Mile, Pallivasal, PO Chithirapuram; d ₹8000 (incl of breakfast) Ambady Estate embodies the warm homestay culture of Kerala. The 75-acre sprawling estate has eight cottages that sit amidst green surroundings. The rooms are high roofed and tastefully decorated in soft hues, with large French windows – some even have a yoga pavilion. Expect authentic Kerala food.

Windmere Plantation Estate Homestay ₹₹₹
☎ 04865 230512; www.windmeremunnar.com; PO Box 21, Pothamedu; d ₹7000–15,500 (incl of breakfast) Experience an English-style farmstay at the plush Windmere plantation cottages nestled amidst cardamom thickets with a panoramic view of tea plantations. The three categories of spacious cottages are stylishly furbished. There's a library, guided plantation strolls, and the in-house cafe serves tea in Kerala-style.

Casa Del Fauno Boutique Homestay ₹₹
☎ 0484 3048769; www.casadelfauno.in; Peak Gardens, Chinnakanal PO, Muttukadu; d ₹5500–6000 (incl of breakfast) This stone cottage with wooden flooring and a fireplace has seven rooms. Ask for the one with a garden and valley view; sunsets here are breathtaking. Three rooms are attached to the main house, while two twin-roomed cottages are slightly away, offering greater privacy.

Nature Zone Resort ₹₹
☎ 0484 6493301; www.naturezoneresort.com; Pulippara, Pallivasal; d tent ₹6000, tree house ₹7700 (incl of full board, trek, bonfire) Nature Zone is a unique camping and tree-house facility on top of a hill. Choose between the 10 African well-furnished tents and plush tree houses. The property sits on a ridge with breathtaking views of the Pothamedu valley. It also has an in-house restaurant and guided outdoor activities like rappelling, birding, trekking and nature walks.

Green Spaces Guesthouse ₹₹
☎ 9844731099; www.greenspacesmunnar.com; Ottamaram, near Oak Fields Resort, Pothamedu Via, Bison Valley Rd; d ₹3500–3900 (incl of breakfast) Finding your way to Green Spaces may get a little confusing but you're likely to forget it all once you see the wooden deck outside the two spacious rooms. This cottage with the feel of a homestay fits perfectly into the hill station set-up. There is a caretaker to organise meals.

PERIYAR TIGER RESERVE

Green Woods Resort ₹₹₹
☏04869 222752; www.greenwoods.in; KK Rd, Kumily; d ₹10,000–14,000, villa ₹19,000, ste ₹20,000–42,000, tree house ₹15,000 (incl of breakfast) Green Woods sits atop a low hill, overlooking the town. There's a multitude of accommodation choices, a pool, in-house restaurant and a shop. The resort has a special treetop pick, Vanya. This is a single tree house (no children allowed) that can be reached by a jeep ride and 30min trek.

Aanavilasam Plantation House ₹₹₹
☏04869 263777; www.aanavilasam.com; Pathumury–Aanavilasam Rd, Thekkady; ste ₹12,949–18,345, pool villa ₹16,186 (incl of breakfast) If absolute privacy is what you seek, Aanavilasam is an ideal choice. The bungalow, with six luxurious though minimalistic rooms, is nestled in seven acres of spice plantation.

Mayapott Plantation Villa Plantation Villa ₹₹₹
☏04868 224271; www.mayapott.com; Kadamakuzhy, Vallakadavu, Kattapana, Thekkady; d ₹9500–10,500 (incl of breakfast and dinner) Mayapott has an *Alice in Wonderland* feel about it. A small white door, camouflaged by drooping creepers, ushers you into a blend of mammoth rock-scape, acres of shady spice plantation and a natural pond. All four rooms have scintillating views.

Pepper County Homestay ₹₹
☏04869 222064; www.peppercounty.com; Kizhakkethalakkal, 1 Mile, Kumily; d ₹3500 (incl of breakfast and taxes) Pepper County offers the company of lovely hosts, Mr Cyriac and his wife, in their house bordering a seven acre spice plantation. Since there are only four rooms, it never gets too crowded, so you can enjoy a peaceful stay.

The Wildernest Bed & Breakfast ₹₹
☏04869 224030; www.wildernest-kerala.com; Thekkady Rd; d ₹4500 (incl of breakfast) Ten simple and tasteful rooms of The Wildernest lie around a lush jackfruit tree. The red oxide floors of the rooms, green metal spiral staircases and stone walls blend in perfectly with the forest nearby. The property lies on the main Thekkady road, which leads up to the sanctuary gate and is walking distance to the key places in town.

The sprawling Ambady Estate sits amidst green surroundings

Eating

MUNNAR

Saravana Bhavan — South Indian ₹₹
☎04865 231129; MG Rd; mains ₹250–500 Tried and tested across Tamil Nadu (and abroad), Saravana Bhavan is the safest option if you are looking at quickly served delicious south Indian vegetarian meals. The small restaurant in the main bazaar area of Munnar is forever lively with visitors and waiters milling about.

Maya Bazar — Multi-Cuisine ₹₹
☎04865 230238; The Silver Tips; mains ₹250–500; 7.30am–10.30pm Largely in favour of north Indian cuisine, Maya Bazar's cinema theme is not out of place. Enjoy a multitude of veg and non-veg dishes with the background score of old Hindi songs.

Saravana Bhawan is a great option for a south Indian vegetarian meal

Sree Krishna Gujarati Marwari Restaurant — Vegetarian ₹₹
☎09656251694; Adimali Rd; mains ₹250–500; 8am–10pm Go here for speedy service of delectable north Indian dishes. The thali is good value for money.

Surya Soma — Multi-Cuisine ₹₹
☎9446327777; mains ₹250–500; 9am–9.30pm Surya Soma is perfectly located for a meal after a bout of shopping. Dig into multi-cuisine veg and non-veg dishes. The food is not extraordinary but decent enough for one meal.

PERIYAR TIGER RESERVE

Sandra Palace — Multi-Cuisine ₹₹
☎04869 224561; opp Lourde Church, Thekkady Junction; mains ₹250–500; 7am–9.30pm A smattering of continental cuisine and an Indian-heavy menu are on offer, but the food is average.

Many places in Kerala organise hour-long shows of the famous Kathakali dance

Kripa
Multi-Cuisine ₹₹
☏ 04869 222972; Lake Rd; mains ₹250–500; 7.30am–10.30pm The large glass windows of Kripa allow you to watch the slow-paced life of Kumily pass you by as you enjoy delicious Kerala fish curry. Try the karimeen, meen polichathu and fish moilee. You can ignore the soups.

Kalavara
Silver Crest
Multi-Cuisine ₹₹₹
☏ 04869 222481; Thekkady Rd; mains ₹500–750; 7.30am–10pm Located in Silver Crest Hotel, the restaurant overlooks the swimming pool and serves decent Indian and Chinese fare. It's a good place to relax in after a day of sightseeing.

The Mirage
Multi-Cuisine ₹₹₹
☏ 04869 224800; KK Rd; mains ₹500–750; 7am–10.30pm A spanking new restaurant at Holiday Vista hotel, serving a long list of multi-cuisine dishes, though it's safest to stick to their north Indian preparations. The restaurant is just off the main Thekkady Junction.

Entertainment

MUNNAR
Thirumeny Cultural Centre
☏ 9447827696; Temple Rd; Kathakali (5–6.30pm), Kalaripayyatu (7–8pm), ₹200 each Thirumeny organises hour-long shows of Kalaripayattu and Kathakali every day in a cosy hall that has a muddy Kalari rink and a stage, with theatre-like seating. You can also see Kathakali artists painting their faces from 5–5.30pm prior to the show.

PERIYAR TIGER RESERVE

Mudra Cultural Centre
☎ 9446072901; www.mudraculturalcentre.com; ₹200 per head/show; 5–7pm Though Mudra's evening cultural extravaganza is held in a bare Kalari rink, the performances are quite thrilling.

Kadathanadan Kalari Centre
☎ 9961740868; www.kalaripayattu.co.in; ₹200 per head; 6–7pm Although not as atmospheric as other centres in Kerala, the Kadathanadan Kalari Centre has a Kalaripayattu show every evening. The athletic agility of performers will leave you speechless.

Activities

MUNNAR

Fun Forest
☎ 8943355440; www.munnarfunforest.com; Second Mile; packages ₹300–500 Tyre walking, spider web, Burma bridge and a zip-line are amongst many attractions for adventure lovers at Fun Forest. Eight kilometres from Munnar, this place, spread over 12-acres, is great for an adrenaline filled day. There are reasonable packages for a group of instructor-led activities. Safety ropes and helmets are available as they take all the necessary precautions.

Carmelgiri Elephant Park
☎ 9446291042; Korandakkadu; elephant ride ₹350 per head for 30 min If you fancy riding elephant-back or washing one, the Carmelgiri Elephant Park is home to six of them. They provide constant entertainment to visitors.

Art of Bicycle Trips
☎ 9538973506; www.artofbicycletrips.com Art of Bicycle Trips organises 10–12 day cycling tours in Kerala. One of their favourites, 'Classic Kerala', covers the hills of Munnar, along with some other significant destinations in the state. Led by accomplished trip leaders, the cycling tour is equipped with a back-up van, medical aid and hand-picked stay options.

Shopping

MUNNAR

KDHP Co (P) Ltd — Tea
☎ 04865 230761; KDHP House; 8.30am–9pm You cannot leave Munnar without picking up a packet of tea. To choose from a wide array, there is no better place than the KDHP (Kannan Devan Hills Plantations) outlet. A multitude of varieties are available at different prices.

Greenland Spice House — Spices
☎ 9446130135; Main Rd; 9am–9pm; Mon closed Munnar is famous for its aromatic spices, especially cardamom. You will find many shops at the market junction, among which Greenland has a large variety.

Sweet Land Home-made Chocolates
☎04865 230759; Main Rd; 9am–9pm Mon closed Choose from an array of home-made chocolates in flavours such as milk, orange and dark chocolate. Some of them come in smarter packing for sale.

Spices Park and Handicrafts Handicrafts
☎9495651433; The Highrange Service Co-op Society Ltd No I 153; 9am–9pm A collection of wooden bric-a-brac, from elephants to Kerala vallams (boats), jewellery and more, sprawls over every inch of the shop. You have a wide choice for gifts.

PERIYAR TIGER RESERVE
Flavours Spices
☎04869 223202; Lake Rd; 8.30am–8.30pm The shopping hub of Kumily, Thekkady Junction is sprinkled with spice shops. There is no difference in rates or quality, so you can pick any.

| Munnar's Art of Bicycle Trips organises 10–12 day tours in Kerala

Red Frog Organic Spices, Art and Antiques
☎04869 224560; www.redfrogindia.com; 8.30am–9pm This shop sells self-branded organic spices and tea as well as curios. An art gallery by the same name is on the opposite side of the road and displays interesting work of local artists.

Chocolate World Home-made Chocolates
☎9947082999; Thekkady Junction; 9.30am–9.30pm You might need to squeeze your way to the counter to order some home-made chocolates, as Chocolate World is a hot favourite. It offers a variety of flavours.

Via Kerala Contemporary Curios
☎0484 2312392; near Periyar Tiger Reserve, Cardamom County; 8am–9pm Via Kerala ticks with people looking for fun souvenirs. It specialises in Kerala-themed curios like cushions, bags and Malayalam-lettered cards.

Kozhikode & Wayanad

Lush coffee-clad Wayanad encompasses an experience which travel cliches cannot capture. Even the rich mix of verdant forests and the coastline at Kozhikode provide plenty of diversity – from architecture and traditional arts to pristine beaches and coffee plantations. Discerning travellers will love this relatively unspoiled section of Kerala.

Trip Planner

GETTING THERE

Kozhikode: Kozhikode Airport has daily flights from New Delhi, Mumbai and Bengaluru. There are trains to Kozhikode from metros like Trivandrum Rajdhani (12432) from New Delhi and Yesvantpur Kannur Express (16527) from Bengaluru. Overnight buses are available from Bengaluru to Kozhikode.

Wayanad: Kozhikode Airport and railway station are the closest (100km), which are connected to all metros. Overnight buses are available from Bengaluru. From Kozhikode many local buses ply till Wayanad.

SUGGESTED ITINERARY (5 DAYS)

Spend a couple of days in Kozhikode visiting the museums, exploring the beaches and the boat building yard in Beypore. After this, drive to Wayanad district that has three towns – Mananthavady, Kalpetta and Sultan Bathery. It is not possible to cover all of these as it easily takes three days to explore just one, so choose ahead in which one you want to stay. Base your decision on the kind of activities you want to engage in.

BEST TIME TO GO

J F M A M J J A S **O N D**

GREAT FOR

Top 5 highlights

- **Boat building Yards of Beypore, Kozhikode** (p272)
- **Kozhikode Beaches** (p274)
- **Tholpetty Wildlife Sanctuary, Wayanad** (p275)
- **Banasura Sagar Dam, Wayanad** (p276)
- **Edakkal Caves, Wayanad** (p277)

Unspoiled Diversity

Chembra Peak is a trekker's delight

After Portuguese explorer Vasco Da Gama entered this port city in 1498, **Kozhikode** (Calicut) catapulted to becoming one of the busiest spice trade junctions in the world. The city still emulates the same hectic pace with a commotion of traffic and commercial activity emanating from the Mananchira Square, the city centre. Verdant undergrowth and palms peeping between flashy new buildings are reminders of the city's original green persona. You must explore the famous boat building yard in **Beypore** and get your fill of the famous Kozhikodan halwa and banana chips here.

Wayanad on the other hand sweeps you into a great outdoors mood with its green cover. The district of Wayanad is spread around three main towns – **Mananthavady** in the northwest, **Kalpetta** in the south and **Sultan Bathery** in the east. It's impossible to cover all in a short time, so depending on your interests, plan your holiday. Sultan Bathery and Kalpetta are better equipped with hotels, but Mananthavady has its own charm, being slightly isolated. The famous Pookot Lake and Banasura Sagar Dam are closer to Kalpetta. Wherever you are planning to stay, you will cross the Muthanga Wildlife Sanctuary and you can make a quick stop here.

Kozhikode

Highlights
1. Boat-Building Yards of Beypore
2. Regional Science Centre & Planetarium
3. Tali Temple
4. Pazhassi Raja & Krishna Menon Museums
5. Kozhikode Beaches

1 BOAT-BUILDING YARDS OF BEYPORE
Come prepared for the deafening sound of a drill whirring into a wooden block in this estuarine port 11km from Kozhikode. Beypore's glorious history is speckled with exalted names since the 1st century AD: vessels for Cleopatra, Lord Horatio Nelson and many more were built in these yards at the edge of the Chaliyar River. Today, only two big yards craft massive dhows or urus (vessels) for merchants in Middle Eastern countries.
Beypore Village

2 REGIONAL SCIENCE CENTRE & PLANETARIUM
Graphic models of dinosaurs, mammoths and other prehistoric animals, as well as educational exhibits, will greet you as you enter the Regional Science Centre and Planetarium. A trip here is a sure-fire hit with kids. Other than the 3D and planetarium shows, the science section is particularly popular. Another fun room both for kids and adults is the Mirror Magic Room with its fun optics: you can

The traditional craft of boat building is still practised in Beypore

float in the air, see yourself vanish, become stick-thin or wide enough to cover the entire mirror.
☏ 0495 2770571; www.rscpcalicut.org; Planetarium Rd, Jafferkhan Colony; entry Science Centre/planetarium/3D show ₹10/25/35; 10.30am–6pm, Onam & Diwali closed; planetarium shows noon, 2pm, 4pm, 6pm; 3D shows 11am, 1pm, 3pm, 5pm

> Tali Temple has elements of typical Malabar architecture

❸ TALI TEMPLE
The 1500-year-old Tali Temple, dedicated to Lord Shiva, has elements of typical Malabar architecture. A wide path surrounds the tiled-roof inner sanctum. You can witness an elaborate ritual here at 9.30am as the door opens to a loud chorus of traditional instruments. Prayers for a child hang in the form of small wooden toy cribs on a tree, while intricate murals decorate the temple walls.
☏ 0495 2703610; www.calicuttalimahakshetra.com; Chalappuram; 4.30–11am, 5–8.30pm

❹ PAZHASSI RAJA & KRISHNA MENON MUSEUMS
The East Hill area of Kozhikode is famous for the Pazhassi Raja Museum and the Krishna Menon Museum with an art gallery. The first, with its wooden floor, is a 200-year-old

building built in 1812. Later converted into a museum to commemorate the local ruler, it now exhibits some rusty coins, models of temples and ancient bronze and stone sculptures. Vimal (☏9847003743), the resident guide can throw more light on details of these interesting exhibits.

The Krishna Menon Museum lies behind this building, with exhibits that focus on the erstwhile defence minister of India, VK Krishna Menon. His personal belongings, awards and medals are displayed on the ground floor. On the first floor of this interesting museum lies a gallery with works of Raja Ravi Varma, one of the greatest and most revered painters of Kerala.

East Hill Pazhassi Raja Museum: adult/child/camera/video ₹10/5/25/250 (videos can be taken only outside); 9am–1pm, 2–4.30pm, Mon closed; Krishna Menon Museum and Art Gallery: ₹2, 10am–5pm, Wed 1–5pm

❺ KOZHIKODE BEACHES

Closer to the city, **Kozhikode Beach** is a breezy stretch along the Beach Road, which has modern sculptures and benches. The more scenic strip of sand, the **Kappad Beach**, lies 19km away from town, but is certainly more attractive. You can also see the inconspicuous weathered monument that is a reminder of Vasco Da Gama's entry into the city.

The scenic Kapaad Beach is great for a lazy day by the sea

Wayanad

Highlights
1. Tholpetty Wildlife Sanctuary
2. Thirunelli Temple
3. Pakshipathalam
4. Kuruva Island (Kuruvadweep)
5. Banasura Sagar Dam
6. Pookot Lake
7. Edakkal Caves
8. Jain Temple
9. Muthanga Wildlife Sanctuary
10. Waterfalls of Wayanad

1 THOLPETTY WILDLIFE SANCTUARY
This sanctuary is doable only if you stay in Mananthavady (24km). If you have received clearance, you can take your own vehicle (only SUVs) into the forest. The flip side of Tholpetty is that the picnickers and noisy groups create an atmosphere not befitting of a sanctuary. Your only chance is to hope for a silent jeep ride (one hour) through the forest. It is closed during the monsoon months.
04936 250853; ₹60; jeep ₹400; camera/video camera ₹25/150; 7am–10am, 3pm–5pm

2 THIRUNELLI TEMPLE
The scenic drive to the Thirunelli Temple adds to the spiritual experience. A barefoot walk to the Papanasini River behind the temple is an effort, though essential if you are participating in a religious ceremony. Non-Hindus are not allowed in the innermost sanctum. It is worth a visit for a view of the temple's exterior with stone carvings, set against a backdrop of mist-covered peaks.
PO Thirunelli Temple; dawn to dusk; 36km from Mananthavady

3 PAKSHIPATHALAM
A formation of large boulders deep in the forest makes for an adventurous trek, which is best done between October and February. The lush deciduous forest is particularly good for birdwatching. Permits are necessary, and can be arranged at forest offices in south or north Wayanad. Reach the Thirunelli Temple, off Mananthavady, at about 8am, to start the 7km trek (after obtaining permission). The DTPC office in Kalpetta organises trekking guides (₹600 per day), camping equipment (₹250 per person) and transport.
04935 210377; Forest Station, Appapara, Thirunelli; ₹1000 (for five people); 8am–5pm; 32km from Mananthavady

Banasura Sagar, the largest earthen dam in the country

④ KURUVA ISLAND (KURUVADWEEP)

A raft or fibre-glass boat plies across the water for a 10-minute ride to reach this dense rainforest island, which has some unusual species of birds and plants (including rare orchids and herbs). A potentially exotic experience can turn slightly disappointing because of the large crowds. Passes from the Forest Department are necessary.

📞04936 245180; ₹50; camera/video camera ₹25/₹100; 9.30am–3.30pm; 17km from Mananthavady

⑤ BANASURA SAGAR DAM

A visit to the largest earthen dam in India – and the second largest in Asia – is worth the time. The sprawling expanse of water has small islands covered in thick foliage and is home to a number of elephants, which can be spotted from the top of the Banasura Hill. The speed-boat facility here is erratic.

📞04936 273562; adult/child ₹15/10; camera/video ₹25/100; 9am–6pm; 25km from Kalpetta

---

Top Tip: *Watch out for leeches*

Leeches can be a menace during the monsoons if you are on a nature trail. Carry small packs of salt to put on a leech if you see one on your skin; once in contact with the salt, it will fall off immediately.

❻ POOKOT LAKE

Arrive early in the morning to avoid the tourist rush. The natural freshwater lake is reasonably well kept, with options for boating. It gets packed on the weekends.
☏ 04936 255207; 15km from Kalpetta; adult/child ₹15/5 (boating extra); camera/video camera ₹20/150; 9am–6pm (boating till 5pm)

❼ EDAKKAL CAVES

Make your way to the steep site of the Edakkal Caves. The trek is worthwhile for two reasons: prehistoric pictorial carvings and jaw-dropping views of Wayanad district. More than 8000-years old, Edakkal's ancient art wows visitors.
☏ 9446052134; 12km from Sultan Bathery; adult/child ₹15/5; camera/video camera ₹20/75; 9am–4pm, Mon closed

❽ JAIN TEMPLE

The 13th-century Jain temple in Sultan Bathery has splendid stone carvings. You can find a board at the entrance, which gives some information on the monument's history.
Sultan Bathery; 8am–12pm, 2pm–6pm

❾ MUTHANGA WILDLIFE SANCTUARY

The sanctuary is closest to Sultan Bathery (15km). Jeeps can be hired with drivers who double as guides. Personal heavy vehicles are allowed inside, but at an extra cost.
☏ 04936 271010; ₹60; jeep ₹400; camera/video ₹25/150; 7am–10am, 3pm–5pm

❿ WATERFALLS OF WAYANAD

Plan a trip during the monsoons in Wayanad to see the many spectacular waterfalls here. Most of these involve some amount of trekking (check with guides). Among those worth seeing are Meenmutty, Karalad and Soochipara.
☏ 04936 202134; www.dtpcwayanad.com; District Tourism Promotion Council (DTPC), Kalpetta

---

✓ *Top Tip: Plan judiciously*

Wayanad is very big and one must plan ahead. Choose the places you'd like to see, and the activities you want to engage in, and then decide on a stay in one of the three regions (Mananthavady, Kalpetta, Sultan Bathery). Maps are available on the Kerala Tourism website (www.keralatourism.org/wayanad.php).

Accommodation

KOZHIKODE

Harivihar Heritage Homestead Heritage Hotel ₹₹₹
0495 2765865; www.harivihar.com; Bilathikulam; d ₹7500 (incl of full board and taxes) The 160-year-old house has a large courtyard, a sprawling garden with a traditional kalyani (pond) and spacious rooms filled with old furniture and artefacts. Yoga and Ayurveda driven, it offers programmes with qualified doctors and instructors.

Harivihar Heritage Homestead is decorated with antique furniture

The Gateway Hotel Hotel ₹₹₹
0495 6613000; www.thegatewayhotels.com; PT Usha Rd; d ₹6750–8000, ste ₹11,000 (incl of breakfast) The Gateway's service is impeccable and it has facilities like Ayurveda, gym and a pool. An all-day multi-cuisine restaurant also offers a menu for guests on an Ayurveda programme, along with continental, Indian and Chinese cuisine.

Kadavu Resort and Ayurveda Center Resort ₹₹₹
0483 2830023; www.kadavuresorts.com; NH 17, Calicut Bypass Rd, Azhinjilam; d ₹6750–9750, ste ₹15,000–20,000, houseboat ₹13,000–16,000 (incl of breakfast) Located in one of the most scenic spots of the city, the plush Kadavu Resort is set amidst a 10-acre coconut grove next to the Chaliyar River, outside the city. Cottages that overlook the waterfront are a better choice as the view is splendid. Ayurvedic massages and pool apart, a houseboat experience is worthwhile.

Westway Hotel Hotel ₹₹
0495 2768888; www.westwayhotel.com; Kannur Rd; d ₹4200–4700, ste ₹5500 (incl of breakfast) The eight-year-old Westway Hotel has reasonably clean and comfortable rooms, two restaurants and a swimming pool.

Renai Kappad Beach Resort Resort ₹₹
0496 2688777; www.kappadbeachresort.in; Chemancheri PO, Thoovapara; d ₹4500–5000 (incl of breakfast) This is the only option if you want to stay at Kappad Beach. It looks a little inefficient, although the rooms are well furnished. Ask for a room on the first floor for better views. It also has a small pool.

WAYANAD

Tranquil Plantation Homestay ₹₹₹
☎ 947588507; www.tranquilresort.com; Aswati Plantations Ltd, Kuppamundi Coffee Estate, Kolagapaa PO, Sultan Bathery; d ₹7500 (incl of full board) This luxury homestay is in a 400-acre coffee estate. Besides massages and a pool, it offers walking trails that have been interestingly mapped.

The Windflower Resorts & Spa Resort ₹₹₹
☎ 9895226611; www.thewindflower.com; VI/108 A, Ammarao, Achooranam Village, Pozhuthana PO, Vythiri Taluk; d ₹14,400, ste ₹9900 (incl of full board) It's difficult to go wrong with this resort. Battery-run vehicles take you from one spot to the other. With an in-house restaurant, and many activities for the day, you will hardly ever have to step out.

Silver Woods Resort ₹₹₹
☎ 9447666033; www.wayanadsilverwoods.com; Manjoora (PO), Pozhuthana; d ₹10,994–24,185 (incl of full board) This resort is an apt pick if you're looking for complete isolation in luxury. You can enjoy a monsoon view of the Banasura Dam catchment area from a Jacuzzi in the sit-out of your suite.

Kliff's View Homestay ₹₹
☎ 04936 218452; Vattathuvayal, Vatuvanchal PO; d ₹6700 (incl of full board) Get a great view of the sunset behind the Nilgiris from a hammock. The common lounge area offers a gorgeous vista of plantations.

Ente Veedu Homestay ₹₹
☎ 04935 220008; www.enteveedu.co.in; PO Kayakkunnu, Pananmara; d ₹3300–4300 (incl of full board) Ente Veedu has rooms with balconies and a view of paddy fields and plantations. It is central for heading out to, Kalpetta (19km), Mananthavady (15km) and Sultan Bathery (23km).

Eating

KOZHIKODE

Paragon Mappila Cuisine ₹₹
☎ 0495 2767020; www.paragonrestaurant.net; Near CH Flyover, Kannur Rd; 6am–11.45pm; mains ₹200–500 If you are arriving

---

Snapshot: Kozhikodan halwa

The famous Kozhikodan halwa has been undergoing a metamorphosis. Earlier, the popular flour-sugar-coconut oil based sweet used to be prepared in four variations: black, white, red and green. The colour infusion was introduced naturally, for example almonds for red and pistachio for green. Today, it is made using jackfruit, mango, grapes, strawberries and even chocolate. Little souvenir packs with mixed flavours are available widely in the range of ₹160–250.

The very sweet and sticky Kozhikode halwa

here for lunch, you might need to jostle for space for a hearty fill of a Kerala meal or Malabar specialties like beef ularthiyath, mutton biryani and kadukka varuval.

Zain's Hotel — Mappila Cuisine ₹₹
☏ 0495 2761482; Convent Cross Rd; 1–11pm; mains ₹200–500 Famous for its typical Malabar biryani, reach Zain's early in the afternoon as this highly popular restaurant gets packed.

Bombay Hotel — Mappila Cuisine ₹
☏ 0495 2366730; Court Rd; 6am–noon; mains less than ₹200 Bombay Hotel has been serving delicious Malabar food since 1949. Even now, the small restaurant gets packed

WAYANAD

Mint Flower Family Restaurant — South Indian ₹₹
☏ 04936 227179; www.hotelmintflower.com; Chungam, Mysore Rd, Sultan Bathery; mains ₹250–500; 8am–9.30pm The reasonable Kerala fare here is sufficient for a quick lunch. Opt for the filling thali, which has a variety of preparations.

Jubilee — South Indian ₹
☏ 04936 220937; Sultan Bathery Market Rd; mains ₹100–250; 7am–10pm Lunchtime is particularly packed as the food is tasty, and time taken to grab a quick combo is short.

Century Restaurant — South Indian ₹
☏ 04935 246166; Kozhikode Rd, Mananthavady; mains ₹100–200; 7am–11pm This eatery is high on taste but low on experience, and is popular with both locals and tourists. Stick to the standard Kerala dishes.

Green Gates — Multi-Cuisine ₹
☏ 04936 202001; www.greengateshotel.com; TB Rd, Kalpetta North; mains ₹100–250; 6am–11pm The slow service at this Kalpetta restaurant is more than compensated by a delicious meal. It's one of the better places for a meal.

The Woodlands — South Indian ₹
☏ 04936 202547; www.thewoodlandshotel.com; Main Rd, Kalpetta; mains ₹100–250; 7am–10pm The cheerful interiors here make it inviting, though it's best to stick to the south Indian preparations that are served here.

Activities

WAYANAD

Windflower Ayurvedic Centre
☎ 9895226611; www.thewindflower.com; VI/108 A, Ammarao, Achooranam Village, Pozhuthana PO, Vythiri Taluk; 9am–6pm One of the few resorts that allows outside guests, they have a host of luxury facilities and Ayurveda services.

Upvan Ayurvedic Centre
☎ 04936 255272; www.upvanresort.com; Lakkidi; 8.30am–5.30pm A small facility with an appointed doctor. Suitable for both short and long duration treatments and therapies.

Santhigiri Ayurveda & Siddha Hospital Ayurvedic Centre
☎ 04936 347775; www.santhigiriashram.org; 18/213, near Collectorate Bungalow, Madiyoorkuni, Main Rd Kalpetta; 8am–5pm An authentic Kerala Ayurvedic centre, run by doctors in association with an extensive ashram of the same name.

Shopping

KOZHIKODE

Kozhikodan Halwa and Banana Chips
Kerala is famous for its fried savouries and snacks but the banana chips of Kozhikode top the list. The extraordinary sticky halwa of Kozhikode is also something you may want to carry back. Both can be found in small bakeries all over town, but the concentration of shops on SM (Sweet Meat) Street is maximum.

Tasara Centre for Creative Weaving
☎ 0495 2414832; www.tasaraindia.com; Beypore; 10am–5pm To pick up exclusive hand-woven and dyed designs on fabric, head to Tasara in Beypore. Tasara has added a contemporary twist to the age-old art of hand weaving, block printing and batik. Call them for directions.

WAYANAD

Uravu Souvenirs
☎ 04936-231400; www.uravu.net; Thrikkaipetta PO; 11am–5pm; Mon–Sat The bamboo by-products of this non-profit establishment make for wonderful souvenirs. The workshop is tucked away in Thrikkaipetta village. Watch out for the many shops in town that make false claims of stocking Uravu products.

♥ If You Like: Treks

Trekking in Wayanad depends on the season. There are no expeditions during the monsoons. Chembra Peak is often spoken of with awe, as it's the highest in the region (6890ft), but try the ascent only if you are extremely fit. For beginners, many estates have thrilling trails where one can encounter plenty of flora and fauna.

Lakshadweep

It's not until you've been to this cluster of islands, 250km off the coast of Kerala, that you realise just how many shades of blue really exist. The waters here are a stranger to pollution, the sands have never seen a plastic bag and the villages haven't been turned into tawdry tourist traps. Whether you swim or try scuba diving, the sea will be the undisputed star of this story.

Trip Planner

GETTING THERE

Agatti: The only airport with access to Lakshadweep is Kochi. Air India has a regular service from Kochi to Agatti. From Agatti, other islands are accessible only by high speed crafts or Pablo boats with the exception of Kavaratti, which can be reached by helicopter. SPORTS (Society for Promotion of Nature Tourism and Sports) – the government organisation offers cruises all year around which combine one to three islands in one package. These all inclusive package tours depart from Kochi to the islands of Kadmat, Minicoy and Kavaratti, depending on which tour package you opt for.

SUGGESTED ITINERARY (7 DAYS)

The government runs several all-inclusive package cruises (p284) and it is best to go for these. Keep about five to seven days in hand. But you should decide on your islands first (only Kadmat, Kavaratti and Minicoy have stay facility since the resorts at Bangaram and Agatti have been closed) and contact the SPORTS office at Kochi who will work out an itinerary keeping ship schedules in mind.

BEST TIME TO GO

J F **M A** M J J A S **O N D**

GREAT FOR

Top 5 highlights

- **Main Beach, Kavaratti** (p283)
- **Marine Aquarium, Kavaratti** (p285)
- **Lighthouse Visits, Minicoy** (p286)
- **Kadmat** (p287)
- **Scuba diving** (p289)

A Sea of Blue

On arriving at this aquamarine paradise that has more palm trees than people, one experiences a strange combination of surprise and gratitude that this tropical island system is a part of India. The distance from land and the efforts of a vigilant government have placed these virgin islands in a time capsule. The simple village folk, whose main sources of income are fishing and coir production, welcome tourists with open arms. While the sea at **Kavaratti** introduces a kaleidoscopic underwater world, mysterious **Minicoy** throws up ancient shipwrecks and lighthouses. **Kadmat** speaks only of serenity. No matter which one you choose, golden sunsets over azure waters await you.

> Shades of blue keep you comapny

Kavaratti

❶ MAIN BEACH
The administrative headquarters of Lakshadweep, Kavaratti offers a small strip of powder sand that accommodates the tourist lodge, water sports centre, and a lone restaurant. Kavaratti may not make the best beach getaway, however it must be visited for the singular purpose of diving.

Highlights
❶ Main Beach
❷ Marine Acquarium
❸ Ujra Mosque

✓ Top Tip: The island trip planner

Be prepared for a whole new tourism experience at Lakshadweep. Here, the government pretty much decides your holiday. While they are eager for tourist traffic, they have decided to keep travel to Lakshadweep a state secret. This lack of clarity bullies most people into booking the government cruise, which comes in an all-inclusive package.

Choose the **Coral Reef** package only if you don't mind travelling with a noisy crowd on a very strict schedule. Choosing from the island stay packages like **Taratashi** or the **Swaying Palm** will be a gentler experience. You should decide on your islands first (only Kadmat, Kavaratti and Minicoy have stay facility since the resorts at Bangaram and Agatti have been closed) and contact the SPORTS office at Kochi who will work out an itinerary keeping ship schedules in mind. Most inter-island transport leaves from Kavaratti but beware that such travel will involve long journeys in a small motorised fishing boat (₹15,000) if the speed crafts (₹2000) are not available, so it's best to not hop too much.

✆0484 2668387; www.lakshadweeptourism.nic.in; I.G Rd, Willingdon Island, Kochi

No matter how beautiful you find the island, always remember that it's nothing compared to what lies beneath: unspoiled coral reefs and stunning psychedelic colours of marine life are a diver's dream. A single dive here may reward you with as many as 100 species of fish.

One of the many world-class dive sites that the professionally managed Lakshadweep Diving Academy (www.lakshadweepdivingacademy.com) will take you down to is the **Wall of Wonder**. This gigantic wall of soft coral that goes deep into a bottomless sea is ablaze with colours of exotic marine life, from bright yellow butterfly fish to the deep purple Crown of Thorns.

A starfish at East Lagoon, Kavaratti

Visit Kavaratti as part of Taratashi package or a combination package with Kadmat which allows for stay on the island; Coral Reef and Samundram package offers only a day trip; helicopter service from Agatti to Kavaratti cost ₹8500 per tourist

Off the Kerala coast, Kavaratti

② MARINE AQUARIUM
One of the few 'sightseeing' options at Lakshadweep, a visit to the aquarium gives you a reason to get off the beach and explore the island. While autorickshaws are available, it's highly recommended that you take the short walk through the lovely village lanes. As you enter the dingy aquarium cum museum with its range of pickled tropical fish specimens, you may wonder why you're seeing them dead in jars when you have the opportunity to meet them alive underwater, but it holds you in morbid fascination nonetheless. There is also a shark pool in the premises with a couple of impatient sharks, which may be worth a look if you don't plan to dive deep enough to meet one.

A visit to the aquarium is included in all packages for Kavaratti

③ UJRA MOSQUE
The ancient mosques in Lakshadweep look nothing like dome-shaped structures with minarets that are seen elsewhere. Here the mosques are white limestone cottages with cheerful red terracotta roofs, reminiscent more of coastal temples than mosques. Of the 300 mosques here, Ujra is the most famous. This collection of three structures including a dargha, is housed in a courtyard of white sand and does not hold regular namaaz. The beautifully designed pillars and verandah with carvings of plants and leaves are a celebrated attraction as is the water tank next door.

Minicoy

> **Highlights**
> 1. Thundi Beach
> 2. Lighthouse Visits
> 3. Townhall

❶ THUNDI BEACH

The translucent emerald waters stretch endlessly in all directions. The shallow lagoon on the southern tip of the island extends over a kilometre into the sea. With its white sea bed that gives the water the appearance of liquid glass, the lagoon is swarming with enormous sea turtles. While the diving facility here is smaller in scale than that on Kavaratti, this crescent-shaped island offers world-class shipwreck dives as shallow as 8m into the sea. These ancient steamer ships lie unnamed and local folklore passed on for generations places their sinking as far back as 1862.

Visit Minicoy as part of 'Swaying Palm' package which allows for stay on the island; Coral Reef & Samundram offer a day trip

❷ LIGHTHOUSE VISITS

Zooming into the stratosphere amidst a dense palm cover, each island offers a pristine white, well-maintained lighthouse that must be visited. The lighthouse at Minicoy, one of Asia's tallest, going well above 47m, is believed to have been constructed in the wake of several shipwrecks in the 1800s. Don't let the steep 200-step climb deter you. Once you reach the top, the island lies spread out below you and all the shades of blue come together in one spectacular sweep. Look out for the antique oil canister and equipment on display as you climb.

Climb up the lighthouse at Minicoy for stunning views

Minicoy lighthouse is walking distance from tourist lodge; entry ₹10/25; 4–5.30pm; Sun closed

❸ TOWNHALL

Minicoy may be in Lakshadweep but its heart is in the Maldives. The cultural practices of this little gem of an island are worth witnessing and Falassery village is the place to see it. Rooted as a matrilineal society, the village operates as a family headed by the Moopan. At its beautifully decorated Townhall, you will see the entire village descend to discuss important matters and celebrate occasions like Republic Day and Independence Day with giant communal meals. Displayed at the Townhall is the star 'jhaldhoni' of the village, crafted by ace boat makers, which is rowed by the males of Falassery in boat races.

A beachside resort at Kadmat

Kadmat

When you're in Lakshadweep you have to constantly remind yourself that you are still in India. On Kadmat, the island most frequented by foreigners, this feeling is more acute. With a beauty quotient that is head to head with Minicoy and a dive facility that rivals Kavaratti, Kadmat has the best of Lakshadweep. It offers a great stretch of beach and endless lagoons on both sides that teem with all variety of marine life. However, the highlights here are the range of spectacular dive sites that go from nine to 40m and cater to all levels of divers. With brilliant visibility, dive sites like Shark Alley or Turtle City make for unforgettable experiences. If you plan to get a diving certification, Kadmat is the place to do it.

Transport from Agatti via high-speed ferry ($2000) or a private Pablo boat (₹15,000) is managed by SPORTS; Alternatively Kadmat can be visited as part of the Marine Wealth Awareness Package

Accommodation

Kadmat Island Beach Resort   Cottages ₹₹₹
☎ 0484 2668387; www.lakshadweeptourism.nic.in; I.G Rd, Willingdon Island, Kochi; **₹26,400 for a 3 night/4 day package (incl of meals and water sports)** The AC and non AC cottages spread out on the beach meet your requirements adequately. Expect the basic facilities like the hot water to run, the phone to dial and the views to be spectacular.

Paradise Hut, Kavaratti   Tourist Lodge ₹₹
☎ 0484 2668387; www.lakshadweeptourism.nic.in; I.G Rd, Willingdon Island, Kochi; **₹6000 per night (incl of meals and water sports)** Paradise Hut is ironically not a hut at all, but a small building on the beach with a restaurant alongside. It offers two double rooms in one unit, which gets a bit awkward if you do not know the couple in the second room. Scrupulously clean, the facilities here are competent but hardly luxurious. The highlight of the lodge is that it offers generous balconies from every room and a roof top that transports you from the bustle below.

Twenty Bedded Tourist Lodge, Minicoy   Cottages ₹₹
☎ 0484 2668387; www.lakshadweeptourism.nic.in; I.G Rd, Willingdon Island, Kochi; **₹6000 per night (incl of meals and water sports)** These compact but incredibly pretty set of 10 cottages are spread out on the beach and come with open-air bathrooms and a modest sit-out, perfect for taking in the sunset. The restaurant facing the beach makes for a great romantic dinner venue.

Eating

Food is not a high point in Lakshadweep. At Kalpeni, you can visit Koya, a small eatery, where you can have rice pancake rotis and crispy reef fish stuffed with spices (₹60). In Kavaratti, try Al Bake for parottas and chicken masala (₹90) or the octopus fry (₹50) at Sandy Beach. If you happen to be travelling by ship package, during the trip to the village, visit Falassery and sample some delicious tuna samosa. Even if you don't have a sweet tooth, try the steamed sweetmeat called fonivara bondi made of coconut flesh and jaggery.

Expert Recommendation
Diving in the deep

Sumer Verma, CEO of Lacadives, has over 7000 dives to his credit and has worked for over 15 years in the diving industry. He is also an underwater photographer.

- **Diving Course:** It is mandatory to know swimming for a diving certification course. A course with PADI (Professional Association of Dive Instructors) will help complete your confined water and theory requirements before heading to the islands. Choose a reputed diving school/centre for learning.

- **For beginners:** Those with a limited time can go on a DSD (Discover Scuba Diving) experience. This involves a hand-held diving one-on-one experience with an instructor under water. You may be taken for half an hour down to 10m underwater.

- **Equipment:** These are included in the price offered by all dive shops and will include masks, fins, and a scuba cylinder with compressed air. The equipment will weigh 15kg on land, but feel luxuriously weightless under water. Choose a reputed dive shop.

- **Instructors:** Diving is always done in pairs or with buddy-instructors for safety. Follow instructor's directions under water to convey discomfort.

- **Fitness:** Diving is suitable for all from 10 years onwards. It's best to consult the doctor for those with medical problems like heart ailments, epilepsy, asthma or any recent surgeries before diving.

- **Period:** Mid-October to mid-May.

- **Dive sites:** Kadmat Island – North Cave, the Wall, Jack Point, Shark Alley, the Potato Patch, Cross Currents and Sting Ray City. Bangaram – Manta Point, Life, Grand Canyon and the sunken reef at Perumal Par. With 25-45m visibility, the wealth of marine life including turtles, fishes, coral make for spectacular diving zones at Lakshadweep.

The sea is abundant with colourful corals and marine life

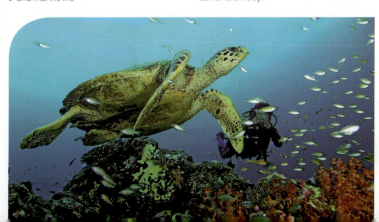

Tamil Nadu

Why Go?

Tamil Nadu remains proudly distinct from the rest of India, welcoming visitors with its wealth of history and culture. Towering temple architecture is the state's greatest drawcard. The temples at **Madurai**, **Rameswaram**, **Tiruchirappalli**, **Chidambaram**, **Kanchipuram** and **Rameswaram** are magnificent in size, grandeur and sculptural elegance as are the Chola temples of **Thanjavur, Kumbakonam** and **Mamallapuram** that are world heritage monuments. Escape the heat of the state's scorching plains to the Western Ghats and go to hill stations like **Ooty**, **Coonoor**, **Kotagiri**, **Kodaikanal** and **Valparai.**

This state is home to the bustling capital of **Chennai**, the blue shoreline of the Coromandel Coast and the former French colony **Puducherry**. Halt at the very end of India in **Kanyakumari** where mighty seas and an ocean mingle over spectacular sunsets.

Close-by is the the Union Territory of **Andaman and Nicobar Islands**. These islands are jewels in the middle of the Bay of Bengal, offering pristine beaches and underwater adventures.

Getting There & Away

Air: Chennai, Coimbatore, Tiruchirappalli and Madurai are Tamil Nadu's four most important airports connected via daily flights to all metros and major cities. While Chennai has daily flights to overseas destinations, Tiruchirappalli, Madurai and Coimbatore have limited international services.

Train: Main cities in Tamil Nadu are well connected to the metros of India. The key railheads are at Chennai, Coimbatore, Erode, Tiruchirappalli , Madurai and Salem. Visit the official railway website www.irctc.co.in for more information.

◾ Colourful fishing boats and the Vivekananda Memorial at the backdrop in Kanyakumari

Tamil Nadu Map

⭐ 12 Best Trips

❶ Chennai & Around (p296) Enjoy the mix of ancient temples and local art as you settle down by the Coromandel Coast for a sundowner.

❷ Mamallapuram & Puducherry (p316) Admire Pallavan temple art at Mamallapuram and sample a slice of French life at Puducherry.

❸ Thanjavur & Kumbakonam (p336) The World Heritage site is a throwback to the pride of Dravidian architecture.

❹ Tiruchirappalli (p350) Scale up the Rock Fort for sweeping hilltop views of the town.

❺ Chettinadu (p358) Marvel at the grand Chettiar mansions and sample fiery Chettinadu cuisine.

❻ Madurai & Rameswaram (p370) Admire the temple culture in both these historic towns.

❼ Kanyakumari (p386) Witness the meeting of the three seas at the tip of the country.

❽ Kodaikanal (p392) Admire nature at its best in this scenic hill station.

❾ Coimbatore & Valparai (p402) Coimbatore is a great base to explore Valparai's lush tea estates.

❿ Ooty, Coonoor & Kotagiri (p414) Take the Nilgiri toy train and visit lush tea gardens.

⓫ Andaman Islands (p434, off map) Gawp at coral reefs and laze on the pristine beaches in this tropical haven.

Thanjavur is home to many stunning temples

Top Highlights

1 Shore Temple, Mamallapuram

Against the timeless waves of Mamallapuram stands the splendour of the Shore Temple (p318). A symbol of Pallavan architecture and maritime influence across the seas, the Shore Temple is a stunning example of a coastal monument. Its towering presence transforms a usual beachside into one that is grand and majestic with a sense of history. Settle on the sands by dusk and watch the darkening silhouette of this monolith against the backdrop of the sea. The sight is sure to take you back to an ancient land.

2 Tranquebar

Located close to Puducherry, this is a quiet, orderly, pretty town set on a long sandy beach with a few fishing boats. Traquebar (p327) was a former colony of the Dutch, who used it as a trading hub before selling it to the British, and remnants of Danish heritage are scattered all over. The most imposing of these is Fort Dansborg which dates back to 1624. Tranquebar is also home to some pretty churches. This is one of the towns which was struck by the devastating 2004 tsunami.

3 Tea Tasting, Coonoor

When a sea of green mossy bushes is all you can see for miles, you know that a hot cup of tea is close by. To taste different varieties of tea in the Nilgiris, head to Highfield Tea Estate (p421) in Coonoor. Free samples are given at the end of a tour to all visitors. Though more formal tea tasting rooms have not permeated the region yet, Tranquilitea (p425) homestay in Coonoor organises a session for their guests with veteran tea planters taking you through the subtle nuances of different varieties.

4 Chettinadu Mansions

The entire Chettinadu region is dotted with huge, lavish mansions (p363) built by one of the wealthiest communities, the Chettiars. Think Burmese teak wood pillars, Japanese tiles and Belgian glass. A typical mansion has a series of courtyards of varying sizes flanked by rooms on all sides. At the entrance usually stands a beautifully carved teak wood door. Go beyond it and you can see till the end of the house as all the doors are concentric. One of the most lavish mansions is the Raja's Palace in Kanadukathan village. Many of them have been converted into hotels.

Chennai & Around

Chennai sits on a bedrock of tradition and antiquity topped by modern leisure options. Take in the city's vignettes of history and heritage and cruise down the East Coast Road to halt along beaches that host kitschy entertainment parks, heritage centres and more. Neighbouring Kanchipuram offers phenomenal temple architecture and the famous silk-weaving culture that goes back 500 years.

Trip Planner

GETTING THERE

Chennai: The Anna International Airport and domestic Kamaraj terminal next door have daily flights to all metros and major cities. Chennai has two railway stations. Interstate trains and those going west depart from Chennai Central station, while trains heading south depart from Chennai Egmore station.

East Coast Road: Chennai airport is 15km from ECR and a cab costs ₹300.

Kanchipuram: Chennai's airport is 62km away. Trains till here leave from Chennai Egmore station six times daily.

SUGGESTED ITINERARY (5 DAYS)

Three days is enough to explore Chennai. Visit historical monuments, temples and shopping hubs during the day and keep the evening for beaches. On the fourth day drive down the East Coast Road along the Coromandel Coast. Next day go to Kanchipuram.

BEST TIME TO GO

J F M A M J J A S O **N D**

GREAT FOR

Top 5 highlights

- Mylapore & Parthasarathy Temple, Chennai (p299)
- Marina Beach & Around, Chennai (p299)
- Churches of Chennai (p303)
- Cholamandal Artists' Village, ECR (p304)
- Kanchi Kamakshi, Kanchipuram (p306)

Southern Star

A visit to **Chennai** is short of delights of the tourist brochure variety. The capital city is now a modern metropolis with spanking malls and swish restaurants, but it has not lost its grip on its heritage and culture. For many, it is as much a gateway to other places in the south as a destination in itself.

If its music and dance remain classical, its popular entertainment offers kitsch and colour, and today the city chimes to both vintage Carnatic music and AR Rahman's techno beats. It needs a keen eye to spot the traditional architecture, antique churches and temples of Chennai, but in this city, the past is always present.

Chase tropical beach culture down the **East Coast Road** along the beachside suburbs of Chennai. Further on, the temples and monuments of **Kanchipuram**, hailed as the 'Varanasi of the south', offer an architectural voyage down the centuries and allow a glimpse into a variegated religious history. It once had a thriving Jain and Buddhist culture and was home to a thousand temples, but time and elements have reduced these to a few hundreds. Kanchipuram is also the home of the ancient silk-weaving culture that has spawned the gorgeous Kanjeevaram sari.

> Chennai is home to the second-longest beach in the world, Marina

Chennai

Highlights
1. George Town & Around
2. Government Museum
3. Parthasarathy Temple
4. Marina Beach & Around
5. San Thome Basilica
6. Kapaleeswarar Temple
7. Theosophical Society

❶ GEORGE TOWN & AROUND

Chennai's foundations as a city were laid in Fort St George by the East India Company. The 17th-century historic fort is the headquarters of the Tamil Nadu government. Visit the **Fort Museum** for interesting military memorabilia from World War I and 18th-century etchings. Popham's Broadway, now known as Prakasam Salai, off George Town, has a cluster of interesting buildings, including **Tucker's Church, Wesleyan Chapel** and **Anderson's Church**. While there is nothing touristy about the fort and its surrounds, it is crammed with period homes, buildings and markets that are best explored during a heritage walk (p300).
Fort St George, Rajaji Salai; 9am–5pm; museum ₹5; 8am–5pm; Sat–Thur

❷ GOVERNMENT MUSEUM

Sprawling over a large campus with four main buildings and 46 galleries, this is one of the best museums in the city. The **Museum Theatre** resembles Italianate architecture and is a throwback to another era. Behind the theatre is a children's museum that displays ancient dolls and toys. The **National Art Gallery** is a stunning piece of architecture combining Mughal and Rajasthani styles. The exhibits include sculptures, Mughal paintings, Tanjores and Raja Ravi Varma's paintings. The **Madras Museum** and National Art Gallery house a large collection of sculptures and bronzes, dating back to early Chola, Pallava and Vijayanagar periods to the time of the East India Company. The art gallery has an impressive collection of contemporary paintings.
www.chennaimuseum.org; Pantheon Rd, Egmore; ₹15; 9.30am–5pm; Sat–Thur

PARTHASARATHY TEMPLE

The British purchased a village in 1676 from the Sultan of Golconda and called it Triplicane, anglicising its poetic Tamil name, Tiru alli keni (the sacred lily tank). The Parthasarathy Temple epitomises the culture emanating from Triplicane. Built by King Dantivarman Pallava in the 9th century, the temple was expanded by the 16th-century Vijayanagar rulers. The presiding deity is Vishnu in the form of Arjuna's charioteer or Partha's sarathy. If it's an auspicious day don't miss the temple prasadam, the famous Iyengar puliodhare (tamarind rice) and sarkarai pongal (sweet rice pudding). **www.sriparthasarathyswamytemple.org; Singarachari St; 6am–noon, 4–9pm**

> The Government Museum has four main buildings

♥ *If You Like: Dance & music*

Chennai breaks into a medley of song and dance kutchery (concerts) to bring the year down. Held annually from December to January end, this season is the city's finest hour with about 60 cultural organisations or sabhas hosting some 1000 performances of dance and music. The ladies dazzle in the best of silks, the city is lit up and the chatterati concentrates on the delights of music and dance on offer. For itinerary and ticket information visit www.kutcheribuzz.com

❹ MARINA BEACH & AROUND

Holding the spot of second-longest beach in the world, Marina Beach is undoubtedly Chennai's pride. The Italianate promenade was built more than a century ago and the name Marina is an ode to its Sicilian inspiration. It's best to stroll along this lively sandy stretch early evening both to take in the refreshing sea breeze and to admire the heritage buildings on the opposite side.

A line of Indo Saracenic buildings stand opposite the entire 4km stretch of the Marina along the South Beach Road. Indo Saracenic is the original hybrid form of architecture developed by the British while in Chennai. The city's first Masonic temple is an elegant all-white structure, with columns, long corridors and arches. The 19th century building is now the Tamil Nadu police headquarters and inaccessible to tourists but you can always admire the impressive structure from outside.

Down the beach road is **Vivekananda House** (formerly Ice House), a circular building built in 1842 to store huge blocks of ice imported from America for the Madras Port. Today the Ramakrishna Mutt has turned the place into a memorial hall for Swami Vivekananda. Further south is **Elliot's Beach** on Besant Nagar, where small and trendy eating joints sell pizzas, dosas, tandoori dishes and Chinese chow.

Swami Vivekananda; adult/child ₹10/5.10am–12.15pm, 3–7.15pm; Thur–Tue

✓ Top Tip: Heritage walks

Storytrails (☏9600080215; www.storytrails.in): It runs walking tours based around themes such as dance, jewellery and bazaars as well as tours specially aimed at children.

The Chennai PhotoWalk (☏9884467463): August 22 is the day Chennai was recorded as a city over 300 years ago. A photo walk takes you past some of Chennai's quaint and historic spots.

Past forward (₹500 per person; two hours): Contact V Sriram for tours of Chennai's cultural history, temples, Islamic heritage and mercantile history.

Snapshot: Mylapore festival

Pongal celebrations (January 14–18) in Mylapore are special annual affairs. With over 12 venues, 30 events and 300 artists Mylapore rejoices in cultural activities that include kolam competitions, folk arts and performances. Women and children take part in drawing elaborate kolams (patterns made of rice flour) along the streets around the Kapaleeswarar Temple.

5 SAN THOME BASILICA

Further down the shore from Marina is San Thome, the first Portuguese settlement in the 16th century. A walk down San Thome with its garden houses, sandy seafront, its many Catholic institutions and San Thome Basilica give a whiff of the Portuguese era. Legend has it that the apostle, St Thomas, who is said to have brought Christianity to the subcontinent, landed in Mylapore in AD 52 where he is believed to have built a tiny chapel with his own hands. The present neo-Gothic cathedral, with its towering 183ft high spire, was built in 1894. A crypt inside the cathedral houses the tomb of St Thomas.

☎ 044 24985455, 24980758; www.santhomechurch.com; **Santhome High Rd**

Women making kolam designs in front of Kapaleeswarar Temple

6 KAPALEESWARAR TEMPLE

The ancient settlement of Mylapore stood before the city of Madras sprang up. Mylapore's landmark is the impressive Dravidian style Kapaleeswarar Temple and its temple tank. This neighbourhood and temple retain a quaint rustic charm. The temple is dedicated to Lord Shiva and was built by the Pallavas of the 15th century and further developed by the Vijayanagar kings in the 16th century.

Kapaleeswarar Temple is built in Dravidian style architecture

Walking along the four roads around the Mylapore temple square is a step back in time. Lined with shops selling silk, temple jewellery, religious paraphernalia, tiffin stalls, vegetable markets and concert halls, this is a bustling square. Notice the Madras terrace roofs (an architectural feature pioneered in the city) of the few 19th-century houses that remain and their quaint vernacular architecture.

☏ 044 24641670, 24611356; www.mylaikapaleeswarar.tnhrce.in; Vadaku Mada Veethi, Mylapore; 5am–noon, 4–9.30pm

❼ THEOSOPHICAL SOCIETY

Cross the bridge over Adyar River to reach the sprawling international headquarters of Theosophical Society, founded in 1878 by Madame Blavatsky and Col Olcott. Its 270 acres of verdant woods remain a green oasis in a dusty city and are a lovely spot just to wander. There are shrines and chapels of all faiths located across the woods – a church, mosque, Buddhist shrine and a Hindu temple as well. The library here has some rare manuscripts. The Theosophical Society's best-known symbol is the 400-year-old Adyar banyan tree which has put in nearly 1000 roots within the complex.

www.ts-adyar.org; Mon–Sat 8.30–10am, 2pm–4pm

If You Like: Churches

Chennai is home to 500 years of church architecture that offers amazing variety. The two prominent clusters of churches in Chennai are around George Town and Santhome.

- **St Mary's Church** (Fort St George; closed to visitors on Sunday): The first Protestant Anglican Church in India, this 17th-century church is located within Fort St George. From Elihu Yale, Job Charnock, Warren Hastings, Wellesley, and Robert Clive, whose marriage to Margaret Maskelyne was sanctified here, the church has heard many illustrious footfalls.

- **St Andrew's Church** (Poonamalee High Rd; Sunday service 9am–2pm): The 19th-century neo-classical church was built for the Scottish communtiy in Chennai. Many refer to it as 'Kirk', (which means Church in Scottish).

- **Armenian Church** (Armenian St, George Town; 9am–2.30pm): The Armenians were the first settlers along with the Jews who came for trade in corals and gems to Chennai. The church has a wooden door topped by a Dutch gable, baroque facade and a three-tiered bell tower.

- **Church of Our Lady of Light** (Luz; Sunday mass for children 10am): Legend has it that a mysterious light safely guided a group of Portuguese sailors tossed by stormy waters and the light disappeared when they struck land. They are said to have built a chapel dedicated to 'Our Lady of Light' in the 16th century.

- **St George's Cathedral** (Gemini Flyover; 10am–6pm): Built in 1816, in the midst of a sprawling compound, this church is a splendid example of classical architecture.

- **St Thomas's Mount** (Parangi Malai; 9am–6pm): Nestorian Christians erected a small church in the 7th-century on the summit of St Thomas' Mount. Marco Polo visited the site in 1293. The Portuguese rebuilt it the 16th century.

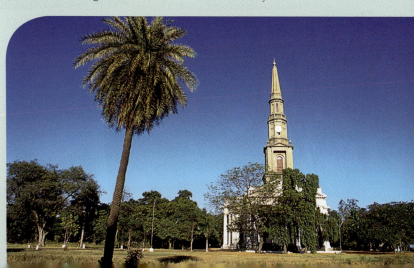

The striking St Andrew's Church is more than a century old

East Coast Road

Highlights
1. Cholamandal Artists' Village
2. Dakshinachitra
3. Crocodile Bank
4. Muttukadu Boat House

❶ CHOLAMANDAL ARTISTS' VILLAGE
There's a tropical bohemian groove floating around Injambakkam village, the site of Cholamandal Artists' Village. Founded in 1965, this four-hectare artists' cooperative is a serene muse away from the world and a quiet chance to see as well as purchase contemporary Indian art direct from the source. The village has many homes of South Indian artists who live and work here. There is a permanent art gallery where the artists' works are displayed and can be bought.
📞044 24490092; www.cholamandalartistsvillage.com; 18km from Chennai; 9.30am–9pm

❷ DAKSHINACHITRA
Dakshinachitra showcases traditional South Indian arts and crafts and local architecture. It has an open-air museum, preserved samples of South Indian architectural styles and artisan workshops. It's a good place to learn about the Dravidian crafts of South Indian states. There are also pottery, silk-weaving, puppetry and basket-making workshops, and traditional theatre performances.
📞044 27472603; www.dakshinachitra.net; 12km from Cholamandal village; adult/student ₹75/30, foreigner/student ₹200/75; 10am–6pm Wed–Mon

A drive down the East Coast Road is an interesting experience

If You Like: Entertainment parks

• **The MGM Dizzee World** (☏9500063716; www.mgmdizzeeworld.com; 1/74 New Mahabalipuram Rd, Muttukadu; adult/child ₹500/400; weekdays 10.30am–5.30pm, weekends and holidays 10.30am–7.30pm, Wed closed): This theme park for family and kids offers 60 adventure and fun rides, water games, a food court and more. It also has an amphitheatre for hosting events.

• **Mayajaal** (☏044 27472860; www.mayajaal.com; 28km from Chennai; entry ₹50; entry free if you have a movie ticket): The popular movie and entertainment complex has a gaming centre, bowling alley, pool parlour, sports village, and a multi-cuisine food court and a bar as well.

❸ CROCODILE BANK

Crocodile Bank is a fascinating peek into the world of reptiles. It does crucial work towards protecting the critically endangered gharial. There are other reptiles here, including the Indian mugger and saltwater crocodiles of the Andaman and Nicobar Islands. If you have a spare evening on the weekend, go for the night safari when you can shine a flashlight over the water and catch the staring eyes of thousands of the bank's local residents. The feeding sessions on Sundays (11.30am, 12.30pm, 4pm, 4.30pm and 5pm) are a hit with most visitors.

☏044 27472447; www.madrascrocodilebank.org; 40km from Chennai; adult/child/camera/video ₹35/10/20/100, 8.30am–5.30pm Tue–Sun; night safari, adult/child ₹60/20, 7–8pm Sat & Sun

❹ MUTTUKADU BOAT HOUSE

Along this stretch of East Coast Road, the TTDC (Tamil Nadu Tourism Development Corporation) runs the Muttukadu Boat House, where you can take a boat trip on the backwaters. Row boats, speedboats, water scooters and motor boats are also available.

All rides are for 30min; row boat 2-seater ₹120, 3-seater ₹150, water scooter ₹550, 6-seater motor boat ₹420, free for children below 5; 9am–6pm all days

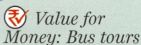 *Value for Money: Bus tours*

To go down the ECR take the TTDC's hop-on, hop-off bus tour (☏044 25383333; www.tamilnadutourism.org/hopontour.html; ₹250) that runs between Chennai and Mamallapuram every half-hour between 9am and 11am, and in the other direction between 4.15pm and 6pm from Tiruvanmiyur.

Kanchipuram

Highlights
1. Kanchi Kamakshi Temple
2. Kailasanathar Temple
3. Ekambareswarar Temple
4. Varadarajaperumal Temple
5. Vaikuntaperumal Temple

❶ KANCHI KAMAKSHI TEMPLE
Kanchi's Kamakshi is one of the three Shakti Peetams in the country after Kashi's Vishalakshi and Madurai's Meenakshi. In honour of Kamakshi's status there are no special sanctums for the mother goddess (Amman) in any other temple in Kanchipuram.

The temple was built in the 11th century but the ornate pillared halls were added in the 17th century by the Vijayanagar kings. The main shrine is topped with a glittering golden roof. There is a separate shrine for Adi Sankara in the outer pathway where he is believed to have attained beatification at the age of 32. The temple has close links to the Kanchi Mutt today.

www.kanchikamakshi.com; 6 Kamakshi Amman Sannadhi St; 5.30am–12.30pm 4–8.30pm

❷ KAILASANATHAR TEMPLE
This is Kanchipuram's oldest and most impressive temple, not for its size, but its historical presence and delicacy of its stonework. It was built in the 8th century by the Pallava king Narasimhavarman II. The low-slung sandstone compound has fascinating carvings, including many of half-animal deities and a large Nandi in early Dravidian architecture style.

♥ If You Like: Heritage museums

The Kanchi Kudil (dwelling of Kanchi) is a novel heritage museum located in a 100-year-old house, renovated to showcase the history of Kanchipuram. Antique household objects and children's toys and a thuli (a cradle made of a long cloth slung over the beams near the ceiling) are on display. Reading material that encapsulates the history of Kanchipuram, its social mores, economy, heritage and the traditional way of life are framed and hung on the walls. If bookings are made in advance, you can have a traditional Tamil meal here.

☏ 044 27227680; www.kanchi.nic.in; 53A, Sangeetha Vidwan Nainar Pillai St; ₹10; 9am–5pm; veg lunch ₹300, non-veg ₹350

📷 *Snapshot: Kanchi Mutt*

The Kanchi Kamakoti Peetam (Salai St; 5.30am–noon, 5–8 pm) is one of the important Hindu religious centres in India. It is believed that the Advaita philosopher, saint Adi Sankara lived in Kanchipuram and was beatified here in 477 BC. He established a Kamakoti Mutt in 482 BC and the Mutt has had an unbroken line of nearly 70 descendants. The current presiding pontiff Sri Jayendra Saraswathi and his successor Vijayendra Saraswathi are the 69th and 70th acharyas respectively to head the peetam.

❸ EKAMBARESWARAR TEMPLE

This temple towers over a sprawling campus area of 40 acres, with a 172ft high rajagopuram. It is a splendid showcase of Pallavan and Chola-style architectures. The present structure, with an 11-storeyed high rajagopuram has impressive embellishments including roaring lions and the 1000 pillar mandapam, or pavilion.

Opp Sankara Mutt; 6am–noon, 4–8pm

❹ VARADARAJAPERUMAL TEMPLE

Also called Devarajaswami Temple, it was built by the Cholas in the 11th century and later by the Vijayanagar kings in the 16th century. It has a 100-pillared hall with exquisite sculptures of horses and mythological creatures, yalis and even sculptures of European soldiers along the praharams (circumambulatory path). The presiding deity is a tall Maha Vishnu. Its large temple tank hosts float festivals thrice a year.

5.30am–noon, 4–8pm

> The Varadarajaperumal Temple has a hall with 100 pillars

❺ VAIKUNTAPERUMAL TEMPLE

This Pallava era temple is roughly 1200 years old. A passage around the central shrine has carved pillars and sculpted wall panels. The main shrine is spread over three levels and contains images of Vishnu standing, sitting, reclining and riding his preferred mount, Garuda.

5.30am–noon, 4–8pm

 Accommodation

CHENNAI

Vivanta by Taj – Connemara — Heritage Hotel ₹₹₹
☏ 044 66000000; www.vivantabytaj.com; Binny Rd; d from ₹13,000 The Taj group has four hotels in and around Chennai but this is the only one with historical ambience, built in the 1850s as the British governor's residence. There's a beautiful pool in the tropical garden, and even the small rooms are large and comfortable.

Park Hotel — Boutique Hotel ₹₹₹
☏ 044 42676000; www.theparkhotels.com; 601 Anna Salai; d ₹13,000–17,000, ste from ₹19,000 This super-stylish large boutique hotel, flaunts design everywhere you look, from the bamboo, steel and gold cushions of the towering lobby to the posters from classic South Indian movies shot in Gemini Studios, the previous incarnation of the hotel site. Rooms have lovely bedding, and stylish touches including glass-walled bathrooms. It's all swish, and that goes for the three restaurants, large open-air pool and luxurious spa as well.

Raintree — Hotel ₹₹₹
☏ 044 24304050; www.raintreehotels.com; 120 St Mary's Rd, Alwarpet; d ₹11,000–13,000 (incl of breakfast) At this 'eco-sensitive' hotel, floors are made of bamboo or rubber, water and electricity conservation hold pride of place, and the heat generated by the AC warms the bathroom water. The sleek, minimalist rooms are stylish and comfortable, and the rooftop has a sea-view infinity pool (which doubles as insulation) as well as a restaurant.

Footprint B&B — B&B ₹₹
☏ 9840037483; www.chennaibedand breakfast.com; Gayatri Apartments, 16 South St, Alwarpet; r from ₹4000 (incl of breakfast) This B&B is located in a quiet street in a leafy neighbourhood. Bowls of pretty flowers and old-Madras drawings set the scene. The nine cosy, spotless rooms have king-size or wide twin beds. Breakfasts (Western or Indian) are generous, wi-fi is free and the hospitable owners can tell you all you need to make the most of your time. Phone or email in advance; walk-ins are discouraged.

Lotus — Hotel ₹₹
☏ 044 28157272; www.thelotus.in; 15 Venkatraman St, T Nagar; d ₹3000–4000 (incl of breakfast) An absolute gem, this hotel offers a quiet setting away from the main roads, a good veg restaurant, and fresh, stylish rooms with wooden floors and cheerful decor.

YWCA International Guest House — Guesthouse ₹
☏ 044 25324234; 1086 Poonamallee High Rd; d ₹1000–1500 (incl of breakfast) The YWCA guesthouse, set

CHENNAI & AROUND

MGM Eastwoods is a boutique property with modern touches

in green and shady grounds, offers a calm atmosphere and exceptionally good value. Run efficiently by an amiable staff, it provides good-sized, impeccably clean rooms, spacious common areas and good-value meals (₹150/225 for veg/non veg).

EAST COAST ROAD

Radisson Blu — Luxury Hotel ₹₹₹
044 27443636; www.radissonblu.com/hotel-mamallapuram; 57 Covelong Rd; d ₹10,000–40,000 Radisson's chalets and villas tease the limits of luxury. A few villas come with private pools and jacuzzis. The restaurant dishes up pastas, grills, tandoor and seafood. Contact their activity co-ordinators for dance classes, a golf session or a ticklish fish spa experience.

Vivanta by Taj – Fisherman's Cove — Luxury Resort ₹₹₹
044 6741 3333; www.vivantabytaj.com; Covelong Beach, Kanchipuram Dist; d ₹15,000–20,000 This resort on the beach is set apart by its quiet elegance and class. The garden cottages and sea-facing villas are truly inviting. Out of the four restaurants here, Bay View dishes up good seafood and is crowded all the time. The resort also offers catamaran rides for an adventure over the waves.

MGM Hotels and Resorts — Resort ₹₹
044 39102400; www.mgmhotels.com; Muttukkadu, ECR; d ₹4500–15,000 The villas and deluxe rooms exude rustic chic and modernity and their lawns overlook impressive vistas of the sea. Here three adults can stay in one room with extra bedding on request. Multi-cuisine buffets and barbeques (Friday dinner, Saturday & Sunday lunch and dinner) draw many people.

TTDC Beach Resort Complex — Resort ₹₹
044 27442361; www.ttdconline.com; ECR, next to IOC petrol bunk; d ₹2500–3500 The TTDC resort comes as a good bargain down this road. All their cottages are basic, intimate and face the sea. They charge ₹600 extra for children above five years of age. The restaurant serves good food and the resort is definitely value for money.

MGM Eastwoods　　　Resort ₹₹
☏044 24490770; www.mgmhotels.com, Injambakkam, ECR; d ₹3200–3500 (incl of breakfast) With 20 chic and well-appointed rooms, a 24-hour restaurant and polite staff, MGM Eastwoods attracts the young, well-heeled crowd.

KANCHIPURAM
GRT Regency　　　Hotel ₹₹
☏044 27225250; www.grthotels.com; 487 Gandhi Rd; d ₹3500 (incl of breakfast) The GRT has the cleanest and most comfortable rooms you'll find in Kanchipuram. The hotel's restaurant, Dakshin is a tad over-priced but offers a big breakfast buffet spread and good seafood and tandoori dishes for other meals.

Sree Sakthi Residency　　　Hotel ₹
☏044 27233799; www.sreesakthiresidency.com; 71 Nellukara St; d ₹1559 Simple wood furniture and coloured walls make the rooms fairly modern, and they are clean. The Sangeetha Restaurant here serves good vegetarian food.

🍴 Eating
Chennai is packed with inexpensive 'meals' joints, serving thalis, idlis and dosas. In the Muslim area around Triplicane High Road, you'll find good biryani joints every few steps. There are also many upmarket restaurants.

CHENNAI
Raintree　　　Chettinadu ₹₹₹
☏044 66000000; www.vivantabytaj.com; Vivanta by Taj – Connemara, Binny Rd; mains ₹475–700; 12.30–2.45pm, 7.30–11.40pm This is probably the best place in Chennai to savour the delicious and spicy Chettinadu cuisine. When the weather is good sit out in the courtyard.

Dakshin　　　South Indian ₹₹₹
☏044 24994101 Sheraton Park Hotel, 132 TTK Rd, Alwarpet; mains ₹550–900; 12.30–2.45pm, 7–11.15pm Dakshin offers cuisines from all four southern states. Traditional sculptures set the scene, and musicians play each night except on Mondays. Try the Andhra fish curry.

Copper Chimney　　　North Indian ₹₹₹
☏044 28115770; 74 Cathedral Rd, Gopalapuram; mains ₹200–575; noon–3pm, 7–11.30pm This is the

Chettinadu food is widely available across Chennai

> *If You Like:* Sweets, kaaram & kaapi
>
> Chennai has a sweet tooth and is fastidious about it. The tiffin, a combination of sweet and kaaram (salty snacks), washed down with filter coffee, is a hit anytime of the day.
>
> • **The Grand Sweets and Snacks** (044 24914213; www.grandsweets.com; 2nd Main Rd, Gandhi Nagar Adyar): Excellent for traditional south Indian sweets, savouries, crunchy snacks, chutneys and pickles. The restaurant serves piping hot vegetarian south Indian tiffin too.
>
> • **Sri Krishna Sweets** (044 243112324/5; www.srikrishnasweets.com; 2&3 Prakasam Rd, Panagal Park, T Nagar): Their Mysorepak (sweet made of gram flour, ghee and sugar) is to die for. It has branches all over the city. The Purasawalkam branch is in a renovated 120-year old house.
>
> • **Adyar Ananda Bhavan Sweets & Snacks** (044 23453045; www.aabsweets. in; 9 MG Rd, Shastri Nagar, Adyar): This is a popular sweets, savouries and tiffin eatery with over 52 branches.

place to go if you're craving for yummy north Indian tandoori dishes that are served in stylishly minimalist surroundings. The fish tikka is superb.

Annalakshmi — Indian ₹₹
044 28525109; www.annalakshmichen-nai.co.in; 1st fl, Sigapi Achi Bldg, 18/3 Rukmani Lakshmipathy Rd; mains ₹180–240, set/buffet lunch ₹575/400; noon–3pm, 7–9pm This place serves fine south and north Indian vegetarian fare in a beautiful dining room adorned with carvings and paintings, inside a high-rise. The buffet option is served in another part of the same premises.

Kumarakom — Kerala ₹₹
044 42034203; www.kumarakomrestaurant.com; 9 Kodambakkam High Rd; mains ₹75-300; noon–4pm, 6.30–11pm You may have to stand in a queue for a table at this popular restaurant done up with dark-wood furniture. The seafood is quite good. Try the prawns masala or karimeen pollichatthu (pearl-spot fish marinated and steamed in a banana leaf).

Hotel Saravana Bhavan — Vegetarian ₹
044 28192055; www.saravanabhavan.com; 21 Kennet Lane; mains ₹60–150; 6am–10pm Delicious lunch and evening south Indian thali meals at the Saravana Bhavans are available from ₹80 to ₹100. This famous Chennai vegetarian chain is also excellent for south Indian breakfasts – idlis and vadas, ice creams, filter coffee and other Indian vegetarian fare including biryanis and pulaos. They have several branches across the city.

Ratna Cafe — South Indian ₹
☎ 9150149001; 255 Triplicane High Rd; mains ₹25–70; 6am–10.30pm

Though often crowded and cramped, Ratna is renowned for its scrumptious idlis and the hearty doses of sambhar that go with it. People come for this dish throughout the day.

Murugan Idli Shop — South Indian ₹
☎ 044 28155462; www.muruganidlishop.com; 77 GN Chetty Rd, T Nagar; mains ₹25–75; 7am–11.30pm

Those in the know generally agree this particular branch of the small chain serves some of the best idlis and south Indian meals in town. We heartily concur.

EAST COAST ROAD

New Town Restaurant & Cafe — Malaysian/Fusion ₹₹₹
☎ 9176066866; 363 Injambakkam; 11am–11pm

Choose from veg/non-veg wraps, or a mezze platter from their fusion menu. Nasi goreng, dry pan mee for a veg option and roti canai curry are some of the dishes to try.

Food Village — Multi-Cuisine ₹₹₹
☎ 044 24493309; 2/161, Injambakkam; 11am–11pm

You can enjoy the quiet ambience of the place if you ignore the mosquitoes under the leafy canopies where the tables are laid out. It offers Kerala vegetarian and non-vegetarian combos, a variety of Lucknowi kebabs and tandoori platters as well.

ECR Dhaba — Chinese/North Indian ₹₹
☎ 044 27472943; 9/76 Kunnukadu, next to Muttukadu Boat House, ECR; 11am–11pm

This dhaba is popular on ECR. The kids can meet the resident cat, emu and pigeons. The dhaba serves regular Chinese and north Indian cuisine.

Madurai Appu — Multi-Cuisine ₹
☎ 044 24490077; www.maduraiappu.com; 2/222, 2nd Avenue, Vettuvankani; noon–11pm

From Chinese to Chettinadu, Madurai Appu offers many cuisines. Choose from their dum biryani, tandoori tangri kebab to Chettinadu non-vegetarian staples and you won't be disappointed. They have branches all over Chennai

 Nightlife

CHENNAI

Zara the Tapas Bar — Bar
☎ 044 28111462; www.zaratapasbar.in; 71 Cathedral Rd; cocktails ₹400–500, tapas ₹225–375; 12.30–3pm, 6.30pm–midnight

Where else in the world would you find DJs playing club music beneath bullfight posters next to TVs showing cricket? Zara is packed on most nights. There's a small space to dance, but most of the acreage is occupied by tables, and it's a good idea to reserve one. And the tapas? The jamon serrano is sacrilegiously minced into a paste, but the tortilla española is authentically good.

Leather Bar — Bar
☎044 42676000; Park Hotel, 601 Anna Salai; 11am–4am This tiny, modish pad has mixologists serving up fancy drinks and DJs spinning dance tunes from around 9pm. How half of Chennai fits into it on Friday and Saturday nights is a mystery.

Dublin — Pub/Nightclub
☎044 24994101; Sheraton Park Hotel, 132 TTK RD, Alwarpet; from 6pm Wed–Sat This Irish pub and nightclub has three levels of dancing and music from hip hop to Bollywood. Until 10pm it's a pub, then it becomes a club, alive till 2am or 3am on Saturday nights.

10 Downing Street — Pub
☎044 43546565; North Boag Rd, T Nagar; noon–midnight An English-themed pub with a small dance floor, 10D is often packed. Wednesday is Ladies' Night, Friday is Retro Night (70s–80s) and Saturday is Club Night.

Activities

KANCHIPURAM
Kanchipuram Ride
Rural Institute for Development Education; ☎044 27268223; www.rideindia.org; 48 Periyar Nagar, Little Kanchipuram RIDE offers fascinating tours (half/full day ₹600/900 per person incl lunch) covering themes from silk weaving and temples to a Tamil cookery class with market visit.

Entertainment

CHENNAI
There's a Bharatanatyam or Carnatic music concert going on somewhere in Chennai almost every evening. Check listings in *The Hindu* or *The Times of India*, or the website www.timescity.com/chennai. The Music Academy (☎044 28112231; www.musicacademy madras.in; 168, old 306, TTK Rd, Royapettah) is the most popular venue; the Kalakshetra Foundation and Bharatiya Vidya Bhavan (☎044 24643420; www.bhavanchen-nai.org; East Mada St, Mylapore) also stages many events.

Shopping

CHENNAI
T Nagar has great shopping for silks, especially at Pondy Bazaar and around Panagal Park. Nungambakkam's Khader Nawaz Khan Road is a pleasant lane of

The famous and colourful silk saris of Kanchipuram are a must-buy in the town

designer shops, cafes and galleries and there are plenty of malls across the city.

Srushti — Handicrafts
☏ 044 42060730; www.srushtihandicrafts.com; 86 Chamiers Rd, Alwarpet; 10.30am–8.30pm This is an artisan outlet with a good collection of bronze and wooden sculptures.

Poompuhar — Handicrafts
108 Anna Salai; 10am–8pm Mon–Sat, 11am–7pm Sun This large branch of the fixed-price state government handicrafts chain is good for everything from cheap technicolour plaster deities to a ₹200,000, 1m-high bronze Nataraja.

Nalli Silks — Silks/Textiles
www.nalli.com; 9 Nageswara Rd, T Nagar; 9.30am–9.30pm The huge, super colourful granddaddy of silk shops, with a jewellery branch next door is a must-visit if you're looking for traditional silk saris.

Rasi Silk House — Silks/Textiles/Handicrafts
☏ 044 24641906; www.rasisilks.com; 1 Sannadhi St, Mylapore This silk shop (formerly Radha Silk Emporium) is over a century old and is located near the entrance of the Kapaleeshwarar temple. It has a good selection of silk saris and cotton saris not just from Tamil Nadu, but across South India and also has an adjoining shop for handcrafts, Tanjore paintings, Salem woodcuts and gift tables.

Sukra — Jewellery
☏ 044 24640699; www.sukra.com; 72 North Mada St, Mylapore; Mon–Sat 10am–8pm Sun closed From traditional and heavy temple costume jewellery for dancers to small and elegant pieces for evening wear and silver objects and jewellery you'll get it all here.

Higginbothams — Books
116 Anna Salai; 9am–8pm Mon–Sat 10.30am–7.30pm Sun If you're fond of books make your way to Higginbothams that is reckoned to be India's oldest bookshop. It opened in 1844 and has a decent collection of books of all genres.

KANCHIPURAM
Shopping in Kanchipuram is only about silk saris. Across the city there are over 100 shops, big and small, state-authorised and private or cooperative society run shops that sell silk saris and cottons. Choose the bigger shops or government affiliated ones if you want a genuine silk sari. Gandhi Road has a line of silk shops on either side of the road and it's best to take a walk at leisure, hopping into one shop after another.

Expert Recommendation
Tamil Nadu's cultural calendar

Dr Srinidhi Chidambaram is a seasoned Bharatanatyam performer and participates in the cultural fests of Tamil Nadu. Here are her top picks.

- **Music Festivals:** The annual **December Season** (www.kutcheribuzz.com; December–January) is the largest congregation of over 600 South Indian classical music and dance performances in one city, held over a period of two months. Carnatic musicians, classical dancers and connoisseurs gather to partake in these cultural festivities, seminars and debates. Be prepared to listen to the saxophone or the guitar set to Carnatic rhythms too. **The Park New Festival** (www.theparknewfestival.com) annually brings contemporary, avant garde work in dance, music, theatre, poetry and more. This is contemporary culture with a twist.

- **Dance Festivals:** The **Natyanjali Festival** is held during MahaShivarathri in February in Chidambaram; the **Mamallapuram Dance Festival** and **Kalakshetra Dance Festival** (www.kalakshetra.net) are both held from December–January.

- **Thiruvaiyaru Thyagaraja Aradhana** (www.thiruvaiyaruthyagarajaaradhana.org): On the banks of the River Kaveri this annual five-day fest is homage to the patron saint of Carnatic music at Thiruvaiyaru.

- **Literary Fests:** The **Poetry Festival** (www.poetrywithprakriti.in; December–January) of reading and sharing by poets and enthusiasts from various language backgrounds and the **The Hindu Lit for Life Fest** (wwwthehinulfl.com), a literary conclave of writers, readers and booklovers make much ado about the written word.

Dr Srinidhi Chidambaram is a renowned Bharatanatyam dancer

Mamallapuram & Puducherry

At Mamallapuram, a World Heritage Site, ancient temples and timeless sculptures stand alongside modern resorts and beachcombers. Not too far is the Union Territory of Puducherry, one of the few places in the country that offers a slice of India's French colonial past. Another face of Puducherry is the Aurobindo Ashram that colours much of the city's personality.

Trip Planner

GETTING THERE

Mamallapuram: The Anna International airport and domestic Kamaraj terminal in Chennai is 50km away. Chennai has two railway stations and is well-connected to all metros. Mamallapuram is 55km from Chennai Central railway station. Take the East Coast Road, SH49, from Chennai.

Puducherry: The closest airport is in Chennai (150km). The railway station at Puducherry has a few trains from Bengaluru and Chennai. Taxis from Chennai airport cost ₹3000–3500.

SUGGESTED ITINERARY (6 DAYS)

Start your trip by spending a couple of days in Mamallapuram. Two days will go by quickly as you'll spend most of your time exploring the temples, mandapams and rock carvings. After this drive to Puducherry (100km) which promises a serene seaside break. A slice of French colonial history and Tamil heritage make this town unique. Take two days to visit the promenade, monuments, Sri Aurobindo Ashram and beaches. Keep the last couple of days to visit Auroville, the Natraja Temple in Chidamabram and Tranquebar.

BEST TIME TO GO

J F M A M J J A S **O N D**

GREAT FOR

Top 5 highlights

- **Shore Temple, Mamallapuram** (p318)
- **Mandapams, Mamallapuram** (p320)
- **Sri Aurobindo Ashram, Puducherry** (p321)
- **Churches of Puducherry** (p322)
- **Natraja Temple, Chidambaram** (p325)

Heritage by the Coast

An elephant blesses the pilgrims outside the Mankkula Vinayagar

Mamallapuram (Mahabalipuram) was once a major seaport and an important seat of the Pallava kings. Saunter through the town's great carvings and temples at sunset, when the sandstone turns bonfire orange and blood red, and modern carvers tink-tink with their chisels on the street, firing the imagination. Many travellers make a beeline here straight from Chennai railway station or airport.

In **Puducherry** (Pondicherry) the characteristic cobble-stoned streets, criss-crossing through the French quarter, are still the most feet-and cycle-friendly in India. One will often find tourists with a map in their hand, tracing their way through different 'rues' (roads). The familiar circular area on the map clearly shows the arterial canal which divides the city into Black Town and White Town (French) quarters. The fairly strong French influence here is evident in the high walls, sparse aesthetics and the clean lines of the architecture. This Gallic touch merges rather interestingly with the essential 'kolam' (religious floor designs) seen outside both French and Tamil houses. Stay in the beautiful White Town for an atmospheric break.

Mamallapuram

Highlights
1. Shore Temple
2. Pancha Ratha
3. Arjuna's Penance
4. Ganesha Ratha & Around
5. Mandapams

❶ SHORE TEMPLE
Standing like a magnificent fist of rock-cut elegance overlooking the sea, the Shore Temple symbolises the heights of Pallava architecture and the maritime ambitions of the Pallava kings. Its carvings showcase excellent proportion and supreme quality, though many have been eroded into vaguely impressionist embellishments.

Originally constructed in the 7th century, it was later rebuilt by Narasimhavarman II and houses two central shrines to Shiva. Facing east and west, the original lingam captured the sunrise and sunset. The temple is believed to be the last in a series of buildings that extended along a submerged coastline.

Combined ticket with Five Rathas Indian/foreigner ₹10/250, video ₹25; 6.30am–6pm

❷ PANCHA RATHA
Carved from single pieces of rock, the Pancha Rathas (five chariots) are low-laying monoliths that huddle in ancient subtlety rather than grandeur. Each temple is dedicated to either a Hindu god, or to one of the Pandavas and Draupadi. Outside each ratha is a carving of an animal on which the gods are mounted.

The Shore Temple overlooks the sea

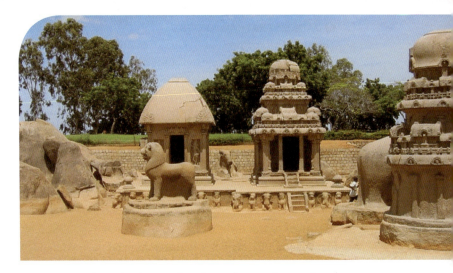

Monoliths at Pancha Ratha are an architectural wonder

Taken together, the theme of God, Pandava and animal mount is remarkable for its architectural consistency, considering that everything here was cut from single chunks of rock. The first ratha as you enter the gate is **Draupadi Ratha**. Behind the shrine of the goddess, a huge Nandi heralds the chariot of Arjuna. Look around the lintels of the middle temple, **Bhima Ratha**, and you'll notice faded faces that some archaeologists believe possess Caucasian features, evidence of Mamallapuram's extensive trade ties with ancient Rome. The final ratha, **Nakula-Sahadeva Ratha**, is dedicated to Indra and has a sculptured elephant standing nearby.
Five Rathas Rd; combined ticket with Shore Temple Indian/ foreigner ₹10/250, video ₹25; 6.30am–6pm

❸ ARJUNA'S PENANCE

This carving is one of the most unpretentious works of ancient India. Inscribed into a huge boulder, the penance bursts with scenes from Hindu myth and everyday vignettes of south Indian life. A herd of elephants marches under armies of celestial beings while Arjuna performs penance. There's humour amid the holy: notice the cat performing penance to a crowd of appreciative mice.
West Raja St

❹ GANESHA RATHA & AROUND

This ratha is northwest of Arjuna's Penance. Once a Shiva temple, it became a shrine to Ganesha after the original lingam was removed. North of the ratha is a huge boulder known as Krishna's Butter Ball. Immovable, but balanced precariously, it's a favourite photo opportunity. The nearby **Kotikal Mandapam** is dedicated to Durga. Close to it is **Varaha Mandapam II**, a cave dominated by an incredible panel of Vishnu's boar avatar. Nearby, the **Trimurti Cave Temple** honours the Hindu trinity – Brahma, Vishnu and Shiva – with a separate section dedicated to each deity.

❺ MANDAPAMS

Mamallapuram's main hill, which dominates the town (and is in turn dominated by a red-and-brownstone lighthouse), makes for an excellent hour or two of low-key hiking. It's also a good spot for enjoying sunsets. Many mandapams are scattered over this low-rise rock, including **Krishna Mandapam**, one of the earliest rock-cut temples in the region. The famous carving depicts both a rural pastiche and Krishna lifting Govardhana mountain to protect his kinsfolk from the wrath of Indra. Other shrines include **Mahisasuramardini Mandapam**, just a few metres southwest of the lighthouse. Scenes from the Puranas are depicted on the mandapam, with the sculpture of goddess Durga considered one of the finest in the country. Above the mandapam are remains of the 8th-century Olakkannesvara Temple, and spectacular views of Mamallapuram.

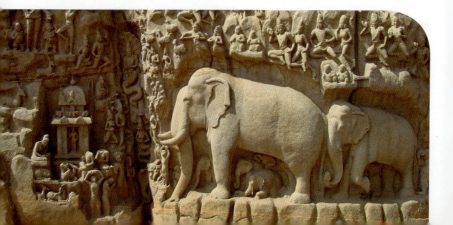

A segment of Arjuna's Penance showcasing elephants

MAMALLAPURAM & PUDUCHERRY

The striking Cathedral of our Lady of the Immaculate Conception

Highlights

1. Sri Aurobindo Ashram
2. Promenade Walk
3. Goubert Avenue
4. Churches of Puducherry
5. Manakkula Vinayagar Koil
6. Government Museum
7. Bharathi Park
8. Chunnambar Boat House
9. Beaches

Puducherry

1 SRI AUROBINDO ASHRAM

Immerse yourself in the serene atmosphere of Aurobindo Ashram, where the flower-covered samadhis of Sri Aurobindo and the Mother are the central attraction for devotees and tourists. A walking path is chalked out for order, while spots are taken by regulars to meditate for a longer time. Founded in 1926, this is where the two spiritual gurus lived.

0413 2233604; www.sriaurobindoashram.org; Francois Martin Str-Manakkula Vinayagar Koil Str; 8am–noon, 2–6pm; children under 3 not allowed; no photography

2 PROMENADE WALK

Puducherry offers a different coastal experience. Instead of shacks serving beer and snacks, you'll come across a long promenade along the sea's rocky edge, with an old jetty in sight. Evenings come alive on Goubert Avenue (Beach Road), with locals and tourists nibbling on local snacks and enjoying the vibrant atmosphere. Benches line the footpath for weary legs, and there is a pleasant break from traffic on this street between 6pm and 7.30am every day.

Goubert Avenue, Beach Rd

Puducherry's rocky beachfront

❸ GOUBERT AVENUE

Puducherry's landmark monuments are located at short intervals on Goubert Avenue, with a **statue of Mahatma Gandhi** at one end and of Marquis Joseph Francois Dupleix (governor of Puducherry between 1742 and 1754) at the other. In between are the **French War Memorial**, the **Old Lighthouse**, statues of Joan of Arc and Jawaharlal Nehru, the **Old Customs House**, and a newly-built **memorial for B.R Ambedkar**. All these are on the right of the street.

❹ CHURCHES OF PUDUCHERRY

There are three important churches in Puducherry. Follow a short trail from the **Eglise de Notre Dame des Anges** (better known as the 'French Church' amongst locals), located on Dumas Street, to the **Cathedral of Our Lady of the Immaculate**

♥ If You Like: Scuba diving

Ron from **Temple Adventures** (☎9789197227; www.templeadventures.com; Colas Nagar; 9am–6.30pm) has started a scuba diving school here. The best season to experience underwater delights is from May to June and from September to October. An introduction to scuba diving can be completed over a weekend, though four days would be ideal.

Top Tip: Getting around the town

- **Grab a map:** Get a map from PTDC office on Goubert Avenue; (9am–5pm); the staff will speedily mark out the important places with rehearsed skill.
- **Rent a two-wheeler:** Rent either a two-wheeler or a cycle on a per-day basis – or longer – from a line of shops on Mission Street to go around Puducherry. You need to leave an original photo id with the owner (this is common practice, so don't be alarmed). J Praja (9894121133, No 106-B Mission Street; cycle/Activa/bike ₹50/200/150 per day).

Conception on Cathedral Street, and finally to the **Church of the Sacred Heart of Jesus** on Subbaiah Salai. All these are known for their masonry and beautiful facades.

❺ MANAKKULA VINAYAGAR KOIL

This more than 300-year-old Ganesha Temple has largely been made famous by Lakshmi the elephant (she was on sick leave when we were there), whose blessings are sought by the many devotees who come from all over the country to visit her. Manoeuvre your way through a lively crowd to pay homage to the depiction of the countless incarnations of this friendly lord.

Manakkula Vinayagar Koil St; shoes ₹1; 5.45am–12.30pm, 4–9.30pm

❻ GOVERNMENT MUSEUM

Housed in a restored century-old villa of a French tradesman (Carvalho), the Government Museum describes a disjointed trajectory of Puducherry's history. This is the only place where you can glimpse the famous Arikamedu excavations. You can also see some artefacts from the Pallava and Chola dynasties, bizarrely juxtaposed with Dupleix's own bed.

₹10, free entry for children; no cameras allowed; 10am–1pm, 2–5pm

Mahatma Gandhi's statue on Goubert Avenue

Bharathi Park is named after the poet

⓻ BHARATHI PARK

Located in the heart of Puducherry and dedicated to the nationalist poet who lived here, this welcome patch of green is a resting spot from the sun. It houses a bright white monument, the Aayi Mandapam, built during the time of Napoleon III.
Victor Simonel St; 6am–9pm

⓼ CHUNNAMBAR BOAT HOUSE

Visit this PTDC-run establishment only if you like boat rides. Avoid the dowdy-looking children's rides and the coffee shop, and head straight to the boarding point. One can take boat rides to the nearby Paradise Island or the backwaters.
7km from Puducherry; adult/child/camera ₹50/25/300; 1.30–6pm

⓽ BEACHES

Though a seaside town, Puducherry is not an ideal beach destination. However, there are a few decent beaches to the north and south of town. Quiet, **Reppo** and **Serenity** Beaches lie north, within 8km of Puducherry. Chunnambar, 8km south, has **Paradise Beach** that offers water sports and backwater boat cruising. Both areas are developing with the opening of high-end resorts.

Around Puducherry

❶ AUROVILLE
About 2200 people from 45 countries inhabit this beachside village and work on projects related to art and culture in tandem with the locals. The Matri Mandir is Auroville's most famous structure. It has an information centre, an open exhibition area, a coffee shop and pavilions. Auroville is about 14km from Puducherry. Rent a two-wheeler, or an autorickshaw for ₹200.
☏ 0413 2622239; www.auroville.org; Visitors Centre; 9.30am–4pm Mon–Sat, 9.30am–12.30pm Sun

> **Highlights**
> ❶ Auroville
> ❷ Chidambaram
> ❸ Tranquebar (Tharangambadi)

❷ CHIDAMBARAM
Located 60km from Puducherry, Chidambaram is a dusty, commercial town that is home to the famous Annamalai University. There is really only one reason to visit Chidambaram – the legendary **Nataraja Temple**. The temple, however, takes Chidambaram to another level, that of a sacred place. 'Chith' means knowledge and 'ambaram' means space. The town is also hailed as the area of cosmic knowledge embodied in the dance of the Nataraja.

The golden dome of the Matri Mandir meditation centre in Auroville

The legendary Nataraja Temple is Chidambaram's main attraction

- **Shrines in the temple:** The Nataraja Temple is unlike any other, as it has both a Shiva and Vishnu shrine in the same complex. Besides its sheer size and grandeur, its architectural and decorative features require time to explore. The Nataraja Temple is also the only Shiva temple in which the deity is not represented by a lingam, but by an elegant, dancing pose of Shiva.
- **Architecture:** The 40-acre complex contains two temples, magnificent gopurams, several tanks, pillared halls and vast praharams. Built by the Cholas around AD 907, the Nataraja Temple's main idols are brilliant examples of Chola bronze sculpture. The temple was later expanded and embellished by several generations of Chola kings. The temple and the deity have been praised in the hymns of the Nayanmars (Saivite saint-poets), including Appar, Sundarar, Sambandhar and Manikkavachagar. The shrine of Nataraja's consort, goddess Shivakamasundari, has some intricately carved pillars and lovely frescoes of scenes from *Devi Mahatmyam* (Tales on Shakti's Power) on the surrounding walls. There is a special and rare sanctum for Chitragupta, the clerk of Lord Yama, who keeps count of the good deeds and sins of mortals.

The vimanam (roof) of Lord Nataraja's sanctum has gilded tiles, crested by nine golden *kalasams*. The front portion of the sanctum is called Kanakasabhai and the inner sanctum is known as Chithsabhai. In the sanctum of Nataraja, numbers rule. From the number of tiles on the roof to the pillars in the sanctum, the maths of the architecture relates to the concept of Shiva, Hindu philosophy and the human body as Ayurveda perceives it. There is a small, crystal lingam in a gold casket which is worshipped with oblations several times a day. There are no electric lights in this sanctum, only oil and ghee lamps illuminate it.

- **Temple tour:** You may need at least half a day to fully explore the temple. Halt by Mukkuruni Vinayagar – the 8ft-tall idol of Ganesha, within the southern tower entrance which is said to answer every prayer.

- **Priests at the temple:** The priests here are known as Dikshitars, a hereditary line of priests who serve Lord Nataraja alone. They look distinctive by the way they tie their hair and wear their clothes.
- **Annual festivals:** Being dedicated to the deity as a cosmic dancer, a dance festival is held annually with classical dancers performing within the precincts of the temple.

❸ TRANQUEBAR (THARANGAMBADI)

Not everyone knows that the Danes were poking around this part of the world well before the French or British. Tranquebar – the 'land of the singing waves' – was established by the Danish East India Company in 1620 as a trading post.

The oldest structure here is the atmospheric **Fort Dansborg**, which today, is home to a fascinating if somewhat moth-eaten museum containing porcelain figurines, crockery, yellowed manuscripts and other relics. The fort affords great views of the sea. Nearby are a couple of churches and the Danish governor's house, which is being renovated into a library.

120km from Puducherry on NH54A; taxi ₹3000-3500; Fort Dansborg entry ₹10, camera fee ₹30, Fri closed

Fort Dansborg by the sea is Tranquebar's oldest structure

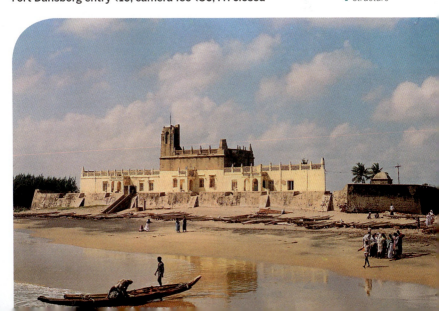

 Accommodation

MAMALLAPURAM

This town has only a few good hotels and resorts. The rest are small hotels and guesthouses offering basic rooms and amenities.

GRT Temple Bay — Resort ₹₹₹
☏ 044 27443636; www.radisson.com/mamallapuramin; Covelong Rd; r ₹8000–9000 (incl of breakfast) This is one of the best luxury resorts in town. It's got everything you need for a relaxing holiday, including a spa, sauna, health club. The rates increase during December/January.

Ideal Beach Resort — Resort ₹₹
☏ 044 27442240; www.idealresort.com; 3.5km north of the town; d ₹5000 This low-key and laid-back beachfront resort 3.5km north of town offers a nice stretch of rooms and cottages located on the beach. It has a landscaped garden and is popular with families. The resort is small and secluded enough to have an intimate atmosphere. There's a lovely poolside restaurant where they sometimes have classical musicians perform.

Hotel Mamalla Heritage — Hotel ₹
☏ 044 27442060; www.hotelmamallaheritage.com; 104 East Raja St; d from ₹2000 This hotel has large, comfortable rooms that come with a mini bar, sparkling bathrooms and the service is friendly. The swimming pool is decent sized, and there's a good rooftop restaurant serving vegetarian food.

Try Residency — Hotel ₹
☏ 044 27442728; 7 Old College Rd; r from ₹800 The rooms aren't too stylish, but they're big and clean. If you need some Western-style amenities, it's not a bad option. There's a wee garden ruled by some ducks and a really tiny pool.

La Vie en Rose — Hotel ₹
☏ 9444877544; East Raja St; d from ₹450 This hotel has its basics in place – simple, decent-sized and clean rooms, friendly staff and a restaurant offering French dishes.

Hotel Sea Breeze — Hotel ₹
☏ 044 27443035; www.hotelseabreeze.net; Othavadai Cross St; r from ₹900 (incl of breakfast)

Le Closerie is a cosy hotel with just five rooms and a natural pool

This is a good beachfront hotel, but the real draw is the swimming pool, which non guests can use for ₹150.

PUDUCHERRY

Villa Shanti   Hotel ₹₹₹
☏ 0413 4200028; www.lavillashanti.com; 14 Rue Suffren; d ₹7000–11,000 (incl of full board) With its high ceilings, white walls and simple wooden furniture, the minimalist furnishings of this recently-launched luxury hotel echo the architecture of the French buildings here. The staff is pleasant and professional. Ideal for those who want a private stay.

Maison Perumal   Heritage Hotel ₹₹
☏ 4843011711 (central reservation); No 44 (old No 58) Perumal St; d from ₹4730 (incl of full board) Built in 1900, this Indo–French heritage hotel, a former Tamil home, has 10 intimate rooms. The central courtyard and verandah in front exhibit the building's Hindu lineage, while the high roofs and minimalistic wooden doors have a French feel to them. The Maison Perumal has a warm and friendly air.

La Closerie   Hotel ₹₹
☏ 0413 4200573; www.lacloseriepondichery.com; 32 Dumas St; d ₹3000–4000 (incl of full board) Plush but reasonably priced, this home-run hotel on Dumas Street has five attractively-furnished rooms. With plenty of refurbished old wooden furniture, a lush garden and a narrow, natural pool in the centre, you are going to enjoy your peaceful time here.

Ajantha Sea View Hotel   Hotel ₹₹
☏ 0413 2349032; www.ajanthaseaviewhotel.com; 50 Goubert Avenue, Beach Rd; d ₹3500–4000 (incl of full board) Ajantha boasts Puducherry's most prestigious address – a sea-facing view on Goubert Street. However, issues over the ownership of the building have left the hotel with only four rooms, besides a bar, ice cream shop and restaurant. Don't expect the ambience of the town's other hotels.

La Maison Tamoule   Heritage Hotel ₹₹
☏ 0413 2223738; la-maison-tamoule.neemranahotels.com; New No 44 (old No 36), Vysial St; d ₹4000–5000 (incl of breakfast) Run by the Neemrana Group, the decently-priced rooms have bright cotton furnishings, copper bath tubs and period wooden furniture. Just a little bit of light filters in through the central courtyard, so take a room on the second floor for access to a sunny roof. One room on the ground floor is for the disabled.

The Richmond   Hotel ₹₹
☏ 0413 2346363; www.therichmond-pondicherry.com; 12, Labourdonnais St; d ₹4296–6445 (incl of breakfast) The Richmond offers economical rooms and plenty of package deals, including complimentary nights,

discount on Ayurvedic massages and free ironing. This hotel, which lies at the edge of the White Town, also has a restaurant and bar.

Hotel De L'Orient   Heritage Hotel ₹₹
☏ 0413 2343067; www.neemranahotels.com; 17 Rue Romain Rolland; r ₹3500–7500 (incl of breakfast) This 1760s renovated mansion presents a plush stay in typical Neemrana style – a small number of rooms with lush furnishings, and a historic hook. The rooms overlook a courtyard restaurant which comes alive in the evenings. All 16 rooms are named after French territories, and are well equipped with large sitting areas and plenty of art.

The Promenade   Hotel ₹₹
☏ 0413 2227750; www.sarovarhotels.com; 23 Goubert Avenue; d ₹5000–8000 (incl of full board) This sea-facing hotel on Goubert Avenue is perfect for families as it has all the amenities of a large hotel. Two restaurants, a 24-hour cafe and a large buffet spread invite a steady stream of guests (which may not be appreciated by those who are looking for privacy). Room numbers 16, 17, 20 and 21 are recommended for families as they are spacious.

L'Escale   Guesthouse ₹
☏ 0413 2222562; www.lescalepondicherry.com; No 31 Dumas St; d ₹1600–2500 Narrow and steep steps from the street open out into a bright lounge and breakfast area on the rooftop, decidedly the most charming part of this warmly-run guesthouse. Immaculately furnished rooms, framed photographs of Puducherry's history, bikes on hire, and the welcoming hosts, all go a long way towards making your stay here a wonderful one.

Mango Hill   Hotel ₹
☏ 9597891966; www.hotel-mangohill-pondicherry.com; Old Auroville Rd, Bommayapalayam; d ₹2500–3800 Mango Hill is ideal for those seeking a relaxing place away from Puducherry town. It has a pool, Ayurvedic spa (though not highly recommended) and a restaurant. Suitable for families and large groups. The place gets busy on weekends and lone travellers and couples may not appreciate the high-activity environment. The Italian and French cheeses (stored in a cellar), are worth sampling here.

Les Hibiscus   Guesthouse ₹
☏ 0413 2227480; www.leshibiscus.in; 49 Rue Suffren; d ₹2500 (incl of full board) Tanjore paintings, incense-doused Ganeshas and other Indian artefacts fit perfectly into this old colonial house in the middle of White Town. With just four rooms, owners Bascarane and Gladys, ensure that the property maintains its quiet and hospitable charm.

CHIDAMBARAM

Hotel Saradharam — Hotel ₹
014144 221366; www.hotelsaradharam.co.in; 19 VGP St; r ₹990, with AC ₹2100 (incl of breakfast) This hotel is a bit worn, but comfortable enough, and a welcome respite from the frenzy of the town centre. For breakfast the hotel lays out a good buffet spread. The hotel has two restaurants – Geethanjali, which is vegetarian and Anupallavi, the multi-cuisine restaurant.

Hotel Akshaya — Hotel ₹
014144 220192; www.hotel-akshaya.com; 17-18 East Car St; r ₹1090, with AC ₹2050–2400 (incl of breakfast) Located close to the temple, this hotel offers a decent selection of rooms. A few non-AC rooms are in better condition than the ones with ACs. The Annapoorani Restaurant does a good south Indian lunch (₹75) and has good veg fare.

TRANQUEBAR

The Bungalow on the Beach — Hotel ₹₹
04364 288065; www.bungalow-on-the-beach.neemranahotels.com; 24 King St, Tharangambadi, Distt Nagapattinam; d ₹3000—6000 (incl of breakfast; 20% discount from Apr–Jul) This is a Neemrana heritage property just across the fort. There are eight rooms in the beautifully renovated former British collector's house. Airy verandahs offer superb sea views.

Eating

MAMALLAPURAM

Restaurateurs near Othavadai Cross Street provide an open-air ambience, decent Western mains and bland Indian curries. If you want authentic Indian food, there are good and cheap vegetarian places and biryani joints near the bus stand. Most places – licensed or not – serve beer, but be sensitive to the 11pm local curfew; if you persuade a restaurant to allow you to linger over drinks, it's the owner, not you, who faces a hefty fine.

Gecko Cafe — Multi-Cuisine ₹
9840734229; www.gecko-web.com; No. 14 Othavadai Cross St; 7am–10pm Two friendly brothers run this cute little spot on a thatch-covered rooftop above the family home. They serve Indian, European and delicious seafood. Mains come

The rooftop Gecko Cafe serves a range of reasonably priced dishes for as low as ₹100–200. The menu choices and prices aren't that different to other tourist-oriented spots, but there's more love put into the cooking here, and the decor is fun: we liked the wall of goddesses, with Lakshmi hanging next to the Virgin and Child.

Le Yogi — Multi-Cuisine ₹
Othavadai St This restaurant serves some of the best western food in town; the steaks, pastas and pizzas are authentic and tasty. You can have a small meal for ₹90–160. The service is good, and the airy dining area, done up with wooden accents and flickering candlelight, is romantic.

Rose Garden — Hyderabadi ₹
Beach Rd Mamallapuram is full of small restaurants serving biryani and Rose Garden is among the better ones. It serves this tasty Hyderabadi rice dish from just ₹50 onwards.

Freshly 'N Hot — Cafe ₹
☎ 044 27443644; **Othavadai Cross St** This cafe does justice when it comes to food. It has a small menu of tasty pizzas, pastas and sandwiches, and offers a range of hot and cold coffees. Don't leave without trying the delicious ice coffees.

Moonrakers — Multi-Cuisine ₹
☎ 044 27442115; www.moonrakersrestaurants.com; **34 Othavadai St** Popular with visitors from Chennai and usually packed on weekend evenings, this place serves seafood, south and north Indian and a few Italian dishes as well. Sit at the top-floor verandah as you sip your beer and nibble a few snacks.

Filter coffee is available at most places in Mamallapuram and Puducherry

PUDUCHERRY

Madame Shanthes — Multi-Cuisine ₹₹
☎ 0413 2222022; **40-A, Rue Romain Rolland; noon–10pm** Rooftop cafe and restaurant, Madame Shanthes is centrally located on Romain Rolland street. Evenings are breezy and relaxed with English retro music playing in the background as the speedy and polite waiters flit around serving great continental dishes. The seafood here is particularly popular. The alcohol choice is limited.

Rendezvous Cafe Restaurant — Multi-Cuisine ₹₹₹
☎ 0413 2339132; **No 30 Rue Suffren; noon–3pm, 6.30–10pm, Tue closed** This popular establishment now

MAMALLAPURAM & PUDUCHERRY

stands in its new avatar, minus the rooftop that many loved. Despite the structural change, Rendezvous still dishes out great seafood. The fish/chicken/mutton and rice combinations are scrumptious and reasonably priced too.

Le Cafe — Cafe ₹₹
Goubert Avenue; 24 hours A historic address on Goubert Avenue, this used to be the old port of Puducherry. The great view of the sea, beach and promenade make up for the slow and disinterested service of this government-run establishment. The chocolate cake and fries here are exceptionally good.

Le Vietnam — Vietnamese & French ₹₹₹
0413 2340111; No 6 Bussy St; 11pm–11pm The novel blend of Vietnamese and French cuisine is far from peculiar (strains of Vietnamese and French music alternate through the day). The ambience is predominantly Vietnamese, with paintings from the East adorning the walls and chopsticks placed on the table, ready for digging into typical preparations like Pho Bo and Chaiyo.

La Terrasse — Continental ₹₹
0413 2220809; No 3 Subbiah Salai; 8.30am–10pm Visit the green and airy La Terrasse for an impressive choice of salads and a continental spread, served in a space resembling a covered garden. The restaurant also has a good selection of fresh juices through the day.

Surguru Spot — Indian ₹₹
0413 4308084; No 12 Jawaharlal Nehru Street; 6.30am–10.30pm The Surguru chain is hugely popular with both Indians and foreigners. Here, you'll get value for money, prompt service and a delicious Indian spread. Visit Surguru for a delightful south Indian breakfast. A busy, no-frills outlet of the same name is located on Mission Street.

Satsanga — Multi-Cuisine ₹₹
00413–2225867; 30–32 Labourdonnais St This popular garden spot serves excellent continental cuisine and has an Indian menu as well. The large variety of sausages, pate and lovely, homemade bread and butter are quite nice and so are the steaks.

✓ Top Tip: Surfing in the south

Surfing as a beach activity is gaining popularity in many parts of South India and surfing schools are also located along the coasts. Popular surfing spots in the south include Kodibengre near Manipal in Karnataka, Varkala, Kovalam in Kerala, Mamallapuram and Manapadu in Tamil Nadu and also Puducherry. Vizag and its big waves is a draw up the Coromandel Coast.

A variety of sculptures are available at Mamallapuram

Nightlife

PUDUCHERRY

Le Club — Club
0413 2227409; 38 Dumas St; 8.30am–11pm One of the most famous restaurants in Puducherry, Le Club is needlessly over priced when it comes to food, but boasts great ambience for a few drinks. With plenty of brands to select from, enjoy this breezy garden.

Asian House — Club
0413 2226139; 7 Beach Boulevard (South); entry with cover charge single/couple ₹700/1000 If you want to shake a leg in Puducherry, there is no better place than Asian House. Loud electronica and dance music and hysterical outbursts can be heard in unison on Saturday nights up to 11pm. The club also invites stags, so hang around with familiar groups.

Activities

PUDUCHERRY

Surf Lessons at Kallialay
9442992874; www.surfschoolindia.com; Bodhi Beach Cafe; 10am–6pm Take beginner to advanced-level surfing lessons on Bodhi beach (near a small fishing village called Tandryankupam) from the enthusiastic duo of brothers, Juan and Samai. On-beach classes are followed by personal or group instructions at the shallow end of the sea. Fee (₹800 onwards) includes rash vest and surfboard. It's essential to know how to swim. Bring your own towel and sunscreen.

INTACH (Indian National Trust for Art and Cultural Heritage) Pondicherry Walks
0413 2225991; www.intachpondicherry.org; 62 Rue Aurobindo St; 9.30am–1pm, 2–6.30pm, Sat closed INTACH organises various guided walks. The walks help one understand the nuances of the architecture and the social fabric of Puducherry, a fascinating blend of Tamilians, French, Christians and Muslims. Prior booking is advised.

Kerala Ayurveda — Spa
0413 6453434; No 27 Muthumariamman Koil St; 9am–7pm Though not an elaborate luxury establishment, one can get reasonably-priced massages (₹1000

onwards), ideal for weary travellers. Abhyangam, Shirodhana and head-and-shoulders massage are the non-clinical, short-duration treatments that you can choose from here.

Shopping

MAMALLAPURAM

Sculptures   Stoneware/Antiques

Mamallapuram wakes to the sound of sculptors' chisels on granite, and you'll inevitably be approached by someone trying to sell you everything from a ₹100 stone pendant to a ₹400,000 Ganesha. There are many art galleries and antique shops here. Nice prints, cards and original art can be found at **Shriji Art Gallery** (11/1 Othavadai St) and beautiful curios culled from local homes at **Southern Arts and Crafts** (044 27443675; www.southernarts.in; 72 East Raja St).

PUDUCHERRY

Auroboutique   Handicrafts

0413 2233705; 12-AJ Nehru St; 9.30am–1pm, 4–7.30pm, Tues closed

Handmade paper products, aromatic candles, incense, soaps and perfumes, crafted by small-scale industries run by the Aurobindo Ashram, are displayed in this small boutique shop.

Nirvana Boutique   Boutique

0413 4209610; 28 Rue Dumas; 10am–1pm, 2–7pm, Sun closed

Amongst many kitsch product shops, this one offers unique Royal Enfield T-shirts and fridge magnets. Colourful bags, cushions and other bric-a-bracs are in plenty.

Via Pondicherry   Boutique

0413 2223319; 22 Romain Rolland St; 9am–1pm, 3–8pm, Sun closed

Designer Vasanty Manet's creations (mostly bags, scarves and clothes) sit cosily at Via Pondicherry on Romain Rolland. The staff here is helpful and offers constructive guidance while you browse through the items.

Sri Aurobindo   Handmade Paper

0413 2334763; 50 SV Patel Salai; 9am–5.30pm Mon–Sat, 10am–1pm Sun One of the small-scale industries that have flourished under the Aurobindo Ashram, it employs many locals. The workshop is open for visitors and also has an elaborate shop with beautiful paper products.

Detour: Arikamedu

Arikamedu is a 1940s excavation site just outside Puducherry. Having created active interest among renowned historians, Arikamedu threw up evidence of being a major port in the Chola Kingdom, which traded with the Romans. It is said to have been in existence before the 1st century. The Pondicherry Museum has a few exhibits related to Arikamedu.

Thanjavur & Kumbakonam

A visit to Thanjavur and the Kaveri delta area is a must if you wish to understand Tamil culture. This is where it all started: the music, dance, temlple architecture, paintings, sculptures, literature and a lifestyle that was based on agricultural prosperity. Neighbouring Kumbakonam has around 188 temples that will demand a two-day stay for a temple tour.

Trip Planner

GETTING THERE

Thanjavur: The closest airport is Tiruchirappalli (50km) which has daily flights from Chennai. From Thanjavur Junction daily trains run to Chennai, Tiruchirappalli, Rameswaram, Bengaluru, and other cities. Private buses ply from Chennai, Tiruchirappalli, Chidambaram and Madurai.

Kumbakonam: This town is 40km from Thanjavur and 100km from Tiruchirappalli airport. Kumbakonam railway station is connected via daily trains to major cities and towns.

SUGGESTED ITINERARY (4 DAYS)

Spend the first day visiting the temples and monuments in the town. The next day you can visit the surrounding areas. After this make your way to Kumbakonam. Even though it is a small town you can spend two days on a temple trail.

BEST TIME TO GO

J F M A M J J A S O **N D**

GREAT FOR

Top 5 highlights

- **Brihadeeswarar Temple, Thanjavur** (p338)
- **Shivaganga Fort, Thanjavur** (p339)
- **Royal Palace & Museums, Thanjavur** (p340)
- **Swamimalai** (p341)
- **Temple Tour, Kumbakonam** (p340)

Cultural Capital

Thanjavur is one of the major towns in the Delta area and the capital of the district of the same name. At first glance it is like any other bustling, dusty town, but look again and you find signs of its past greatness everywhere. The ruins of forts, palaces and ramparts, the cultural medley of the many communities that live here and the presence of dance and music even in the street displays are testimony to this.

Legend goes that it was named after a demon called Thanjan, who was slayed by Lord Vishnu on the banks of the Kaveri. Prosperity gave the people here the luxury of exploring the finer aspects of life. Once known as the 'rice bowl' of Tamil Nadu, the Kaveri delta is now drying up.

Apart from its fabulous temples **Kumbakonam** has an aura that derives from its antiquity and reputation as a seat of secular and spiritual studies. The acerbic wit of its inhabitants lends an invigorating presence to the town.

Bharatanatyam performances take place regularly at Brihadeeswarar Temple

Highlights

1. Brihadeeswarar Temple
2. Punnainallur Mariamman Temple
3. Bangaru Kamakshiamman Temple
4. Shivaganga Fort
5. Schwartz Church
6. Royal Palace & Museums
7. Saraswathy Mahal Library

Thanjavur

❶ BRIHADEESWARAR TEMPLE

This magnificent Shiva temple is so massive that it's called 'Periya Kovil' or Big Temple. Built in AD 1004 by the greatest of the Chola dynasty emperors Rajaraja Chola I, it's spread over 33,000sq ft. The main sanctum's roof is carved from a single granite block. The vimanam of the sanctum is 13 storeys high and the lingam inside is 12ft tall. It is said that the granite blocks, of which it is mostly built, were rolled up to the site on special ramps all the way from the quarries of Tiruchirappalli, 56 km away. The temple took only six years to build.

In 1987 it was declared a Unesco World Heritage Site. It's got lovely frescoes on the outer walls. To see the temple bathed in orange glow, when it looks the best, try and visit it during sunrise or sunset. In the morning, the tawny granite begins to assert its dominance over the dawn sunshine, and in the evening, the rocks capture a hot palette of reds, oranges, yellows and pinks on the crowning glory of Chola temple architecture.

4km from Thanjavur railway station; 7am–noon, 4–9pm

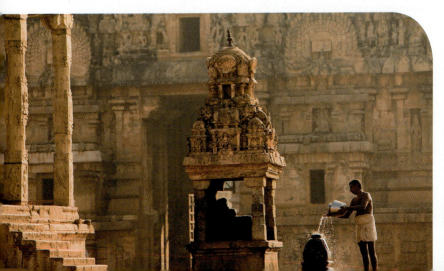

The massive Brihadeeswarar Temple is also known as Big Temple

❷ PUNNAINALLUR MARIAMMAN TEMPLE

A manifestation of goddess Kali, Mariamman is a favourite folk deity in Tamil Nadu. In this temple, built in the 18th century, she is worshipped both in the form of an deity and an ant hill which predates the temple by many years. The goddess is credited with healing powers.

5km from Brihadeeswarar Temple; 6am–8.30pm

The Royal Palace is full of colourful art

❸ BANGARU KAMAKSHIAMMAN TEMPLE

The temple got this name because the idol of goddess Kamakshi is made of pure gold, 'bangaru' in Telugu. The finely adorned deity is credited with granting every righteous wish. It is said to have been brought here from Kanchipuram for safe-keeping during a Muslim invasion and then it remained here.

2km from Brihadeeswarar Temple; 6am–noon, 4–9pm

❹ SHIVAGANGA FORT

Built in the16th century by the Vijayanagar dynasty, the fort encircles the Big Temple, as if to protect it. It was strengthened and modified by the Maratha rulers of Thanjavur in the 17th century. The 35-acre complex includes most of Thanjavur's tourist attractions. Its ramparts remain intact as does the moat, although there is now no water in it. The Shivaganga tank is a large one and the park nearby, though small, is interesting for children as it has a small zoo and play area. The Rajagopala beerangi (cannon) near the eastern gate of the fort, is said to be the biggest one in India.

❻ SCHWARTZ CHURCH

Christian Schwartz, a Danish missionary built this small and simple church in 1779. Although evangelism faced stiff opposition in Thanjavur at the time, he played a mentor's role in the life of King Serfoji II, the Maratha ruler of Thanjavur. A sculpture in the church depicts Schwartz on

⑦ ROYAL PALACE & MUSEUMS

Thanjavur's royal palace is a mixed bag of superb art and random royal paraphernalia. The labyrinthine complex was built by the Vijayanagar kings and later added to by the Maratha rulers. It is still owned and maintained by the descendants of the last Maratha ruler of Thanjavur. Though a little decrepit now, the Rajaraja Museum and Art Gallery inside it are definitely worth a visit; both display the finest of Chola bronzes and stone sculptures.

Indian/foreigner/camera ₹10/50/30; 9am–1pm, 3–6pm

⑧ SARASWATHY MAHAL LIBRARY

Within the palace complex, this ancient library has a huge collection of palm leaf and other rare manuscripts. The library staff has interesting information on how the manuscripts were preserved through the centuries.

10am–1pm, 3–6pm

Kumbakonam

Highlights

① Adi Kumbeswarar Temple
② Mahamaham Tank
③ Nageswarar Temple
④ Sarangapani Temple
⑤ Chakrapani Temple
⑥ Ramaswamy Temple
⑦ River Kaveri
⑧ House Of Srinivasa Ramanujam

① ADI KUMBESWARAR TEMPLE

A sculpturally magnificent Chola temple that dates before the 7th century, it was enlarged by later rulers. The main sanctum has scenes from Hindu mythology in bas relief on the ceiling and the 12 zodiac signs, while the chain links hanging from it are made of stone – a fine example of Chola sculpture. Outside the temple an elephant will bless you with his trunk as you give him a banana or some coins.

The shrine of Kumbeswarar's consort is also spectacular. The four feet tall idol is sheathed in gold plating and stands on a golden base. Devotees seek her blessings to build their homes. In the praharam around the sanctum

Detour: *Thiruvaiyaru & Swamimalai*

- **Thiruvaiyaru:** This small town 13km away, is the birth place of 18th-century Carnatic saint-composer, Thyagaraja. Thiru means 'sacred', ai means 'five'; and aru means 'river'. The town is at the confluence of five rivers and bathing at the Kaveri here is said to be as holy as bathing at Varanasi. The presiding deity at the Shiva temple is also called Panchanatheeswarar or Aiyarappan which means Lord of the Five Rivers.

  Saint Thyagaraja's samadhi on the banks of Kaveri River comes alive during the annual Carnatic music festival every January. Reputed musicians join people in singing Thyagaraja's compositions, creating a special musical experience.

- **Swamimalai:** Located 31km from Thanjavur, this town is famous for its temple of Lord Muruga in his incarnation as Swaminatha, the mentor of Swami or Shiva. The temple commemorates the legend that even as a little boy, Muruga was so full of wisdom that he was able to explain the concept of 'Om' to his father, Shiva.

  Swamimalai is also where the world famous Thanjavur bronze icons are manufactured, especially the exquisite dancing Nataraja. Individual sculptors and little factories jostle for space in the small town to turn out the much-sought after icons. Many are willing to explain and demonstrate the actual process of making the icons, something well worth watching.

Swamimalai is famous for making bronze Nataraja icons

> ### 📷 Snapshot: History of Kumbakonam
>
> Kumbakonam predates the Sangam age (3BC–AD3) and was a Chola city until the 12th century. The Cholas were succeeded by Pandyas and then Vijayanagar kings. In the 17th century, the city fell into the hands of the Marathas; in the 18th century it was invaded by Tipu Sultan. It was under British rule, in the 19th century, the town emerged as a centre of both Hindu culture and European education. It also attracted commerce. Today it is best known as a pilgrim centre.

is an amazing palliarai (bedroom of the goddess). Its walls and ceiling are painted in rich Tanjore style, in vegetable dyes and ornamented with pure gold leaf and precious gems. Amidst the many shrines in the praharams of the temple is one to Jurahareswarar (Shiva, who destroys fevers).

3km from bus terminus and railway station; 6am–12.30pm, 4–8.30pm

❷ MAHAMAHAM TANK

The sacred waters of the Mahamaham tank is believed to score over even the Kaveri River in ridding people of their sins. It spreads over three acres. There are 19 wells inside the tank, and along its banks are shrines for 16 lingams. In the Kasi Viswanathar Temple on the north bank are idols of nine river goddesses, including Ganga and Yamuna. Every 12 years, the Mahamaham Festival, akin to the Maha Kumbh Mela, takes place in this tank, in February–March. The last was held in 2004.

2km from Adi Kumbeswarar Temple

❸ NAGESWARAR TEMPLE

This 12th-century Chola temple is dedicated to Shiva in the guise of Nagaraja, the serpent king, and is considered by some to be holier than Adi Kumbeswarar. The temple has an idol of Nandi, the sacrificial stone and the flag. Legend says that Adi Sesha, the serpent god, and Surya worshipped Shiva

> ### ♥ If You Like: Festivals
>
> The bi-monthly pradosha pujas, sacred to Shiva, draw huge crowds. The **annual float festival** in Panguni (Mar–Apr) takes place in the Mahamaham Tank. The annual **Brahmotsavam festival** takes place in Chithirai (Apr–May) and lasts for 10 days. The procession of Sarangapani in his silver chariot is held during the first day of **Uttarayan** (14 or 15 Jan). The Float Festival takes place in Vaikasi (May–Jun) in the Hema Pushkarni.

THANJAVUR & KUMBAKONAM

here. This spacious temple has a striking rajagopuram and wide praharams.
500m from Adi Kumbeswarar Temple; 6.30am–noon, 4–9pm

> Adi Kumbeswarar is a magnificent example of a Chola Temple

❹ SARANGAPANI TEMPLE

This Vishnu temple is the biggest one in Kumbakonam, with an 11-tiered gopuram which is 44m tall. It is third in line of importance among the 108 divya desams of the Vaishnavites, the first two being Srirangam and Tirupati.

The sanctum is shaped like a chariot with 12 sculpted columns. Look out for astounding stone trellis work inside. According to legend, Sarangapani, as an incarnation of Vishnu married the goddess Komalavalli, who did penance here before the arrival of her Lord, so devotees are expected to visit her shrine first, before entering that of Sarangapani.
Next to temple tank, Hema Pushkarni; 6am–noon, 4–8.30pm

❺ CHAKRAPANI TEMPLE

This Vishnu temple is neither as ancient nor as big as the other temples in Kumbakonam, but it is has special significance as a place of healing. Chakrapani means 'he who holds the chakra'. Here Vishnu is worshipped as Sudarshana, a fiery incarnation, with a third eye and eight arms, all holding weapons. Installed near the entrance are brass statues

of Maratha king Serfoji and his queen, who became great devotees after the king was cured of a severe stomach ailment after worshipping in this temple.
Half km from Adi Kumbeswarar Temple; 7am–noon, 4.30–9pm; Brahmotsavam (Feb–Mar) & Navaratri celebrations Sep–Oct

❻ RAMASWAMY TEMPLE

Built by King Raghunatha Nayak in the 17th century, this Vishnu temple illustrates the fondness of the Nayak rulers for sculpture and painting. In the mandapam outside the main sanctum are 62 frescoes depicting scenes from Vishnu's ten avatars. Paintings on the walls of the inner praharam portray scenes from the Ramayana, culminating in a large Thanjavur painting of the coronation of Rama that stretches over an entire wall and sparkles with gold foil and gem stones.
Less than 1km from Adi Kumbeswarar; 6am–noon, 4–9pm

The Ramaswamy Temple has 62 frescoes in the main mandapam

❼ RIVER KAVERI

The best time to go here is after the monsoon when the river runs fairly full. There are a few ghats, such as Sarkarai Padithurai and Bhagavatha Padithurai which are favoured by bathers. Nearby Mutt Street is the Kanchi Kamakoti Peetam Mutt, where the morning and evening worship of the lingam by the Sankaracharya attracts a lot of devotees. The 17th-century Raja Veda Patashala is a centre for Vedic studies and it's a lovely experience to listen to the chanting of the Vedas by students.

❽ HOUSE OF SRINIVASA RAMANUJAM

The simple house, off Sarangapani Sannidhi Street, where the maths genius, Srinivasa Ramanujam was born and spent much of his life, is in fairly good shape and was renovated and opened to the public some years ago.
10am–5pm

Detour: Temples around Kumbakonam

- **Airavateswarar Temple, Darasuram** (4km): The Airavateswarar Temple is a Unesco World Heritage Site. It has ornate carvings and the main sanctum is in the shape of a chariot, resting on wheels and pulled by horses.

- **Srinivasa Perumal Temple, Nachiar Kovil** (10km): This Vishnu temple is better known as Nachiar Kovil, after the name of goddess Andal. The main sanctum is for Nachiar accompanied by Vishnu's sanctum. Note the large stone Garuda idols that make for an arresting feature in the temple. The town is also famous for brass lamps, especially the traditional one with five wicks, and varying in height from 1ft to 5 or 6ft.

- **Uppiliappan Kovil,** (4km from Nachiar Kovil): The temple is in Thirunageswaram. Vishnu is called Uppiliappan, 'He who eats no salt'. Legend has it that Vishnu agreed to eat saltless food made by Lakshmi due to his love for her.

- **Tribhuvanam,** (5km from Uppiliappan Kovil): The temple of Sarabhamurti, an incarnation of Shiva as part-beast, part-bird and part-human, meant to subdue the fury of Vishnu in his avatar as the ferocious Narasimha, is an ancient Chola one. It has a chariot-shaped hall and a 130ft tall tower.

- **Gangaikondacholapuram** (36km from Kumbakonam): A Unesco World Heritage Site, this temple was built by King Rajendra Chola, to celebrate his conquest of lands up till present-day Bangladesh. He brought back water from the Ganges River from his conquests and poured it into Ponneri, the huge tank here or the town which held the waters of the Ganga.

The main sanctum of Airavateswarar Temple is in the shape of a chariot

Accommodation

THANJAVUR

Tanjore Hi — Boutique Hotel ₹₹₹
☎ 04632 252111; www.tanjorehihotel.com; 464 East Main St; r from ₹9341 (incl of breakfast)
A 1926 house revamped by a German architect, Tanjore Hi has stylish rooms done up in blue and white, with wooden flooring, LED lighting and large contemporary art prints. The brightly decorated top-floor restaurant serves a range of good international and Indian dishes.

Hotel Ramnath — Hotel ₹
☎ 04632 272567; www.hotelramnath.com; 1335 South Rampart; r ₹900, with AC ₹1200
Among the best from a bunch of hotels close to the bus stand, Hotel Ramnath is a decent budget option with clean, though not very big, pine-furnished rooms.

Hotel Valli — Hotel ₹
☎ 04632 231580; www.hotelvalli.com; 2948 MKM Rd; d ₹605–715, with AC ₹1463
Located near the railway station, this green-painted hotel has spic-and-span rooms. The staff is friendly, and the hotel has a good Indian restaurant.

Hotel Gnanam — Hotel ₹
☎ 04632 278501; www.hotelgnanam.com; Anna Salai; d from ₹2518 (incl of breakfast)
With the best overall value in town, Hotel Gnanam has stylish, comfortable rooms. The more expensive ones have lovely clean bathrooms with a bathtub, and there

Rooms at Tanjore Hi are done up in blue and white with large art prints on the ceiling

If You Like: Filter coffee

Kumbakonam is famous for 'degree' coffee. 'Degree' refers to the purity and thickness of the milk, as well as the temperature at which the ingredients are mixed (100 degrees for the milk, and the coffee decoction must always remain on a double boiler). The tip is to brew the coffee in a brass filter – it is far more aromatic. Kumbakonam filter coffee is a unique experience. Don't miss it.

---

is free wi-fi in the lobby. You can be sure of good meals and other modern amenities.

KUMBAKONAM

Paradise Resort — Resort ₹₹₹
0435 3291354; www.paradiseresortindia.com; Tanjore Main Rd, Darasuram; d ₹5996–10,193
Located 5km from the town, this charming resort occupies large, lush grounds that even include a small village. The luxurious rooms have antique doors, carved wood furnishings and big bathrooms. You can enjoy cooking demonstrations, bullock cart rides, Ayurveda and yoga here. The multi-cuisine restaurant, done up with Burmese woodwork has some great south Indian specialities.

Hotel Raya's — Hotel ₹
0435 2423170; www.hotelrayas.com; 18 Head Post Office Rd; r ₹990, with AC ₹1320–2280 Friendly service and spacious, clean rooms make this one of the best hotel options in town. They have a convenient car service for out of town trips. The restaurant offers good vegetarian and non-vegetarian fare in clean surroundings.

Hotel Kanishka — Hotel ₹
0435 2425231; 18/450 Ayekulam Rd; r ₹770–880, AC ₹1100–1238
This is a cheerful place with small, simple and stylish rooms done up with yellow or pink walls. It's owned by a young couple who keep the hotel family-friendly. There is free wi-fi in the reception area.

Eating

THANJAVUR

Although there are many small eateries and restaurants in Thanjavur, you still get the best filter coffee and the softest idlis in the smaller cafes. The three-course ilai sappadu is like a thali meal (served on banana leaves) which is the best lunch option.

Sri Venkata Lodge — South Indian ₹
Gandhi Rd; thalis ₹50; 5.15am–10pm
A friendly, popular vegetarian place does a nice thali.

Vasanta Bhavan — Indian ₹
1338 South Rampart; mains ₹50–70; 6am–11pm The most appealing of the several vegetarian restaurants close

to the bus stand, Vasanta Bhavan has air conditioning. It offers biryani and north Indian curries, as well as usual southern favourites.

Hotel Gnanam	Indian ₹₹

Anna Salai; Sahana mains ₹95–115; Diana ₹140–250; 7am–11pm The hotel has two restaurants – Sahana – which does a decent selection of fresh, tasty, mainly vegetarian dishes. The hotel's pricier non-veg restaurant Diana is a good option if you are craving for northern dishes or local Chettinadu fare. They have beer also.

Sathars	Indian ₹₹

167 Gandhiji Rd; mains ₹80–160; noon–4pm, 6.30–11.30pm Good service and quality food make this place popular, and the upper floor is air-conditioned. You can get biryani, five types of chicken tikka kebabs, good paranthas, and mutton, seafood and plenty of vegetarian dishes as well.

KUMBAKONAM

Hotel Sri Venkkatramana	Indian ₹

TSR Big St; thalis ₹50–65; 5.30am–10pm; Sun closed This place serves fresh vegetarian food and is very popular with the locals.

Taj Samudra	Multi-Cuisine ₹

 **0435 2401332; 80 Nageswaran South St; mains ₹100–170; 11am–3pm, 7–11pm** If you're craving for Chinese or north Indian, make your way to Hotel Taj Samudra's restaurant, that offers a decent selection. But if you'd rather stick to the usual south Indian fare, you won't be disappointed.

Shopping

THANJAVUR

Thanjavur Paintings

The famous Thanjavur paintings are done on glass or on specially prepared wooden surfaces and painted with vegetable dyes. The uniqueness of the Thanjavur painting is the embellishment with gold leaf and gemstones. The more commercially crafted paintings use synthetic dyes and artificial gold leaf and glass stones. The theme is always religious, of either gods and goddesses or

---

Snapshot: Kumbakonam's betel

Locals in Thanjavur and Kumbakonam love chewing betel and the leaves grown here are small, deep green and tangy to the extent of being almost spicy. It is usually taken after a meal with a dab of lime paste, a spoon of betel nut shavings roasted in ghee, a clove and a cardamom – this acts both as a digestive, as well as a mouth freshener. It is never sweet. Of course, the locals chew it all the time and carry their own little vetrilai pettis, little metal boxes with compartments for the betel leaves and all the other ingredients. The older pettis have now become collector's items.

THANJAVUR & KUMBAKONAM

scenes from Hindu mythology. For better crafted paintings you might try the antique shops on **South Keezha Veedhi** or the **Poompuhar** showroom on **Gandhiji Road**. Bronze icons and the ubiquitous Tanjore plates (brass plaques with decorative silver inlay work) and brass lamps can be bought at all government showrooms.

Dolls

Not so expensive but still cute is the thalaiyatti bommai (head-nodding doll). Made of clay or papier mâché and brightly coloured, they come in pairs and rock even with gentle breeze. A variation is the dancing doll which can shake its head like a Bharatanatyam dancer. Look outside the Punnainallur Mariamman Temple for these, or on carts outside the palace complex.

Colourful papier mâché dolls are called thalaiyatti bommai locally

KUMBAKONAM

Brass vessels and lamps

Kumbakonam is famous for its brass vessels and lamps. Although brass utensils are not as popular as they once used to be, those who want them for decorative value, can get some attractive pieces here. **RS & Co** and **Karpaga Vilas Stores,** are both on Big Street, near Kumbeswarar Temple.

Silk saris

One of South India's well known silk weaving centres, Kumbakonam's bigger stores all carry a good selection but you can also go directly to the weavers along Gandhi Adigal Saalai.

Tiruchirappalli

Situated on the banks of Kaveri River, Tiruchirappalli (or Trichy as it is popularly known) is best known for the imposing Rock Fort Temple perched on a picturesque hillock. It is now a thriving industrial hub in Tamil Nadu, but for travellers the main draw is the footprints of history left behind by ancient empires which once ruled this culturally rich southern part of the country.

Trip Planner

GETTING THERE

Tiruchirappalli International Airport has daily flights to all the metros and to a few international destinations as well. Tiruchirappalli Junction station is on the main Chennai–Madurai line with daily trains to Chennai, New Delhi, Mumbai, Kolkata and Bengaluru. From Chennai, it is 412km and takes between six to seven hours by bus. A Volvo costs ₹500–700.

SUGGESTED ITINERARY (3 DAYS)

Spend a day at Srirangam exploring the Sri Ranganathaswamy and Jambukeswarar temples. Next day, stop by at the Lady of Lourdes Church and prepare to climb up to the Rock Fort Temple. Spend your final day picnicking at Mokambu and shopping in Tiruchirappalli's bazaars.

BEST TIME TO GO

J F M A M J J A S O **N D**

GREAT FOR

Top 5 highlights

- **Sri Ranganathaswamy Temple** (p352)
- **Jambukeswarar Temple** (p352)
- **Rock Fort Temple** (p351)
- **Lady of Lourdes Church** (p352)
- **Mukkombu Picnic Spot** (p353)

On the Rocks

Located in the heart of Tamil Nadu, **Tiruchirappalli**, known during the British period as Trichinopoly, is one of the oldest cities in the state. The town is dominated by a rocky outcrop and on one such rock is the famous Rock Fort Temple, which can be seen from nearly every part of town. Devotees from all over the country come to visit the well-known Sri Ranganathaswamy Temple. Today, Tiruchirappalli is a big, crowded and busy industrial hub where the modern and the traditional jostle for space. Despite all modern conveniences, the city retains its spiritual moorings.

Its earliest settlements date back to 2nd century BC. Later, it served as the capital of the imperial kingdoms of the Cholas and the Pandyas. It was also the theatre for battles between the British and French and the victory of the former played a key role in deciding which imperial power would rule over South India.

> The climb up to Rock Fort Temple is worth it for the views

❶ ROCK FORT TEMPLE
The 7th-century Rock Fort Temple, perched 83m high on a massive rock outcrop, lords over Tiruchirappalli with stony arrogance. A huge fort was built on top of the hill

TAMIL NADU

Highlights
1. Rock Fort Temple
2. Lady of Lourdes Church
3. Sri Ranganathaswamy Temple, Srirangam
4. Sri Jambukeswarar Temple, Srirangam
5. Mokambu Picnic Spot

by the Nayakar kings of Madurai and the British, and hence the name Rock Fort. Constructed by the Pallavas, it consists of two main temples. Midway up the hill is **Thayumanaswamy Temple** dedicated to Shiva, where he is worshipped in the form of a mother to commemorate his acting as a midwife for his devotee. This is the biggest temple on the rock. On the hill's summit stands the smaller **Ucchi Pillayar Vinayagar Temple**, dedicated to Lord Ganesha. The climb of more than 400 stone-cut steps is steep but the panoramic view of Tiruchirappalli and Kaveri River makes it worthwhile. The temple is also known for its stunning architecture.
www.thiruchyrockfort.org; 6am–1pm, 4–8pm

② LADY OF LOURDES CHURCH
This lovely 20th-century church took 13 years to build. It's a replica of the famed Basilica at Lourdes in France with a spire soaring up 213ft. It is situated on the grounds of St Joseph's college and has gorgeous stained glass windows.
Salai Rd; 7am–8pm, 5.30am–8pm Sun

The vimanam at Sri Ranganathaswamy Temple is made of 95kg gold

③ SRI RANGANATHASWAMY TEMPLE, SRIRANGAM
Located in Srirangam, the river island formed by the Kaveri and Kolidam, this temple is considered to be the

> ## 📷 Snapshot: Legend of Sri Ranganathaswamy Temple
>
> After the battle in which Rama defeated the Lankan army, Vibhishana, the brother of slain demon Ravana, left home for Sri Lanka. Rama gifted him an idol of Vishnu. The upset gods did not want their deity to leave and asked Ganesha to create obstacles in Vibhishana's journey. When Vibhishana halted at Srirangam, Ganesha appeared as a cowherd and convinced him to take a dip in the Kaveri, promising to hold the idol aloft. Ganesha laid down the idol at the spot where the temple is located today. Vibhishana was unable to move the idol. Vishnu assured Vibhishana he would keep an eye on Sri Lanka and so the idol faces southwards.

foremost Vishnu temple in India. Spread over 156 acres, the complex has 21 magnificent gopurams, of which 20 were constructed between the 3rd and 17th centuries. The last was completed as recently as 1987 and, at 73m, is the highest tower in South India. The temple has 49 shrines dedicated to Vishnu, and reaching the inner sanctum from the south, as most worshippers do, requires passing through seven gopurams. The main idol is of Vishnu in a reclining pose. There is a golden vimanam made of 95kg gold in the sanctum sanctorum, where only Hindus are allowed.
9km from Tiruchirappalli; www.srirangam.org; special darshan ₹250; 5.30–7.30am, 9.30am–noon, 1.15–5.45pm, 7–8.45pm

❹ SRI JAMBUKESWARAR TEMPLE, SRIRANGAM
Located a kilometre from Sri Ranganathaswamy Temple, this is amongst the five most revered Shiva temples in the country. It is dedicated to Shiva, Parvati and water. The spring in the sanctum is believed to be eternal. There is a special puja at noon. The priest dresses in a sari with the paraphernalia of the goddess and worships the Lord.
8km from Tiruchirappalli; 6am–1pm, 3–9pm

❺ MUKKOMBU PICNIC SPOT
On the banks of the Kaveri River, this is a popular spot with locals. However, it's not much of a place if the river is dry.
18km from Tiruchirappalli; adult ₹4; 6am–6pm

Accommodation

Sangam Hotel — Hotel ₹₹
☏ 0431 2414700; www.sangamhotels.com; Collector Office Rd; d ₹3400–5500 (incl of breakfast) One of the oldest and most popular hotels in the city, Sangam has an old-world charm. The recently-renovated deluxe rooms are better than the standard ones, which look a bit worn out. The hotel has good dining options; Chembian, their multi-cuisine restaurant, that serves a good breakfast spread and the 24-hour coffee shop Cascade that has several options in the menu for children. The Egyptian themed bar, Soma is the perfect place for a drink in the evening. The hotel also has a swimming pool.

Grand Gardenia — Hotel ₹₹
☏ 0431 4045000; www.grandgardenia.com; 22-25, Mannarpuram Junction; d ₹3000–4000 (incl of breakfast) This stylishly designed hotel has rooms with wooden flooring and leather couches. It has two popular restaurants on its premises, Kannappa, famed for its Chettinadu food, and the multi-cuisine roof-top restaurant Golden Palm. Grand Gardenia offers a convenient 24-hour check-out facility. However, not being in the heart of the city, you have to take a taxi to visit the sites.

Breeze Residency — Hotel ₹₹
☏ 0431 4045333; www.breezeresidency.com; 3/14 McDonald's Rd; d ₹2900–3500 (incl of breakfast) One of the older and more popular hotels in Tiruchirappalli, Breeze Residency, only a kilometre from the railway station, has large and comfortable rooms. Most of the bathrooms have tubs. The hotel has a swimming pool, fitness centre and a shopping arcade in the lobby for those last minute souvenirs. The bar, Wild West, with pictures of cowboys and leather bar stools, is where the city's elite catch up for a drink.

Hotel High Point — Hotel ₹
☏ 0431 2416766; www.hotelhighpoint.in; Manghalam Towers, 9 Reynolds Rd, Cantonment; d ₹2500–3300 (incl of breakfast) Located on the top floor of a shopping complex with a food court and a multiplex below, Hotel High Point is a convenient stopover. The spacious rooms have modern cane furniture and contemporary art. There is an in-house restaurant and bar, but of course the food court, just below has a larger variety.

SRM Hotel — Hotel ₹
☏ 0431 2421303–06 ; www.srmhotels.com; Race Course Rd, Khajamalai; d ₹2250–2500 (incl of breakfast) Spread over five and a half acres, SRM Hotel is at a distance from the city centre, but only around a kilometre from the airport. Most rooms overlook lovely trees in the property. The glass capsule lifts are

a sign of its modern design and the large, elegant lobby overlooks the swimming pool. It also has a fitness centre and two restaurants, one of them open round the clock. The hotel provides free pick-up and drop to and from the airport, railway station, bus stand and city centre.

PL.A Krishna Inn — Hotel ₹
0431 2406666; www.plahotels.com; 8A Rockins Rd, Cantonment, opp Central Bus Stand; d ₹2100–2500 (incl of breakfast) This is a small but elegant hotel and in spite of the heavy traffic on the road, you are not disturbed by street noises inside the rooms, which are compact are comfortable. Wi-fi is free but connectivity is usually a problem. The hotel does not provide complimentary bottles of water. There is a multi-cuisine restaurant but the breakfast spread is primarily south Indian.

PL.A Rathna Residency — Hotel ₹
0431 2405500; www.plarathnaresidency.com; No 4 Dindigul Rd; d ₹2100–2300 (incl of breakfast) The extremely helpful staff and great location (close to the Central Bus Stand) make Rathna Residency a preferred choice. Fusion, the open-air coffee shop, offers a variety of beverages and refreshments and has a great ambience, making it a good option during the evenings. The hotel offers free wi-fi.

Sangam is one of the oldest hotels in town

Eating

Kannappa — Chettinadu ₹
0431 4045005; 22-25 Mannarpuram Junction; mains ₹100–150, 11am–11.30pm Located on the ground floor of Grand Gardenia hotel, Kannappa is known for its Chettinadu food. The chicken biryani and Chettinadu chicken are extremely popular. However, the restaurant is done up simply, and service is slow, especially on weekends when the place is crowded. Be prepared to share a table if there's no place.

Chembiam — Multi-Cuisine ₹₹
0431 2414700; Hotel Sangam, Collector Office Rd; mains ₹150–250; noon–3pm, 7–11pm Besides good food Chembiam has a great ambience. There is live Carnatic instrumental music on weekend evenings and it

Payasam, a perfect finish to a typical Tamil meal

is adorned with paintings depicting history and culture of the place. It has an extensive menu of south Indian, north Indian, Chinese and continental dishes and the service is prompt. Try the chicken biryani (₹190) but if you prefer continental, go for the cannelloni legumes (₹200), which has just the right amount of vegetables and cheese.

Sangeethas   Vegetarian ₹
☏ 0431 2415545; Annexe, Hotel Anand, 1, VOC Rd, near Central Bus Stand; mains ₹50–150; 6am–3pm, 4.30pm–12am Traditional vegetarian south Indian food is its USP. Breakfast, comprising dosa, idli, vada and upma is served from 6– 11.30am. For lunch you can order an unlimited thali (₹100) comprising of sambhar, rasam, poriyal (any dry vegetable, beetroot is the most popular), keerai (a green leafy vegetable), kolumbu (a curry vegetable), rice, curd and papad. For dinner a variety of south Indian and north Indian food is available.

Hotel Femina Complex   Street Food ₹
107-C Williams Rd, Cantonment; mains ₹25–100; 4–10pm Satisfy your craving for street food like chaat and pav bhaji at the Hotel Femina Complex. Every evening, stalls are set up here selling pani puri (₹25), kulfi, corn, and other lip-smacking delights. The atmosphere is festive with many people sitting around or just hanging about on the pavement.

Golden Palm
Roof Top   Multi-Cuisine ₹₹
☏ 0431 4045000; 22-25 Mannarpuram Junction; buffet ₹300; noon–4pm, 7–11.30pm The food here is good, but the ambience even better.

Located on the roof of the Grand Gardenia, the restaurant has both a covered area and open-air seating. While lunch is a la carte, dinner is generally a buffet comprising Indian and continental fare.

Shopping

Poompuhar — Handicrafts
0431 2704895; West Boulevard Rd, Singathorpe; 10am–8pm, Sun closed Tamil Nadu government's showroom offers handicrafts from across the country. So not only can you buy Tanjore paintings and wood carvings from Tamil Nadu, but also Rajasthani miniature paintings and sandalwood products from Karnataka. Since it's a government store, you are assured of quality and price.

Sarathas — Textiles
0431 2702077; No 45, NSC Bose Rd; 9am–9.30pm Touted as the country's largest textile store, the 1.5 million sq ft Sarathas caters to all your textile needs – from a handkerchief and a sari to towels and bedcovers and upholstery as well. A member of the staff accompanies you around the store making sure that you find just what you are looking for.

Femina Shopping Mall — Mall
0431 4200610; 107-C Williams Rd, Cantonment; 9.30am–10pm A large departmental store in the Hotel Femina Complex, it sells everything from clothes (men, women and children) to bags, accessories, imitation jewellery and cosmetics. There is also a large variety of burqas.

Chudidar House — Clothes
0431 2400946; No 4 D Maan Sarovar Building, Collector Office Rd, Cantonment; 10am–9pm Check out the beautiful collection of readymade salwar suits as well as material at Chudidar House, which opened recently in a shopping complex next to Hotel Sangam. It also stocks a decent collection of lehangas.

Rathna Stores — Utensils
0431 2715333; Siva Complex, 9&10, NSB Rd; 9.30am–10.30pm Tamil Nadu is known for its steel utensils so do visit Rathna Stores just to see the sheer variety. The entire gamut is available, including plates, bowls, serving spoons, tiffins as well as serving and cooking utensils.

✓ Top Tip: Shopping at Rock Fort

The steps leading to Rock Fort have shops selling idols of Lord Ganesha made from various materials such as granite, wood, soft stones and even grain. You can also buy imitation jewellery, cosmetics, hair accessories, and more such stuff. Costumes of various gods and goddesses can also be hired for school children performing on stage. Shops on the lower levels are cheaper than those higher up.

Chettinadu

Visit Chettinadu to experience the rich cultural heritage of the prosperous Chettiar merchants who hail from the area. Marvel at their palatial mansions, allow the fragrant aroma of the famed Chettinadu cuisine, garnished with hand-pounded spices, to whet your appetite and then head off to the antique shops for some leisurely shopping to pick up a timeless relic from a bygone era.

Trip Planner

GETTING THERE

Karaikudi, the largest town in the Chettinadu region, is close to both Madurai (90km) and Tiruchirappalli (75km). Both these towns have airports that are connected to all metros. The Chettinadu station has daily trains to Chennai.

SUGGESTED ITINERARY (2 DAYS)

Spend the first day visiting some of the temples and admiring the palatial homes of the Chettiars. The next day, try your hand at tile making or sari weaving and then head off to the antique market in search of a special artefact. Don't leave without sampling the fiery Chettinadu cuisine, flavoursome and redolent with the spices of the region. The cuisine has many loyal followers and can be found in restaurants all over the country.

BEST TIME TO GO

J F M A M J J A S **O N D**

GREAT FOR

Top 5 highlights

- **Thiruvenkadamudaiyan Temple** (p360)
- **Chettinadu Mansions** (p363)
- **Thirumayam Fort** (p361)
- **Athangudi Palace** (p361)
- **Antique Market** (p362)

Palatial Homes & Fiery Food

A typical Chettinadu mansion with a huge courtyard

The town of **Karaikudi** and 74 villages sprawled across the 1550sq km area in Sivagangai and Pudukkottai districts of south Tamil Nadu form the Chettinadu region. It is the homeland of the enterprising Chettiar community who dominated the business and financial sectors of Tamil Nadu and had flourishing trade links with Southeast Asian countries. Influenced by the architectural styles they saw during their travels abroad, the Chettiars built impressive mansions in the art deco style with airy courtyards and spacious rooms, embellished with things brought from Italy, Belgium, Japan and Burma. The money from their ventures financed these grandiose constructions.

The Chettinadu region evolved its distinctive cuisine redolent with aromatic spices. The region is also known for tile making and weaving. A number of shops stock relics from the Chettinadu mansions which have been razed or refurbished, and with a good eye and luck, you can come away with a steal.

The Chettiar community has nine clans with each having its own temple dedicated to Shiva. Marriage within the clan is strictly forbidden. These are always consecrated at the native village with all relatives making a beeline for their ancestral village for this function no matter where they are based.

Highlights
1. Thiruvenkadamudaiyan Temple
2. Pillaiyarpatti Vinayagar Temple
3. Thirumayam Fort
4. Athangudi Palace
5. Antique Market
6. Pudukkottai Museum

1 THIRUVENKADAMUDAIYAN TEMPLE
Popularly known as 'Then Tirupati' (literally South Tirupati), the temple is located in Ariyakudi. Built during the 17th century by Nagarathar Natukottai Chettiars, it is dedicated to Vishnu in his form as Srinivasa Perumal. The temple has an impressive 80ft high gopuram. Locals believe that unwed girls will soon meet their prince charming if they pray here. The 'Then Tirupati' epithet signifies that prayers can be offered here to Lord Balaji of Tirupati if one can't visit Tirupati itself.
About 4km from Karaikudi; Karaikudi-Rameswaram route; 7.30am–12.30pm, 4.30–8.30pm

2 PILLAIYARPATTI VINAYAGAR TEMPLE
This rock cut temple was built by Pandyan kings in the 4th century. The image of Karpaga Vinayaka and a Shiva lingam were carved by a sculptor called Ekkattur Koon Peruparanan, who left behind his signature on a stone inscription seen in the sanctum.
12km from Karaikudi; Karaikuki-Madurai Rd; 6am–12.30pm, 4–8.30pm

Snapshot: Origin of Chettinadu
Legend says the Chettiars originally hailed from a port city in the Bay of Bengal from where they were displaced in the 13th century after a massive cyclone hit the area. They started looking for a dry area where such destruction could never revisit them, and discovered Chettinadu and settled here. Even today their houses are built at a height to signify that they are prepared in case there is another cyclone-like disaster.

❸ THIRUMAYAM FORT

The fort was built in the 17th century around a rocky outcrop at Thirumayam by one of the Sethupati kings of Ramnad, Vijaya Raghunatha Devan. Only a portion of the original fortification survives today. The top of the rock has the bastion of the fort and a cannon of British origin. Two rock-cut temples here are dedicated to Shiva (Satyagirisvara) and Vishnu (Sathyamurthiperumal).

35km from Karaikudi; Karaikudi-Trichy Rd; Indian/foreigner/ video camera ₹5/100/25; 9am–5.30pm

> Only a part of the ancient Thirumayam Fort remains

❹ ATHANGUDI PALACE

Sprawling across 60,000sq ft, Athangudi Palace is a typical specimen of Chettinadu architecture. It was erected in 1932 by Nachiappa Chettiar, a wealthy trader. The front of the house is on one street and the back opens onto another, with a series of courtyards in between. Each courtyard is surrounded by Burmese teak pillars or iron pillars imported from Britain. The ceramic tiles are all Japanese and the glass is Belgian; the flooring is in Italian marble. Apparently it took 300 artisans three years to complete the mansion at a cost of six lakh rupees. Earlier the palace was let out for film

The kottan or woven basket is a popular gift from Chettinadu

shootings; however, this was not permitted after a part of the upper floor was destroyed.
15km from Karaikudi; Indian/foreigner ₹30/100; 9.30am–5.30pm

❺ ANTIQUE MARKET

You cannot leave Chettinadu without a visit to the antique market in Karaikudi (p368). With old Chettinadu homes being razed to the ground, everything from tiles to teak wood pillars have found their way here. It's a small, narrow street comprising around 12–15 shops selling everything from brass idols, Thanjvur paintings, Raja Ravi Varma lithographs, old enamel kitchenware as well as posters and calendars. The shops are small and crammed and unless you are looking for something specific, you can spend an entire day rummaging through stuff. The old, restored furniture is also quite a draw. Only some shops are open for a few hours on Sunday.
Muneesvaran Kovil St, Karaikudi, Sivagangai Distt; 9am–8pm

❻ PUDUKKOTTAI MUSEUM

Relics of bygone days are on display in this wonderful museum located in a renovated palace building in Pudukkottai town. Its eclectic collection includes musical instruments, some remarkable paintings and miniatures.
Indian/foreigner ₹5/100; 9.30am–5pm Sat–Thu

Snapshot: Chettinadu mansions

The Chettiars were, and continue to be, one of the wealthiest communities of South India. One of the ways they displayed their wealth was by building huge mansions, almost like palaces. These properties were typically spread over an acre of land and had the entrance on one street and the back gate on another.

The Chettiars were traders and travelled across Southeast Asia and Europe. Their mansions reflect the influences of places they visited. Most have Italian marble floors, Japanese ceramic tiles, Belgian glass mirrors and Burmese teak wood pillars.

Most mansions are similar in architecture. There is the front hall, which was used by the men of the family, followed by a series of open courtyards flanked by teak wood or iron pillars. On both sides of the courtyards are small rooms, which were used as storerooms. Behind these is a huge dining hall. At the end of the courtyards are the women's quarters and the kitchen area. The Raja's palace in Kanadukathan village is one of the grandest properties, but unfortunately it's no longer open for public viewing. However, it makes a great photo-stop. While a large number of these mansions have been razed to the ground, quite a few have been converted into hotels. Many of them organise tours of different mansions for visitors curious to get a glimpse of how the Chettiars lived.

| Intricate sculptures are a mark of grand Chettinadu mansions

| The mansions were made using imported material from various countries

Accommodation

Chidambara Vilas Heritage Hotel ₹₹₹
☏ 9585556431; www.chidambaravilas.com; TSK House, Ramachandrapuram, Kadiapatti, off Thirumayam Fort, Pudukkottai Distt; d ₹7500–8500 (incl of breakfast & taxes) This 108-year-old palatial mansion with large halls and courtyards, Burmese teak wood pillars, colourful ceramic tiles and beautifully carved woodwork, has been converted into a luxury heritage hotel. The hotel has 25 rooms and suites that have been recently restored and retain the essence of the hotel's architectural heritage. Beautiful furniture such as a large, carved four-poster bed adorns the double rooms and some even have a pankha. The bathrooms are modern. Enjoy a traditional Chettinadu meal at the Kalyanakottagai restaurant. You can interact with the chef and take a cooking lesson in Chettinadu cuisine. The hotel does not serve alcohol but you can carry your own.

Saratha Vilas Heritage Hotel ₹₹
☏ 9884203175; www.sarathavilas.com; No 832 Main Rd, Kothamangalam, Karaikudi, Sivagangai Distt; d ₹6500–7500 (incl of breakfast & taxes) An old mansion built by a wealthy Chettiar merchant in the early 1900s, Saratha Vilas is a typical stately Chettinadu home, complete with a well in the backyard. It has been restored to its former glory and converted into a hotel by two French architects, who have used traditional arts from across the country. While the master bedrooms have antique four-poster beds and other carved furniture, the twin rooms are done up in a more modern style. Bernard Dragon, one of the architects, stays on the property and happily chats with guests. The hotel is closed in May and June.

The master bedrooms at Saratha Vilas have antique furniture and four poster beds

Visalam Heritage Hotel ₹₹
☏ 04565 273301; www.cghearth.com; Kanadukathan, Karaikudi, Sivagangai Distt; d ₹6500 (incl of breakfast & taxes) This 70-year-old mansion, built by a father for his daughter, is now a luxury heritage hotel. The house still retains its old-world charm with large verandahs and a pillared courtyard. The spacious rooms are decorated with traditional furniture and Athangudi tiles. Meals

at the hotel are extremely interactive with guests encouraged to accompany the chef to purchase ingredients. You can even choose a chicken for your meal from the poultry stock. However, there is no room service or a bar.

The Bangala   Heritage Hotel ₹₹
☏ 04565 220221; www.thebangala.com; Devakottai Rd, Senjai, Karaikudi, Sivagangai Distt; d ₹6500 (incl of breakfast & taxes) One of the first heritage hotels to have come up in this region, The Bangala is still run by the family who owns it. Unlike other heritage hotels, it wasn't their home but more like a club house. While some rooms are part of the original building, most are in a newer wing overlooking the pool. The staff is helpful and the family a mine of knowledge on local culture and cuisine. Gardens and little seating areas add to the charm. Traditional Chettinadu meals are served for lunch and dinner.

Chettinadu Mansion   Heritage Hotel ₹₹
☏ 04565 273080; www.chettinadumansion.com; SARM House, behind Raja's Palace, Kanadukathan, Sivagangai Distt; d ₹6500 (incl of breakfast & taxes) Built in 1902, all rooms at Chettinadu Mansion have brightly painted walls and a private balcony that overlooks Kanadukathan village. The hotel provides bullock cart rides to the village and organises cooking sessions with the chef. There's also a swimming pool and an Ayurvedic massage centre. The room service is restricted to just ordering tea and coffee. No alcohol is served in the hotel.

Thappa Gardens   Resort ₹₹
☏ 04565 2221777, 221888 ; www.thappagardens.com; 687, Main Rd, Ariyakudi Village, Karaikudi, Sivagangai Distt; d ₹4500–5500 (incl of breakfast) This resort has individual cottages. The rooms have Athangudi tiles on the floor and are done up with traditional furniture. Each cottage has a verandah overlooking a private garden. Besides Chettinadu cuisine, the multi-cuisine restaurant serves good north Indian food as well. This is one of the few hotels in the region with a bar. There is a wading pool for children.

Hotel Nachiappa Palace   Hotel ₹
☏ 04565 230077; www.hotelnachiappapalace.com; 4, Subramaniyapuram 1st St , near SBI Main Branch, Karaikudi, Sivagangai Distt; d ₹850 (incl of breakfast) A budget hotel in the heart of Karaikudi, it offers clean rooms and bathrooms. Unlike other hotels where the stay itself is part of the experience, Nachiappa is just a basic stopover.

Eating

Chettinadu's cuisine is mostly non-vegetarian, but there is enough variety for vegetarians as well. All hotels provide for in-house guests, but if you're coming specifically for a meal, it's best to inform in advance.

The Bangala — Chettinadu ₹₹₹
04565 220221; www.thebangala.com; Devakottai Rd, Senjai, Karaikudi, Sivagangai Distt; meals ₹850 (veg), ₹1000 (non veg); 12.30–2.30pm, 7.30–10pm For a traditional Chettinadu meal, served on a banana leaf with informative and helpful staff telling you exactly what you are eating, head to The Bangala. However, make sure you call them at least three hours in advance; chances are you won't get any food if you turn up unannounced, especially in the low season. Each meal (both veg and non veg) has at least 10–12 dishes. Oh, and you can ask for seconds, thirds…fourths.

Friends — Chettinadu ₹
04565 236622; TT Nagar 1st St, 100 Feet Rd, near Periyar Statue, Karaikudi; mains ₹90–120; noon–11pm If you want to have authentic Chettinadu food but don't want to go to a hotel, Friends is your best bet. This restaurant, in the heart of Karaikudi, has an AC and non-AC section; and food is served on banana leaves. Try chicken Chettinadu and the mushroom gravy or simply have a veg meal for ₹75.

Chettinadu Court — Multi-Cuisine ₹
9846344305; SARM. House, Kanadukathan, Sivagangai Distt, next to Chettinaduu Mansion; mains ₹150–200; noon–3.30pm, 7–9pm If you want something other than Chettinadu food, visit the multi-cuisine restaurant at Chettinadu Court. Try their finger chips which are basically French fries but have pepper masala. But if you are looking for something more filling, there's always chicken biryani or chapatti and chicken curry.

Karaikudi Annalakshmi — Vegetarian ₹
9442538500; 100 Feet Rd, Karaikudi, Sivagangai Distt; mains ₹80–100; 6.30am–9.30pm Annalakshmi is one of the few pure vegetarian restaurants in the region. It's a basic place where service is prompt and the food decent. Try the kuzhi panniyaram. It's similar to idli but is lightly fried and often has onions and chillies in it.

Chetinadu Mansion — Chettinadu ₹₹₹
04565 273080; SARM House, behind Raja's Palace, Kanadukathan, Sivagangai Distt; fixed meals ₹600; 12.30–3pm, 7.30–9pm Savour the authentic ambience of a traditional Chettinadu meal served in the dining hall of what was once a palatial Chettiar house. You need to let the hotel know in advance whether you are vegetarian or non-vegetarian. If you are an outside guest, inform them a day in advance. Not only is the food good, the staff is knowledgeable about Chettinadu culture and cuisine.

CHETTINADU

Thappa Gardens Multi-Cuisine ₹
☎ 04565 2221777; www.thappagardens.com; 687, Main Rd, Ariyakudi Village, Karaikudi, Sivagangai Distt; mains ₹100–150; 11am–3pm, 7–11pm The restaurant here has a north Indian chef and hence you'll be served a perfect naan, authenctic dal makhani and butter chicken. Their kathi rolls are also quite good.

Activities

Tile Making
☎ 04565 281353; Sri Ganapathy Tiles; A Mutthuppattinam, Karaikudi Main Rd, Athangudi, Sivagangai Distt; 9.30am–6.00pm The Athangudi tiles take their name from the village of Athangudi where craftsmen have been making these handmade tiles for decades to adorn some of the palatial homes and nearly all the hotels in the region. You can also try your hand at tile making and get creative by designing your own tiles. The tiles take more than 10 days to dry, but if you leave your contact information with the tile unit, they will courier them to your home. There's also a huge variety of colourful tiles available for sale. A typical 8x8 inch tile costs ₹50.

Sari Weaving
☎ 04565 273286; Sri Mahalakshmi Handloom Weaving Centre; 19/6 KM St, Kanadukathan, Sivagangai Distt; 10.00am–5.00pm A visit to a sari weaving centre can be exciting as you can try your hand at weaving one yourself, or weaving even a few lines on one already on the loom. Each handloom cotton sari takes approximately 16 hours to weave. It may take you longer, but if you have the time and inclination, then you can discuss the colour and pattern and weave your own exclusive sari. Weaving demonstrations, as well as your attempt at weaving is free of charge. There is always a beautiful collection of saris at the centre available for sale.

Sari weaving is one of the most popular activities in the region

Shopping

Karaikudi is known for its antiques and many items from old Chettinadu mansions find their way to shops here. If you have an eye for antiques, you can often strike a great bargain. Prices are quoted randomly and haggling is a good idea. But some products can be fake.

Old Chettinadu Crafters — Antiques
☎ 9842423062; Murugan Complex, 37/6, Muneesvaran Kovil St, Karaikudi, Shivagangai Distt; 9.30am–8pm, 10am–1pm Sun This shop stocks a collection of brass idols, prints of Raja Ravi Varma paintings, old posters, tin cans, utensils and other knick-knacks. J Murugesan, the shop owner, is helpful and if you are looking for something specific, he will try to source it for you.

M.M. Crafters — Antiques
☎ 9842664547; Murugan Complex, 49, Muneesvaran Kovil St; Karaikudi, Sivagangai Distt; 9.30am–8pm, 9.30am–3pm Sun Besides the usual collection of old paintings, posters, brass idols and wooden carvings, the shop also keeps old and restored furniture pieces.

Mangalam Arts — Antiques
☎ 9442515350; 49/1 Muneeswaran Kovil St, Karaikudi, Shivagangai Distt; 10am–8pm, 10am–3pm Sun At Mangalam Arts you can find old Chettinadu pillars with which to adorn your house. They are available from ₹9000 onwards. The shop also has a huge collection of Tanjore paintings, prints of Raja Ravi Varma paintings

There are many takers for antique brass idols in Chettinadu

and old posters and calendars. There's also a collection of brass pots and idols.

RMR Silks — Saris
☎ 04565 233066; No 93, MM St, Karaikudi, Shivagangai Distt; 9.30am–8.30pm, 10am–2pm Sun Chettinadu saris have a typical check pattern. The traditional cotton sari, worn without a petticoat, was as thick as a bed sheet and did not need ironing or starch. While these are no longer practical and hence hardly available, you can always check out the large collection of what are considered Chettinadu cotton saris today.

Expert Recommendation
Chettinadu sampler

Author of cookbook *Flavours of Chettinad*, **Seetha Muthiah**, is an authority on Chettinadu cuisine and has inspired many in the community to make it famous.

For Chettiars, meals are about feasting. And yet Chettinadu cuisine is not about the exotic but a canny combination of spices that ensures outstanding results. The cuisine has also assimilated the influences from the community's extensive travel, especially in east Asia, be it enamelware for pickling or eastern spices for flavouring.

• **Mutton kola:** This is both a tasty starter and a snack made of minced meat and spices sauteed with various lentils and nuts and then deep fried. Vegetarians can try the raw jackfruit or beetroot kola.

• **Mutton kari kulambu:** Tangy and not too spicy, this is a winner and is typical of Chettinadu meals. It is made of dried meat in curry, or can be kola kulambu – meat ball in a curry.

• **Chettinadu chicken fry:** This popular dish is typical of Chettinadu. The chicken is marinated and then cooked in a combination of spices, including red chillies and fennel, until it is dry, absorbing the spices. It can be eaten with rice or chapatti.

• **Chettinadu pulao:** This is a vegetarian rice dish made with large pieces of potatoes and carrots.

• **Vadagam and vathal:** Seasoned balls and fritters are special to Chettinadu cuisine.

• **Paal paniyaram:** Chettinadu cuisine has a range of desserts but the big favourite is pal paniyaram. These are sweetened dumplings in cardamom-flavoured milk.

Mutton kola is eaten mostly as a starter or snack

Madurai & Rameswaram

Envelop yourself in Tamil history in the ancient city of Madurai, where you can get lost in the corridors of the celebrated Meenakshi Temple and wander around its bazaars to experience a destination which has changed little over the years. Further south on the seashore lies the island of Rameswaram that is home to the famous Ramanathaswamy Temple.

Trip Planner

GETTING THERE

Madurai: Madurai Airport has direct flights from Chennai and connecting flights from other metros. Madurai Junction station has daily trains to New Delhi, Mumbai, Bengaluru, Kolkata and Chennai.

Rameswaram: The nearest airport is in Madurai (170km). Rameswaram Railway Station has daily trains to Chennai and Madurai. Regular buses ply between the two places. An AC bus costs ₹300–400.

SUGGESTED ITINERARY (4 DAYS)

Spend the first day exploring the Meenakshi Temple, Gandhi Museum, Thirumalai Nayak Palace and the bazaars around the temple. Next day visit the Thiruparankundram Temple in the morning and the Jain caves in the evening. On the third morning, make your way to Alagar Kovil, and in the evening drive three hours to Rameswaram. The next day attend the morning aarti and carry on to Dhanushkodi later in the day.

BEST TIME TO GO

J F M A M J J A S **O N D**

GREAT FOR

Top 5 highlights

- Meenakshi Sundareswarar Temple, Madurai (p372)
- Thiruparankundram Temple, Madurai (p374)
- Gandhi Memorial Museum, Madurai (p372)
- Ramanathaswamy Temple, Rameswaram (p376)
- Panchmukhi Hanuman Temple, Rameswaram (p376)

Temple Cities

The stunning 1212-pillared corridor at Ramanathaswamy Temple in Rameswaram

Situated on the banks of Vaigai River, **Madurai** is as old as Tamil civilisation itself. Bustling and chaotic, Madurai is known as 'the city that never sleeps' because of the numerous street stalls around the bus stand and railway station that serve piping hot food round the clock.

Today considered the cultural capital of Tamil Nadu, Madurai is dominated by and is almost synonymous with the celebrated Meenakshi Temple. It was once the capital of the Pandyas, one of the three dynasties (the other two being the Cholas and the Cheras) which held sway over South India for most of its early history. The Nayak kings who ruled during the 16th and 17th centuries contributed extensively to the architecture of the city.

Located 170 km from Madurai, the island of **Rameswaram** is connected to the mainland by Pamban Bridge, one of those marvels of engineering which leaves one awestruck. The town itself is only a few streets near the Ramanathaswamy Temple, but if you explore further you can't escape the intimate connection this town has to the *Ramayana*.

Madurai

❶ MEENAKSHI SUNDARESWARAR TEMPLE

One of the most famous temples of South India, it houses the deities of goddess Meenakshi (with eyes like a fish), said to be an avatar of goddess Parvati and Sundareswarar or Lord Shiva. With elaborately carved pillars, this colossal temple, which was built between the 8th and 17th century is considered an architectural marvel. Its main attraction is 14 magnificently carved towers. Four of these elaborately sculptured rajagopurams, each nine-storeys high, stand in each of the cardinal directions to mark the entrances to the temple. Eight shorter but exquisitely carved ones line the concentric squares that lead to the deities in the centre. Two golden pinnacles rise over the sanctums of the temples which are dedicated to Shiva and Meenakshi. The thousand-pillar hall has been converted into a museum and houses stone sculptures of gods and goddesses.

www.maduraimeenakshi.org; special darshan ₹50/100; 5am–12.30pm, 4–10pm; Thousand Pillar Museum adult/child ₹5/2; 7am–1pm, 4–8pm; no photography

Thirumalai Nayak Palace is a fusion of Dravidian and European architectural styles

❷ GANDHI MEMORIAL MUSEUM

Housed in the 16th-century summer palace of Rani Mangammal of the Nayak dynasty, the Gandhi Museum showcases many personal items belonging to Mahatma Gandhi and other exhibits. Spend some time going through the special exhibition on 'India Fights for Freedom' where the entire history from the Battle of Plassey to Independence Day has been depicted in 30 panels. Among the exhibits at the museum, the most

✓ Top Tip: Bus tours

A comfortable way of touring Madurai is to opt for one of the three tours conducted by the **Madurai Sightseeing Company** (☏8939039000; www.maduraisightseeing.com; ₹400 per adult). The first tour (Mon–Sat 8am–2pm) takes you to the Meenakshi Temple, Mariamman Theppakulam and Nayak's Palace. The darshan is not part of the tour, but they give you time for it. The tour also includes one hour of shopping. The second tour (Mon–Sun 3–9.30pm) takes you to Alagar Kovil and the Jain caves, and the third tour (Sun only 7.30am–2pm) takes you to a larger number of Jain caves. All tours are in an AC bus with an English speaking guide; hotel pick-ups are available.

significant is the blood-stained cloth worn by Gandhi at the time of his assassination.

☏0452 2531060; www.gandhimmm.org; Tamukkam; camera ₹50; 10am–1pm, 2–5.45pm, Fri closed

❸ THIRUMALAI NAYAK PALACE

Constructed by Nayak king Thirumalai in 1636, the palace is an architectural fusion of Dravidian and European styles designed by an Italian architect. The current structure is only one-fourth of the original palace; the rest was destroyed by Thirumalai Nayak's grandson, who wanted to move the capital to Tiruchirappalli and build his own palace. The pillared corridors and sculptures on the walls are striking. Unfortunately, guides are difficult to get, so if you want to understand more about the Nayak rulers and Thirumalai, watch the sound-and-light show held every evening.

2.5km from Meenakshi Temple; adult/child (Indian) ₹10/5, (foreigner) ₹50/25; camera/video ₹30/100; 9am–5pm; Sound-and-Light show adult/child (English) ₹50/25, (Tamil) ₹25/10; English 6.45pm Tamil 8pm ,

❹ MARIAMMAN TEPPAKULAM

This huge tank is the largest in Tamil Nadu. Built by Thirumalai Nayak in 1645, the mud excavated from this tank was used to make bricks for his palace. During the float festival

Highlights

❶ Meenakshi Sundareswarar Temple
❷ Gandhi Memorial Museum
❸ Thirumalai Nayak Palace
❹ Mariamman Teppakulam
❺ Thirupparankundram Temple
❻ Alagar Kovil Temple
❼ Jain Rock Caves

♥ If You Like: Festivals

- **Jalli Kattu:** This takes place during Pongal on 15 and 16 January. Jalli Kattu is a show of valour, where young men try to overpower a raging bull among cheering crowds.

- **Chithirai:** This month-long festival is held in April. On the first 15 days people celebrate the marriage of goddess Meenakshi with Shiva or Lord Sundareswar and the deities are paraded in their wedding attire around the temple streets. The next half of the month is a celebration of Meenakshi's brother, Lord Alagar.

in January, the tank is filled with water and idols of goddess Meenakshi and her consort Lord Sundareswarar are brought here in colourful floats.

2km from Meenakshi Temple

❺ THIRUPARANKUNDRAM TEMPLE

The antiquity of this cave temple atop a hill can be gauged from the fact that poets as far back as the Sangam age (3BC–3AD) have sung paeans to it. The current structure was built by the Pandya kings in the 8th century, while the seven-tiered gopuram and 48-pillared mugha mandapam were added by the Nayak kings in the 16th and 17th centuries. The temple is considered to be one of the six abodes of Lord Murugan (Karthikeya), and is venerated as the place where he married Indra's daughter, Devasena (or Deivayani). This tradition has made it a favoured temple for couples to tie the knot. The Panguni Uthiram festival in March/April, when the wedding is re-enacted, is a huge draw.

8km from Madurai; 5.30am–12.30pm, 4–8.30pm

❻ ALAGAR KOVIL

Located on the foothills near Madurai, Vishnu is worshipped in this ancient temple as Lord Alagar (brother of Meenakshi). This is one of the 108 divya desams (sacred shrines) of Lord

📷 Snapshot: Legend of Meenakshi Temple

The Pandya king Malayadwaja and his wife Kanchanamalai conducted a yagna to invoke the gods to bless them with a child. A girl child appeared out of the holy fire. However, she had three breasts and it was prophesised that the third breast would disappear when she met her husband. As soon as she set eyes on Lord Shiva, her third breast disappeared. Shiva then came to Madurai and married the goddess who had been crowned as queen. Meenakshi and Shiva as Sundara Pandiyan then ruled over Madurai for a long time.

The Keelakuyilkudi Jain cave is located close to Madurai

Vishnu. Do visit the kalyana mandapam, a hall with beautiful sculptures where marriages are solemnised. Before visiting Alagar Kovil, devotees usually pray at the Karrupanaswamy Temple, devoted to a village diety, considered the guardian of the village as well as a guard of Lord Alagar. This temple adjoins Alagar Kovil and what makes it unique is that there is no idol – just a sword representing Lord Karrupanaswamy.
20km from Madurai; www.alagakovil.org; 5.30am–noon, 4–8pm

❼ JAIN CAVES

Several Jain caves dating back to the 3rd century BC lie around Madurai. Prominent among them is **Thenparankundram**, right behind the cave temple of Thiruparankundram, 8km from Madurai. Stone engravings dating back to the 2nd century BC establish that the hill served as a monastery for Jain monks. There are three Tamil Brahmi inscriptions and over 10 rock beds in this cave. **Keelakuyilkudi**, 8km from Madurai, is another Jain site. On top of the cave is a sculpture of Mahavira cut into the rock.

Rameswaram

Highlights
1. Sri Ramanathaswamy Temple
2. Gandamadana Parvatham
3. Panchmukhi Hanuman Temple
4. Abdul Kalam's House
5. Dhanushkodi

❶ SRI RAMANATHSWAMY TEMPLE
This is one of the 12 Jyotirlingam shrines revered by Hindus and devotees from across the country and the only one located in South India. The 1212-pillared Third Corridor is considered the longest corridor in the world. The temple has 22 wells where pilgrims bathe before a darshan. While devotees queue up alongside the wells, priests throw water on them. As a result the whole temple becomes wet and slippery. At 5.10am there is a puja, where Shiva as a spatikalingam (a type of crystal) is worshipped. This is considered one of the main pujas.
2km from railway station, entrance from East Gate; special darshan ₹50, bathing in the 22 wells ₹25; 5am–1pm, 3–9pm

❷ GANDAMADANA PARVATHAM
This shrine on top of a hillock is the highest point in Rameswaram so the views are stunning. There is an imprint of two feet on a chakra, believed to be those of Lord Rama.
4km from railway station; 6.30am–6.30pm

❸ PANCHMUKHI HANUMAN TEMPLE
Besides having a rare idol of Hanuman with five faces, the temple has a small water tank with stones floating in it. The

Crossing the long Pamban sea bridge is an experience in itself

MADURAI & RAMESWARAM

> ### 📷 Snapshot:
> ### Legend of Sri Ramanathaswamy Temple
>
> After killing Ravana, Lord Rama returned to the mainland and wanted to pray to Lord Shiva to expiate himself from the sin of killing the demon king. He directed Hanuman to bring the lingam from Mount Kailash, but since Hanuman was delayed, Sita prepared one of sand, which Rama sanctified and worshipped. The lingam in the temple is believed to be the same one. When Hanuman returned with the Vishwalingam from Mount Kailash, Lord Rama assured him that it would be placed north of the main lingam and devotees would worship both.

priest will tell you that it was stones like these that were used to make the legendary bridge between India and Sri Lanka, which the monkey army of Lord Rama used to cross the sea and invade Sri Lanka to rescue Sita.

2km from railway station; 7am–7pm

❹ ABDUL KALAM'S HOUSE

At this house of former Indian President APJ Abdul Kalam, which has been converted into a museum by his family, numerous photographic exhibits trace his life from childhood to his term as President. Also on display are books written by him and the various awards he has won, including the Padma Bhushan and the Bharat Ratna.

Muslim St; entry free; 10am–noon, 4–6pm, Fri closed

❺ DHANUSHKODI

With the Bay of Bengal on one side and the Arabian Sea on the other, Dhanushkodi is a great place for a drive. However, it may be bumpy, but the beautiful landscape makes up for that. Once a flourishing seaside town, Dhanushkodi was destroyed by a cyclone in 1964, and is now only a ghost town.

20km from railway station; entry not allowed after 6pm; jeeps seating 5–6 persons ₹1000–1200 round trip, mini vans seating 12–15 persons ₹2000–2500

> ### 📷 Snapshot:
> ### Pamban Bridge
>
> This 2.3km long bridge, which connects Rameswaram to mainland India, is the second longest sea bridge in the country. Next to the crossing for vehicles is the cantilevered railway bridge that can be raised to let ships and barges pass through, and if lucky, you may get to see one.

Accommodation

MADURAI

The Gateway Hotel — Luxury Hotel ₹₹₹
☏ 0452 6633000, 2371601; www.thegatewayhotels.com; No 40, TPK Rd, Pasumalai; d ₹6000–8000 (incl of breakfast) Surrounded by 62 acres of landscaped gardens atop Pasumalai hill, The Gateway Hotel is one of the highest points in Madurai. Each cottage has two or three large and airy rooms with a common verandah. The property has a pool and an Ayurveda centre as well. However, it's more convenient for those who have their own vehicles. Otherwise you need to book cabs to reach town (20km) and a round trip will cost between ₹630–730.

Heritage Madurai — Luxury Hotel ₹₹
☏ 0452 3244187; www.heritagemadurai.com; 11, Melakkal Main Rd; Kochadai; ₹4500–8000 (incl of breakfast) One of the main attractions of this hotel is that each villa comes with a small 2ft deep pool. The deluxe rooms are comfortable with really large bathrooms. Heritage Madurai has a swimming pool and a golf simulator as well.

Fortune Pandiyan Hotel — Hotel ₹₹
☏ 0452 4356789; www.fortunehotels.in; Race Course; d ₹4600–7500 (incl of breakfast) One of the oldest hotels in Madurai, Fortune Pandiyan, is set amidst landscaped gardens and offers a fitness centre, swimming pool with a special kids section and a spa that has Indonesian therapists. Most of the rooms have been recently renovated. There's a multi-cuisine restaurant, Orchid, and a bar, The Ranch, which is a popular watering hole for the city's elite crowd.

GRT Regency — Hotel ₹₹
☏ 0452 2371155; www.grthotels.com; 38, Madakulam Rd, TPK Rd, NH 7, Palanganatham Signal Junction; d ₹4750–5750 (incl of breakfast) Everything about the GRT spells class. This beautiful hotel has large and elegantly furnished rooms, an Ayurvedic massage centre, fitness centre and a pool. Its multi-cuisine restaurant, Ahaaram, hosts a number of food festivals throughout the year.

Sangam Hotel — Hotel ₹₹
☏ 0452 4244555; www.sangamhotels.com; Alagarkoil Rd; d ₹4750–5750 (incl of breakfast) One of the older hotels in Madurai, Sangam is popular with both locals as well as outsiders. The deluxe rooms have a see-through glass partition between the bathroom and the room, allowing you to soak in the Jacuzzi and still watch TV. There's a pool, too, and a beautiful multi-cuisine restaurant called Madurai. It is adorned with lovely paintings and is set around a small waterbody. It offers a lunch buffet (₹425 weekdays, ₹475 weekends) and a la carte dinner.

Royal Court   Hotel ₹₹
☏ 0452 4356666; www.royalcourtindia.com; opp railway station, 4, West Veli St; d ₹4000–4700 (incl of breakfast) Located in the heart of the city, just a 10-minute walk from the Meenakshi Temple, Royal Court offers a choice of regular and executive rooms. There's also a fitness centre and a rooftop restaurant with lovely views of the Meenakshi Temple. The hotel provides accommodation for drivers.

The inviting rooms of Sangam Hotel

JC Residency   Hotel ₹₹
☏ 0452 4200399; www.jcresidency.com; 14, Lady Doak College Rd; d ₹3500 (inc of breakfast) Elegantly designed, the JC Residency is a welcome addition to Madurai's hotel scene. The rooms have carved furniture and oil paintings depicting various chapters from the Bible adorn the walls. The staff is warm and helpful, but the service is slow.

Hotel Park Plaza   Hotel ₹₹
☏ 0452 3011111; www.hotelparkplaza.net; 114-115, West Perumal Maistry St; d ₹2800–3850 (incl of breakfast & dinner) Located close to the Meenakshi Temple, Park Plaza is good value for money. Book a few weeks in advance and you may get a temple-view room. While all the front office staff speak fluent English, the rest are not as proficient and you may have some trouble communicating with them.

Heritage Residency   Hotel ₹
☏ 0452 2665501; www.heritageresidency.com; 144/1-A, NH 7 Bypass Rd, K Salai Pudur; d ₹2500–3000 (incl of breakfast) A recently opened hotel, Heritage Residency, offers neat rooms that are done up brightly and have elegant furniture. However the bathrooms are small. It has a rooftop swimming pool, fitness centre and a multi-cuisine restaurant, Nlabagam.

Madurai Residency   Hotel ₹
☏ 0452 4380000; www.madurairesidency.com; 15, West Marret St; d ₹2300–2700 (incl of breakfast) The first thing that catches your eye in this hotel is the colourful mural depicting life in Madurai. The rooms are clean and spacious but the bathrooms are small in comparison. It has a rooftop multi-cuisine restaurant, Megan but it's open only for dinner from 7 to 11pm.

RAMESWARAM

Until a few years ago Rameswaram had only lodges and dharamshalas. Now, however, several hotels have come up.

Daiwik Hotel — Hotel ₹₹
📞 04573 223222, 301401; www.daiwikhotels.com; NH 49 Madurai Rameswaram Highway; d ₹3500–4500 (incl of breakfast) This tastefully designed hotel has the only spa in Rameswaram. The rooms are elegantly furnished and all the suites have a separate living room. Ahaan, the vegetarian restaurant, offers a buffet for lunch and dinner (₹304 incl of taxes). The hotel has rooms for drivers, is walking distance from the bus stand and around two kilometres from Ramanathaswamy Temple.

Hotel Royal Park — Hotel ₹
📞 04573 221680, 221321; www.hotelroyalpark.in; Semma Madam, Ramnad Highway; d ₹2000–2500 Located on the highway, this is the first hotel you come across as soon as you enter Rameswaram. It's a modern hotel with a spiritual mooring. The lobby has sculptures of Rama and Sita and an installation of the kalpavriksha – a golden tree meant to fulfil one's heart's desires. The rooms and bathrooms are modern and have all necessary amenities. A pure vegetarian restaurant, Bhojan, offers buffet meals.

Hotel Queen Palace — Hotel ₹
📞 04573 221013, 221131, 9442100704; www.hotelqueenpalace.com; near bus stand, NH Rd; d ₹1600–3000 This budget hotel has clean and modern rooms and suites, though the bathrooms are a bit small. Only two kilometres away from the temple, its triple-bed room is ideal for a family. Hot water is a problem as the water is solar heated and often not avialble in the morning.

All suites at Daiwik Hotel have wooden flooring and a separate living room

Hotel Vinayaga   Hotel ₹

📞04573 222361; www.vinayagahotel.com; 5, Railway Feeder Rd; d ₹1800–2000 The hotel is just five minutes away from the railway station and offers simple, clean rooms and bathrooms. The staff is pleasant and always willing to help. The vegetarian restaurant offers local dishes. The travel desk can organise trips to Dhanushkodi.

Hotel Sunrise View   Hotel ₹

📞0452 2523030; www.hotelnorthgate.com; Goripalayam; d ₹2000–3000 (incl of breakfast) Sunrise View is opposite the temple entrance and hence perfect if you are visiting Rameswaram primarily for this reason. Most of the rooms overlook the sea, however a strong smell of fish generally pervades the hotel. Though there is no restaurant, room service is available.

Hotel Tamil Nadu   Hotel ₹

📞04573 221277; www.tamilnadutourism.org; near Agni Theertham; d ₹1500–2000 (incl of breakfast) This TTDC hotel boasts one of the best locations in town. The large property with plenty of trees is right next to the sea, also called Agni Theertham, where pilgrims are required to take a dip before going to the temple. The sea-view rooms are a better choice so it's best to book in advance. This is the only hotel in Rameswaram that has a bar.

A typical south Indian vegetarian thali is easily available in both the cities

Eating

MADURAI

The joy of this city's culinary delights lies in its stand-alone restaurants and messes. And since the city never sleeps you can get a meal anytime of the day and night at the food stalls near the bus stop and railway station.

Murugan Idli Shop   South Indian ₹

📞0452 2341379; 196 West Masi St; mains ₹40–50; 6am–midnight Murugan Idli almost has a cult status. And while most think it's all about the idlis, there is a lot more to try out at this no-frills restaurant near Meenakshi Temple. You can have your fill of dosas, idlis and utthapam, sambhar and chutney on a clean banana leaf. You must try the famous Madurai summer drink – jigar thanda – a combination of milk, sugar syrup, malai and ice cream for ₹15.

Sree Mohan Bhojanalaya — Vegetarian ₹
☏ 0452 2346093; 33, Dhanappa Mudali St, opp Hotel Temple View, West Tower St; mains ₹85–135; 7am–10.30pm If you want simple, home-style cooked north Indian veg food in unlimited quantities, climb up to Sree Mohan Bhojanalaya and order from a variety of thalis offering puris, aloo parathas or chapattis. Sharing thalis is not allowed, but you may be asked to share a table.

Dhivya Mahal Restaurant — Multi-Cuisine ₹
☏ 0452 2342700, 2342790; 21, Town Hall Rd; mains ₹80–200; noon–11pm A small nondescript restaurant divided into booths by aquariums, Mahal has been around for decades. An extensive menu offers everything from vegetable au gratin (₹90) to fish and chips (₹150). A 'must try' are their ice creams, including jackfruit and black currant. Don't expect food to be served quickly especially if you are in one of the corner booths.

Phil's Bistro — Multi-Cuisine ₹₹
☏ 0452 2583444; Door No 444, East 9th St, near Rajmahal Kalyana Mandapam, KK Nagar; mains ₹150–350; noon–3pm, 6–11pm One of the few stand-alone restaurants serving continental food in Madurai, Phil's Bistro, run by chef Philip, specialises in Italian and American food. So you get wood-fired pizzas such as Popeye's pizza (with spinach and cheese, ₹160) and chicken pepper steak (₹300), both worth trying. His take on fusion food is also good. Service is prompt.

Amma Mess — Non-Vegetarian ₹₹
☏ 0452 4360361; 136, Alagar Kovil Rd, Tallakulam; mains ₹120–250; 11am–5pm, 7–11pm One of the most popular places for non-vegetarians, Amma Mess is perpetually crowded. It is known for its rabbit chops (₹160), mutton biryani (₹150), crab omelette (₹160) and pigeon roast (₹180). However it offers absolutely nothing for vegetarians. Even dosa is served with mutton curry and not sambhar. Service is fast and they always try and accommodate you even if it means sharing a table.

Sri Gobu Iyengar Kadai — South Indian ₹
☏ 9788730177; 37/35 Mela Chitrai St; mains ₹30–40; 7–10.30am, 3–7.30pm, Mon closed Very close to the north and west gates of the Meenakshi Temple is a small kadai (shop) specialising in filter coffee (₹11) and tiffin items such as bhajji, idli and utthapam since 1932. It's the perfect place to stop just before or after the temple darshan.

KB Konar Mess — Non-Vegetarian ₹
☏ 0452 2538311; 117 Alagar Kovil Main Rd, Tallakulam; mains ₹80–150; 11am–noon This is another basic but popular place for non-vegetarians,

where meals are served on banana leaves. Try the kari dosai (mutton dosa,₹110), which is like a miniature utthapam with meat toppings, and liver curry (₹90).

British Bakery — Cafe ₹

0452 4374477; 31 A ½ West Veli St; near railway station; mains ₹40–100; 7.30am–10.30pm A small cafe selling coffee, pizzas, sandwiches, pastries, cakes and snacks like bhelpuri, British Bakery is an apt place to grab a quick bite.

RAMESWARAM

Being a temple town, non-veg food is not easily available in Rameswaram. Pure veg food can be had at various messes and bhojanalayas around the temple.

Ahaan — Multi-Cuisine ₹₹

04573 301401; Daiwik Hotel, NH 49 Madurai Rameswaram Highway; buffet ₹304 (incl taxes); noon–3pm, 7–10pm Try the lunch and dinner buffet here, with a decent variety of north Indian, south Indian, Chinese and ample desserts.

Ashok Bhawan — Vegetarian ₹

9965117001; No 6 West Car St, near Indian Bank; mains ₹60; 7am–4pm, 7–10pm For a simple home-cooked style veg thali, either north Indian (₹60) or south Indian (₹50), head to Ashok Bhawan, a five minute walk from the temple. Service is prompt and the food wholesome.

Hotel Saravana Bhavan — South Indian ₹

9597077203; Thittakkudi Corner; mains ₹15–60; 5am–10.30pm Saravana Bhavan never disappoints. Have a plate of idli (₹16) or an onion dosa (₹35) for breakfast and then a full south Indian thali or meal for lunch. This place is also a five-minute walk from the temple and hence ideal for a stopover after darshan.

> Phil's Bistro is one of the few places in Madurai where you can get Italian food

Ambika Bhojanalaya — North Indian ₹

☎ 0457 223834; Middle St; mains ₹60–80; 8.30am–3pm, 6.30–10pm Thronged by pilgrims from north India wanting to eat dal, rice, chappati and vegetables, Ambika Bhojanalaya offers unlimited thalis. The menu changes every day for both lunch and dinner, ensuring a variety.

🛍 Shopping

MADURAI

Pothys — Clothing

☎ 0452 4262333; 159, West Masi St; 9am–9.30pm Part of a large chain with stores in Chennai and Coimbatore, the four-floored Pothys is crowded with customers wanting to purchase saris, readymade clothes and material for men, women and children, imitation jewellery, bags and also cosmetics.

Bhima — Jewellery

☎ 0452 4231500; www.bhimajewellery.com; 137 West Masi St; 9.30am–9.30pm Just two buildings away from Pothys, Bhima is a large jewellery store that has two more branches – in Thiruvananthapuram and Nagercoil. It specialises in gold, diamond and platinum jewellery, hallmarked and hence with an assurance of quality.

Ranee Saris JSV TEX — Saris

☎ 0452 2330931; 157-A, South Masi St, near KVB Bank; 10am–9pm, 10am–7pm Sun One of the oldest sari shops in Madurai, it specialises in cotton saris, especially wax prints, batik and tie-and-dye. You are required to sit on a mat while a sales girl shows you a huge variety of saris. They do not accept credit cards.

Uttara — Boutique

☎ 0452 4353556; www.uttara-inca.com; Second Floor, 73, Chandragandhi Nagar, Bypass Rd; 9am–9pm, 2–9pm Sun A chic boutique selling ethnic wear for women, Uttara is trying to revive the sungudi style – an old art of tie-and-dye particular to Madurai but not commonly available now. You can pick up from a limited but beautiful range of saris, kurtas and suit materials. Their collection of terracotta jewellery is worth checking out.

> ### ✓ Top Tip: Shopping at Pudhu Mandapam
>
> The Pudhu Mandapam, opposite the Meenakshi Temple is a 17th-century mandapam, where sculptures jostle for space with shops selling various trinkets. You can buy everything from cosmetics and lace to utensils, books and toys. There are also tailors present who specialise in stitching clothes within a few hours and delivering them to your hotel. Most shops are open from 11am and 8.30–9pm.

Poompuhar — Handicrafts
☎ 0452 2340517; 12, West Veli St; 10am–8pm, Sun closed Run by the Tamil Nadu Handicrafts Corporation, the collection of traditional Tamilian handicrafts here is considered quite superior. Choose from a range of brass and stone idols, Tanjore paintings, as well as a host of things from other states, such as sandalwood products from Karnataka.

Cottage Arts Emporium — Handicrafts
☎ 0452 2623614; www.cottageartsemporium.com; 44 North Chitrai St; 9am–8.30pm Walking distance from the north gate of the Meenakshi Temple, the emporium houses one of the largest collections of handicrafts in Madurai. It's run by Kashmiris and an entire floor is devoted to Kashmiri carpets. You can buy traditional jewellery all the way from Ladakh down to the Toda tribes of the Nilgiris. They also keep some traditional Chettinadu jewellery

> Shopping at Pudhu Mandapam is an experience that should not be missed

pieces. The prices, however, are on the higher side.

Khadi Gramodyog Bhavan — Handicrafts
☎ 0452 2339758; 108, TPK Rd; 9am–9pm, Sun closed A good place to pick up typical Madurai souvenirs such as brass idols of goddess Meenakshi or miniature models of the Meenakshi Temple.

RAMESWARAM

Kalam Sea Shell Mart — Souvenirs
☎ 04573 221294, 222194; 27-A Muslim St; 7am–9pm Housed next to ex-president APJ Abdul Kalam's house and run by his family members, the Kalam Sea Shell Mart sells everything from soft toys to bone china and cheap Chinese imports ranging from lamps to nail cutters. Make your way carefully around this small store, else you might bump into something breakable.

Kanyakumari

Upon reaching the tip of the country you'll be greeted with the surreal sight of the waters of three seas, the Bay of Bengal, the Arabian Sea and the Indian Ocean, merging into one another. There are certain times of the year when you can see the sun set and the moon rise simultaneously at this unique spot. Kanyakumari is surrounded by hills bordered by the sea, fringed with coconut trees and paddy fields.

Trip Planner

GETTING THERE

Thiruvananthapuram International Airport (90km) is the nearest airport with daily flights to all metros and a few international destinations as well. The Kanyakumari Railway Station is connected via daily trains to all the metros. Vivek Express (15906) which leaves on Saturdays runs all the way to Dibrugarh in Assam, covering 4241km in 85 hours, making it the single longest train ride in the country. It stops at 54 places on the way. Taxis from Kovalam cost ₹1500.

SUGGESTED ITINERARY (2 DAYS)

Sightseeing in Kanyakumari will not take longer than a day but you should spend a night to catch both a sunset and a sunrise. Next day make your way to Suchindram Temple and also visit Padmanabhapuram Palace.

BEST TIME TO GO

J F M A M J J A S **O N D**

GREAT FOR

Top 5 highlights

- **Kumari Amman Temple** (p387)
- **Vivekananda Memorial** (p389)
- **Seafront** (p389)
- **Beach View Park & Viewing Tower** (p389)
- **Triveni Sangam** (p389)

Meeting Point

Statue of Tamil poet Thiruvalluvar are next to each other

The end of India is not just the end of the road – it has far more appeal. You feel a whiff of accomplishment upon making it to the tip of the country, the terminus of a narrowing funnel of rounded granite mountains, green fields plaited with glinting rice paddies and slow-looping turbines on wind farms. There's a sense of the surreal here. You can see the confluence of three great water bodies, the sunset merging into the moonrise and the Temple of the Virgin Sea Goddess within minutes of each other. Beyond that, **Kanyakumari** (Cape Comorin) is a friendly town. A temple lies at the tip of Kanyakumari and leading north from it is a small bazaar lined with restaurants, stalls and souvenir shops.

❶ KUMARI AMMAN TEMPLE

Located on the tip of the subcontinent, at the confluence of mighty seas and the ocean, stands goddess Kanyakumari, worshipped as the guardian of seas and the vanquisher of evil. This temple is more than 1000 years old and was built by the Pandya kings of Madurai and later renovated by the Cholas and Nayaks. The setting is gorgeous and the nearby crash of waves from three seas can be heard through the twilight glow of oil fires clutched in votive candles. The

Highlights
1. Kumari Amman Temple
2. Gandhi Memorial
3. Kamaraj Memorial
4. Swami Vivekananda Wandering Monk Exhibition
5. Vivekanandapuram
6. Vivekananda Memorial
7. Seafront
8. Beach View Park & Viewing Tower
9. Triveni Sangam

shoreline around the temple has a couple of tiny beaches and bathing ghats. Souvenir shops lead back from here to the main road.
4.30am–12.30pm, 4–8.15pm

2 GANDHI MEMORIAL
Appropriately placed at the end of the nation is this memorial dedicated to Mahatma Gandhi, who visited Kanyakumari twice. It resembles an Orissa temple. The central plinth was used to store some of the Mahatma's ashes. Exhibits are limited to a few uncaptioned photos. Guides may ask for more, but ₹10 is enough.
Admission by donation; 7am–7pm

3 KAMARAJ MEMORIAL
Just next to the Gandhi memorial is a shrine dedicated to K Kamaraj, the former chief minister of Tamil Nadu, also known as 'the Gandhi of the South'. There is a rare collection of photographs, but no context or explanation.
7am–7pm

4 SWAMI VIVEKANANDA WANDERING MONK EXHIBITION
This newly refurbished exhibition details Swami Vivekananda's life from 1888 to 1893, as a wandering monk.

Swami Vivekananda Memorial is built in different architectural styles

Photos, letters and other exhibits detail his growth in these five years.
Main Rd; ₹10; 8am–noon and 4–8.15pm

5 VIVEKANANDAPURAM

This ashram, 3km north of town, provides a snapshot of Indian philosophy, religion, leaders and thinkers. Vivekananda Kendra, devoted to propagating Vivekananda's teachings, has its headquarters here, with some tourist accommodation.
☏ 04652 247012; www.vivekanandakendra.org; ₹34; 8am–4pm

6 VIVEKANANDA MEMORIAL

Four hundred metres offshore is the rock where Swami Vivekananda meditated. A two-mandapa memorial was built in 1970, and reflects architectural styles drawn from all over the country. The statue on the smaller island is of Tamil poet Thiruvalluvar. Built in 2000, it is the work of more than 5000 sculptors and honours his 133-chapter work *Thirukural* – hence its height of 133ft.
Ferries 7.45am–4pm; tickets ₹30 (return) Memorial entry ₹10; 8am–5pm

7 SEAFRONT

There's a crowded beach here and ghats that lead to a lingam half submerged in a wave-driven tidal pool. There is also a memorial to victims of the 2004 tsunami.

8 BEACH VIEW PARK & VIEWING TOWER

Make your way here to get one of the best sunset views. Climb the spiral Viewing Tower for panoramic vistas.

9 TRIVENI SANGAM

A sandy patch at the Triveni Sangam – where the Bay of Bengal, Arabian Sea and the Indian Ocean meet – is packed with people who come to watch the waves lash the rocky shore.

Detour: Suchindram Temple

Located 11km before Kanyakumari, this temple is famous for its Sthanumalayan deity (Brahma, Vishnu, Mahesh in one sanctum) and for a wealth of architectural and sculptural details. The pillars of 'Alankara Mandapam' produce notes when struck lightly. The mesh of figures on the seven-storeyed gopuram is characteristic of 17th-century Dravidian architecture.

Accommodation

Some hotels, especially mid-range places around the bazaar, have seasonal rates hence the tariff doubles in April and May, and from late October to January.

Seashore Hotel — Hotel ₹₹
☏ 04652 246704; www.theseashorehotel.com; East Car St; r ₹3450–6500 This is one of the fanciest hotels in town, and has shiny, spacious rooms with gold curtains and cushions and glassed-in showers. All rooms except the cheapest ones have panoramic sea views and the 7th-floor restaurant is one of Kanyakumari's best. There is free wi-fi in the lobby.

Manickhan Tourist Home — Hotel ₹
☏ 04652 246387; www.hotelmaadhini.com; North Car St; r ₹800–1800 This hotel has large rooms that come with a TV and clean bathrooms and if you're willing to shell out a bit, you'll get superb sea views as well. The staff is friendly. Prices tend to rise in December, January and May.

Santhi Residency — Hotel ₹
☏ 04652 247091; Kovalam Rd; r ₹1000–1500 This small and old restored house has a more subtle sense of style as compared to other hotels. The only decoration in each simple room is a picture of Jesus Christ. It is a quiet and clean place with a nice patch of leafy garden.

Hotel Tri Sea — Hotel ₹
☏ 04652 246586; www.triseahotel.com; Kovalam Rd; d ₹800–1800 As you walk west of the town you can't miss the high-rise Tri Sea, which offers huge, airy rooms, most with balconies facing the sea. The colour schemes are hectic but there are flatscreen TVs and a rooftop pool. Interestingly the hotel has viewing platforms to watch the sunrise and sunset.

Hotel Tamil Nadu — Hotel ₹
☏ 04652 246257; www.ttdconline.com; Beach Rd; r from ₹900–1700 Despite the usual quirks of a government-run hotel, this TTDC property has a great location if you want to get away from the bustle of town; balcony rooms have ocean, though not temple views.

Saravana Lodge — Hotel ₹
☏ 04652 246007; Sannathi St; r ₹300–1000 It's basic, but you can get a reasonable deal at this place that is just outside the temple entrance. All rooms have private bathrooms, though there's no hot water. The better rooms are on the upper floors of the new block at the far end from the entrance.

Hotel Sun World — Hotel ₹
☏ 04652 247755; www.hotelsunworld.com; Kovalam Rd; d from ₹1500–1000 Everything's bright and glossy at this place, where most rooms have a private balcony with fabulous views of the sea.

Hotel Sivamurugan — Hotel ₹
☎ 04652 246862; www.hotelsivamurugan.com; 2/93 North Car St; r ₹1000–2000 This well-appointed new hotel has spacious and spotless rooms. The 'super-deluxe' rooms have sea views past a couple of buildings. There's 24-hour hot water, which not all competitors can claim.

Eating

Sangam Restaurant — Multi-Cuisine ₹
Main Rd; 7.30am–11pm It's as if the Sangam started in Kashmir, trekked across the entire country and stopped here to open a restaurant that features culinary picks culled from every province along the way. The food is good and the joint is bustling. The biggest downer is a height-and-weight machine by the front door that calculates your BMI.

Sri Krishna — Cafe ₹
Sannathi St If you need fresh juice, good ice cream, pizzas, chips and burgers, try this clean and bustling corner cafe.

Hotel Seaview — Multi-Cuisine ₹
East Car St; 6am–11pm This hotel has an excellent AC multi-cuisine restaurant specialising in fresh local seafood and north and south Indian favourites. The vibe is upmarket and waiters are very attentive. It's also probably the best breakfast spot in town, with buffet, continental and American options.

Hotel Tamil Nadu has a great location and some rooms overlook the ocean

Hotel Triveni — South Indian ₹
Main Rd This sea-facing restaurant is clean, has efficient service and good-value, mainly south Indian vegetarian dishes.

Hotel Sarvana — Vegetarian ₹
Sannathi St; 6am–10pm A popular spot with plenty of north and south Indian vegetarian dishes, and lunchtime thalis.

Geetha Bhavan — North Indian ₹
East Car Rd; 6am–10pm If you're craving for good north Indian food, make your way to Geetha Bhavan, you won't be disappointed.

Ocean Restaurant — Multi-Cuisine ₹₹
Seashore Hotel; East Car St; 7am–10.45pm This 7th-floor restaurant is the only one with a sea view and with great food and service. There's good grilled fish and plenty of Indian veg and non-veg choices.

Kodaikanal

Kodaikanal is one of those fortunate hill stations which retains its old-world charm despite its growing popularity and commercialisation. Here you can still see beautiful flowers blooming on roadsides and feast your eyes on lush greenery. Add to these delights, numerous gardens, walks and sights, and you have all the trappings of an ideal getaway, either for a short break or for a longer, more leisurely holiday.

Trip Planner

GETTING THERE

The nearest airport and railway station is in Madurai (120km). Both have daily connections to all the metros and other major cities in the country. Private buses from Chennai can take 10–11 hours and cost ₹800–1000. From Bengaluru buses take 9–11 hours and cost ₹600–900.

SUGGESTED ITINERARY (3 DAYS)

This hill station is compact and the central town area can easily be explored on foot. Spend the first day boating on the lake, strolling through Coaker's Walk and enjoying the vast variety of flowers at Bryant Park. Next day, head to the Kurinji Andavar Temple and stop over at Chettiar Park. Leave a little early on the third day and drive through the surrounding forest with stops at Silent Valley View and Berijam Lake.

BEST TIME TO GO

J F M **A M J** J A **S O** N D

GREAT FOR

Top 5 highlights

- **Kodaikanal Lake** (p394)
- **Bryant Park** (p394)
- **Coaker's Walk** (p394)
- **Chettiar Park** (p395)
- **Berijam Lake** (p397)

Evergreen Escape

Sometime in 1821, an American surveyor, Lt BS Ward, trudged 7,000 ft (2,133m) up the upper Palani hills and came upon a plateau, which he felt would be an ideal retreat for American missionaries looking for a break from the heat of the plains. The Europeans who followed agreed and hence 'Gift of the Forest' – Kodaikanal was found.

Kodaikanal does not have the commanding heights of the Himalayan ranges or its snow-capped peaks as a backdrop, but it has an extravagance of green. The morning glories and hydrangeas give the roadside a colourful and cheerful feel, while the gardens and parks exhibit horticultural ingenuity. The slopes around the hill station have forests where nature takes its own course with tall pines and clearings that have come to be a film director's and tourist's delight. The sheer cliffs all around command great views of the **Vaigai Dam** and the plains below.

April to June, when the clouds don't eclipse the sun, is the best time to visit. However, the rest of the year has its own charm, minus the crowds; the hotels are cheaper, and the mist, which creeps up without warning, adds to the mystique.

> Kodaikanal Lake is at the heart of the hill station

TAMIL NADU

Highlights
1. Kodaikanal Lake
2. Bryant Park
3. Coaker's Walk
4. Kurinji Andavar Temple
5. Chettiar Park
6. Silent Valley View
7. Pillar Rock
8. Green Valley View Point
9. Berijam Lake

❶ KODAIKANAL LAKE
Right in the heart of the hill station is the 45 hectare Kodaikanal Lake designed almost like a star. Made in 1863, today it's a popular spot where boating is the favourite activity though you can also hire a bike and cycle around it. There is also a good walking path encircling it and horse riding is available too.

Boating ₹50–190 (30 min), free for children below 5, cycle hire ₹20–50 (30 min); 9am–6pm

❷ BRYANT PARK
Located on the eastern side of the lake is the 20 acre Bryant Park, a lovely botanical garden with a mindboggling variety (740) of roses. There's also a greenhouse for orchids, ferns and other plants. The park is popular with fitness enthusiasts who frequent it for their morning or evening walks, lovers who get cosy in the shade of one of the many ancient trees and also families with children. There's a separate play area with swings.

Adult/child/camera/video camera ₹30/15/50/100; 9am–6pm

❸ COAKER'S WALK
Built by Lt Coaker in 1872, Coaker's Walk is a one-kilometre paved pedestrian path running along the edge of steep slopes. Take a stroll and admire the breathtaking views of the valley

Boating is a favourite activity at the lake

Snapshot: Flower show

Every year, usually in the last week of May, the annual flower and vegetable show is organised at Bryant Park as part of a week-long summer festival that also includes boat races on the lake. The flower show lasts only two days but you can see a profusion of varieties like pansies, carnations, roses, dahlias, poppy and much more. If you do decide to visit Kodai during that time, make your hotel bookings way in advance as most places get sold out.

below. Benches are placed strategically along the way for those who simply want to sit and soak in the scene. There's also a telescope house for closer views of the valley. Coaker's Walk should ideally be visited before 3pm as the mist starts to settle in by late afternoon.
Entry ₹5, camera ₹10; 6am–7pm

❹ KURINJI ANDAVAR TEMPLE
The Kurinji Andavar Temple commands a great view of the hill station, the Vaigai Dam and the Palani hills. Built in 1936 by a European lady who converted to Hinduism, the presiding deity of the temple is Murugan celebrated here as the Lord of the kurinji flower, that blossoms once in 12 years. There are several kurinji shrubs in the compound too.
5km from Central Bus Stand; 6am–7pm

❺ CHETTIAR PARK
On the way to the Kurinji Andavar Temple is Chettiar Park. It is small but full of flowers, paved paths and swings – a perfect hang-out place for the whole family.
4km from Central Bus Stand; adult/child (below 10yr) ₹15/10, camera/video camera ₹25/50; 9am–5pm

❻ SILENT VALLEY VIEW
True to its name the valley is silent, but unfortunately the people visiting the viewpoint are not. If they were, the experience would be better. Expect a large number of people chattering and marvelling at the view. Though there is an iron mesh at the edge, parents should be alert. Also make sure you go on a clear day or else the mist blankets it out.

View of Pillar Rock

Early mornings or late afternoons are better. Permission is required from the forest department office near the bus stand (8–10am) and only a limited number of vehicles are allowed from 10am–4.30pm.

Berijam Lake Rd, close to Pillar Rock; ₹150 per vehicle

❼ PILLAR ROCK

A 7km hike from Kodaikanal Lake brings you to a set of three rocks that are 122m high, shoulder to shoulder and are referred to as Pillar Rock. The cave on the far side of the pillars was earlier aptly named Devil's Kitchen because of the mist which mysteriously appeared to emanate from it. Now it goes under the rather prosaic name of Guna Cave after the shooting of an eponymous Tamil film there.

7km from Kodaikanal Lake; ₹3; 7am–6.30pm

❽ GREEN VALLEY VIEW POINT

Located around 5km from Kodaikanal Lake, next to the golf club, is Green Valley view point, from where on a clear day you can see views of the Vaigai Dam.

✓ Top Tip: Walk to Vattakanal

The trek to Vattakanal village, about 4.5km from the town centre, is a great experience. On the way, if you're lucky, you'll spot gaur (bison) or giant squirrels, go past La Saleth Church, a lovely blue and white structure, making your way through an unpaved track passing through Pambar Shola forest, a bridge above some falls and snack stalls selling tea, coffee, omelettes and corn.

The valley is almost 5000ft deep and was earlier known as Suicide Point. There are barbed wires now; however monkeys continue to be a hazard.
5km from Kodaikanal Lake

 BERIJAM LAKE
An hour's drive from Kodaikanal is the 15km long Berijam Lake, surrounded by forests. Boating is prohibited on this calm and serene freshwater lake as it is a source of water for the neighbouring villages. To visit the lake, you need to take permission from the forest department office near the bus stand from 8–10am. Only a limited number of vehicles are allowed between 10am and 4.30pm.
Berijam Lake Rd, close to Pillar Rock; ₹150 per vehicle

♥ *If You Like: Waterfalls*

- **Silver Cascade Falls:** These falls lie 8km before Kodai on the Madurai-Kodai route (Laws Ghat Road). The excess water in the Kodai Lake falls 180ft through piles of rocks to form the waterfall. Since it's on the way to Kodai, it also serves as a pit stop for vehicles. There are several shops selling fruit and forest products around it. Beware of monkeys.

- **Bear Shola Falls:** An ideal picnic spot just 3km from the bus stand. Earlier, bears would come here to drink water – hence this name. Cars need to be parked around half a kilometre away, from where it's a 10-minute walk. The best time to visit the falls is during the monsoon season.

Bear Shola Falls is a popular picnic spot

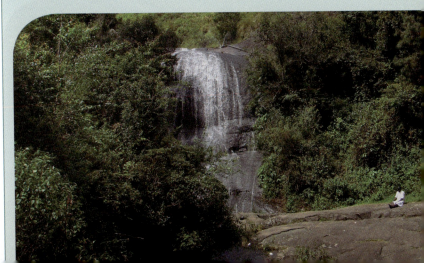

Accommodation

The Carlton   Hotel ₹₹₹
📞 04542 248555; www.krahejahospitality.com; Lake Rd; d ₹7915–8721 (incl of breakfast & dinner) The cream of Kodai's hotels is this five-star colonial-era mansion that overlooks the lake. The property, spread over five levels, offers beautiful views of the lake from most of the rooms which are spacious and comfortable. Every evening a fire is lit in the lounge and tambola and other games are organised for guests. The bar, serving Indian and foreign liquor, is open till 11pm. It also has its own jetty for guests to go boating on the lake.

The Fern Creek   Hotel ₹₹₹
📞 9360213034; www.theferncreek.com; Fern Hill Rd; d ₹7000 (incl of full board) The Fern Creek is a residential property converted into a hotel. While the original house has been transformed into the reception area and the dining room, seven Swiss luxury tents have been put up in the garden. Flowers, shrubs and trees of different sizes abound, giving enough privacy to each tent. All the tents have attached bathrooms. There's also a recreation room where guests can play chess, carom and other board games.

Kodai Resort Hotel   Hotel ₹₹
📞 04542 241301, 240632; www.kodairesorthotel.com; Noyce Rd; d ₹3900 (incl of breakfast) Conveniently located close to Coaker's Walk is Kodai Resort Hotel with 50 independent cottages. Each one has a private deck offering splendid views of the surrounding hills. The hotel offers amenities such as a health club and massage parlour. On rainy days, one can hang around in their den playing table tennis, board games or reading a book. However, the cottages are all on

The lounge at The Carlton is a favourite spot during chilly winter evenings when a fire is lit

The recreation room at The Fern Creek has wooden flooring and stone walls

different levels and you need to climb several stairs to reach the restaurant or the lobby.

Villa Retreat — Hotel ₹₹
04542 240940; www.villaretreat.com, Coaker's Walk; d ₹2878–4677 (incl of breakfast) Villa Retreat is an old stone-built property with breathtaking views of the valley and Vaigai Dam. The rooms are compact and clean. For best views choose the Classic Rooms. Meals are a combination of north and south Indian cuisine and are served in the dining room overlooking the valley.

Lilly's Valley Resort — Resort ₹₹
04542 244307, 9442241558; www.lillysvalley.com; 17/178 Sivanadi Rd; d ₹2950–3450 (incl of breakfast) This resort is a bit far from the centre of the hill station and you need to take a taxi to reach the lake and other areas. However, it is well worth it as it offers beautiful views of the valley and the rooms are spacious. The pine wood panelling and furniture give the rooms a nice feel. If you are travelling in a large group you can book the Ganesh Giri, a 110-year-old bungalow in the resort that sleeps eight to ten people (₹5950–7450).

Richwin Hotels — Hotel ₹
04542 242699, 245657; www.richwinhotels.com; 22/33-2, Anthoniyar Kovil St, Coaker's Walk; d ₹1439–2998 This budget hotel offers compact clean rooms and bathrooms. Some rooms in the hotel have an attached balcony for better views. It's centrally located and is walking distance from Coaker's Walk and Bryant Park. Service is efficient.

Top Tip: Guided tours

If you are interested in taking a guided tour of Kodaikanal and surrounding areas, make your way to the bus stand. Several taxi and tour operators have set up shop there. A guided city tour will cost approximately ₹250 per person. A trip to the forest, including Berijam Lake and Silent Valley View, costs around ₹275 per person with a guide. From April to June, government buses run at half hour intervals between 8am and 3pm. They charge ₹80 for adults and ₹40 for children.

Eating

Tava
Vegetarian ₹

04542 241153; Hotel Jewel Complex, Seven Road Junction; mains ₹75–125; 11am–8.45pm, Wed closed For homely north Indian fare head to Tava. The food is simple and tasty. It's a delight to find regular chappatis (made on the tava) here instead of the standard tandoori roti and naan. The food is pure vegetarian and besides regular food, Tava also offers snacks such as pav bhaji and sev puri. It's usually crowded so expect a 15–20 minute wait, but the meal is certainly worth it.

Cloud Street
Cafe ₹

PT Rd; opp government tourist office; mains ₹180; 8am–9pm
This simply decorated cafe on the first floor, has lovely views of the hill station and surrounding areas. You can sit at the balcony or on easy chairs inside and relax while you read from their collection of books and magazines. You can also play a board game, as the food takes a while to reach the table. The menu includes pizzas, pastas, sandwiches, coffee and cakes. They also have wi-fi connectivity.

Astoria
South Indian ₹

04542 245524; Anna Salai; mains ₹80–100; 7–10pm For a pure veg south Indian meal head to Hotel Astoria, next to the bus stand. While you will be served idli and dosa during breakfast, lunch is generally a south Indian thali comprising rice, sambhar, curd, poriyal (a dry vegetable), keerai (some leafy vegetable) and of course poppadam (papad).

Tibetan Brothers Restaurant
Chinese ₹

PT Rd; mains ₹100–150; noon–4pm, 5.30–10pm Colourful posters of Tibetan monasteries greet you as soon as you enter this small, no-frills restaurant. The menu is extensive and has a collection of Tibetan and Chinese dishes. If you haven't had Tibetan food before, you must try it, just to know what it's all about. But if you are familiar with the nuances of the cuisine and enjoy it, you will be disappointed. You are better off ordering the Chinese dishes.

The Silver Oak — Multi-Cuisine ₹₹₹
☏ 04542 248555; The Carlton, Lake Rd; buffet ₹750 (lunch) ₹850 (dinner); 1–3pm, 7.30–10.30pm
The lunch and dinner buffets at the Carlton are popular with locals and have a high rating with guests too. Lunch is served on the lawns on clear days and generally there is a barbeque. Dinner is in the restaurant and is a combination of north Indian, south Indian and continental. Try and go early as by 9–9.30pm most of the food has been polished off and you usually have to wait really long for it to be replenished.

 Shopping

Lord's Spices — Spices
☏ 9488056982; Bus Stand Complex; 9.30am–9.30pm Go here for its selection of fresh spices such as cloves and cardamoms or dry fruit like walnuts and almonds; they all make wonderful gifts. They also have a variety of herbal pastes and gels such as sandal paste and aloe vera gel. Their handmade soaps, innovatively packed, make good gifts too.

Danish Display — Handicrafts
☏ 04542 242455, 9842142495; 1 CLS Complex, Anna Salai; 9.30am–9.30pm There is nothing Danish about it, but if you are keen on handicrafts, this is the best place to find a good variety. Take your pick from a range, including wood carvings, brass statues, scented handmade candles and wooden bangles. They also have some woollens on sale. The prices of handicrafts are slightly higher than in the plains.

The Cocoa Bean — Chocolates
☏ 04542 240414; Maratha Shopping Complex, Anna Salai; 9.30am–9.30pm There's something about home-made chocolates and hill stations and Kodai is no exception. The Cocoa Bean sells several varieties of chocolates made with personal attention at home. There are also chocolate cookies you can binge on. Another must-try is their selection of home-made pickles and jams, especially the date pickle and blueberry jam.

The Eco Nut — Organic Food
☏ 04542 243296; PT Rd; 10.30am–5.30pm, Sun closed If you are a health food freak and like organic stuff, then Eco Nut is the place to be in. It specialises in food that is grown organically in Kodai. Here you can find dry fruit, nuts, cereals, hand-pounded brown rice and wheat bread herbs, biscuits, and home-made muffins.

Coimbatore & Valparai

Nestled between the Annamalai and Nilgiri ranges, Coimbatore is a wonderful base to explore the scenic beauty of neighbouring areas. The rolling tea estates of Valparai carpet the hillsides so perfectly they could be mistaken for manicured gardens. The crisp air and breathtaking views as you drive out a couple of hours from Coimbatore make it well worth a halt.

Trip Planner

GETTING THERE

Coimbatore: Coimbatore Airport, 21km from city centre, has direct flights from all the metros. Coimbatore Junction on Railway Road is the main railway station, where trains arrive from all metros. Buses from Chennai take over nine hours and cost ₹600–800; from Bengaluru they take six to seven hours and cost ₹500–650

Valparai: Coimbatore is the closest airport and railway station to Valparai, which is 104km from Coimbatore.

SUGGESTED ITINERARY (6 DAYS)

Arrive in Coimbatore and spend three days exploring the town's many highlights such as Perur Patteeswarar Swamy Temple, Echhanari Vinayaga Temple and GD Naidu Museum. You can next spend a night at the forest lodge at Topslip in the Annamalai Hills and go for a jungle safari. Then drive up to Valparai and spend a couple of days or more relaxing at a tea estate and enjoying the lush, green scenery from numerous viewpoints and adjoining dams.

BEST TIME TO GO

J F M A M J J A S **O N D**

GREAT FOR

Top 5 highlights

- **Perur Patteeswarar Swamy Temple, Coimbatore** (p404)
- **Echhanari Vinayaga Temple, Coimbatore** (p405)
- **Dhyanalinga Yogic Temple, Coimbatore** (p406)
- **Azhiyar Dam, Valparai** (p406)
- **Tea Estates, Valparai** (p407)

Kovai Calling

Valparai's lush tea estates

Coimbatore offers pleasant weather through the year and all necessary urban conveniences without the jostling for space seen in many other towns. The friendly people add to its charm. 'Kovai' to locals, Coimbatore is the second largest city of Tamil Nadu and the hub of 'Kongu nadu' culture. A traditional centre of the textile industry, the city is today a prosperous hub for trade and commerce.

It is uniquely located as a launch pad for exploring the Western Ghats. The three hill stations of the Nilgiris – Ooty (Udhagamandalam), Coonoor and Kotagiri – as well as Topslip and Valparai in the Annamalai range are close by. The journey is as good as the destination, so do slow down and take in the sights. Be prepared for sudden encounters with elephants, deer and bison. If you are lucky enough to sight wildlife, take care not to startle them. There are also amusement parks on the outskirts of the city.

About 100 km away is **Valparai**, which retains an elegance of the past because it is not frequented by hordes of tourists. It has lovely tea estates and several trekking options.

Coimbatore

Highlights
1. Perur Patteeswarar Swamy Temple
2. GD Naidu Museum
3. K Sreenivasan Art Gallery & Textile Museum
4. Eachanari Vinayagar Temple
5. Dhyanalinga Isha Yoga Centre & Temple

❶ PERUR PATTEESWARAR SWAMY TEMPLE
Located 6km from Coimbatore in the town of Perur, the Patteeswarar Swamy Temple is dedicated to Lord Shiva. It is popular with locals who come to pray for their ancestors. The lingam is a swambhyu (self manifested), around which Chola king Karikalan built the sanctum sanctorum in 2nd century AD. In the 17th century the Kanakasabai (Golden Hall of Dance), which has a statue of Nataraja, was added. The pillars have stone carvings of various manifestations of Shiva and the roof has stone chains with a lotus at the centre. The ceiling has beautiful paintings made from vegetable dyes. www.perurpatteeswarar.in; 5.30am–1pm, 4–8.20pm, temple closes 9pm

❷ GD NAIDU MUSEUM
This museum has a large collection of electronic items. You can see a collection of transistors and music systems from old spool players to vinyl to the latest USB drives. Do check out the old IBM computer – the size of a two-wheeler – but with just enough memory space to match a regular pen drive.

Kovai Kuttralam Falls are a popular getaway during the monsoons

♥ If You Like: Theme parks

- **Maharaja World** (☏04222 6504128; Neelambur; adult/child ₹400/350; 10.30am–6.30pm): Located 20km from Coimbatore, Maharaja World has a combination of wet and dry rides. Thrill seekers should try the Yellow Canyon ride. There is also a multiplex which screens the latest Tamil movies as well as a mini golf course.
- **Black Thunder** (☏04254 226632-40; www.btpark.org; 40km from Coimbatore; Ooty Main Rd, Mettupalayam; adult/child ₹500/450; 930am–5.30pm): This water theme park has several water rides and a few dry rides as well as a 5D theatre. Swimming costumes are not mandatory in the water. Some water areas are meant only for women and children.

There is an optical illusion section for children and a guide to help them understand different aspects of science.

☏0422 2222548; 734 Avinashi Rd; 8am–5pm, Sun closed

❸ K SREENIVASAN ART GALLERY & TEXTILE MUSEUM

Art lovers should definitely visit K Sreenivasan Art Gallery & Textile Museum to see the eclectic collection of Indian art such as Thanjavur paintings, copies of works of modern masters such as MF Husain, oil paintings by little known artists as well as lithographs of Raja Ravi Varma and European artists. In the textile section are charkhas, handlooms and textiles from across the country.

☏0422 2574110; kasthurisreenivasanartgallery.com; Culture Centre, Avinashi Rd; 10am–1pm, 2–6pm, Sun closed

❹ EACHANARI VINAYAGAR TEMPLE

This 15th-century temple is 10km from Coimbatore. The idol of Lord Ganesha here was meant for the Perur Patteeswarar Temple but the chariot broke and it was installed at Eachanari. The deity (6ft by 3ft) is one of the biggest Vinayaka idols in South India. The temple is popular with people who have bought a new vehicle.

☏0422 2672000; www.eachanarivinayagar.com; Pollachi Main Rd, Eachanari; 5am–10pm

✓ Top Tip: Waterfalls

The surrounding areas of Coimbatore and Valparai are dotted with waterfalls such as **Kovai Kuttralam**, 35km from Coimbatore, and **Monkey Falls**, located on the way to Valparai. However, the falls often dry up due to poor monsoons. Nevertheless, if you go in the monsoon months make sure to visit.

> **Detour: Topslip**
>
> Topslip, 75km away, is a base to explore the Indira Gandhi (Annamalai) Wildlife Sanctuary. Regulated treks through the forest, accompanied by forest guards (₹200 per person, minimum five people), with vehicle (₹125 per person) and elephant safaris (₹200 per person) provide an excellent opportunity to experience the diverse flora and fauna of the area. You can watch the safari elephants being fed at the elephant camp at 8.30am. Government accommodation is available. For a more varied experience combine the trip with a visit to Parambikulam, 20 km away in Kerala. There are regular buses from Pollachi bus stand to Topslip and Parambikulam. For accommodation, safaris and trekking contact Wildlife Warden Indira Gandhi Wildlife Sanctuary and National Park (📞04259 238360; 176 Meenkarai Rd, Pollachi).

❺ DHYANALINGA ISHA YOGA CENTRE & TEMPLE

Situated 30km away, in the foothills of the Velliangiri mountains, the massive Dhyanalinga Isha Yoga Centre & Temple complex has lovely sculptures, gardens and a lotus pond. There is a teerthkund (tank) where devotees are encouraged to take a dip but are charged ₹20 to do so. No particular religion is meant to be practised here and the place is meant for meditation. The Dhyanalingam, which is over 13ft high and the largest mercury-based lingam in the world, is considered a representative of Lord Shiva and you will find devotees prostrating themselves before it.

📞0422 2515345; www.dhyanalinga.org; Isha Yoga Centre, Semmedu (PO); 6am–8pm

Valparai

Highlights
1. Azhiyar Dam
2. Tea Estates
3. Sholaiyar Dam
4. Loam's View Point

❶ AZHIYAR DAM

Azhiyar Dam, located on the foothills of Valparai, is a welcome stopover either on your way to Valparai or from Pollachi. There is a children's park and if you climb more than 100 steps to reach the top of the dam you will be rewarded with a breathtaking view. The reservoir is on one side, on the other a green carpet made of treetops stretches out. Boating is available.

39km from Valparai; boating adult/child ₹40/30; 9am–5.30pm

❷ TEA ESTATES

Valparai is known for its rolling tea estates and it's best to take either long walks or drive through the lush green slopes. You can stop to talk to women plucking tea leaves or even try your hand at it to understand that a lot more than just a few leaves go into making your morning cup of tea. There are no guided tours of tea estates.

❸ SHOLAIYAR DAM

Around 30km from Valparai on the Chalakudy River is the 6km-long Sholaiyar Dam, amongst the longest dams in Asia. While the view from the dam is beautiful, the drive from Valparai to Sholaiyar is spectacular.
30km from Valparai; 9.30am–6.30pm

❹ LOAM'S VIEW POINT

On the way to Valparai is Loam's View Point. Stop here to take in the beautiful view of Azhiyar Dam and the lush Western Ghats.
9th hairpin bend

✓ *Top Tip: Trekking*

Valparai is best enjoyed on foot. There are many trekking routes in the Annamalai range, but they can be undertaken only with forest guards after due permission. The forest officers will give you the best option available depending on the season, number of people and your fitness level.

Try not to miss the 2km Poonajai trekking route that will take you through thick teak forests, a tribal settlement and a pond, where one can take a dip. Contact the Wildlife Warden, Indira Gandhi Wildlife Sanctuary and National Park.

Valparai's tea estates are best enjoyed by taking long walks

Accommodation

COIMBATORE

Surya – Vivanta By Taj   Luxury ₹₹₹
☎ 0422 6681000; www.vivantabytaj.com; 105 Race Course Rd; d ₹10,000–12,000 (incl of breakfast)
Spacious rooms, courteous staff and good food are trademarks of Taj hospitality and Vivanta By Taj does not disappoint. It has three restaurants, a pool and health club. However, some things can irk you, such as being asked to pay for wi-fi.

Le Meridien   Luxury ₹₹₹
☎ 0422 2364343; www.starwoodhotels.com ; 762 Avinashi Rd; d ₹7500–9000 (incl of breakfast) Le Meridien lives up to its classification of 'luxury' – the rooms are spacious and comfortable, and each of the twin beds in a room is almost the size of a queen bed. Those overlooking the swimming pool are quieter than the others.

The Residency   Hotel ₹₹
☎ 0422 2241414; www.theresidency.com; 1076 Avinashi Rd; d ₹5500 (incl of breakfast) One of the older and more popular hotels in the city, it has spacious and bright rooms and the staff is courteous and helpful. Rooms on the higher floors have a good view of the city. The swimming pool and health club were undergoing renovation at the time of writing this.

The Arcadia   Boutique Hotel ₹₹
☎ 0422 4567777; www.hotelthearcadia.com; 4 Avinashi Rd; d ₹3500–3750 (incl of breakfast)
This boutique hotel scores high on aesthetics, whether it is the huge paper flowers in the reception or the paintings in the elevator. The rooms too are comfortable and stylish with appropriate use of lighting, bright curtains and primarily white decor. It provides all regular amenities including free wi-fi.

Hotel Alankar Grande   Hotel ₹₹
☎ 0422 4378888; www.alankargrande.com; 10 Sivasamy Rd, Ramnagar; d ₹3100–3950 (incl of breakfast) The hotel has a lot of plus points – it is well located in the

The plush Tamil Nadu suite at Le Meridien

heart of the city, is close to the bus stand and commercial activity at Gandhipuram, the rooms are neat and clean and the staff is efficient. The only drawback is that the TV in the room only broadcasts local channels.

Rathna Residency — Hotel ₹₹
📞 0422 4225666; www.rathnaresidency.com; 355 Variety Hall Rd; d ₹3000–3500 (incl of breakfast) Compact but clean rooms and a welcoming staff make Rathna Residency a pleasant choice. Besides a 24-hour check-in desk, the hotel has three restaurants: Valayapatti, serving Chettinadu cuisine, Fusion, a fine-dining restaurant and Palms, a multi-cuisine roof-top restaurant that has lovely views of the city.

Hotel Vaidurya — Hotel ₹
📞 0422 4297777; www.hotelvaidurya.com; 73 Geetha Hall Rd; d ₹1000–2000 (incl of breakfast) Located conveniently opposite the railway station, Vaidurya is a no-frills, value-for-money hotel. Rooms are small but clean. There's a small TV in each of them but no refrigerator. Room service is provided till 10.30pm. The staff is courteous, efficient and speaks English.

VALPARAI

Sinna Dorai — Tea Estate ₹₹
📞 0422 4567777; www.sinnadorai.com; 4 Avinashi Rd; d ₹6500 (incl of full board) Set amidst beautiful tea estates, Sinna Dorai is a destination in itself. Beautifully furnished cottages with long glass windows ensure that you wake up to breathtaking views. The idea is to be one with nature and hence there is no TV in the rooms but if you can't do without your daily dose of soaps, there's one in the common room. You can go for long walks, play chess, read, or just laze around. The fixed menu of the day, though limited, offers both non-vegetarian and vegetarian options and is homely and well-made.

Green Hill Hotel — Hotel ₹
📞 04253 222562, 222861; www.valparaigreenhillhotels.com; State Bank Rd; d ₹1100–2500 (incl of breakfast) A basic hotel in the centre of Valparai, it has a restaurant serving south Indian food. The rooms are no-frills but are value-for-money. There is plenty of car parking available.

Hotel Holiday Break — Hotel ₹
📞 04253 222255, 9894523929; www.hotelholidaybreak.com; near Thulasi Kalyana Mandapam, behind Gandhi Statue; d ₹850–990 (incl of breakfast) Only a few months old, Holiday Break provides clean and comfortable accommodation. The rooms are well furnished and if you are travelling with family, you can book a family room that sleeps four persons for ₹1500. There's no restaurant, but 24-hour room service is provided.

Eating

COIMBATORE

Being cosmopolitan, Coimbatore offers a range of eating places. While traditional south Indian restaurants are value for money, for a wider variety of cuisines one needs to head to the hotels.

Kovai Biryani Hotel — Indian ₹
☏ 0422 2545549; No 3 VCV Layout, opp Senthil Hospital; noon–10.45pm; mains ₹100–150 As the name suggests, this is where you must head for traditional Coimbatore biryani. Located in the bustling RS Puram area, the restaurant is basic and small with wooden tables and chairs but the food is splendid. Try the chicken biryani for ₹102 (half plate) and the muttai (egg) parotha for ₹57.

The Cascade — Chinese ₹₹
☏ 0422 2568888, 8098787878; Avinashi Rd; noon–2.40pm, 7–10.40pm; mains ₹200–350 Besides traditional Chinese dishes, this restaurant keeps adding a twist to its menu. Try the Volcano Prawns, that are deep fried prawns with a semi-cooked egg white on top (₹285), and the Tom Yum, a clear soup (₹195). Quick service and a family-friendly ambience has made the place popular with local folk.

Southeast — Multi-Cuisine ₹₹₹
☏ 0422 4378888; Hotel Alankar Grande, 10 Sivasamy Rd, Ramnagar; 12.30–3pm, 7.30–11pm At ₹625 (with taxes) for the buffet, you couldn't get a better spread of both north Indian and south Indian cuisine than at Southeast. While biryani is on offer almost daily, a few Chinese dishes also make it to the table, especially during the weekends.

The Pavillion — Multi-Cuisine ₹₹₹
☏ 0422 2241414; The Residency, 1076 Avinashi Rd; 12.15–2.45pm, 7.15–11.45pm buffet ₹750 (weekdays) ₹850 (weekends) For a large spread of Indian and continental cuisine, it's best to opt for the buffet at The Pavillion in The Residency hotel. From salads, appetisers to desserts, everything on offer is quite delicious.

Sri Krishna Sweets — Sweets ₹
☏ 0422 2458333; 169-F, NSR Rd, Saibaba Colony; 9am–9.30pm; sweets ₹100 One of the oldest chain of sweet shops in Tamil Nadu, this one is a must-visit for all those with a sweet tooth. Try some of their unusual offerings, such as green chilly halwa, a sweet halwa with an aftertaste of chilly (₹380 per kg).

Sree Annapoorna — Vegetarian ₹
☏ 0422 4382121; 418 Mettupalayam Rd, opp Avinashi Lingam College; 6.30am–10.30pm ₹70–100 Sree Annapoorna has a reputation for wholesome, value-for-money, pure vegetarian south Indian meals. Don't

get side-tracked by the variety of north Indian and Chinese items on their menu – most are not available and even if they are, it's not their forte. Stick to south Indian fare and you won't be disappointed.

VALPARAI
The town is so small that it doesn't have any stand-alone eating places. Most hotels don't allow outside guests at their restaurant.

Green Hill Hotel — South Indian ₹
📞 04253 222562; State Bank Rd; 8am–10pm; mains ₹70–100 This is one of the few places where you can go and eat in town. The hotel's restaurant on the ground floor, next to the car parking area, is very basic. There's a selection of veg and non-veg south Indian food on offer.

Top Touch Bakery — Sweets ₹
📞 9487373232; Main Rd; 8.30am–10pm; sweets ₹100–120/kg Don't go by the name for Top Touch Bakery is more of a sweets shop. Try the jaggery halwa and the coconut halwa, both for ₹100 per kg.

Bharath Bakery — Bakery ₹
📞 04253 222674; opp Murugan Temple, Main Rd; 9am–10pm Known for its plum cake (₹200/kg) and mushroom puffs (₹14 per piece), Bharath Bakery offers a variety of delectables such as cupcakes (₹10 per piece) and jackfruit chips (₹250/kg).

🛍 Shopping

COIMBATORE
Coimbatore is a shopper's delight for jewellery and primarily Indian wear and saris. Most shops are open from 10am to 9pm on all days.

Karpagam — Jewellery
📞 0422 4506001; www.karpagamjewellers.com; No 491 Cross Cut Rd; 10am–8.30pm Besides their beautiful gold and diamond jewellery, check out their innovative range in gold and terracotta, gold work on handbags and gold watches. They also have a large range of hand-made jewellery.

Kirtilals — Jewellery
📞 0422 2398899; www.kirtilals.com; 601 Raja St; 10am–8pm This is a well organised store, but it may become a bit irksome because of the amount of walking you need to do. While gold earrings are displayed in one room, for diamonds you need to go to another

| Gold jewellery is popular in all the states of South India

> ### 📷 Snapshot: Naksh jewellery
>
> Coimbatore is known for its traditional Naksh jewellery where idols of gods and goddesses are created in 22 karat gold. You can buy pendants, earrings, bangles or necklaces with Ganesh, Lakshmi or Murugan and other icons.

and for bangles yet another. The organised set-up works if you are there to buy a specific item, but it can be tedious if you are browsing.

Ramraj Cotton — Clothing
☎ 0422 2393147; 340–341 Oppanakara St; 9.30am–9.30pm Head to Ramraj if you're looking to buy a crisp cotton veshti (dhoti or lungi) and matching white shirt – the preferred attire of most middle-class Tamilian men. You can buy fabric for shirts, but only in white or cream. There is also a limited range of cotton saris and salwar suit material.

PSR Silks Cotton — Saris
☎ 0422 2498694; www.psrgroup.in; No 942 Cross Cut Rd, Gandhipuram; 10am–9.30pm This multi-storied sari shop offers everything from handwoven Kanjeevaram silk saris to fancy embroidered ones. There's also a wide range of pavadai and half saris (lehangas). The latest styles of salwar suits and material are also available.

RMKV — Clothing
☎ 0422 2255100; Brookefields, Brooke Bond Rd; 10am–9.30pm A wide range of Indian wear for women is available, though the western line is limited. For men and children there's a lot to choose from in both Indian and western styles. Don't be put off by the large crowds – the billing is efficient.

Grasp — Clothing
☎ 0422 4204039; 1 Thirugnana Samvandam Rd, Race Course; 10am–9.30pm This is where you can get really good deals for the entire family. Various big brands are available at half the rates. Accessories such as belts and handbags are available.

Selva Gold — Jewellery
☎ 0422 2230132; 171 Cross Cut Rd, Gandhipuram; 9.30am–9.30pm Want to look like you're decked up in gold but don't want to pay the high prices? Selva Gold offers perfect imitation or gold-plated items. They have a good collection of necklaces, earrings and bangles.

VALPARAI
Valparai is small and there aren't too many shops. However, you can buy tea and spices.

TMD Enterprises — Tea
Main Rd; 10am–7.30pm A shop with a variety of teas from neighbouring estates. You can buy spices like pepper and cloves as well as pickle.

Expert Recommendation
Coffee cultivation

Pushpanath Krishnamurthy is first a coffee lover and second an expert on coffee cultivation

Legend has it that a 17th-century Islamic Sufi stole seven seeds from Yemenis and planted them on the peaks of the Sahyadri Range. The hill is called Baba Budan, named after a Sufi saint, in today's Chikmagalur district of Karnataka.

• Indian coffee is a shade growing coffee and it is rare because all the coffee grown in India, is in natural conditions, dependant on monsoon rain and thrives in shade growing areas. As a result Indian coffee is grown in forest like conditions.

The popular coffee bean of India is the Coffea Arabica grown in the hilly regions of Karnataka. While Arabica is sensitive and needs care, Robusta beans grow in forest areas alongside other trees and spices.

• Coffee cultivation faces an ecological threat. A walk alongside the River Kaveri reveals how climate change, gales, unpredictable rains and insect attacks are creating havoc to coffee cultivation.

• Centre for Social Markets (CSM) a non-profit based in Bengaluru, is partner with Karnataka Growers Federation (KGF) and has produced a landmark study on how indigenous people have been affected by modern coffee cultivation technologies.

| Coffea Arabica is a popular coffee bean in the country

Ooty, Coonoor & Kotagiri

Ooty's reputation as 'Queen of the Hills' is hard to beat, and your Nilgiri experience is incomplete if you haven't visited this bustling hill station. Move on to tranquil Coonoor to get a quintessential feel of a tea country and end your trip with quaint Kotagiri, the perfect mountain getaway with its natural beauty, treks and colonial ambience.

Trip Planner

GETTING THERE

Ooty: The closest airport is in Coimbatore (95km). The main railway station with frequent trains to other cities is Coimbatore Junction. From Bengaluru it is 265km by road.

Coonoor: Coimbatore airport is 78km away and the railway station, Coimbatore Junction, is 70km away.

Kotagiri: The nearest airport is in Coimbatore (76km). The railway station is 68km away. There are regular buses from Coimbatore to these three places.

SUGGESTED ITINERARY (7 DAYS)

Arrive in Ooty and spend around three days exploring the town's many highlights. From here take take the toy train up to Coonoor (25km) and spend the next two days relaxing in tea estates and enjoying the scenery at numerous viewpoints. Next on the Nilgiris circuit is Kotagiri (18km) which is relatively unexplored and can fill another two full days in the calm tea-scaped hills steeped in Raj ambience. Those who are fond of the outdoors can explore the many hiking trails.

BEST TIME TO GO

J F **M A M** J J A S **O N D**

GREAT FOR

Top 5 highlights

- **Botanical Gardens, Ooty** (p416)
- **Nilgiri Mountain Railway, Ooty** (p419)
- **Lady Canning's Seat, Coonoor** (p420)
- **High Field Tea Estate, Coonoor** (p421)
- **Kodanad Viewpoint, Kotagiri** (p422)

Nilgiri Magic

View of the Nilgiris and tea gardens

Although **Ooty** (Udhagamandalam) has a repertoire of travel cliches, which ensure a typical hill station experience, it cannot be missed. This place is a delight for shutterbugs. Tea plantation-clad hills, strewn with bright Lego-like houses, interspersed with lush patches of fern and eucalyptus, the hills immediately put you in a good mood after leaving behind the heat of the plains. Enjoy simple pleasures like the sight of fresh carrots and turnips temptingly lining the roads, and the whimsical weather, specially nearing the monsoons.

Visit **Coonoor** for a pleasant change from the run-of-the-mill hill station holiday. Enjoy the peaceful bellflower-lined streets (preferably on foot). Around town are numerous viewing lookouts, which are best explored early in the mornings to avoid the rush of tourists. The weather patterns here are starkly different from neighbouring Ooty, with the rains arriving in November. Expectedly, the summer months, from April to September, are the best time of the year to visit.

Kotagiri is another colonial charmer, but it also has an indigenous cultural fabric that comes from the diverse tribal groups of the Nilgiris – the most prominent being the Badagas. Going beyond the perpetually misty views of the tidy tea-lined valleys, a visit to Kotagiri offers an experience that's simple and fulfilling.

Highlights
1. Doddabetta Peak
2. Tea Factory & Museum
3. Botanical Gardens
4. Boat House
5. Thread Garden
6. Rose Garden
7. St Stephen's Church
8. The Nilgiri Mountain Railway (Toy Train)
9. Tribal Research Centre Museum

Ooty

1 DODDABETTA PEAK
The peaceful 9km stretch of fern and eucalyptus-lined bumpy road off Ooty, ends in a bevy of tourists making a beeline for the lone telescope, some worn out children's swings and snack food joints. The reasonably well-kept Doddabetta Peak itself offers a great view of the Hecuba, Kattadadu and the Kulkudi summits. A short stop is enough to stay away from a chartered holiday experience.
₹5; 8am–5pm

2 TEA FACTORY & MUSEUM
A commendable educational effort which caters to a variety of travellers – one cannot really brag about the museum or the presentation of the loud speaker-enabled guide – but the limited information on tea brewing is enough for mass consumption. There is a channelled walk through the factory that ends in a small sampling of tea. There is also a counter to buy spices and chocolates, as well as, of course, varieties of Nilgiri tea.
Doddabetta Rd, Ooty; adult/child ₹5/2; camera ₹10; 9am–6pm

3 BOTANICAL GARDENS
Established in 1847, the Botanical Gardens of Ooty are less appreciated for the horticultural experience and more for a pleasing backdrop for photo enthusiasts. One cannot help join the photo-frenzy with temptingly beautiful varieties

Snapshot: Colonial connections
While a few British expeditions had set off earlier to the Nilgiris, it was only after John Sullivan, Collector of Coimbatore, built the Pethakal Bungalow in 1819 at Kotagiri, that British interest in the mountain region grew. And with them came potato cultivation and tea plantations. Sullivan set foot in Wotokymund (Ootacamund) in 1821 and chose it as the perfect sanatorium for English soldiers. Thus began the shaping of this nondescript village into a buzzing hill station.

of flowers and the large cacti in the glasshouse. Its vast expanse is even dotted with a lone bench or two, to absorb all the cheer around. The wilting plants at the sales counter are a rather sad contrast to the lush gardens outside.
Government Botanical Garden; adult/child/camera/video ₹20/10/30/75; 7am–6.30pm

❹ BOAT HOUSE

> **📷 *Snapshot: The 12-year Kurinji bloom***
>
> Strobilanthes, the carpety blue flower better known as the Kurinji, crops up in conversations every 12 years in the Nilgiris. Though there are over 40 species of flower across this mountain range, the Kurinji is the most popular. Uniquely, it blooms just once every 12 years, and spreads like sponge over high hillsides, however the blooming period is short. The next flowering is in 2018.

This is a single stop for a full day of entertainment if you have an appetite for boating, horse riding and carousels. Especially recommended if you are travelling with children, for whom the cotton candy stands, fruit vendors, food court, mini train can be engaging. Given the number of tourists that visit the Boat House, it has been well maintained.
₹5; camera/video ₹10/100; boating ₹320 onwards; horse riding ₹50 onwards; 8am–6pm

❺ THREAD GARDEN

The Thread Garden is a laudable effort to replicate flower varieties in thread. The brainchild of Antony Joseph, six crore metres of thread have been put to use by 50 ladies over 12 years, to create this mind-boggling array of 150 varieties of flowers. However, the dimly-lit presentation in a shed-like enclosure tends to dampen your interest a bit.

Botanical Gardens is home to a range of colourful flowers

Take a joyride in the iconic Toy Train

☎ 0423 2445145; www.threadgarden.com; opp Boat House; adult/child/camera ₹15/10/30; 8am–6pm

❻ ROSE GARDEN

Paler in comparison to the grand Botanical Garden, this too winds up as a photography destination for most people. There are over 1000 varieties of roses, out of which a green one is bound to catch your attention.

Ooty Centenary Rose Garden; adult/child/camera/video ₹15/10/30/75; 7am–6.30pm

❼ ST STEPHEN'S CHURCH

Established in the 19th century, this historic landmark is one of the oldest churches in the region and stands testament

✓ Top Tip: How to buy tea

Claims of 'best', 'most fragrant' and 'international quality' tea leaves at most shops in the city can be slightly perplexing, if you're looking to buy some. With estates moving towards branding their own product, the advertising hullaballoo is even stronger. Here are a few tips on making a reasonable decision about which kind of tea to buy. Depending on taste, there are multiple flavours available. Besides that, you should be checking for freshness in the smell (not musty), uniformity in colour, and also check that no colour additives are present. Rub a little between your fingers; if it comes onto your skin immediately, then the tea is sure to be adulterated. Some tried and tested brands include Tranquilitea (only online purchase), Chamraj and Glendale.

to the colonial past of the city. Walk around to the back of the church to see the cemetery, and trace the graves of John Sullivan's wife and daughter.
9.30am–4.30pm

❽ THE NILGIRI MOUNTAIN RAILWAY (TOY TRAIN)
The Unesco-listed World Heritage Site is worth every jostle once you have squirmed your way into a comfortable position along with all the other tourists. Started in 1908, the train still runs partially on steam locomotive engines (on the Coonoor–Mettupalayam stretch), and chugs its way from Ooty to Mettupalayam in 3½ hours. It twists and turns over 250 bridges, through 16 tunnels and deep gorges, across forests and tea plantations. Book ahead to ensure a ride, though having a ticket is no guarantee of a great seat.
www.irctc.co.in; first class/second seater ₹155/23; 2pm–5.35pm

❾ TRIBAL RESEARCH CENTRE MUSEUM
Though not extensive, the Tribal Research Centre Museum does give you an idea about the history and current life of the tribes of the Nilgiris. Engross yourself in the decent collection of artefacts and items of daily use of the tribes before moving on to the rest of the displays at the museum, which may seem somewhat cheerless and unrelated.
M Palada; 10am–5pm; Mon–Fri

Coonoor

❶ SIM'S PARK
Meet keen morning walkers at Sim's Park. This 1874 creation of one JD Smith started out as a pleasure resort and gradually developed into a botanical garden. If visiting in May, look out for the annual fruit and flower show.
Adult/child ₹20/10, camera/video ₹30/75; 8am–6.30pm

Highlights
1. Sim's Park
2. Lamb's Rock
3. Lady Canning's Seat
4. Dolphin's Nose
5. Droog Fort
6. Highfield Tea Estate
7. Ralliah Dam

❷ LAMB'S ROCK
Eight kilometres out of town, a forest-fringed road leads upto Lamb's Rock, a favourite viewing point that buzzes with tourists. On weekends, the narrow road is packed with cars. From here, you can get a view of the sprawling Coimbatore plains, as well as a large jagged rock, at least a few hundred feet tall, buried deep in the forest.

❸ LADY CANNING'S SEAT
Tucked between trees, this viewing point is ahead of Lamb's Rock on the same road. Named after the wife of Lord Canning (one of the British viceroys), the spot commands a brilliant view of the tea estates and distant mountains. Off the main road, it is a short climb to the top.

❹ DOLPHIN'S NOSE
This is another viewing point, which has a splendid panorama of the Catherine Falls in Kotagiri. It can, however, be noisy and crowded. Visit in the mornings to avoid the rush – but be prepared to be greeted by the previous day's trash. Dolphin's Nose is 10km from Coonoor town and stands at a height of 1000ft above sea level.

❺ DROOG FORT
The weathered 18th-century fort of Tipu Sultan, Droog (also known as Bakasura Malai) can be reached by a combination of road travel (13km) and a short trek. Though the fort itself is in ruins, the view of the valleys below makes it a picturesque trek. It's a great spot for a picnic lunch – after all, one would need refuelling after the climb up to the spot.

📷 Snapshot: Tribals of Nilgiri hills

A number of tribal groups exist in the Nilgiris: Todas, Kotas, Kurumbas, Irulas, Paniyas and the Kattunayakans. Each group has its unique cultural traits, and is found in different parts of the mountains. Exposure has led to many of these tribes leading urban lives and working in various sectors of trade and industry. Only a few still inhabit the forests, and these pockets are fiercely protected by the government and anthropologists alike. Find out more about them at the Tribal Research Centre Museum (p419) in Ooty.

Droog is not recommended for older people due to the strenuous nature of the walk involved.

> Ralliah Dam is a good spot for a picnic

❻ HIGHFIELD TEA ESTATE

This 50-year-old factory off the Sim's Park–Kotagiri Road is one of the few that allows visitors a short tour inside to see the tea-making process. You can also wander around the plantation to click photographs. The trip is definitely worth it, despite the heavy scent of tea that hangs on to you long after you have left. There is also an in-house store selling tea leaves and herbal oils.

☎ 0423 2230840; pay what you feel; 8.30am–6.30pm

❼ RALLIAH DAM

Officially a part of Kotagiri, this can be considered Coonoor's secret. A short walk through a thicket leads you to the still waters of the Ralliah Dam, built in 1941 to provide water to the town (a function it still performs). It is an excellent spot for small groups. If you walk along the bank, you reach a small Toda settlement. There is an occasional guard who volunteers as a guide, and can be paid a small amount. Ralliah Dam is about 11km from Coonoor on the Kattabettu–Kotagiri Road. Ask for directions at Elithorai village to reach the dam.

Kotagiri

Highlights
1. Kodanad Viewpoint
2. Toda Shrine
3. Catherine Falls
4. Pethakal Bungalow
5. Nehru Park
6. Kallur Peak
7. Banagudi Shola (Sacred Forest)

1 KODANAD VIEWPOINT
A significant spot featuring dramatic views – including India's largest earthen dam (Bhavanisagar), Tipu Sultan's garrison base (Ali Rani Koli), the meeting point of the Western and Eastern Ghats, and the Moyar River twisting into a horseshoe shape – the Kodanad viewpoint is a pleasant change from the regular hill station vistas. It lies about 18km outside Kotagiri town.

2 TODA SHRINE
On your way back from Kodanad, do not miss a Toda mund (tribal shrine) just off the main road. It has a characteristic small door, thatched roof and carvings on the outside. More interestingly, three large rounded boulders represent the essentials of a marriage proposal made by a man: to lift three stones, eat three ragi (finger millet) balls (each weighing as much as one of the stones), and to drink three glasses of butter milk. The tradition is still followed symbolically.

3 CATHERINE FALLS
The 249ft-high waterfall is best seen from the opposite Coonoor hillside (likewise, one can get a clearer view of Dolphin's Nose viewpoint from Kotagiri). Head further than the vandalised spot for a closer look. The point is about 8km outside Kotagiri town.

4 PETHAKAL BUNGALOW
This bungalow houses the **Interpretation Centre of the Nilgiris Biosphere Reserve** and has a collection of well-kept memorabilia, presenting a quick history of the British presence in the Nilgiris, and also of the pre-colonial tribal era. Look out for an identical picture of Ooty taken in 1870, and then in 1970. Even if the door is locked, one can call a displayed number and an attendant will let you in.
✆ 9488771571, Sullivan Memorial, Nilgiri Documentation

Centre, Kannerimukku; ₹10; 10am–5pm (closed for lunch 1pm–2pm)

❺ NEHRU PARK
A pleasant park on Johnstone (now Kamraj) Circle, it is believed to be the place where a young Jawaharlal Nehru learnt horse riding. Step in to see the Kotha Temple through a locked gate.
Johnstone Circle; adult/child/camera/video ₹5/2/20/75; 6am–9pm

❻ KALLUR PEAK
The Kallur Peak is a short walk from Adubettu near the Aravenu hill. Apart from the picturesque view of the Mettupalayam plains below, you can see the Nilgiri Toy Train chugging along the meandering track.

❼ BANAGUDI SHOLA (SACRED FOREST)
This is a sacred forest with ancient shrines still worshipped by tribals. To absorb the rich biodiversity of this 21-hectare grove, it's best to opt for a guided hike with A Bhoopathy (☏9786971735) or his team from Nature Watch. Dolmans or burial tombstones which are thousands of years old, a host of birds, reptiles and animal species, and a Kurumba settlement, subsist in this forest area. You'll also come across a village close by belonging to the Toriya tribe.

Bird's-eye-view of Kotagiri

 Accommodation

OOTY

Red Hills
Nature Resort　　**Heritage Cottage ₹₹₹**
☎ 0423 2595755; The Nilgiris, Ootacamund; r from ₹7000 (incl of full board) Visit Red Hills for a spectacular view of the Avalanche and Emerald lakes from your room. The 1875 property, on the outskirts of Ooty, attracts only those who want to stay away from the city din. The long drive up is worth your while for the vantage location, organic garden, Moby the dog and personalised treks.

Destiny　　Heritage Cottage ₹₹₹
☎ 9487000111; www.littlearth.in/sherlock; The Nilgiris, Ootacamund; d ₹5358–7886 (incl of full board) The 2km bone-rattling truck ride on a forest road ends in a 100-acre farm geared up to ensure you rough it out in luxury. A spa overlooking the hills, horse-riding, bonfires, fishing, zip-lining and other adventure sports ensure an activity-centric holiday. The western farm theme spills over into the names of rooms, creatively christened 'Billy the Kid', 'Butch Cassidy', etc.

Lymond House　　Homestay ₹₹
☎ 0423 2223377; www.serendipityo.com; 77 Sylks Rd; d ₹4094–4747 (incl of full board) The British style cottage (1855) still retains a colonial air in its high ceilings, fireplaces, lush garden and a small driveway. Sit out in the gazebo to enjoy the Ooty weather or meet other travellers by the bonfire in the evenings. A handwritten note on laundry details in your room brings a smile to your face. There's also an in-house restaurant.

Tranquilitea　　Heritage Bungalow ₹₹
☎ 9443841572; www.tranquilitea.in; The Bungalow in Ooty, The Nilgiris, Ootacamund; d ₹4000–7500 (incl

| Destiny is located in a 100-acre farm surrounded by hills

of full board) Proximity to town and a view of the race tracks are the best things about this cosy three-room refurbished colonial bungalow. You can be sure to have your privacy intact as no other room is let out even if you book only one room. Ideal for a group.

King's Cliff   Heritage Cottage ₹₹
☏9487000111; www.kingscliff-ooty.com; Havelock Rd, Ooty; d ₹3568–5846 (incl of full board) Slide back in time at this 1920s 'Shakespearean' themed cottage, complete with elaborate tapestry, fireplaces and wooden floors. It's delightful to see that the management has painstakingly tried to match the upholstery from an old photograph. Dig into the baked goodies and be pampered by the well-trained and attentive staff.

Sherlock   Themed Cottage ₹₹
☏9487000111; www.littlearth.in/sherlock; The Nilgiris, Ootacamund; d ₹2500–5846 (incl of full board) The Sherlock Holmes-themed cottage sits tucked on a hill at the far end of Ooty. Apart from the great view, a sprawling garden and frequent visitors like deer and bison, the century-old cottage gives you a chance to indulge in Holmes-related pictures, books, and little nooks and corners; the dining room is named after Irene Adler.

I-India   Heritage Cottage ₹
☏0423 2448959; www.iindiaecolodge.in; 273 Grand Duff Rd, Valley View; d ₹2400–3000 (incl of full board) This newly furbished 100-year-old cottage, away from the city, has a comforting hill station feel about it. The establishment is great value for money with clean 'no frills' rooms, a cheerful common area with wide French windows, and a fantastic view of the valley. Run by a small team, the personalised attention is a welcome change.

COONOOR

The Gateway Hotel   Hotel ₹₹₹
☏0423 2225400; www.thegatewayhotels.com; The Gateway Hotel, Church Rd; d ₹6096–9863 (incl of full board) This colonial building with an old-world charm comes with all the contemporary amenities, as you'd expect from a 5-star Taj Hotel property, including a spa. Opt for the fireplace room, or the one with a personal garden. The Hampton Bar is a decent place to get a drink.

Tenerife Tranquilitea   Homestay ₹₹
☏9443841572; www.tranquilitea.in; Tenerife Rosery Tea Gardens; d from ₹4000 (incl of full board) Guest privacy is the focus here; no other rooms are let out if you have booked one. A sunny garden in front of the room, a tea lounge, and undivided attention ensure an exclusive stay. To add to the experience, the tea-tasting tour is educational and fun.

Spectacular sunsets can be seen from the gazebo at Lazy Hills

De Rock   Garden Resort ₹₹
0423 2103030; www.de-rock.com; 2/16 E, Lamb's Rock, Guernsey; d ₹3000–3300 (incl of full board)
A cosy three-room setup is perched on the edge of a hill by Lamb's Rock. The rooms have a brilliant view of the valley, especially at night. The staff is endearing and spoils you silly.

180° McIver   Heritage Bungalow ₹₹
9715033011; www.serendipityo.com; 1–4 Orange Grove Rd; d ₹3857–5875 (incl of full board) A unique 180-degree view of the valley is best experienced from a wide garden in front of this 115-year-old bungalow. The refurbished wooden floors, high ceilings and fireplaces ensure a luxury stay – and the grand bathroom can become a quick favourite.

Acres Wild   Farm Stay ₹₹
9443232621; www.acres-wild.com; 571, Upper Meanjee Estate, Kannimariamman Kovil Street; d ₹3597–4796 (incl of full board)
Single and double unit cottages sit wide apart in this farmhouse, located on uncultivated land. One can spot a fair amount of wildlife in the evenings here. But the most fascinating part of Acres Wild is the cheese cellar and the workshop area.

KOTAGIRI

La Maison   Luxury Homestay ₹₹₹
9585471635; www.lamaison.in; Hadathorai, Nihung Post Office; d ₹6900–8900 (incl of breakfast)
French couple Anne and Benoit's cheerful white luxury bungalow is the perfect homestay if you want every meal served 'fresh from the garden' (and also if you want to binge on cheese and wine!). Anne experiments with a host of homegrown veggies and flowers in the food. The open jacuzzi by the tea plantation is the most coveted spot on the property.

Lazy Hills   Luxury Homestay ₹₹
9941943921; www.lazyhills.in; 4/657/3, Adubettu, Arvenu; d ₹4510 (incl of breakfast) The earthy and minimalistic architecture of the two dwellings here (a tree house and luxury room) gives just the right amount of intimacy and privacy. At Lazy Hills, you'll be consumed by the silence of the valley. And if the clouds allow, you could be treated to a spectacular sunset. Only guests over 21 years allowed.

Cassiopeia — Guesthouse ₹₹
0423 2233323; www.serendipityo.com; Kenthony Rd, Elada, Kodanad; d ₹4228 (incl of breakfast) Newly constructed Cassiopeia sits on the edge of Pristine Valley, overlooking a large expanse of acacias and tea estates. A three-bedroom house, it's perfect for a large group. Admire the Rangaswamy Peak in the distance as you lounge in the flower-lined balcony on the first floor.

The Sunshine Bungalow — Guesthouse ₹₹
9486553104; www.thesunshinebungalow.com; Club Road; d ₹5900 (incl of full board) One of the oldest English properties in Kotagiri, Sunshine Bungalow has been refurbished with modern furniture but has retained its old-world charm. Poster beds, elaborate furnishings and wooden flooring give a grand air to the house. Choose one of the front facing rooms to ensure that you get enough natural light in your room.

Twin Tree — Hotel ₹₹
04266 275333; www.twintreekotagiri.com; 5/39-A Corsley Rd, opp Riverside Public School; d ₹3560 (incl of full board) Quiet and clean, Twin Tree has a cosy set of rooms away from the busy city junction. The good thing about this place is that there is an in-house cafe and it's great to kill some time here if you are feeling too lazy to step outside. A great view of tea plantations and a pleasant garden make for a comfortable and hassle-free stay.

Masters Garden — Guesthouse ₹₹
9486553104; Masters Cottage, Club Rd; d ₹11,800 (incl full board for 4 adults) Yet another renovated old colonial bungalow, overlooking a lush valley, Masters (or Lord's) Garden is an ideal spot if you want to stay away from the town. The guesthouse has two rooms which are let out to a single group only.

The luxurious homestay La Maison is ideal for a few lazy days

Eating

OOTY

Shinkows — Chinese ₹₹
☎ 0423 2442811; 38/83 Commissioners Rd; noon–3.45pm, 6.30–9.45pm The apparent nostalgia sweeps in this 1954 restaurant, even if you are visiting for the very first time. Yellow checked table cloths, chatty waiters and the obvious familiarity of locals make an endearing backdrop. Old timers will tell you that dishes like No 5 (chicken and mushroom soup) and No 26 (pork and broccoli dish) is what keeps them coming back time after time to Mr Pao Chun's famous establishment.

Nahar Restaurants — Multi-Cuisine ₹₹
☎ 0423 2442173; 52-A Charring Cross; 1.30–3.30pm, 7–8.30pm A set of restaurants right on the main Charring Cross, the speciality is vegetarian food. Expectedly, it is swarming with crowds in the tourist season. Visit the Sidewalk Cafe for Continental and Chandan for Indian and Chinese fare.

Hotel Blue Hills — Multi-Cuisine ₹₹
☎ 0423 2442034; Commercial Rd 1pm–10pm Though nondescript to look at, Hotel Blue Hills serves excellent non-vegetarian food like brain masala and various chicken delights. This is good place to catch lunch if you are roaming around Commercial Street.

Earl's Secret at Kings Cliff — Multi-Cuisine ₹₹₹
☎ 9487000111; www.kingscliff-ooty.com; Havelock Rd; 12.30–2.45pm (buffet), 7.30–10pm (a la carte) They serve large spreads of Thai and continental food (recommended). The restaurant seats 85 in cosy pockets of the heritage bungalow, of which the sunny glasshouse is welcome on a cold, rainy day.

Lymond House — Continental ₹₹₹
☎ 9843149490; www.serendipityo.com; Sylks Rd; 12.30–3pm, 7.30–10pm The blackboard menu lists the dishes of the day, while some retro favourites and the garden add to the setting for a long lunch. Great homemade desserts and personalised attention by Joe, the restaurant manager, completes an enjoyable experience. Prior booking is required.

Earl's Secret at Kings Cliff has elegant seating in a glasshouse

COONOOR

Quality Inn — Multi-Cuisine ₹₹
0423 2236400; www.qualityrestaurant.net; Bedford, Upper Coonoor; 12.30–10.30pm
If you are roaming around Coonoor town, the slow, laid-back service of Quality Inn might be your best bet. The fare here is moderately good; the large lunch buffet is recommended.

180° McIver — Multi-Cuisine ₹₹₹
9715033011; Orange Grove Rd; noon–2.45pm, 7–9.45pm The McIver Villa has an in-house continental restaurant run by French chef, Pierre Mazou who uses organic ingredients only. Long, lazy lunches (with a view of the valley) are the order of the day. Book ahead if you are part of a large group.

KOTAGIRI

Orange Pekoe (Spice Inn) — Multi-Cuisine ₹₹
04266 211000; www.orangepekoeleisurehotel.com; Ooty-Kotagiri Rd; 11am–10.30pm This new establishment is just off the main road as you enter Kotagiri. Though the mixed cuisine is nothing to write home about, the place is clean, and good for a quick meal.

Hari Mess — South Indian ₹
04266 272148; Mettupalayam Rd; noon–3.30pm, 7–9.30pm Run by a trio of brothers, this is a place loved for its unassuming home-made food and

Lymond House is all about homemade desserts and long meals

hospitality. It's easy to overlook the dinginess when you have sumptuous non-vegetarian combos prepared by the affable family.

Nahar — Multi-Cuisine ₹₹₹
04266 273300; www.naharretreat.com; Kota Hall Rd; 9am–9pm The ambience in Nahar's might have a busy and chartered-holiday feel to it, but the food is better than that served at most other hotels. The restaurant prepares multi-cuisine fare but stick with north and south Indian, to be on the safe side. Nahar also serves Jain food.

BS Bakery
Aravenu Rd; 8am–8pm Check out the baked snack, 'varkey', ready to be packed in newspapers and doled out with speed. This crunchy snack is best consumed when slightly warm. Arrive early morning or in the evenings, when the batch is fresh.

 Activities

OOTY

This may well become an unexpected golfing break as two golf courses allow non-members to play by paying a green fee.

The Wellington Gymkhana Club — Golf

☏0423 2230256; www.wellingtongymkhanaclub.com; Wellington, Barracks Post; 8pm–6.30pm; ₹400 for 18 holes Established in 1873, the club is spread over 63 acres and has impressive facilities, including a Golf Pro gym and lockers. One must book in advance as weekends are packed with regulars. Note that only guests of members are allowed; you can ask homestay owners for admission.

| Fabrics with intricate embroidery at Needle Craft

The Ootacamund Gymkhana Club — Golf

☏0423 2442254; www.ootygolfclub.org; Ooty–Mysore Rd; 7am–10pm; ₹1100 for guests of members, for 18 holes The Ooty Gymkhana has a 18-hole golf course. Non-members are allowed to play after paying a small fee. Book in advance.

Shopping

OOTY

Higginbothams — Books

☏0423 2442546; Oriental Building, opp Collector's Office; 9am–1pm, 2–6pm Visit the century-old building which houses Higginbothams bookshop, bursting with books on old wooden shelves. Fredrick Price's *Ootacamund: A History* is recommended reading for gripping tales of Ooty.

If You Like: Volunteering

Volunteer at the 17-year-old **Keystone Foundation** (📞04266 272277; www.keystone-foundation.org; Keystone Centre, Groves Hill Rd, PB No 35), which works with the indigenous communities of the Nilgiris to enhance the quality of life and the environment. Get in touch with the Kotagiri-based organisation only if you want to commit a month or more of your time. Apply for a range of fascinating, on-ground projects undertaken by Keystone.

Chellaram — Tea
📞0423 2442229; New No 47, Commercial Rd; 9.30am–1.30pm, 3–7.30pm Buy the best quality Nilgiri tea from here. Apart from tea you can shop for herbs, spices and eucalyptus oil here. Also pick up the regular souvenirs from this age-old establishment.

King Star — Chocolates
📞0423 2450205; 54, Commercial Rd; noon–9pm Home-made chocolates are an essential part of the Ooty shopping landscape with plenty of shops selling a vast array. Pick up a mixed box from the oldest establishment in Ooty (1942), whose ownership, sadly, is now fragmented. The chocolates might taste just the same as in any other shop, but buying from this small, dingy shop is a romantic travel experience.

Modern Stores — Chocolates
📞0423 2447353; 144 Garden Rd; 9.30am–9pm The cleaner and glitzier Modern Stores up ahead on Garden Road has far surpassed King Star in its popularity to grab a bag of chocolates. This store too is over 50 years old (though it does not look like it).

Mohans — Ethnic Jewellery
📞0423 2442376; opp Collector's Office; 10am–1.30pm, 3–8pm A distinct shopping establishment near St Stephen's Church, Mohan's has been around in the city since 1947. Though they claim to sell Toda jewellery, locals are confident that the tribe has stopped making their traditional ornaments, and these might be imitations. The shop is good for other bric-a-brac which make for interesting souvenirs to take home.

COONOOR

Transcultural Mission — Handicrafts
📞9626343774; 28/C Quill Hill; 9am–4.30pm Pamela Bennyalves's nine-year-old initiative to work with mothers of slum children has resulted in a superb range of hand-embroidered products, out of a small workshop in Upper Coonoor. Pick up bed sheets, pillow covers, towels, etc; a large percentage of the proceeds goes back to the women.

Green Shop — Tribal Products
☎ 0423 2238412; Jograj Building, Bedford Circle; 9.30am–7.30pm An initiative of the Kotagiri-based Keystone Foundation, Green Shop's range consists of products sourced from local tribes of the region, with a view to providing them with a sustainable means of living. This fair-trade establishment has Kurumba paintings in veg dyes (₹275), organic food, pottery, handicrafts, garments and oils, among other products.

Vishal Marketing Co. — Tea
☎ 0423 2232500, ISSU Building, Coonoor; 9.30am–1.30pm, 3.30–8pm Owing to the patronage of most resorts and homestays, this otherwise nondescript store on Bedford Circle simply can't be missed if you're shopping for some tea. The owner, Mr Parekh, stocks the best of the region's top-20 brands. The teas range in price from ₹100 to ₹8000 per kg.

Cee Dee Jay's Baker's Junction (Cedrick's Nilgiris) — Cheese
☎ 0423 2222223, 27 Stanes School Rd; 10am–9pm, Sun closed If you are craving for fresh bread and some local cheese, visit this departmental store just off Bedford Circle. The shop stocks a variety of aromatic cheeses from the Acres Wild and Gray Hill farms in Coonoor.

Needle Craft — Needlework
☎ 0423 2230788; Erin Villa, Singara Estate Rd; 10am–5.30pm The beautiful Erin Villa is home to Needle Craft, which stores products from missionary establishments. Look out for delicately made (if slightly overpriced) silk embroidery, handmade lace, cut-work and cross-stitch work.

KOTAGIRI

Green Shop — Local Produce
☎ 04266 273887; www.lastforest.in; Johnstone Square; 9.30am–7.30pm An initiative of the Keystone Foundation, the Green Shop is great for buying souvenirs which have been sourced from the local tribes of the region. Paintings, honey, oils, clothes and organic foods are the best picks.

Riverside Tea Promoters — Tea
☎ 04266 272769; Aravenu (PO); 8.30am–7.30pm Though you may want to pick up tea leaves when leaving Ooty, you can also buy a souvenir pack from this shop.

Women's Co-operative — Handicrafts
10am–5pm; Mon–Sat The Women's Co-operative is focused on Toda products, especially embroidered goods like shawls, bags, tablecloths, etc. Honey and candles are also available here. The shop is run-down and dusty, but it is the best place to get a good bargain on these authentic products (instead of the more glitzy shops in town).

If You Like: Eco adventures

Nature Watch (☏9786971735) is an adventure company with a focus on eco-tourism and conservation. The group has an assortment of backpacking trails across the Nilgiris, catering to all levels. They can customise your package according to your needs: discuss your health and ability in detail and get recommendations from the small but efficient team for the right trip for you. For longer trails through forests, you need to get permission from the government; contact at least eight days in advance.

One Day Package (Beginners)

- **Peaks:** Solur, Hebbanad, Rangaswamy, DarshkalHullikkal Droog
- Rangaswamy Pillar
- Dolphin Nose to Catherine Falls
- Ridge-way trail from Catherine Falls to Mullur
- Bikkapathi peak to Hebbanad peak

Trekking in the Nilgiris is an experience that should not be missed

- Aderly to Burliar

Special Treks (Advanced)

- Kodanad to Thengumarahada
- Rangaswamy to Aracode
- Garikaiyoor to Kallampallayam
- Solur to Bokkeypuram
- Hebbanad to Anaigatty

Beginners can choose a day package for hiking in the Nilgris

Andaman Islands

The Andamans & Nicobar archipelago beckons travellers to discover the hidden beauty of its tiny and remote islands. This idyllic paradise boasts pristine beaches and underwater explorations that provide encounters with an exquisite marine ecology. The population is a mix of South and Southeast Asian settlers, and Negrito ethnic groups that's baffled anthropologists.

Trip Planner

GETTING THERE

Port Blair: Port Blair airport has flights from all major cities from the country including New Delhi, Mumbai, Kolkata, Bhubaneswar, Chennai and Kochi. There are boats that run weekly from Chennai (044 25226873, Chennai Port); and fortnightly from Kolkata (www.shipindia.com) to Port Blair. From Port Blair's Phoenix Bay Jetty ferries run regularly to Havelock, Ross and Neil Island.

SUGGESTED ITINERARY (7 DAYS)

After you arrive in Port Blair, spend two days here, visiting the Anthropological Museum, Cellular Jail, Corbyn's Cove Beach and Ross Island. Then it is time for island hopping. Make your way to Havelock Island and spend three days exploring its pristine white beaches and scuba diving. Next in line is Neil Island that has five beautiful beaches where you can spend a couple of days.

BEST TIME TO GO

J F M A M J J A S **O N D**

GREAT FOR

Top 5 highlights

- **Port Blair** (p435)
- **Ross Island** (p436)
- **Radhanagar Beach, Havelock** (p437)
- **Elephant Beach, Havelock** (p437)
- **Scuba Diving** (p439)

Diver's Haven

Beautiful corals and clear waters make the Andamans a top diving destination

Nestled in the Bay of Bengal, Andamans is one of the prettiest archipelagos you can possibly imagine. Its emerald green waters surrounded by primeval jungle are proof of its isolated exclusivity. Here snow white beaches melt under orange and purple sunsets. Watch the sunrise or sunset (depending on which side of the island you are) and swim in the tranquil bays. It is one of the most popular diving destinations in the country with stunning corals and a kaleidoscopic marine life and several renowned dive schools. It has an ecologically diverse zone inhabited by turtles, saltwater crocodiles, many varieties of fish and over 250 species of birds.
Remember not to damage coral and shells, or carry them back – it is punishable by law.

Port Blair & Islands

❶ PORT BLAIR
Green and laid-back, Port Blair has a mixed immigrant culture, tinged with a bit of colonial nostalgia. You can spend a couple of days here before you make your way to the beach delights of **Havelock** and **Neil**. A visit to **Cellular Jail** is a

Highlights
❶ Port Blair
❷ Ross Island
❸ Havelock Island
❹ Radhanagar Beach, Havelock
❺ Elephant Beach, Havelock
❻ Vijaynagar Beach, Havelock
❼ Neil Island

Quick Facts: Reaching Havelock

- **Ferry** (☎03192 212355, 236677; www.makruzz.com): All departures are subject to weather conditions. The government ferry from Port Blair to Havelock takes 2.5hr and departs at 6am, 11.30am & 2pm (₹150–250). The MV Makruzz private ferry takes 90min; ₹815 premium ₹950 deluxe. Coastal Cruise (www.coastalcruise.in) is another new entrant that has the same rates as Makruzz.
- **Sea Plane** (☎03192 244312, 9531828222): Nine passengers per plane; leaves Port Blair at 7.45am and 12.45pm, 20min; ₹4100/person (one way).

must, especially to expose youngsters to the sacrifices made by our freedom fighters. **Corbyn's Cove** is the popular tourist beach, while **Chidiya Tapu**, a 30km drive is a gorgeous spot to catch the sunset.

❷ ROSS ISLAND

Ross Island is just 20 minutes from Port Blair and is good for a half-day trip. It used to be the bustling administrative headquarters of the British, till an earthquake in 1941 destroyed quite a bit of it. The Navy has preserved the island's past as it was left by the British in 1945. Walk by the old ruins and crumbling buildings that stand like ghosts from the 19th century; don't miss the once-grand ballroom.

Boats leave from the jetty at the Water Sports Complex at 8.30am, 10.30am, 12.30pm & 2pm (Wed closed) and take 20min to reach; ₹75/ person; admission to island ₹20 (carry ID)

❸ HAVELOCK ISLAND

Corbyn's Cove is a popular beach off Port Blair

With crystal blue waters, white-sand beaches and lush forests, peace and quiet find a new definition on Havelock Island. The most action you'll get here is in the water itself – snorkelling, swimming and scuba diving – though there are a

few occasional musical nights with beers on the beach. Here's a promise though: the waters of Havelock are so pristine and mesmerising, you won't be complaining about the lack of phone and internet connectivity. After a glimpse of that soft white sand and the gradients of blue in the ocean, you will understand why this tiny island has become a favourite amongst beach connoisseurs. To experience the full beauty of Havelock, visit the individual attractions described below. It is easy to rent cabs, autos or two-wheelers to get around.
Scooter ₹400 per day; cycle ₹100 per day; shared jeep/taxi ₹20 per person per ride; autos, maximum ₹250

❹ RADHANAGAR BEACH, HAVELOCK

Also called Beach No.7, this is the most spectacular stretch of sand in Havelock, framed by the wave-lashed ocean on one side and tall rainforests on the other. The beach is amazing at sunset since it faces the west. Walk for about 10 minutes down the sandy strip and you will come to Neil's Cove, a beautiful and quiet spot, abundant with rocks, perfect for sunbathing. Further up you'll come to a quiet lagoon where the shallow water is great for swimming and snorkelling.
12km from the jetty, auto ₹150

❺ ELEPHANT BEACH, HAVELOCK

Getting to Elephant Beach is a bit complicated, but well worth the effort for the stark beauty of its white sands. The bleached driftwood and gnarled tree trunks rising from the sea make it a picture postcard perfect scene. With bright corals, it is one of the best spots in the island for snorkelling. If you are adventurous, you can take a 40-minute walk (the

---

📷 *Snapshot: Cellular Jail*

The Cellular Jail (GB Pant Rd; 8.30am–5pm, Mon closed and daily for lunch 12.30–1.30pm; entry ₹10, camera ₹25; Sound and Light Show from Mon–Wed at 6.45pm, ticket ₹20) that imprisoned Indian freedom fighters is now a national memorial. With seven wings stretching out from a central tower (only three exist now), the 698 cells were meant for maximum isolation. The gallows and torture instruments on display stand testimony to the cruelty inflicted.

Havelock is dotted with beaches that are safe for boating and swimming

path goes down from the road between Radhanagar Beach and Govindpuri and it's clearly marked) that involves getting your feet wet as you wade through shallow water. Otherwise opt for the glass bottom boat ride from the jetty.
A 40min walk or 20min boat ride from the jetty

⑥ VIJAYNAGAR BEACH, HAVELOCK

Popularly known as Beach No.5, this is where most diving centres, hotels and restaurants are located. Despite the commercial row of stalls, the beach is clean and inviting, though swimming can be hard as the waters are shallow and interspersed with rocks. This beach faces the east and is good to watch the sun's first rays arriving in India.
6km from Havelock Jetty

⑦ NEIL ISLAND

A stone's throw across the sea from Havelock and 40km from Port Blair is the small and quiet Neil Island with five beautiful beaches that have ample character. With plenty of unbleached, live coral under the surface, and a large school of fish, this is a dream spot for divers. The island is best visited through your resort or the dive shop at Havelock, who can organise tickets and boats and provide equipment for your diving or snorkelling trip there. Lakshmanpur (Beach No 1) is very pretty and has a swampy dense forest just behind the pristine white sand stretch. Snorkelling here is good fun, but swimming can be a bit tedious because of the abundant coral.

Beach No 2 is famous for its 'natural bridge', which rises out of the water and is made entirely of carved rock. One thing's for certain – you can kiss your cell phone reception good bye when your boat departs for Neil.

Ferry leaves Port Blair from Phoenix Bay Jetty at 6.30am, takes 2hr and costs ₹195; the Rangat Ferry leaves Havelock Jetty once a day (timings vary) and costs ₹150

If You Like: Scuba diving

Diving is the number one activity here and Havelock is the favourite spot for it. With shallow waters continuing for miles, the island is one of the best places for beginners. If you don't have the time to complete your PADI (Professional Association of Dive Instructors) or SSI (Scuba Schools International) certification then you have the wonderful opportunity of testing the waters and indulging in a single day diving experience. This isn't offered all over the world, and so it's a good spot to jump in and get on the action underwater. For more experienced divers, dive centres on Havelock offer a series of magical experiences including night diving and wreck diving. Prices between dive shops rarely vary. Though hotels have their own dive shops, non-residents are welcome too.

- **DiveIndia** ☎03192 214247; www.diveindia.com; located between Beach 3 & 5; bookings instructor 9932082205; PADI open water course for 4 days ₹20,000; PADI scuba diver course for 3 days ₹15,000; SSI course ₹17,000.
- **Barefoot Scuba** ☎9566088560; www.diveandamans.com; Beach No.3 You can pre-book a full course online.
- **Andaman Bubbles** ☎03192 282140, 9449036747; www.andamanbubbles.com; Beach No.5.
- **Doongi Dives** ☎3192 212028; www.doongidives.com; Beach No.5.
- Rates for Discover Scuba Diving/single-day experience (dive till 12m) for all dive centres ₹4500.

Andamans colourful coral reefs are a highlight of underwater excursions

Accommodation

PORT BLAIR

Sinclair's Bay View — Hotel ₹₹₹
03192 227824; www.sinclairshotels.com; South Point d ₹6000–10,000 The big and comfortable rooms here have the best views in town, opening right out to the water. Eat breakfast out on the deck where you'll have a breathtaking view of the sea, and if possible stay in an attic suite – romantic and cosy with a different floor for the kids.

Fortune Resort Bay Island — Hotel ₹₹₹
03192 234101; www.fortunehotels.in; Marine Hill; d ₹6800, with all meals ₹8,600 This 30-yearold ITC property is full of atmosphere with a fabulous sea-facing bar and restaurant (food is indifferent though). The rooms on the terraced slope are ideal for a family stay.

SeaShell — Hotel ₹₹
9933239625; www.seashellportblair.com; Marine Hill; d ₹4500–6000 This swanky hotel with clean rooms, a decent multi-cuisine restaurant – Salt n Pepper – and one of the best rooftop bars in the city, Amaya, makes it a great stay option. The tasteful bar hosts live performances regularly. Even if you don't stay here, drop by for a drink.

Sun Sea Resort — Resort ₹
03192 244442; www.sunsearesort-andamans.com; M.G.Road, Middle Point; d ₹2000–4800 This hotel has clean rooms and friendly staff. It's not fancy, but if you want to spend a couple of nights it's a good place to 'come home to'. Take a room towards the back of the hotel as the ones at the front tend to let in too much sound from the main road.

HAVELOCK ISLAND

Barefoot at Havelock — Hotel ₹₹₹
9840238042; www.barefoot-andaman.com; Beach No 7, Radhanagar Village; d ₹5000–

The Wild Orchid has cosy cottages, perfect for couples

20,000 Located on the pristine Radhanagar Beach, Barefoot remains Andaman's most exotic property where you can choose from a selection of tents or villas. Besides a great bar and a beautiful circular restaurant, there is a spa as well. Barefoot is the proud owner of one of the last sea swimming elephants in the world – Rajan. You can book in advance to enjoy a swim or bathing session with this big boy, but be warned – it all depends on his mood!

Silver Sands Resort   Resort ₹₹
☏ 03192 282493; www.silversandhavelock.com; Vijaynagar Beach; d ₹6000–12,000 Silver Sands is the last resort on Beach No 5 and as a result has one of the nicest, smoothest sands on this stretch. The resort is a favourite with honeymooners. The stand-alone rooms are done up tastefully.

> Sinclair's Bay View has vast and comfortable rooms, some of which are sea-facing

Munjoh Ocean Resort   Resort ₹₹
☏ 03192 212028; www.munjoh.com; Vijaynagar Beach; d ₹7000–10,000
The resort has a series of luxury villas and its cottages and suites are scattered over a zigzag base of canals. The spa offers incredible treatments and the bonus is the extremely quiet private beach. They have their own dive centre, the small but functional Doongi Dives. The beach chalet, comes with a kitchen and can accommodate two couples.

The Wild Orchid   Beach Resort ₹₹
☏ 03192 282472; www.wildorchidandaman.com; Vijaynagar

Avoid snorkelling during low tide as its easy to step on corals and damage them

Beach; d ₹3500–6000 This upmarket place is definitely one of the 'hubs' on the island. Their small but classy cottages are perfect for young couples looking for a bit of peace and quiet balanced with a bit of activity. Don't miss the wonderful restaurant, The Red Snapper that offers good seafood and brilliant evening gigs.

Symphony Palms Beach Cottages ₹₹
☎03192 232425; www.symphonypalmshavelock.com; Govindnagar Beach; d ₹4500–6500 This resort has rows of beautiful glass fronted cottages that come with modern amenities. They have a restaurant, Charcoal and a bamboo bar on stilts, Venom, though the selection of alcohol is limited.

NEIL ISLAND
Dancing Dugong Beach Resort Resort ₹₹
☎03192 214247; www.diveindia.com; d ₹4500 DiveIndia's new resort at Neil is probably one of the best stay options on the island. Since it is linked to the dive shop, it is popular with those coming for scuba diving. The luxury cottages are great to come home to after a day in the sea. The divers who stay pep up the evenings with great story-sharing experiences.

Pearl Park Beach Resort Beach Huts/Cottages ₹₹
☎03192 233880, 9434260132; www.andamanpearlpark.com; Beach No 1; d ₹1200–7000 Pearl Park offers five types of cottages. The traditional Nicobari cottage is pretty, with a thatched roof but no AC. If you want

air conditioning, opt for the deluxe cottages. Beyond the gardens that surround the property, their 'sunset point' is great at dusk.

Tango Beach Resort — Resort ₹
☏ 03192 282583, 9474212842; www.tangobeachandaman.com; Beach No 1; d ₹1700–5000 This beach resort offers a variety of rooms and cottages. Though the thatched huts are more charming, the rooms fitted with ACs would be more comfortable for city dwellers. The restaurant looks right onto the sea and they even have a small library.

Eating

PORT BLAIR

Annapurna — North/South Indian ₹
☏ 03192 234199; MG Rd One of the most popular eating spots in Port Blair, they serve north Indian food but it is best to stick to the south Indian fare – their dosas, idlis and coffee are all good and make for a great breakfast.

Lighthouse Residency — Restaurant ₹
MA Rd, Aberdeen Bazaar At this bustling restaurant the air conditioning is cranked up, the beer, cold and seafood, fresh. Choose from the display of red snapper, crab and tiger prawns. The BBQ fish is quite nice.

HAVELOCK ISLAND

The Lee Meridian
German Bakery — Restaurant ₹
The circular restaurant is large and airy and quite the hang-out spot in Havelock. They offer an extensive breakfast menu and also serve Chinese, north Indian, Mexican, and Israeli delights, not to mention the usual pizzas and pastas.

Fat Martin Cafe — Veg/South Indian ₹
This tiny spot is just off the main road and serves a wide selection of south Indian food. Try their vast range of dosas, which includes the unique nutella dosa.

Full Moon Cafe — Multi-Cuisine ₹₹
DiveIndia premises Govindnagar Beach This cafe is a hit and almost everything on their vast menu is a success, and people flock here from all over the island to get a pancake, falafel roll, grilled fish, salad, pasta or

---

 Snapshot: Careful with coral

Generally, you should only snorkel during high tide here. At low tide, it is easy to step on corals, irreparably damaging the delicate organisms. Even the sweep of a strong flipper kick can do harm. You could also risk a painful sea-urchin spine if you set foot on the seabed. Divers should be extra cautious about descents near reefs; colliding with coral at a hard place with full gear can be environmentally disastrous.

anything thats on the menu. This is a great post-diving hub.

The Red Snapper — Seafood ₹₹₹
☎ 03192 282472; www.wildorchidandaman.com; **Wild Orchid Resort; Vijaynagar Beach** Wild Orchid's restaurant, The Red Snapper, is considered one of the best places around here. However it is pricey (₹1500 for a meal for two). They serve a great fish fry and have a selection of fresh seafood to choose from. Their desserts are heavenly, especially the crème caramel. On most nights, Wild Orchid's restaurant is the best place to hang-out. Swing by for drinks and live bands or Bollywood theme evenings. The bar closes at 10.45pm.

B3 – Barefoot Bar & Brasserie — Continental ₹₹₹
Village No 1; Havelock Jetty You'll spot B3 easily by its beautiful wooden deck on the first floor. The menu has Western dishes and offers the best pizzas in town. The Caprese salad is so fresh you'll want another.

Clown Fish Cafe — Italian ₹₹₹
Main road, adjacent to Andaman Bubbles Though their menu isn't extensive, whatever they dish out is quite good. Their thin crust pizzas are

It is easy to find fresh seafood at most restaurants

nice and come loaded with fresh tuna, if you like. Do try their fresh juices.

NEIL ISLAND

Dhaba Delights — Bengali ₹
Grab a Bengali meal at the main market (₹130/thali). Delicious, hot and authentic, these generous portions won't leave you complaining.

Moonshine — Restaurant ₹
Beach no 1 This restaurant on the road to Beach no 1 makes excellent home-made pasta that can be washed down with cold beer.

ANDAMAN ISLANDS

Expert Recommendation
Getting the best of the Andamans

India's leading dive operation and instructor centre was founded by ad guru **Prahlad Kakkar** 15 years ago. His new dive centre is at Chidiya Tapu, South Andamans.

• **Diving & Snorkelling:** Havelock Island (Beach no 5, Barefoot Dive Centre, Andaman Bubbles) has popular sites for diving and snorkelling. There are two major sites at Cinque Island, accessible only from Chidiya Tapu, 25km from Port Blair. The first is shallow with colourful corals. The deeper diving site flows with currents and offers beautiful marine life including sting rays and turtles that come to feed here. Red Skin Island is a good place for beginners to start off their underwater adventures. Go snorkelling at Wandoor. A good variety of fish and coral life and if you're lucky, even a saltwater crocodile await here. At Chidiya Tapu the waters are filled with healthy coral, beautiful snappers, fusilier, rays, turtles and the occasional manta. Mundapahad is for beginners and the old shipwreck is a site for advanced divers and home to anemones, clown fish, schooling snapper and resting rays, and colonies of colourful corals.

• **Birdwatching:** Let not the beauty of its beaches and marine lives overshadow Andaman's flora and fauna. The marriage of mangroves, rainforests with migratory birds and flowers at Chidiya Tapu, also called Bird Island, is truly unique.

• **Children's special:** Lacadives, Reef Watch and local group Annette have collaborated to host regular trainings and school programmes at Wandoor on marine environment consciousness and on basic snorkelling tips.

Havelock Island has popular sites for diving and snorkelling

Andhra Pradesh

Why Go?

With unexplored beaches along the state's pristine coastline, the low, cool Eastern Ghats and a host of handicraft hubs to visit, Andhra Pradesh surprises you with its variety. Its capital, **Hyderabad**, is a haven for history lovers with every nook and corner of the Old City shrouded in the history of the Qutb Shahis.

From the beach city **Visakhapatnam**, cruise south along the coastline, stopping at the craft and weaving centres of the state – the villages of Etikoppaka, Uppada and Pedana and then move on to scenic **Araku Valley**. Then swerve back inland to explore the city of **Vijayawada**, Kondapalli and places around. Andhra Pradesh also offers a tryst with one of the richest deities of India, Sri Balaji of **Tirupati**. If this pilgrimage centre does not stir your spiritual sensibilities, the ancient temples of **Srisailam**, Kanaka Durga and Mangalagiri sure will.

Getting There & Away

Air: Rajiv Gandhi International Airport in Hyderabad is the state's only international airport. It has multiple daily flights to all metros and major cities in the country. Other important airports are in Visakhapatnam, Vijayawada, Tirupati and Rajahmundry.

Train: The key travel hubs of the state are well connected by the South Indian and Eastern Railway network. Overnight trains from other South Indian destinations are also easily available. Only a few places need to be further accessed by road. The key railway stations are in Hyderabad, Tirupati, Visakhapatnam, Vijayawada and Rajahmundry.

▋ The icon of Hyderabad's landscape is the imposing Charminar in the Old City

Andhra Pradesh Map

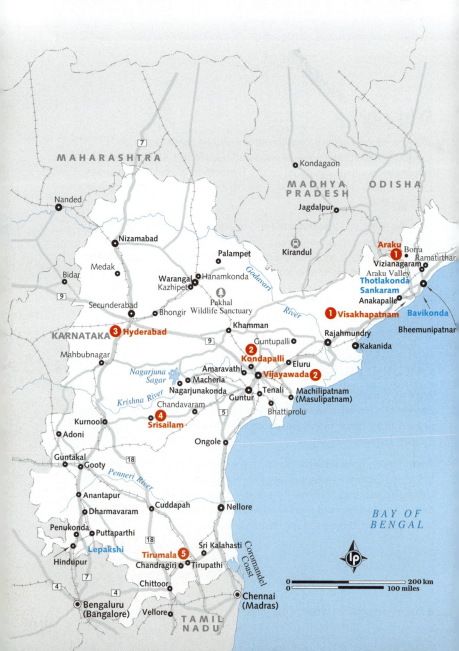

⭐ 5 Best Trips

① Visakhapatnam & Araku Valley (p452) Enjoy the breezy city of Visakhapatnam at the edge of the Bay of Bengal and then move to Araku Valley for a leisurely trip in the beautiful lush hills.

② Vijayawada & Around (p466) Use Vijayawada as a base to explore weaving hubs like Mangalagiri, Uppada and Pedana. You can also visit Kuchipudi village and toy towns, Etikoppaka and Kondapalli from here.

③ Hyderabad (p472) The capital still retains its ancient charm. Add to that, a burgeoning modern city and you have a perfect milieu of the new and old.

④ Srisailam (p492) This town is home to one of the oldest temple complexes in the country.

⑤ Tirupati (p498) A trip to the sanctum of Tirupati Balaji can be overwhelming, but an experience that you will not forget in a hurry.

Traditional souvenirs at Sri Venkateswara Swamy Temple

Top Highlights

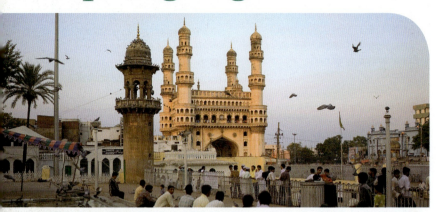

1 Charminar & Around

You can't escape the legacy of the Qutb Shahi kings while roaming around the streets of Old Hyderabad which take you back to a bygone era. Start at the busy junction of Charminar (p474), the quintessential historic symbol of Hyderabad and an erstwhile mosque. A profusion of ittar, bangles, surma, pearls, antiques and crumbling restaurants dot the market lanes that emanate from this central node. After this, go to Chowmahalla Palace, Golconda Fort, and the Qutb Shahi tombs to unearth secrets from the 16th century.

2 Beaches around Visakhapatnam

You can choose from a vast stretch of sandy hideouts or join in the evening fun at Rushikonda (p456), the most scenic beach of Visakhapatnam. This is the only beach in the region where the gentle topography and soft waves allow travellers to enjoy a range of water sports. Closer to town, the RK Beach (p454) straddles the edge of the city and is buzzing with activity in the evenings. Nestled between low mountains, Yarada Beach (p457) is scenic and secluded.

3 Srisailam

Presumably one of the oldest temple complexes in the country, Srisailam (p492) is the abode of Lord Mallikarjuna (Shiva) and Goddess Bhramaramba (Parvati), perched on the Nallamalai Hills. The temple has been mentioned in ancient scriptures dating back to 1st century AD. Mud coloured walls enclose the two shrines and a large courtyard, which take hours to manoeuvre by slow lines. The town is swathed in people during the Shivratri festival, when lakhs of devotees descend here in the months of February/March.

4 Coastal Andhra Cuisine

Long clubbed together with all other 'south Indian food', coastal Andhra cuisine is unique in its spices and flavouring. Distinct from other seafood, it's a heady mix of masala crab, spicy prawns and curried fish. Unlike the rest of Andhra Pradesh's food, the only similarity is that the base remains one of rice. The best way to sample it though, is as a prawn biryani! Try out Sea Inn or any other of Visakhapatnam's restaurants (p463) famed for this simple yet delicious cuisine.

Visakhapatnam & Araku Valley

Visakhapatnam may be an industrial city, but it has diverse attractions – from pristine beaches and the country's oldest shipyard to the only natural harbour on India's east coast. Once a part of the Kalinga kingdom, it also has a fascinating mix of Buddhist and Hindu history. Nearby lies the lovely hill station, Araku Valley, covered with thick coffee plantations.

Trip Planner

GETTING THERE

Visakhapatnam: The airport is 7km from the city centre and has daily flights to all metros and major cities. Visakhapatnam Railway Station has trains from main South Indian hubs, from New Delhi and also Ahmedabad. A number of state and private buses also arrive from main cities in the state.

Araku Valley: Visakhapatnam Airport is 109km away. It's best to take the Visakhapatnam-Kirandul train from Visakhapatnam to Araku which goes through the hills.

SUGGESTED ITINERARY (6 DAYS)

Two days is enough time to explore the beaches of Visakhapatnam. On the third day make your way to Araku Valley and spend a couple of days here. On the fifth day go to Etikoppaka and then Rajahmundry, from where you can visit Yanam and Uppada for a day.

BEST TIME TO GO

J F M A M J J A S **O N D**

GREAT FOR

Top 5 highlights

- Rushikonda Beach, Visakhapatnam (p456)
- Kailasagiri, Visakhapatnam (p456)
- Simhachalam, Visakhapatnam (p457)
- Tribal Museum of Habitat, Araku Valley (p458)
- Borra Caves, Araku Valley (p458)

Sea Meets Hills

The clean and clear coastal stretch of **Visakhapatnam** (popularly called Vizag) along the Bay of Bengal will dazzle you with its beauty. The old beach-resort vibe exists despite the fact that Vizag is Andhra Pradesh's second largest city, famous for shipbuilding and steel. Its beaches are alternately peaceful or bustling with a festive atmosphere. Here, luxury resorts sit peacefully alongside stalls selling local Andhra bites, and a few days easily go by in the blink of an eye.

Once done with coastal delights, explore the Buddhist sites, the ancient temple of Simhachalam, and the Araku–Ananthagiri loop. Just 114km from the city, the low hills of **Araku** are covered with thick coffee plantations, relatively untouched tribal settlements, waterfalls and umpteen viewing points, making them a favourite local getaway. In the same trip, you can loop around the fringes of the **Ananthagiri** reserved forest, making it a two day-long trip, relaxing in its green confines and seeing local tribal life at close quarters. A great way of experiencing the ghats is to take the Visakhapatnam–Kirandul passenger train that meanders from Vizag to Araku through the hills.

Spectacular view of the curved coastline from Kailasagiri Park

Visakhapatnam

Highlights

1. Indira Gandhi Zoological Park
2. RK Beach
3. Visakha Museum
4. INS Kurusura Submarine Museum
5. Rushikonda Beach
6. Kailasagiri
7. Thotlakonda & Other Buddhist Complexes
8. Dolphin Nose, Yarada Beach
9. Simhachalam Temple

❶ INDIRA GANDHI ZOOLOGICAL PARK

This massive zoological park can be explored from your car; you can stop at the moated enclosures at your own pace to see the animals. Once inside, you can also opt for a battery-operated vehicle. The lush expanse of more than 600 acres is part of the Kambalakonda Wildlife Sanctuary of the Eastern Ghats. There are seating pavilions and other public conveniences, in case you want to take a rest from the birds, mammals and reptiles.

☏ 0891 2552081; adult/child/camera/car/video ₹15/5/15/200/100; 9am–5pm, Mon closed

❷ RK BEACH

The Ramakrishna Beach runs along the main seaside avenue of the city. Two decades ago this was a virgin beach that locals rarely visited, but today it is a different story. Seating areas, a park, sculptures and sightseeing options make this an interesting spot to explore. The Kali Temple, Matsyadarshini Aquarium and the Victory At Sea memorial, built as a homage to the war martyrs of the 1971 war, are

The park at RK Beach offers great views of the sea

GETTING AROUND

Autos are a convenient way of getting around – the lack of meters being the only impediment (minimum charge ₹20–30). However language gap can be a problem at times if you do not know Telegu. Chaturya Travel Zone has a decent fleet of cars and Hindi speaking drivers. Discuss your plan in detail before booking and feel free to ask for a deal if you are hiring the car for a long trip (☏9246666844; 49-32-6/6, Ramakrishna Nagar, Shankaramatam Rd). Taxis can be hired at ₹8–10/km. For detours to places such as Araku Valley, fixed packages starting from ₹3000 are available.

a few of them. The beach is not safe for swimming, but a stroll is recommended in the evening as it provides much entertainment in the form of food and people-watching.
Matsyadarshini Aquarium adult/child/camera/video ₹25/1/20/50; 9am–9pm

❸ VISAKHA MUSEUM

Located in an old colonial Dutch bungalow and home to ancient artefacts and naval and wartime display, a visit here gives you fascinating snippets of the maritime history of the city. Do not miss a part of the Pakistani submarine, Ghazi, which was found after the 1971 war. A visit to Visakha Aquarium, where you can see some marine creatures is interesting for children.
☏0891 2549215; off Beach Rd; adult/child ₹5/2; Tue–Fri 11am–7pm, Sat–Sun noon–8pm, Mon closed

❹ INS KURUSURA SUBMARINE MUSEUM

Highly recommended on the itinerary, this unique submarine museum lies on RK Beach. The 91.3m-long and 8m-wide technical wonder was once a Soviet built submarine, used by the Indian Navy. In 2001 it was placed on Beach Road to be used as a learning exhibit for the public. It's the only place in India where you can enter the 300ft submarine, and see how the insides work. Guided tours of the submarine are a special hit with children.
Beach Rd; adult/child/camera/video ₹40/20/50/200; Tue–Sat 2–8.30pm, Sun 10am–12.30pm, 2–8.30pm, Mon closed

The ropeway to Kailasagiri offers great views

5 RUSHIKONDA BEACH

Stretching right below Sugar Loaf Hill, this spectacular moon-shaped beach stretch is the most popular tourist hot spot, 20km from town. With its growing popularity, it now has a busy picnic vibe and it's worth a day trip. There are plenty of eating joints, shacks selling knick-knacks made of shell and coconut vendors. APTDC also offers two water rides: a motor boat and a jet ski. The full length of the beach can be seen from a restaurant on the hill. Swimming is forbidden here due to the strong currents.

Motor boat ₹300/3 people per ride; jet ski ₹200, life jacket included; 9.30am–5.30pm

6 KAILASAGIRI

This park is located high up on a hilltop and reaching there involves an exciting ride up an aerial tramway, but if you're not up for that you can also drive. It has a toy train, ropeway, horse rides, exhibits, swings, eating joints and sculptures of Shiva and Parvati. If you gloss over the kitschy sculptures you will be rewarded with panoramic views of the city, the curved coastline of the Bay of Bengal and green hills on the other side. If travelling with kids a visit here is worth it.

Walkers/two wheelers/cars ₹5/20/50; ropeway ₹60, train AC/non AC ₹75/50 for a 20min ride; 8.30am–8.30pm

7 THOTLAKONDA & OTHER BUDDHIST COMPLEXES

It's believed that Emperor Ashoka propagated Buddhism in this part of the country as is evidenced by the city's few Buddhist complexes. The most accessible and well-maintained one, Thotlakonda, is 15km from the city. A low hilly area lined with bougainvilleas ends in a large expanse with the remains of a 2000-year-old monastic complex, heralded by a Buddha statue near the gate. Excavations have thrown up some stunning relics and rock-hewn sculptures. The view of the sea is exquisite. Pavuralakonda and Sankaram are other Buddhist sites that have been excavated.

₹30; 7am–6pm

❽ DOLPHIN NOSE, YARADA BEACH

Start driving to Dolphin Nose hill from the city side and see the houses get smaller in the distance as you reach the residential naval colony here. The trip makes for a pleasant evening drive. You can visit the lighthouse on top of the hill and then loop across to drive amidst the lower slopes until you start seeing the coastline of Yarada Beach. This is not a touristy beach but the drive is scenic.

Lighthouse Indian/foreigner/child/camera/video ₹10/25/3/20/25; 3–5pm

❾ SIMHACHALAM TEMPLE

One of the most important pilgrim centres for Hindus, the Simhachalam Temple, stands atop a hill, 16km from the city. Dedicated to the man-lion avatar of Lord Vishnu, Narsimhaswamy, the temple is a visual and spiritual treat. Arrive as early as 6am to line up for the free darshan or you can come in slightly later and pay ₹100 for a quicker darshan.

The ancient temple's carved columns look beautiful as the sound of temple percussions in the background awes you into reverence. Do not miss seeing the kappastambham; you will find many devotees hugging this with fervour in order to pray for a child. There is also a 'go-daan' section (offering for cows) and head tonsuring facility (₹10).

📞 0891 2010452; entry free or ₹20/100; two wheeler/four wheeler ₹10/30; 6.30am–9pm

The heavily carved Simhachalam Temple is located on a hill

Araku Valley

Highlights
1. Padmapuram Botanical Garden
2. Tribal Museum of Habitat
3. Katiki Waterfall
4. Borra Caves

❶ PADMAPURAM BOTANICAL GARDEN
Spend a day exploring the sightseeing options around Visakhapatnam in Araku Valley. Start with Padampuram Botanical Garden and Horticulture Centre at the end of the main Araku Road. The garden needs sprucing up, but is good for a walk or a toy train ride.

☎9440203188; adult/child ₹10/5; 8am–noon, 1–5pm

❷ TRIBAL MUSEUM OF HABITAT
A short distance from the Botanical Garden, the Tribal Museum of Habitat is an an interesting place to stop. Ignore the rest of the ill-maintained 10-acre area and head straight for the single hall that functions as a museum. The exhibits tell you a lot about the 17 indigenous and isolated tribal communities of the valley.

Adult/child ₹10/5; 8am–1.30pm, 2.30–6.30pm

❸ KATIKI WATERFALL
The Katiki Waterfall lies 15km from the APTDC Hill Resort in Ananthagiri. The last 8km of the road can only be covered with a four-wheel drive. Jeeps are available from a junction on the main road but are quite pricey.

₹1000 full jeep/₹150 per person if sharing

❹ BORRA CAVES
Close to the Katiki junction, the Borra Caves offer a wonderful opportunity to see spectacular low hanging stalactite and stalagmite formations. The short and steep climb to the main gate is flanked by local tribals selling fruits, cashew and spices sourced from the hills.

☎0891 2788820; adult/child/camera/mobile photography/video ₹60/45/100/25/100; 10am–1pm, 2–5pm

Expert Recommendation
Crafts & textiles of Andhra Pradesh

Sharan Apparao heads Apparao Art Galleries and is a curator and connoisseur of art, design and craft.

- **Crafts:** Silver filigree from **Karimnagar** is a treasured collectible. Andhra also has a lively toy craft culture. **Nirmal**, in Adilabad town is home to colourful papier mâché toys; Etikopakka dolls, toys and lacquerware are popular. **Kondapalli** wooden dolls have been treasures for centuries. Leather puppets are now repurposed as lampshades, wall crafts and gift items.

- **Paintings:** Cherai scroll paintings depicting mythological stories and themes of battles and amorous couples and Kalamkari hand painted textiles in vegetable dyes from **Kalahasti** are lovely crafts.

- **Textiles:** Andhra's enduring craft heritage includes textiles, dyeing and printing and handloom fabrics. Southern **Machilipatnam** led in production of vegetable-coloured block printed textiles, inspired by Persian panels and once used as awnings and panels in interiors. Today they are sold as home textiles and dress materials. Tie-and-dye or ikat fabrics and saris in silk and cotton are produced in **Pochampally.** The village of **Chirala** makes red, black and white tie-and-dye telia rumals woven with pre oiled yarn to make it weather resistant for fisherfolk. **Jamdani** weaves of Paithani saris, zari weaves of **Gadwal** and **Venkatagiri**, the lesser known **Upaddas** and **Putapakkas** found their way to many a woman's wardrobe. No narration of the textiles history is complete without including the zari embroideries of the royal karkhanas to the humble but vibrant cotton needle crafts of the nomadic gypsies, the lambadas of Andhra.

The gorgeous Ikat fabrics are produced in Pochampally, a weavers village

Accommodation

In Visakhapatnam, it is advisable to stay close to Beach Road as the interiors are often clogged with heavy vehicles since NH5 runs through the city.

VISAKHAPATNAM

The Park — Luxury ₹₹₹
☎0891 2754181; www.theparkhotels.com; Beach Rd; d ₹9000–11,000, ste ₹15,000–20,000 (incl of breakfast) One of the prettiest hotels in the city, it is inspired by the region's Buddhist legacy. The elegantly styled rooms and chic ambience of The Park, along with its location by the beach make it one of the best luxury addresses for your stay in Visakhapatnam.

The Gateway Hotel — Hotel ₹₹₹
☎0891 6623670; www.thegatewayhotels.com; Beach Rd; d ₹8000–9000, ste ₹18,000 (incl of breakfast) Each of the thoughtfully placed rooms at The Gateway has a view of either the sea or the pool. Black and white sketches of Andhra themes adorn the walls of the galleries, ensuring that the mood of the hotel matches your travel plans. The service is impeccable.

Novotel — Hotel ₹₹₹
☎0891 282222; www.novotel.com; Beach Rd; d ₹6500–13,500 (incl of breakfast) Novotel is the latest addition to the beachside hotels at Visakhapatnam and has stylish

The restaurants at The Park Hotel are a favourite with locals

interiors and facilities. You can also avail discounts with the flexi prices policy. The hotel has a pool and many restaurants. Ask for a sea-facing room to make your stay complete. Another plus is the spa that offers a range of soothing therapies.

Best Western Ramachandra — Boutique Hotel ₹₹
☎0891 2579777; www.bwramachandra.co.in; 8-8-36, Main Rd, Gajuwaka; d ₹3500–5500, ste ₹7000 (incl of breakfast) Access to Best Western lies in the busy Gajuwaka area, but the spic and span smart rooms, with rich interiors, ample buffet spread at breakfast and service a notch above the rest, make this a top pick for the family. The rooms are small so check if you are planning to add an extra bed for children.

Palm Beach — Hotel ₹₹
☎0891 2754026; www.palmbeachhotel.in; Beach Rd; d

₹5500–7500 (incl of breakfast) An exclusive private beach area for guests is the highlight of this hotel! One cannot really bathe in the sea near the RK Beach, but this is one spot that you can get into the water, under watch. The lush money plants in the hotel add a refreshing splash of green to the corridors. Ask for the first floor rooms with a wide terrace overlooking the pool and the beach. The hotel also has two restaurants.

Ambica Sea Green — Hotel ₹₹
0891 2821818; www.ambicaseagreen.com; Plot No 1, Kirlampudi Layout, Door No 7-24-3/2, Beach Rd; d ₹4500–5500, ste ₹6500 (incl of breakfast)
While opting for Ambica Sea Green, ensure that you book the sea-facing rooms; this is the only charm of the otherwise reasonably priced hotel. Ambica lies right next to the Victory Memorial on RK Beach and also overlooks the Submarine Museum. Evenings by the beach are especially great for a stroll.

Budhil Park — Hotel ₹₹
0891 2795353; www.hotelbudhilpark.com; 48-8-12, 1st Street, Dwaraka Nagar; d ₹3450–3900 (incl of breakfast) Of all the hotels in the town, Budhil Park is one of the few that is centrally located in the business hub and yet peacefully cut off from the main road. There are 41 rooms with modern amenities, and the two dining options make this a comfortable budget stay.

Jukasotel — Boutique Hotel ₹₹
0891 3050100; www.jukaso.co.in; 47-10-19, 2nd Lane, Dwarakanagar; d ₹3000–4000 (incl of breakfast)
Trendy Jukaso Hotel's uniquely designed rooms, modern facilities and excellent hospitality make it a good choice for travellers who want to stay in the middle of town.

Sun Ray Village Resort — Resort ₹₹
9490700147; www.sunrayvillageresort.com; Amatam, Ravivalasa Panchayathi, Savaravilli, Bogapuram Mandal, Vijayanagaram; d ₹3222–12888 (incl of breakfast)
Usually a weekend getaway for locals, Sun Ray Village Resort gives you a chance to drive through the countryside along the NH5, 63km from the city. It has sprawling manicured lawns dotted with furnished villas. Cycling, swimming, basketball, an activity room, gym, gaming zone, a special kids area and access to multiple dining options make it a great choice.

APTDC Beach Resort — Resort ₹
0891 2788826; www.aptdc.in; Rushikonda Beach; d ₹2000–2600, ste ₹3800–6600 (incl of breakfast)
Though the APTDC property is not plush, it has a vantage spot on a hill, with a brilliant view of the Rushikonda Beach. The spacious rooms have

private balconies and reasonable furnishings with a flat-screen TV. There is no wi-fi facility or swimming pool, but an in-house restaurant and access to the beach makes up for this.

55 Lawsons Bay Guesthouse ₹
☏ 0891 6627555; www.55lawsonsbay.com; 4-72-2/31, Lawsons Bay Colony; d ₹2500–3000 (incl of breakfast) Not too far from Beach Road, 55 Lawsons Bay offers newly built, clean spacious rooms. The guesthouse is also good value for money with its fine location and facilities. Though no meals are served in this intimate nine-room property, the staff can help you order out.

White Villa Guesthouse ₹
☏ 0891 2792215; www.whitevilla.com; 50-50-20/A, TPT Colony, opp Apseb Substation Seethamadhara; d ₹1800–3000 (incl of breakfast) The newly built White Villa has everything in the making for a great budget stay, with facilities like wi-fi, room service and spacious rooms. Though the service is a little tardy, the youthful staff is warm and go out of their way to help with meals ordered in the rooms and fixing travel plans for you.

ARAKU & ANANTHAGIRI

Vihar Holiday Resort Hotel ₹
☏ 08936 249333; www.viharholidayresorts.com; Araku; d ₹2300, ste ₹2900 (incl of breakfast) Apart from the APTDC options, Vihar Holiday Resorts is a cosy and clean stay with 12 rooms and an in-house restaurant. The property is close to the Araku main road, where the Botanical Garden and Museum are situated.

Haritha Valley Resort APTDC Resort ₹
☏ 08936 249202; www.aptdc.gov.in; Araku; d ₹1200, ste ₹2000–2750 (incl of breakfast) Haritha Valley Resort lies at the base of the hills, close to the Botanical Garden and the Tribal Museum. Each villa unit has four spacious but sparsely furnished rooms that overlook a central garden. There is a swimming pool and an in-house restaurant as well.

Haritha Hill Resort APTDC Hotel ₹
☏ 08936 231898; www.aptdc.gov.in; Araku; d ₹1850–2850, ste ₹6100 (incl of breakfast) Haritha Hill Resort stands at the edge of a hill overlooking coffee-scaped mountains and has lush manicured lawns separating the cottages. This is a much more scenic property with an in-house restaurant (with slow service) at the edge of the valley. Non AC rooms are suitable for the cooler weather here so you can budget accordingly.

Jungle Bells APTDC Camp ₹
☏ 0891 2788820; www.aptdc.gov.in; Tyda; d ₹1200–2250 (incl of breakfast) An eco-tourism project, Jungle Bells at Tyda is a nature camp set up with decently furnished rooms

without TV or internet facilities. The newer wooden cottages are spacious and give a great feeling of being in the hills, with mildly creaking wooden floors and a sit-out to enjoy the weather.

Eating

VISAKHAPATNAM

Zaffran   Multi-Cuisine ₹₹₹
☎ 0891 282222; Novotel Hotel, Beach Rd; mains above ₹750–1000; 12.30–3pm, 7.30–11.30pm There is no better accompaniment to a meal in Visakhapatnam than a view of the ocean. Enjoy the stunning blue expanse along with a variety of multi-cuisine dishes here. The Mughlai food is especially delicious and the service is impeccable.

> Authentic Hyderabadi biryani is available at most places in Visakhapatnam

Zodiac   Multi-Cuisine ₹₹
☎ 0891 398844; 47-10-34&35, Dwaraka Nagar, Diamond Park, Sreekanya Rd; mains ₹500–750; noon–3.30pm, 7–11.30pm The in-house restaurant of Fortune Inn, Zodiac is an ideal place to try the spicy local Andhra cuisine. If too hot for you, you can mix it with subtler dishes as the restaurant serves other cuisines too to choose from.

Vihar   Multi-Cuisine ₹
☎ 9908483936; Rushikonda Beach; mains ₹200–500; 11am–11pm The view from this hilltop cafe is reason enough to come here for a drink or a meal. You can sit outside and enjoy a breezy view of the action on the Rushikonda Beach below. The restaurant also serves alcohol.

Punjabi Grill   North Indian ₹
☎ 0891 6625777; Matsyadarshini, RK Beach Rd; mains ₹200–500; 11am–11pm If you're craving for north Indian cuisine head straight to Punjabi Grill and relish a plate of juicy butter chicken. The decor and ambience is nothing to write home about, but the fare is good.

Hyderabad House   Andhra ₹
☎ 0891 6463939; Siripuram VIP Rd; mains ₹200–500; 11am–11pm Head here to try the famous Hyderabadi biryani. The menu is mostly non-veg.

Kondapalli wooden toys – dolls and elephants – are popular souviners in the region

Pastry, Coffee N Conversation Cafe ₹
0891 6512953; Dutt Island, Siripuram; 11am–10.30pm Better known as PCNC, this charming cafe is done up with cane and wood furniture. You can read a book as you enjoy a coffee, drop by for a quick dessert or even stop in the morning and get sandwiches and other snacks packed for a day at the beach. It serves an interesting selection of chocolate cakes, which includes a Snickers cake, a Kit Kat cake and an Oreo cake. There's music to jive as well.

Sea Inn Seafood ₹₹
0891 2790403; Rushikonda, along Vizag–Bheemli Rd; noon–9pm, Mon closed Also known as Raju ka dhaba, after the owner, this is your one-stop shop for local food. Try the prawn biryani and fried seafood dishes. They've been around for two decades. It's unpretentious, clean and the food is lip-smacking. However, they do not accept credit cards.

Venkatadri Vantillu Andhra ₹₹
Praveen Plaza, CBM Compound, VIP Rd For an authentic Andhra dosa or tiffin, head to this restaurant that seems more like a local canteen. Try their speciality 'sponge' dosa.

ARAKU VALLEY & ANANTHAGIRI
APTDC Resorts Multi-Cuisine ₹
The APTDC resorts are the best places to eat in Araku Valley and Ananthagiri. There aren't too many options available in the hills, so stick to the safe and clean food of these establishments. The menu mainly consists of South Indian and also Chinese dishes.

Shopping

Lepakshi Handicrafts
0891 2508037; Main Rd, Jagdamba Centre; 10am–8.00pm The Andhra Pradesh chain of emporiums is your best bet at picking souvenirs from Visakhapatnam. Not only can you get your hands on local favourites like Kondapalli toys and saris, but also knick-knacks from other South Indian states.

Eastern Art Museum Handicrafts
0891 2562775; 10-1-9/1, Waltair Uplands Rd; 10am–8.30pm For handicrafts from across India and Andhra Pradesh, the Eastern Art Museum offers both reasonable and slightly higher priced items.

Detour: Getaways from Visakhapatnam

If you are driving down to Vijayawada (p466), 350km away, these places are good options to stop by on the way.

- **Etikoppaka:** This small unassuming village, 65km away, is home to the traditional art of lacquer finished wooden artefacts. Over 200 villagers are involved in making unique colourful toys, games, bangles, boxes, dolls and other bric-a-brac with the soft 'ankudu' wood, finished with vegetable dyes. To know better about this art form, visit the **Handicrafts Production Centre** (08931 220202; www.etikoppaka.in; Hasthakala Nilayam; 9am–6.15pm) run by CV Raju, whose forefathers were instrumental in propagating it in the village.

- **Rajahmundry:** This town (190km), on the banks of Godavari River can be used as a hub to explore Yanam and Uppada. It falls a little ahead of mid distance to Vijayawada. The **Arthur Cotton Museum** (adult/child/mobile/camera/video ₹2/1/5/10/20; 9am–1pm, 3–6.30pm) here is named after the British irrigation engineer responsible for creating the Dowleswaram Barrage built on the river. You can also visit the pink-stoned ISKCON temple or go for a cruise organised by **APTDC** (9848629341; day-long cruise adult/child ₹650/550).

- **Yanam:** A reminder of India's colonial past, Yanam lies between Uppada and Rajahmundry. It's 63km away. This is the third of four enclaves of Puducherry. The small town has very few remnants of French architecture and history, but makes a scenic stop besides the Godavari River.

- **Uppada:** The small village, 23km from Yanam, is a well-known sari-weaving centre of the state. You can hear the rhythmic clicking of wooden looms in the narrow lanes; almost every household is occupied with this craft. Famous for the intricate 'jamdani' designs, it's a delight for shoppers. Visit **Annapoorna Handlooms** (9866506467; Main Rd; 10am–7.30pm), the saris here are at least 30–50% cheaper than the showrooms in the city.

View of the Godavari Bridge from Rajahmundry

Vijayawada & Around

Bordered by the massive Krishna River, Vijayawada may not be the conventional holiday destination, but it works well as a hub for those who are hooked on to crafts and culture. Its proximity to places like Mangalagiri, Kondapalli, Kuchipudi and Pedana make it an essential stopover on your coastal Andhra sojourn for a taste of history and architecture, besides craft traditions that go back centuries.

Trip Planner

GETTING THERE

The Gannavaram Airport is 18km from the city and connected to all the metros and major cities in the country. The railway station is on the South Central Railway zone network and provides more frequent service with connections from most important nodes in the country: Chennai, Bengaluru, New Delhi, Mumbai, Hyderabad, Kolkata and other prominent South Indian cities as well. Overnight APSRTC buses and private operators are available from parts of Andhra and bordering states.

SUGGESTED ITINERARY (4 DAYS)

A holiday in Vijayawada means that you would be taking day-long trips around to cover the weaving and craft centres and possibly a day of sightseeing within the city. Four days is ample time for this.

BEST TIME TO GO

J F M A M J J A S **O N D**

GREAT FOR

Top 5 highlights

- **Kanaka Durga Temple** (p467)
- **Undavalli Caves** (p467)
- **Kondapalli Toy Village** (p468)
- **Pedana** (p469)
- **Mangalagiri** (p469)

Weaving Magic

Look beyond the busy roads of **Vijayawada**, and let the city's green surrounds weave their magic over you. Its intersected by canals, lined with ghats and ringed by rice fields. The Kanaka Durga Temple, several crafts and textile hubs like Kondapalli, Pedana and Mangalagiri or Uppada, add to Vijayawada's charm as the heart of Andhra culture and heritage.

Undavalli Caves are carved out of sandstone hills

❶ KANAKA DURGA TEMPLE
Located atop the Indrakeeladhri Hill, on the banks of Krishna River, is the most popular temple of Vijayawada – Sri Durga Malleswara Swamy (Kanaka Durga) – where the deity is seated on a silver throne. The ceiling is done up with murals. Visit early morning to beat the long queues for a quick darshan. Else, buy a ₹100 ticket to speed up the lines. Beware of touts asking for money for a simple teeka. Devotees offer red saris to the goddess. Ladoo, pullihora and chakrarchana are the main prasadams.
☏ 0866 2423600; www.kanakadurgatemple.org; 4am–9pm; photography not allowed

Highlights
❶ Kanaka Durga Temple
❷ Undavalli Caves
❸ Victoria Jubilee Museum
❹ Kondapalli Toy Village
❺ Kondapalli Fort
❻ Pedana
❼ Mangalagiri
❽ Kuchipudi

② UNDAVALLI CAVES

Carved out of sandstone hills, the Undavalli Caves, 10km from Vijayawada date back 4–5 centuries. One of the caves houses a massive form of a sleeping Lord Vishnu hewn out of a single granite block and there is a cave shrine for Narasimga, a Vishnu avatar. The view from the top has emerald green fields open up before you. Smaller, but equally interesting are the Mogalrajapuram caves, at the base of Indrakeeladhri Hill.

Indian/foreigner/video ₹5/100/25

③ VICTORIA JUBILEE MUSEUM

This museum is a fine example of Indo-colonial architecture showcasing porcelain, bidriware coins and sculptures. The large portrait of Queen Victoria on the opposite wall of the entrance is impressive. The museum's foundation was laid in 1887 to mark the Golden Jubilee celebrations of Queen Victoria's coronation.

Adult/child/camera ₹3/1/20; 10.30am–5pm, Fri & public holidays closed

④ KONDAPALLI TOY VILLAGE

Travel 22km from Vijayawada to enter the colourful world of Kondapalli bommalu (toys). The village has about 200 resident artisans, and every household is involved in making these traditional toys that were once an essential part of Sankaranti and Navaratri festivals. Shops and houses will happily welcome you to their work places.

☏9346660234; S Nageswara Rao; 32-64 Toys Colony, Killa Rd; 10am–6pm

Colourful wooden toys being made at Kondapalli

⑤ KONDAPALLI FORT

The drive up to the 14th-century Kondapalli Fort is mesmerising. Though the maintenance of rooms inside leaves much to be desired,

the weathered stone walls and winding passages still speak of stories of bravery by the Reddy dynasty and later rulers like Bahamanis, Gajapatis of Orissa, Krishnadevaraya of Vijayanagara kingdom and even the Qutb Shahi dynasty.
Adult/child/foreigner/camera/video ₹5/3/500/20/100; 10.30am–5pm

6 PEDANA
This town's claim to fame is Kalamkari, the art of block printing on fabric. The distinct designs in browns, blacks, red, blue and green are created from vegetable dyes. Almost the entire village community is involved in this craft. Halt at Kanti Textiles, the largest manufacturer, to watch artisans at the workshop, and shop at discounted prices. Pedana is 73km from Vijayawada, off Machilipatnam.
9885324329; Kanti Textiles

The famous Kuchipudi dance originated at a village by the same name

7 MANGALAGIRI
This town, 14km away, has three main highlights: sari weaving units and two temples dedicated to Lord Narasimhaswamy. Shop at the main market for Mangalagiri cotton and silk saris. The main temple marks the centre of the town. The other temple of Sri Panakala Lakshmi Narasimhaswamy stands on a hill.
Sri Panakala Lakshmi Narasimhaswamy 6am–4pm

8 KUCHIPUDI
Birthplace of the famous dance form by the same name, Kuchipudi village is 53km from Vijayawada, in the same direction as Pedana. A school of some 150 Kuchipudi students, a statue of Siddhendra Yogi who popularised the dance, and the office of guru and dancer, Pasumarthy Keshav Prasad stand testimony to the birthplace of this beautiful dance. The village temple hosts an annual festival in the beginning of the year, where many famous artistes perform.
9949618846; Sri Pasumarthy Keshav Prasad

Accommodation

VIJAYAWADA

The Gateway Hotel — Hotel ₹₹
0866 6644444; www.thegatewayhotels.com; 39-1-63, MG Rd; d ₹4750–6750, ste ₹8500–18,300 (incl of breakfast) Vijayawada's most sought after address for a luxurious stay, The Gateway is located close to the business district and offers five types of room options, a gym and pool. It has two restaurants, and one of them serves typical Andhra food, including an Andhra thali, which are its biggest asset after a tiring day of sightseeing.

Fortune Murali Park — Hotel ₹₹
0866 3988008; www.fortunehotels.in; 40-1-28, MG Rd, Labbipet; d ₹4200–5200, ste ₹6500–15,000 (incl of breakfast)

> A few restaurants in Vijayawada serve a typical Andhra thali with a variety of vegetables

ITC's Fortune Hotel is close to the shopping hub of Vijayawada. The hotel is a comfortable option and is good value for money. It has a health club, a 24-hour coffee shop and a Chinese restaurant.

Minerva Grand — Boutique Hotel ₹₹
0866 6678888; www.minervagrand.com; MG Rd, Labbipet; d ₹3600–4100, ste ₹5500 (incl of breakfast) Choose from one of the 40 stylish rooms of this boutique hotel. You could also ensure that you book the Imperial category if you plan to put an extra bed for children. The hotel is situated in a cosy corner just off the main MG Road.

The Kay Hotel — Hotel ₹₹
0866 6635555; www.thekayhotel.com; 48-12-4/1 Gunadala; d ₹2900–4300, ste ₹10,000 (incl of breakfast) This hotel is well worth its price for its spacious and aesthetic rooms. The wi-fi facility is chargeable. And the best part is that it is located at a comfortable distance from the traffic clogged highways of the city.

Quality Hotel DV Manor — Hotel ₹₹
0866 6634455; www.hoteldvmanor.com; MG Rd; d ₹4200–5800, ste ₹6700–7500 (incl of breakfast) Sink into the plush sofas and comfy beds of DV Manor. It is walking distance from the shopping hub, and its modern amenities make for a comfortable stay.

Eating

Eating at the in-house restaurants of any of the listed hotels is a good idea. You can be assured of quality, cleanliness and tasty food.

VIJAYAWADA

Bay Leaf — Andhra Cuisine ₹₹
☎0866 6644444; 39-1-63, MG Rd; mains ₹500–750; 7am–11pm This is your best bet to get authentic Andhra food in the city. Gateway hotel's Bay Leaf restaurant serves a host of fiery Andhra specialties. Add the nattu kodi mamsam, mutton curry or soor vindaloo to complement a regular thali. The Gateway has three more options: GAD, Sugar & Spice and G Bar.

Orange — Multi-Cuisine ₹₹
☎0866 6635555; 48-12-4/1, Gunadala; mains ₹200–500; 11am–11pm The bright ambience of the 24-hour coffee shop at Kay Hotel is inviting. Quick service and tasty food do the trick.

MACHILIPATNAM (FOR PEDANA)

Vani — Vegetarian ₹₹
☎08672 222228; www.bandaruladdu.com; 18/6-A, opp TDD Kalyana Mandapam; mains ₹200–500; 8.30am–11pm Indian sweets, chole bhature, thalis, dosas and a range of other multi-cuisine delights are served here. It's a viable stop while going to Pedana.

If You Like: Sweets

Those with a sweet tooth travelling in this belt of Andhra must not miss these two delicacies:

- **Bandar Ladoo:** The famous ghee-soaked sweet, made of chickpea flour, sugar, saffron and cashews, is known to be the best in the Machilipatnam area. You can get these in any of the sweet shops of Vijayawada.

- **Pootharekulu:** The wafer-thin sweet is an Andhra speciality. It's a roll made of sheets or crepes of rice flour with jaggery stuffing. It is a traditional delicacy from Atreyapuram village, 25km from Rajahmundry.

Shopping

Lepakshi — Handicrafts
☎0866 2573129; Gandhi Nagar; 10am–8pm, Sun closed Andhra's one-stop shop for handicrafts from the state, offers a large array of items for souvenirs. The prices are reasonable with not much difference from the craft hubs.

Kalanikethan — Saris
☎0866 2488333; 27-33-4, Gudavallivari St, Goverorpet; 10am–9.40pm Lazy or tired to visit individual weaving centres? Visit Kalanikethan instead for a large collection of traditional saris, but pricier. A couple of storeys full of Uppada, Mangalagiri and Kalamkari saris are available here.

Hyderabad

Andhra's capital is spectacularly diverse. It is a city that is reminiscent of its illustrious and opulent past when the Qutb Shahi dynasty reigned. Today, this original home of the Kohinoor diamond has turned into a fast growing cosmopolitan centre set against the backdrop of forts, palaces, vibrant markets and of course aromatic biryani joints.

Trip Planner

GETTING THERE

The glitzy Rajiv Gandhi International Airport connects Hyderabad to most airheads in the country. The Hyderabad Deccan railway station (better known as Nampally) is well connected to cities like New Delhi, Kolkata, Mumbai, Bengaluru, Chennai and all major South Indian cities. Overnight buses are run privately and by the state from Chennai, Bengaluru and other major cities of Andhra Pradesh.

SUGGESTED ITINERARY (4 DAYS)

If you want an easy paced holiday in Hyderabad, keep at least four days for sightseeing options that will interest you. Charminar and surrounding areas can take an intensive day itself. Add another for Pochampally, Nagarjuna Sagar Dam and Ramoji Film City. Once you have covered the essentials, keep another day or two to relax or shop.

BEST TIME TO GO

J F M A M J J A S **O N D**

GREAT FOR

Top 5 highlights

- **Charminar** (p474)
- **Golconda Fort** (p476)
- **Hussain Sagar Lake & Necklace Road** (p479)
- **Ramoji Film City** (p480)
- **Biryani** (p485)

Kohinoor of the South

Charminar illuminated by the Old City's busy bazaar

With four centuries of history mingling with the urban city, **Hyderabad's** draw lies in its milieu of a unique cultural backdrop. You are likely to encounter a mixed vibe – malls, traffic jams, a burgeoning nightlife and new suburbs popping up to accommodate the fast paced development. The IT hub, Hi Tech City, is the one example that you will soon get acquainted with. At the same time, weathered monuments and tombstones sprinkled over the city are a gentle reminder of its distinctive history. You will be traversing past three areas: across the Musi River to hop into the **Old City**, on the other side of Hussain Sagar Lake to **Secunderabad**, and the modern city.

The 16th-century ruler, Mohammad Quli left his imprint on a large part of Hyderabad: even the city is christened after his wife, Hyder Mahal. Besides the name, other remnants of the dynasty – palaces, mosques and tombs – are scattered all across the city. Historically, Hyderabad was a lucrative region for trade with its gold mines, pearl industry, and most of all, diamonds, that brought enormous wealth to its rulers and merchants. In fact, the Kohinoor diamond was found in the Golconda area. The city was declared a princely state in the late 18th century and was ruled by seven Nizams until the country gained independence from the British. Inheriting the tastes of their ancestor, Asaf Jahi, each of the Nizams continued to fervently promote art, food, culture and literature. With Hyderabad still sporting its Islamic heritage proudly, their rich and delectable cuisine is one of the city's main attractions.

Highlights
1. Charminar
2. Nehru Zoological Park
3. Mecca Masjid
4. Golconda Fort
5. Qutb Shahi Tombs
6. Chowmahalla Palace
7. Salar Jung & H.E.H. The Nizam Museum
8. Hussain Sagar Lake & Necklace Road
9. Lumbini Park
10. AP State Archaeological Museum
11. Chilukur Balaji Temple
12. Birla Temple
13. Ramoji Film City

❶ CHARMINAR
This icon of Hyderabad's landscape lies in the Old City. The imposing Charminar with its four minarets makes for a striking image as you jostle through a busy market that surrounds it and make your way to the building's first floor. Built in 1591 by Qutb Shah, it was originally constructed as a mosque from the four sides of which the city would emanate. You can spiral up the dark, narrow staircase to get a view of the area spread around. Intricate Islamic motifs still peep out from the graffiti-scrawled walls of Charminar. Use a guide to hear anecdotes about the building, the favourite being that of an underground 8km tunnel connecting it to Golconda Fort.

Adult (incl SAARC countries)/foreigner/video ₹5/100/25; guide ₹150; 9am–5.30pm

❷ NEHRU ZOOLOGICAL PARK
If you are travelling with children, this zoological park, also called the Hyderabad Zoo, can be a daylong sightseeing option with 380-acres to explore on battery run vehicles, cycles, trains and a canter safari. The well-maintained zoo

GETTING AROUND
The minimum auto fare in the city is ₹16, but most probably you will have to pay a premium on this so gear up to whet your bargaining skills beforehand. Taxis cost ₹1000/8hr/80km, typically for a full day sightseeing trip. Trips out of the city cost about ₹1200 plus a tip of ₹200 for the driver.

Mecca Masjid, one of the oldest mosques in the city

lets you get close with animals that reside in large enclosures which almost emulate their natural habitat. If you want a quick spin, then the 40-minute ride in the battery vehicle takes you to the main enclosure trail of tigers, lions, leopards, birds, reptiles, elephants, bears, rhinos and a few more animals. The zoo is kept plastic free to a large extent, so leave your bottles and polybags outside at the bag section.
☎ 040 24477355; www.hyderabadzoo.in; adult/child/camera/video ₹20/10/20/100; battery vehicle adult/child ₹40/20/40min; cycles on rent ₹20/hr; train ₹15/15min; safari adult/child ₹25/10/30min; Apr–Jun 8am–5.30pm, Jul–Mar 8.30am–5pm, Mon closed

❸ MECCA MASJID

The best view of one of the city's oldest mosques is from the top of Charminar, but if you prefer to be on ground level, you can walk into a grey sea of pigeons at Mecca Masjid's main front yard. It is said that almost 8,000 labourers toiled for more than 50 years as the granite structure emerged to accommodate over 10,000 worshippers, making it one of the largest in the world. Women are allowed only in the front open area and are advised to dress modestly.
Charminar area; 5am–8pm

❹ GOLCONDA FORT

Zigzag through the one-way, stone-walled pathway to Golconda Fort, the well-known symbol of the Qutb Shahi dynasty, originally built by the Kakatiyas in the 13th century. Use a guide to take you around the fort that was once the keeper of the Kohinoor and Hope diamonds. Stories of secret clapping signs from the front gate which could be heard till the King's Durbar on top of the hill, stables and the women's quarters; of a secret tunnel to Charminar; of a separate gate for royal corpses that had to be transferred to the Qutb Shahi tombs, will keep you engrossed.

☎ 040 23512401; Makki Darwaza Rd, Toli Chowki; adult/foreigner/camera/ video ₹5/100/25/25; 9am–5pm; Sound & Light show (English) adult/child ₹130/70, 7–8pm; guide ₹650/2hr

❺ QUTB SHAHI TOMBS

Many travellers tend to bypass this on the sightseeing trail, but the Qutb Shahi tombs are a respite from the overwhelming Charminar and Golconda experience. The large green expanse dotted with seven humungous tombs gives you a chance to appreciate the distinct architecture in peace. All but the last Qutb Shahi ruler were laid to rest in these black asphalt, octagonal tombs with a bulbous top.

Fort Rd, Toli Chowki; adult/child/camera/video ₹10/5/20/100; guide ₹200/one hr; 9.30am–5.30pm

View of Hyderabad from Golconda Fort

HYDERABAD

> *If You Like: Parks*
>
> **KBR** (Kasu Brahmananda Reddy National Park, 4.30am–8.30pm): This park in the city offers residents and visitors a verdant respite from the busy streets. This is a huge park which spreads over 400 acres and even houses a villa known as the Chiran Palace.
>
> **NTR Gardens** (adult/child ₹20/10; 12.30–8.30pm): Named after the actor, director and later Andhra Pradesh's chief minister, the park provides an affable ambience for families with restaurants, a variety of plants, swings and even a small waterfall. The late chief minister's samadhi is an opulent addition adjacent to the park.

❻ CHOWMAHALLA PALACE

More than 200 years old, this former palace lies close to Charminar and has been restored as a vast showpiece of the Nizam's collection of personal photographs, old cars and antiques. The clock tower and pillared Durbar with grand chandeliers are the most striking features of the palace. The original 45 acres of the palace have now shrunk to only 12 acres, and house history-laden sections of the royal family's personal belongings.

☏ 040 24522032; www.chowmahalla.com; Khilwath Rd, Moti Gali, Charminar; adult/foreigner/child/camera/video ₹40/150/10/50/100; 10am–5pm, Fri closed

❼ SALAR JUNG & H.E.H THE NIZAM MUSEUM

You can spend considerable time exploring the 38 galleries of the Salar Jung Museum near the Charminar area, right in front of the erstwhile Musi River. The museum houses an impressive collection of art and artefacts not just from India, but Persia, Syria and Egypt. The man behind the museum was Mir Yousuf Ali Khan, better known as Salar Jung III. He took it upon himself to make the museum a robust repository of unique art from around the world. Just a kilometre away from Salar Jung lies the **H.E.H The Nizam's Museum**, where you can take a quick tour of souvenirs and gifts given to the seventh Nizam on the occasion of silver jubilee celebrations of his reign in 1936. Go there only if you have time to spare.

Salar Jung Museum ☏ 040 24576443; www.salarjungmuseum.in; Door No 22-8-299/320, Salar Jung Rd, Naya Pul, Darul

Shifa; adult/foreigner/child ₹10/150/5; 10am–4.15pm, Fri closed H.E.H Nizam Museum ☎040 24521029; www.hehnmh.com; Purani Haveli; 10am– 5pm; Fri closed

❽ HUSSAIN SAGAR LAKE & NECKLACE ROAD

Hyderabad's answer to Mumbai's Marine Drive, the road skirting the Hussain Sagar Lake, comes alive in the evening with walkers, ice cream carts, hawkers and people enjoying the lake. When lit, the road looks like a string of pearls, and is thus christened Necklace Road. Hazrat Hussain Shah Wali originally constructed the lake in AD 1562, but its popularity now derives from the monolithic statue of Gautam Buddha, which was erected in 1992. It looks lovely when lit up. Many entertainment joints have sprung up around this; children are likely to enjoy Lumbini Park the most.

❾ LUMBINI PARK

Lumbini Park is rather special as it allows one access to the impressive Buddha statue in the middle of Hussain Sagar Lake. The 7.5-acre well-manicured property teems with visitors during evenings and weekends. It's child-friendly and it's best to let the kids make a bee line for the swings, a toy train, viewing deck and pop-up fountains while adults take a breather in the pleasant surrounds. Speedboats make furious trips to the statue and back and slower steamers glide with a larger crowd. The laser show at 7.15pm each evening dazzles a 2000 capacity crowd.

Adult/child ₹10/5; speedboat ride ₹300 for 4 people; steamer ₹50 per person; laser show ₹55; 9am–9pm

❿ AP STATE ARCHAEOLOGY MUSEUM

Popularly known as Hyderabad Museum, the erstwhile palace of the Nizam's daughter displays, amidst many unique

---

✓ *Top Tip: Packing in the maximum in one day*

You can combine a triple trip to Pochampally, Nagarjuna Sagar Dam and Ramoji Film City as they lie in the same direction, but you will have to plan your day and time at each place accordingly.

The Buddha statue stands impressively in the middle of Hussain Sagar Lake

exhibits, reproductions of Ajanta paintings, an Egyptian mummy and an exclusive copy of a Quran with Emperor Shah Jahan's seal on it. The museum has a collection of Buddhist antiques dating back to the 3rd century, a numismatics gallery, extensive bidriware, porcelain, arms and bronze sections.

✆ 040 23232267; www.museums.ap.nic.in; 5-10-193 I Floor, HACA Bhavan, PG Rd, near Control Room; adult/child ₹10/5; 10.30am–5pm; Fri closed

⓫ CHILUKUR BALAJI TEMPLE

Head for the 'Visa God' and join hundreds circumambulating this temple sanctum at Chilukur, popular among those who want visas to go overseas, especially students. After each circle, devotees systematically slash out numbers on a card marked with 108 blocks as they chant 'Govinda' and concentrate on the visa application which they bring along to be blessed. This unique temple lies 33km from the city and makes for an interesting stop. You will have to leave your mobile phones, cameras and any other belongings except the card and offerings at a locker room outside.

www.chilukurubalajitemple.com; Chilukur; 5am–3pm, 3.30–8pm

A special coach takes visitors around Ramoji Film City

⑫ BIRLA TEMPLE

The white marble extravaganza once commanded a high vantage point from where one could see a large part of the city. Today, one needs to go up Naubath Pahad, a low hill surrounded by residential colonies and multi-storeyed buildings to see the magnificent Birla Temple. Climb the temple steps to reach the sanctum of Lord Venkateshwara. Take a moment to admire the view of Hussain Sagar Lake from here. The temple combines South Indian and Orissa forms of architecture. Just a short drive away, you can also visit the planetarium, an observatory and museum by the Birla Group.

☏ 040 23233259; 7am–noon, 2–9pm

⑬ RAMOJI FILM CITY

If the idea of seeing movie sets and famous actors is appealing drive 34km outside the city, to Ramoji Film City –the largest film studio complex according to the Guinness Book of World Records. Vast gardens, kitschy statues and open-air films sets, dotted over 1500 acres, requires a whole day visit. The Film City organises movie shows, and has several restaurants and a hotel if you want to spend a night.

☏ 08415 246555; www.ramojifilmcity.com; NH 9, Abdullapurmet; adult/children ₹700/600 (incl general tour); 10am–4.30pm

Detour: Day-long trips from Hyderabad

The following destinations are viable day-long trips that can be added to the Hyderabad itinerary.

• **Pochampally:** Situated 42km from Hyderabad, Pochampally is a weavers' village, where. 'ikat' like designs on cotton and silk are painstakingly woven on mechanised and pit looms. You can shop at **Pochampally Handloom Park** (08685 80000000; Kannumukula). **Pochampally Handloom Weavers Co-op Society** (08685 222628; 9am–6pm, Sun closed) and **Raj Kumar Handlooms** (08685 222794; 9am–7pm, Sun 11am–6pm) are two of the best options. The latter can also guide you to smaller villages where weavers work on pit looms in clusters of 20–25. There's also a spartan museum, **Chenethakala Kendram** (₹5; 10am–6pm, Mon closed), and a temple dedicated to Vinobha Bhave Nagarjuna.

• **Nagarjuna Sagar Dam:** Drive out 165km to visit the largest stone masonry dam in the world, built on the Krishna River. You can book an overnight stay or stop over at the restaurant in the APTDC property, Vijay Vihar on the banks. Ahead lies the Launch Station of **Nagarjunakonda** (₹5), a small island with a Buddhist museum, with excavations dating back to the 3rd century (adult/child ₹90/60; 9.30am, 1.30pm/3hr). If you have time, you can visit the **Ethipothala Falls**, 22km from Nagarjunakonda (adult/chid ₹20/15; 9am–5.30pm).

• **Warangal:** The heart of Andhra Pradesh, Warangal, 195Kkm away, was the capital of the Kakatiya Dynasty from the 12th–14th century. Remnants of the unique architectural style of the era can still be seen in **Warangal Fort** (Indian/foreigner/camera ₹5/100/25; 9am–5.30pm), the **Thousand Pillar Temple** (5.30am–8pm), dedicated to Shiva, and **Bhadrakali Temple** (5am–1pm, 3–8.30pm) with many shrines in the large complex.

The decorative gateway of Warangal Fort

Accommodation

Taj Falaknuma Heritage Hotel ₹₹₹
☎ 040 66298585; www.tajhotels.com; Engine Bowli, Falaknuma; d ₹24,000–5,00,000 (incl of breakfast) This once glorious abode of the Nizams is a scorpion-shaped palace, which sits 2000ft above the city of Hyderabad. Now a luxury heritage hotel run by the Taj Group, it's your entry ticket to a royal world. You can stay in one of the 60 luxuriously furnished rooms or even drop in for a pre-booked dinner to experience the opulence of a past era. If lucky, Mr Faiz, former guard to the Nizam and one of the oldest employees here, will take you on a guided tour. A dining table that seats 101 people, Belgian glass chandeliers and other exotic British and French works of art created for the Nizam are painstakingly preserved for your viewing pleasure.

The Park hotel has contemporary rooms

The Park Hotel ₹₹₹
☎ 040 23456789; www.theparkhotels.com; 22 Rajbhavan Rd, Somajiguda; d ₹7700–9700 (incl of breakfast) The hotel's contemporary rooms with historic references to the rich textiles and Nizam's jewels are done up aesthetically. The service is impeccable, along with facilities like an infinity swimming pool overlooking the Hussain Sagar Lake, a health club and spa. It has multiple options to eat and drink including Aish, a fine dining restaurant offering Nizami cuisine.

jüSTa Boutique Hotel ₹₹
☎ 040 66336644; www.justahotels.com; 5-4-187/5,SM Modi Complex, Karbala Maidan, Necklace Rd, Rani Gunj; d ₹6000–8000, ste ₹11,000 (incl of breakfast) This hotel in Rani Gunj gives you brilliant views of Necklace Road and the Hussain Sagar Lake. Specifically ask for the lake facing rooms as some of those at the back of the hotel are pretty dingy. It has a good in-house restaurant.

Daspalla Hotel ₹₹
☎ 040 23455678; www.daspallahyderabad.com; Road No 37, Jubilee Hills; d ₹5650–6950, ste ₹9500 (incl of breakfast) The latest addition to the city's luxury hotels, Daspalla, provides excellent access to the dining and shopping hubs of the city. A pool, gym and a choice of three bars and multi-cuisine restaurants give ample options for a good meal.

Ebony　　　　　　　Boutique Hotel ₹₹
☎040 40319696; www.ebonyhotel.in; 8-2-120/C/98/1&2, Road No 2, Banjara Hills; d ₹5000–5500, ste ₹8000 (incl of breakfast) The elegantly styled rooms and chic ambience of Ebony is perfect for those who do not like the fuss of a large hotel. Services like wi-fi, 24-hour express check-in and check-out and a rooftop bar and restaurant make for a comfortable stay.

Lemon Tree Premier　　　　Hotel ₹₹
☎040 44212121; www.lemontreehotels.com; Plot No. 2, Survey No 64, HITEC City, Madhapur; d ₹4099–6099, ste from ₹7099–9099 (incl of breakfast) This is one of the most coveted business hotels in the city. But with its bright and cheerful rooms, modern amenities like a spa, pool and fitness centre, three restaurants, a bar and coffee shop, its becoming popular with those on vacation as well.

Bikanervala　　　　Boutique Hotel ₹₹
☎040 66661111; 6-3-190/2, Road No 1, Banjara Hills; d ₹4600–6600, ste ₹9600 (incl of breakfast) North Indian travellers might love the ease of living in the commercial hub of Hyderabad with one of their favourite food joints located on the bottom floor. The boutique hotel has 31 spacious rooms with modern decor; opt for the ones facing the lake and the road.

Courtyard by Marriot　　　　Hotel ₹₹
☎040 27521222; www.marriott.com; 1-3-1024 Lower Tank Bund Rd; d ₹4500–7500 (incl of breakfast) This hotel lies parallel to the breezy Necklace Road and provides value for money with its plush rooms, combined with good hospitality and services like wi-fi, pool and fitness centre. The Marriott, which lies across the street, can be accessed by a private bridge.

Minerva Grand　　　Boutique Hotel ₹₹
☎040 67198888; www.minervagrand.com; 8-2-616, Road No 11, Banjara Hills; d ₹4200–5200, ste ₹6500 (incl of breakfast) Situated right in the city's corporate hub, Minerva is good value for money with its boutique ambience, modern amenities and stylish rooms. The hotel also has a multi-cuisine restaurant and wi-fi service. If you wish to stay in the heart of Hyderabad, close to the dining and shopping areas, Minerva Grand is a good choice.

La Serene　　　　Boutique Hotel ₹₹
☎040 42408080; www.laserene.in; Plot No 174, Kauvri Hills, Phase II, Jubilee Hills; d ₹3500, ste ₹4500–7500 (incl of breakfast) La Serene is a good choice offering modern amenities and comforts besides the personalised services of a well established boutique hotel. It lies centrally in the commercial hub, yet away from the clogged streets of the Jubilee and Banjara Hills area. The

decor is too bright, but the rooms are spacious and clean.

Mercure — Hotel ₹
☎040 67122000; www.mercure.com; 5-9-208 Chirag Ali Ln, Abids; d ₹2750–3750, ste ₹5250 (incl of breakfast) There's a touch of the local in the modern boutique rooms of Mercure hotel. There's also a spa and a vegetarian restaurant. This hotel is at a comfortable distance from most sightseeing spots.

Taramati Baradri — APTDC Hotel ₹
☎040 20030352; Ibrahimbagh; d ₹2000, ste ₹2500 (incl of breakfast) A respite from the crowded cityscape, Taramati Baradri is an APTDC venture. Travellers who would like to stay in the erstwhile caravan station of Ibrahim Quli Qutub Shah will appreciate the connection. It has been named Taramati after the favourite courtesan of the seventh Sultan of Golconda. The current landscape emulates the Persian gardens of old, but now a restaurant and bar, souvenir shop and an amphitheatre sprawl over the open spaces of this basic but clean hotel. This is also a much coveted venue for musical shows and plays in the city.

Taj Mahal Hotel — Heritage Hotel ₹
☎040 66120606; www.hoteltajmahalindia.com; 4-1-999, Abid Rd; d ₹1850–2000, ste ₹2150–2750 (incl of breakfast) The bright, white bungalow and its period look makes Taj Mahal a good pick for those who would like to experience the historic ambience of Hyderabad. Opt for the first floor rooms for a better view and for distance from the buzz of the restaurant, which is extremely popular amongst locals. The high ceilings, wooden furniture and vintage decor of the rooms make up for the slightly dull lighting.

Eating

An amalgam of Andhra and Nizami cuisine with infusions of continental fare and other south Indian staples make Hyderabad a gastronomic delight. The Ramadan period is special when special food joints make an appearance till the wee hours of the morning.

N Grill — Continental ₹₹₹
☎040 64644141; www.ngrill.com; 788, Road 36, near Croma, Jubilee Hills; mains above ₹1000; noon–3.30pm, 7–11.30pm With an avant-garde ambience, chic grey coloured interiors and an open-air section, N Grill has been created in a remodelled old home. The menu is decidedly continental, focusing on a delicious range of steaks, soups, pastas, salads and risottos.

The Water Front — Multi-Cuisine ₹₹₹
☎040 65278899; www.waterfronthyd.in; Eat Street Complex, Necklace Rd; mains above ₹1000; noon–3pm, 7–11pm

♥ *If You Like: Biryani*

Every foodie comes to Hyderabad with an idea of hitting the best biryani haunts to taste the city's signature dish. Below are some of the top joints. Along with the biryani, also try the Irani chai and desserts like khubani ka meetha and a local fried snack, lukhmi.

- **Paradise** (☎040 66313721; www.paradisefoodcourt.com; Sarojini Devi Rd, Paradise, Secunderabad; mains ₹250–500; 11am–11pm): Established in 1953, Paradise has been dishing out variations of biryani for the last six decades. The higher the floor, the more plush the decor and costlier the biryani. There are three more branches in the city.

- **Pista House** (☎9396500786; Charminar area; mains less than ₹200; 7am–11pm): Another food lover's paradise, it is packed at lunchtime, with hasty service and shared seating; however, this only adds to the old Hyderabad experience.

- **Bawarchi** (☎040 27605308; www.bawarchihyd.com; RTC 'X' Rd; mains below ₹200; 11am–11pm): The large lettering on Bawarchi's cards announces 'We have no branches'! When you see this, you should be at the RTC Road. Come early at lunchtime and in the evenings before the biryani runs out.

- **Cafe Bahar** (☎040 23237605; 3-5-815, Hyderguda; mains ₹250–500; 11am–11pm): A wave of chatter hits you when you open the door to Cafe Bahar's AC section. Again, there's always a problem finding a seat during lunchtime. Only one more branch exists in the city.

- **Shadab** (☎040 2456648; opp Madina Building, Ghansi Bazaar; mains ₹200–500; noon–midnight): Shadab is one of the oldest restaurants, where brilliant Nizami food is dished out from behind greying counters. Sit upstairs if you want to eat at your own pace. A colourful faluda counter is engrossing to watch if not to eat at.

| Don't leave the city without trying biryani from one of these joints

A soothing, fine-dining option on the fringes of the Hussain Sagar Lake is all you need after a hectic day of sightseeing. The restaurant serves multi-cuisine fare which is best enjoyed if you have a seat by the window. It's better to reserve a table in advance.

The Blue Door — Mediterranean ₹₹₹
040 23555003; www.bluedoor.in; Plot No 1179, Road No 45, Jubilee Hills; mains above ₹1000; 7am–11pm Virgin white walls, bougainvilleas, wavy wall tops and steps leading up to a bright blue door emulate a Mediterranean ambience to perfection. And the food only adds to this! The Blue Door is only a few months old and hits the nail on the head with a sumptuous Greek menu. Don't leave without trying the traditional desserts.

♥ If You Like: Haleem during Ramadan

During Ramadan, a number of temporary food stalls pop up around the city, which serve iftar (meal to break the fast) till the wee hours of the morning. Haleem made from wheat, barley, beef (mutton and chicken haleem are also available), and cooked slowly for seven to eight hours with a generous helping of spices, is nothing short of divine. The food eaten after the fast is also known as 'nihari'.

So. Food & More — Continental ₹₹₹
040 23558004; www.notjustso.com; above Little Italy, 550 F Aryans, Road No 92, Jubilee Hills; mains above ₹1000; noon–11.00pm A whiff of lemon grass and other herbs draws you to the semi-open, rooftop restaurant. With plenty of plants and a pleasant view of a large green patch amidst the traffic downstairs, So. Food & More is atmospheric and offers fresh grills, bakes and salads. A live wok adds to the versatile cuisine.

Angeethi — North Indian ₹₹₹
040 66255550; www.bjngroup.in/restaurants; City Centre, 5th Floor, Road No 10, Banjara Hills; mains ₹750–1000; 12.30–3.30pm, 7.30–11.30 pm On the topmost floor of City Centre Mall, Angeethi's bright yellow walls with green windows cannot be missed. The aesthetics inside are equally delightful, and the same goes for the delicious range of north Indian dishes on the menu.

Chutneys — Multi-Cuisine ₹₹
040 30628484; Shilpa Arcade, Road No 3 Banjara Hills; mains ₹500–750; 7.30am–11pm Largely south Indian, Chutneys is a safe bet if this is what you're looking for. You will get a great option of dosas, idlis, vadas and Andhra meals served in a family ambience here. They even have Chinese dishes but it's best to avoid that. Chutneys has four other branches across town.

Rayalseema Ruchulu   Andhra ₹₹₹

☏ 040 64515252; 36th Square, Level 5, Opp SVM Mall, near Peddamma Gudi, Jubilee Hills; mains ₹500–750; noon–4pm, 7–10.30pm This is your 'head-to' destination for authentic spicy Andhra cuisine, especially non-vegetarian fare. Choose between the four branches of Rayalseema. The original branch, Lakdi Ka Pul, is more family friendly. The Kundelu mamsam (rabbit) and prawns iguru are definately worth a try.

The fine-dining Tadka restaurant at Ohri's Banjara

Ohri's   Multi-Cuisine ₹₹₹

☏ 040 23302200; www.ohris.com; Sri Ram Nagar Colony, Banjara Hills; mains ₹500–750; 7.30am–11.30pm The multi-storeyed hotel Ohri's in Banjara Hills is home to many restaurants, providing a range of cuisines on each floor. It's difficult not to find something to your taste here.

Southern Spice   Andhra ₹₹

☏ 040 23353802; 8-2-350/3/2, Plot No 34, Road No 3, Banjara Hills; mains ₹500–750; noon–3.30pm, 7.30–10.30pm For an unfussy mealtime special, try the authentic Andhra thali at Southern Spice. You can find a quiet spot for yourself at the restaurant and enjoy the spicy dishes characteristic of Andhra meals. Add a fish and prawn dish to your order for some extra zing. The restaurant offers other multi-cuisine dishes as well, but go for the Andhra food and you won't be disappointed.

Eat Street   Multi-Cuisine ₹₹

☏ 040 65278899; Necklace Rd; mains ₹250–500; 7.30am–11pm An open-air food court overlooking the Hussain Sagar Lake, this is one of the best family options as it caters to a variety of tastes; snacks, ice creams, fast food, south Indian fare and other dishes are available.

Famous Ice Cream   Dessert ₹

☏ 040 65972958; Mozam Jahi Market; below ₹200; 10am–midnight Dishing out the best natural fruit ice creams since the last sixty years, Famous presents you with unique flavours like anjeer (fig), melon, mango and sapota (chiku). Plastic chairs in clusters separate the other honcho, Shahi, though both serve exactly the same thing.

Karachi Bakery   Bakery ₹

☏ 040 24603502; Mozam Jahi Market; below ₹200; 10am–midnight

Started in 1953, Karachi Bakery has been dishing out the best bakery items in Hyderabad; the soft crumbly biscuits (especially the fruit flavour) are the most popular in its vast repertoire. With its growing popularity, a few more branches have been launched in the city and the biscuits have made their way into many multi-brand stores. If you miss buying them in the city, you can find them at the airport as well.

After a hectic day of sightseeing undwind with a cocktail at one of the clubs

 Nightlife

Liquids — Club
☏ 040 66259907; 5th Floor, Bhaskar Plaza, Road No 1; 7.30pm–midnight
Be ready to bring down the house rubbing shoulders with the youngsters of Hyderabad at this pricey and loud but popular watering hole of the city.

Hard Rock Cafe — Bar
☏ 040 64636375; www.hardrock.com; 1st Floor, GVK One, Road No 1, Banjara Hills; noon–11.30pm
Hyderabad's rock and roll scene took an upturn with the arrival of international chain Hard Rock Cafe. Often the venue for live gigs, there is never a dull night here.

Over The Moon — Bar
☏ 040 30512844; www.daspallahyderabad.in; 8th Floor, Road No 37, Jubilee Hills, CBI Colony; mains above ₹1000; noon–11pm The latest addition to the pub landscape of the city, Daspalla's Over The Moon is the current favourite for downing drinks in a semi open-air lounge with a view to die for.

Bottles & Chimney — Club
☏ 040 27766464; www.bottlesnchimney.com; Old Cargo Office, opp Begumpet Airport; mains ₹750–1000; 8pm–midnight One of the old favourites, Bottles & Chimney, has regular DJ nights to let your hair down. The pace of this club picks up around nine and continues till midnight.

10 Downing Street — Club
☏ 040 66629323; www.10downingstreetindia.com; Begumpet; mains ₹750–1000; 11am–midnight 'TDS' as it's affectionately called, is an iconic watering hole in Hyderabad. It's cosy and has a warm familiarity. The moment you enter, you know that the English styled pub is a regular haunt for partygoers.

The Bar — Bar
☏040 66824422; Novotel Hotel, Hi Tech City; mains ₹750–1000; 5pm–3am This is your post party haunt when you need that one last beer. The Bar at Novotel is alive and kicking till the wee hours of the morning.

⊛ Entertainment
Art and culture flourished under the rule of the Nizams and continue to do so even today.

La Makaan — Cultural Space
☏9642731329; www.lamakaan.com; lane adjacent to CBay, opp GVKOne Road No 1, Banjara Hills; 10am–10pm, Mon closed The cosy amphitheatre, cafe and workshop space of La Makaan is a cultural mainstay of the city. Stay abreast with events listed through their website, so you can catch what you like.

Snow World — Theme Park
☏040 65990167-70, 9866699475; www.snowworldindia.net; Lower Tank Bund Rd; adult/child ₹400/250 (incl of snow apparel); 11am–9pm For an hour-long thrill of sliding down snow-covered hills and roaming the -5 degree centigrade play area with swings, polar bears, penguins and alpine trees, go to Snow World. Do not expect an exceptional ambience but it is something that the children will surely enjoy. Mobile phones are not allowed inside.

Ocean Park — Theme Park
☏040 24193236; www.oceanparkindia.net; Gandipet; adult/child ₹400/250; 11am–9pm Situated 15km from the city, Ocean Park is a popular weekend spot for water-themed rides. The ambience cannot be compared to international amusement parks but the place is reasonably clean and has enough rides for you to spend the whole day. Carry an extra pair of clothes and your own towels.

⊛ Activities
Greater Hyderabad
Adventure Club — Adventure Club
☏040 23350008; www.ghac.in; 8-2-350/B/B, AK Enclave, adjacent lane to Pizza Corner, Road No 3, Banjara Hills; 9.30am–6.30pm, Sun & 2nd Sat closed Pioneers of Hyderabad's outdoor and adventure scene, GHAC is a not-for-profit organisation that organises reasonably priced hiking, bouldering, nature and adventure-themed trips around Hyderabad and even further away. Contact them prior to your arrival to check if something interesting is on the cards.

Society to Save Rocks — Treks
☏040 23552923; www.saverocks.org; 1236, Rd No 60, Jubilee Hills To understand the boulder-strewn topography of Hyderabad, join the guided Rock Walks to areas around the city on the third Sunday of every month. Book ahead to ensure a spot.

INTACH Hyderabad — Walking

📞 040 23525322 Heritage walks of the Charminar area are organised by The Indian National Trust For Art and Cultural Heritage (INTACH). They are free of cost and conducted in the mornings (6am or 7am) for about two hours. Contact Anuradha Reddy of the Hyderabad chapter for walks around Golconda Fort, temples of Hyderabad and other historical rockscapes.

🛍 Shopping

Kedarnathji Motiwale — Pearls

📞 040 66712345; www.kedarnathji.com; next to Bata, Pathergatti; 10am–8.30pm, Sun 10am–7.30pm Shop at the oldest proprieters in the business here. Beware, there are plenty of posers with the same name. Notice the many black and white photographs of famous personalities who've shopped here.

Mangatrai Ramkumar — Pearls

📞 040 24577339; www.mangatraipearls.com; Pathergatti, near Charminar; 10.30am–8.30pm, Sun closed Mangatrai has been in the business since 1905. There are many other branches in the city, but the one near Charminar is the oldest.

Kalanjali — Clothing & Artefacts

📞 040 23231309; www.kalanjali.com; 5-10-194, Hill Fort Rd, Saifabad; 10am–8.30pm The variety of clothes, accessories, handicrafts, artefacts and furniture makes Kalanjali the 'one-stop' destination to pick up Andhra-themed souvenirs.

Lepakshi — Handicrafts

📞 040 23212902; www.lepakshihandicrafts.gov.in; Gunfoundry, Abids Rd; 10am–8pm, Sun closed This multi-storied store house of souvenirs from the South Indian states ensures that you don't have to go elsewhere to pick up bric-a-brac. The Kondapalli toys are especially eye catching.

Bidri Crafts — Bidri

📞 9849156921; opp State Bank of India, Gunfoundry; 11am–9pm, Sun closed The shop has a small but superb collection of this Persian art introduced to South India in a town called Bidar, near the state's border.

A variety of ittars are available at shops in the Charminar area in the Old City

Berket & Son — Hookahs & More
S No 5/4/365, Poo Petrol Pump, Moazam Jahi Market; 10am–10pm Shop for dry fruits and vintage hookahs, mehendi, ittar, surma, oils and more in the twin shops of Berket & Son.

Royal Perfume Centre — Ittar & Surma
Beside Machli Kaman, Gulzar House, Charminar area; 11am–10pm Take a short walk from Charminar till Machili Kaman and you'll pass by plenty of ittar (traditonal perfume) and surma shops. But Royal Perfume Centre is easy to find as it lies just below the Machli Kaman Darwaza. It sells a variety of ittars.

Kareem Bangles Store — Bangles
040 24576980; 20-4-1227, Lad Bazar, Charminar area; 10.30am–10.30pm, Sun 10.30am–1.30pm Though you will find laquerware bangles elsewhere in Lad Bazaar, Kareem's easy location at the beginning of the market and the variety of bangleware is hard to resist.

Anonym — Clothing & Accessories
040 23552386; 550F Aryans, Road No 92, Jubilee Hills, next to Little Italy; 11am–9pm A trendy boutique of clothing and accessories with an accent on Pochampally weaves lies in the heart of Jubilee Hills. Lovers of this traditional weave are sure to find something unique here.

> **Snapshot: Pearls sheen**
>
> Hyderabad defies all geographical logic when it comes to the business of pearls. The city was a former trading centre of diamonds and pearls during the rule of Qutb Shahi kings. These were acquired from Ceylon (Sri Lanka), Goa and Arab countries. and made their way to this landlocked city. These days imported pearls from China, Indonesia, Australia, Tahiti, Venezuela and Japan can be bought here. It's the credibility of the ancillary industry of drilling, polishing and stringing that popularly lures buyers to Hyderabad.

Shilparamam — Arts & Craft
040 23100455; Hi Tech City Main Rd; adult/child ₹25/10; 10.30am–8.30pm, Sun 10.30am–9pm A cultural village-like ambience, with rows of shops selling ethnic clothing, accessories, toys and artefacts makes this worth a stop. Large gardens, food stalls, an amphitheatre promise time well spent browsing or shopping.

Joshi Masala Stores — Andhra Pickles
040 24656080; www.joshimasala.com; 4-5-795, Badichowdi, Sultan Bazaar; 9.30am–9.30pm, Sun 10am–1pm Joshi Masala Stores, with outlets elsewwhere in the city offers a variety of Andhra pickles. Choose from flavours like allam, gongura, tomato and chintakaya, along with podis (dry powered spice eaten with rice and idli).

Srisailam

Witness the spiritual fervour of Hindu devotees at Srisailam Devasthanam, the hilltop abode of Lord Mallikarjuna Swamy and Goddess Bhramaramba (incarnations of Shiva and Parvati). The ancient temple by the Krishna River finds mention in the Skanda Puranas and is one of the 12 jyotirlinga temples of India. Srisailam is a scenic blend of Saivite pilgrims, tribal communities and a mighty river bank.

Trip Planner

GETTING THERE

The closest airport is in Hyderabad, 200km away, which has daily flights to all metros and major cities. Kurnool (190km) is the key railway junction if you want to visit the town but has limited options compared to Hyderabad. Overnight APSRTC and private buses run from several towns of Andhra Pradesh and Karnataka.

SUGGESTED ITINERARY (2 DAYS)

A two-day trip is sufficient to explore this religious town. On the first day take it easy and just complete the darshan of the temple. The next day you'll get sufficient time to see other places that are close by.

BEST TIME TO GO

J F M A M J J A S O **N D**

GREAT FOR

Top 5 highlights

- **Srisailam Devasthanam** (p493)
- **Akka Mahadevi Caves** (p495)
- **Patal Ganga** (p495)
- **Nagarjunasagar Srisailam Interpretation Centre** (p495)
- **Mallela Teertham** (p496)

Gateway to the Gods

Srisailam Devasthanam's sculptured gopuram is visible from afar

Spiritual fervour runs high in this small town. But a trip to **Srisailam** is not just about devotion and religion; it's a great way to see the state's scenic countryside and the life of Chenchu tribals around.

Numerous legends surround the origins of this ancient temple on the Nallamala Hill of Andhra Pradesh. This is where Lord Rama installed the Shiva lingam. Dedicated to Mallikarjuna and Bhramaramba Devi (Shiva and Parvati), it is a special pilgrimage for Saivite Hindus. Many kingdoms held the temple in great honour and contributed to its advancement. Shivratri is the busiest time of the year when thousands arrive to worship Shiva.

❶ SRISAILAM DEVASTHANAM

After snaking past many hairpin bends for the last 75km, you reach the massive gate of the town. The temple's yellow gopuram can

Highlights
1. Srisailam Devasthanam
2. Akka Mahadevi Caves
3. Patal Ganga
4. Paladhara Ganga
5. Nagarjunasagar Srisailam Interpretation Centre
6. Mallela Teertham
7. Farahabad

be spotted behind a busy market street lined with shops selling religious paraphernalia and bric-a-brac. Leave your footwear on the left of the gate and walk down the pillared path towards the temple. Metal barricaded lines segregate the devotees by the ticket amount (special darshan ₹100) and the lines inch ahead at snail's pace, specially on Mondays and festival days. The ₹100 ticket will help in getting in faster.

The Mallikarjuna Swamy temple comes first and there is a silver door to the main sanctum. Devotees throw flowers at the head of the door and consider it lucky if it stays on the top ledge. Before this, there is a place to break coconuts as offering right in front of the Nandi that faces the temple. The Shiva lingam is surrounded by an intricate silver encasement.
📞08524 288883; www.srisailamonline.com; 6.30am–9.30pm

❷ AKKA MAHADEVI CAVES

Named after the famous 12th-century poet, Akka Mahadevi, the caves are supposed to be the hallowed ground where she worshipped a natural Shiva lingam. You can reach this spot only by boat. APTDC has boat services to the caves, which can be combined with a trip to the Srisailam Dam and an

Stone carvings of goddess Shakti and at Srisailam Devasthanam

aerial ropeway ride to the Patal Ganga ghats on the Krishna. The boat ride to the cave takes 20 minutes.
Adult/child ₹270/200; 9.30am–noon

❸ PATAL GANGA

The ghats at the Krishna River are known as Patal Ganga. Many devotees take a dip in the river at the ghats. It's best to reach here taking the aerial ropeway at the APTDC centre. You can combine this visit with a boat ride to the dam.
Adult/child ₹50/35; 6am–12.45pm, 1.45–5.30pm; combo of boat ride and ropeway adult/child ₹90/65, 9am–5pm

Krishna River's gushing water at Srisailam Dam

❹ PALADHARA PANCHADHARA

Located 6km from town, about 250 steps lead into a small valley where two perennial springs attract plenty of devotees as these symbolise water flowing from the forehead of Lord Shiva. It is said the Adi Sankara spent considerable time meditating here. Incidentally 'pala' also means milk and many feel that it refers to the gush of white water that comes down the small cliff. Do not expect a large waterfall throughout the year. During the summer, it is no more than a trickling stream.

❺ NAGARJUNASAGAR SRISAILAM INTERPRETATION CENTRE

The Srisailam Tiger Reserve is still finding its feet as a tourism highlight but a small Interpretation Centre is surprisingly well maintained and provides information on how the local Chenchu tribes have been inculcated in the tiger programme and protection of the jungles. There is a

The scenic Mallela Teertham waterfall

small museum with pictures of local villages and tigers. A deer enclosure often has a few animals and makes for a quick stop for children.
Adult/child ₹5; 8.30am–6.30pm

6 MALLELA TEERTHAM

On the route back to Hyderabad from Srisailam, 50km into the drive, you hit a small village called Vatvarpalli. From here, make an 8km detour on the right to the waterfalls of Mallela Teertham, past Chenchu settlements. The drive is scenic and gives you a chance to see the Andhra countryside, though the road is a little bumpy. You have to walk down more than 300 steps to reach the base of the waterfalls, with thick foliage all around.
Adult/child ₹10/5; 8am–5pm

7 FARAHABAD

If interested, you can have a tryst with the Nagarjunasagar Srisailam Tiger Reserve forest at Farahabad. Jeep drives for about an hour and a half are the best way to go around the jungle here.
Jeep ₹800/ 6 people; 7am–4pm

♥ If You Like: Legends

Among the legends surrounding the Srisailam Devasthanam, some of the popular ones go like this:

- **The Chandravathi Tale:** The daughter of local ruler Chandragupta Pattana decided to come and live on a hill after an altercation with her father. She saw a cow standing over a stone and shedding milk on it. On closer investigation, Chandravathi saw that it was a self-manifested lingam and started worshipping it, using jasmine garlands (mallika pushpam). Soon after, the hill came to be known as Srisailam, the abode of Lord Mallikarjuna Swamy.

- **Parvatha:** Son of Silada Maharishi is said to have performed penance to please Shiva to make him live inside his body. He assumed the shape of a big hill, Sriparvatha (Srisailam) and Shiva decided to grace the top of the hill as Mallikarjuna Swamy.

Accommodation

Haritha Resorts — Hotel ₹
📞 08524 288320; www.aptdc.gov.in; d ₹1250–1800 (incl of breakfast; weekend rates are slightly higher) This APTDC run resort is the best possible accommodation here. Reasonably clean and spacious rooms stand in a quiet complex with an in-house restaurant. The AC rooms are better than others, which are, however, cosier. All rooms have a TV.

Temple Accommodations — Guesthouse ₹
📞 08524 287351; www.srisailamonline.com; d non AC ₹1250–1800 There are seven guest houses run by the Devasthanam that provide basic accommodation facilities. You can choose depending on your budget, though the higher priced rooms are cleaner and more spacious. Carry your own bedspreads as the upkeep of the rooms can be slightly shoddy.

Eating

There are only vegetarian options in the temple town. Most places are basic and offer reasonably tasty meals.

Pesarattu and ginger chutney is a must-try

Hotel Ilapuram — South & North Indian ₹
Mains less than ₹200; 6am–11pm This small restaurant is right next to the Devasthanam office, near the temple. You can get south and north Indian vegetarian food here.

Hotel Sahasra — Multi-Cuisine ₹
📞 9490537300; less than ₹200; 7am–11pm Sahasra lies close to the main entrance of the town and is usually not too crowded. Like all other restaurants, it is simply furnished and the food is basic.

Haritha Restaurant — Multi-Cuisine ₹₹
Mains ₹200–500; 6am–11.00pm The in-house restaurant of APTDC's Haritha Resorts is a clean place to catch meals. The restaurant is closed during non-meal times in the afternoon. Of the multi-cuisine options, the Chinese fried rice is good.

Shopping

Arts and Craft Society — Handicrafts
📞 08524 288200; beside Vasavi Choultry; 8am–9pm The shop has a small collection of religious souvenirs.

Tirupati

The holy hill of Tirumala is always packed with tens of thousands of devotees, many of whom endure long journeys to see Lord Venkateswara at his home. The temple is often compared to the Vatican as a place of worship that is incredibly rich and receives the highest number of pilgrims. Absorb yourself in the chants of 'Govinda', as you line up with pilgrims to visit one of the world's most famous temples.

Trip Planner

GETTING THERE

The airport is 14km from the city. The Tirupati station has express trains that connect from Chennai, Bengaluru, Hyderabad and Vijayawada and there are special trains that connect directly to Tirupati from Mumbai. State buses and Volvos connect Tirupati from Chennai, Hyderabad and Bengaluru.

SUGGESTED ITINERARY (3 DAYS)

Keep one entire day for Venkateswara Swamy Temple and the next day to roam around town and visit the other highlights. On the third day you can visit temples outside the town.

BEST TIME TO GO

J F M A M J J A S **O N D**

GREAT FOR

Top 5 highlights

- Tirumala (p500)
- Sri Kalyana Venkateswara Swami Temple, Narayanavanam (p503)
- Sri Kalahasti Temple (p502)
- Sri Govinda Raja Swami Temple (p502)
- Sri Kalahasti (p502)

The World of Vishnu

The towering temple spire can be seen from afar

Astounding statistics have always preceded the grand reputation of the Venkateswara Temple at Tirumala, in Chittoor district of Andhra Pradesh. The temple is said to receive over 1 lakh pilgrims daily and gains an income of ₹60 lakh every day through hair sold from tonsured heads. It is also one of the world's richest religious bodies, earning ₹22.5 lakh daily in cash offerings.

The temple's prosperity is evident in the well-organised, self-sufficient city that has been built around it on the hill of Tirumala, which stands amidst seven peaks, looking down at the town of Tirupati. The Tirumala Tirupati Devasthanams (TTD, www.ttdsevaonline.com) trust does an excellent job of convening all operations related to the pilgrimage centre.

Snapshot: Bald & beautiful

Donate your entire treasure of tresses, or just three locks, at Tirumala's free tonsuring service centres. This traditional offering commemorates the sacrifice made by a princess, Neela Devi, when she offered her locks to Lord Vishnu to fill up a small bald patch on his head. It's not odd to witness a sea of bald heads in this town. The practice is very common, and even women unflinchingly donate all their hair.

Highlights

1. Sri Venkateswara Swamy Temple, Tirumala
2. Papavinasanam, Tirumala
3. Japali Hanuman Temple, Tirumala
4. Shila Thoranam, Tirumala
5. Sri Varahaswami Temple, Tirumala
6. Sri Padmavati Devi Alayam (Alamelu Mangapuram), Tirupati
7. Sri Govinda Raja Swami Temple, Tirupati
8. Sri Kalahasti
9. Sri Kalyana Venkateswara Swami Temple, Narayanavanam
10. Temple Museum, Tirumala

Base yourself in Tirupati, the service town, and visit the many ancient shrines here, sprinkled over a 40km radius, all with a considerable fervent following. Free and frequently scheduled buses ply between temples (there are also free food halls and locker facilities).

1 SRI VENKATESWARA SWAMY TEMPLE, TIRUMALA

If you are staying in Tirupati, leave early to cover the 18km stretch to Tirumala by road. Intensive checking at the toll is essential to proceed.

After inching through a shoulder-rubbing queue for at least three hours, you get a glimpse of the black statue of Lord Balaji (Vishnu), which lies in the sanctum of the temple. The experience is overwhelming, amidst constant chanting – and getting forcefully pushed by professional ushers to accommodate the thousands that visit here each day. End your spiritual tryst with the sumptuous big ladoo (copyrighted by the TTD).

₹300 (Seeghra Darshan)/₹50 (normal); Darshan timings are different through the week; Mon 7am–5pm, Tue 8am–2pm, Wed 9am–2pm, Thur 9am–5pm, Fri 9.30am–9pm, Sat & Sun 7am–9pm

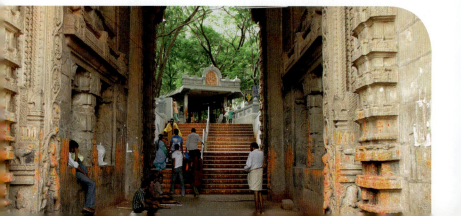

The walking path to Tirumala temple

❷ PAPAVINASANAM, TIRUMALA

Located 5km from the main Tirumala shrine, Papavinasanam is a holy bathing site of 10 channelised outlets of a river, monitored by a dam. Pilgrims throng here to cleanse themselves of their sins.
7am–5pm

❸ JAPALI HANUMAN TEMPLE, TIRUMALA

A 500m-long path of easy steps from the main road leads to a cool forested area, which houses an Anjaneya (Hanuman) temple. Legend goes that Lord Ram and wife Sita visited this spot. A natural pond (known as the Rama Kund) in front of the temple adds to the beauty of the verdant landscape. Make sure that you plan well so as to avoid landing up at the lunch break, when the temple closes.
₹2; 8am–1.30pm, 3pm–8pm

Sea of bald heads in Tirumala

❹ SHILA THORANAM, TIRUMALA

A quick stop is enough to witness the geological wonder, Shila Thoranam, which lies in a park close to Tirumala Temple. This rock formation is fantastic enough but other than that, there is nothing spectacular about the park (it is often swarming with tourists).
6am–5pm

❺ SRI VARAHASWAMY TEMPLE, TIRUMALA

This temple is in the same complex as the Balaji Temple. Varaha is the boar-faced Vishnu avatar. It is said that one must come here before visiting the Tirumala Temple, as this was originally Varaha's abode before Lord Vishnu arrived. He had to seek permission from Varahaswamy to take residence at Tirumala hills.

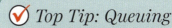

✓ *Top Tip: Queuing*

All devotees have to keep to a well-constructed narrow path, lined by metal guards so that nobody jumps the queue. Free milk is served to pilgrims; many come without eating to pay homage, so this refreshment is a relief during the tiring wait. There are also clean loos built along the line.

✓ Top Tip: Book ahead

To avoid the slow, snaking lines, book online in advance (at least one week). Reserve a spot on www.ttdsevaonline.com to reach a 'waiting lounge' directly, as per your designated darshan timing. From here, one joins the common line to the sanctum but the time taken is less than an hour.

❻ SRI PADMAVATHI DEVI ALAYAM (ALAMELU MANGAPURAM), TIRUPATI

This temple, 4km from Tirupati town, is dedicated to Lord Vishnu's spouse, Sri Padmavathi Devi. Expect meandering lines in metal barricades, and a brief glimpse of the deity.
5am–5pm

❼ SRI GOVINDA RAJA SWAMY TEMPLE, TIRUPATI

Situated in the middle of the bustling market street of Tirupati, the Govinda Rajaswamy Temple is famous for the impressive statue of a reclining Vishnu. Like the others around here, it is a busy temple with slow-moving queues of hundreds of devotees.
4.15am–9.30pm

❽ SRI KALAHASTI

The only Shiva temple in the region, it's worth the 34km drive from Tirupati. The name is derived from Sri (spider), Kala (snake) and Hasti (elephant), animals that worshipped Shiva to gain salvation. Besides housing impressive statues, the temple bears centuries of history. Enter the temple and take a deep, narrow-creviced pathway to enter. Narrow steps lead down to a shrine for Ganesha. Don't forget to see the 'Vaayulingam', a lamp that burns inside the innermost sanctum without any air; there are no doors or windows, but the lamp flickers relentlessly.
**www.srikalahastitemple.com;
6am–9.30pm**

Top Tip: Must read

Hindu mythology can seem extremely complicated but Dr Devdutt Patnaik's book, *Seven Secrets of Vishnu*, simplifies the symbols, stories, rituals and perspectives in straightforward, storytelling parlance, making your experience in the temple town even more enjoyable.

⑨ SRI KALYANA VENKATESWARA SWAMY TEMPLE, NARAYANAVANAM

If you have time, a trip to this temple, 37km from Tirupati is worth it. It is said that Lord Vishnu wedded Padmavathi Devi here. The peaceful environs of the shrine are a pleasant relief from the frenzied pace of the other temples close to Tirupati town. One will often see young, unmarried girls visiting this temple for a special puja and praying for a good husband.
6am–1pm, 3pm–8pm

⑩ TEMPLE MUSEUM, TIRUMALA

The temple museum in Tirumala is a sparkling clean building which houses paintings, sculptures and photographs related to the history of Sri Venkateswara Swamy Temple.
8am–8pm

📷 Snapshot: Inside Sri Venkateswara Swamy Temple, Tirumala

One quickly gets over the exhaustion of getting to the temple, as a number of bewildering experiences and quirky sights keep you engaged inside the shrine. Here, you'll see the glass-encased money-counting section. Peep in to find sombre, half-naked priests sorting through cash and coins with dexterity. The sheer quantity of money that is offered is astounding. If you are travelling abroad, say a prayer to Lord Vimana, marked with a red arrow on the gold gopuram. A weighing scale in the temple premises is often seen with people donating rice or wheat (even gold) as much as the weight of a person. There is also a rough stone where devotees jostle to scribble their wishes with their fingers, in the hope that they come true.

| Devotees lining up to see the idol at Sri Venkateswara Temple

Accommodation

If you're looking for lavish accommodation and proximity to all the temples, stay in Tirupati; Tirumala has basic guesthouses.

TIRUPATI

Minerva Grand　　　　　Hotel ₹₹

☏ 0877 6688888; www.minervagrand.com; Renigunta Rd; d ₹3800–11,000 (incl of full board) This hotel has minimalistic white decor, soothing ambience and well-furnished rooms. A multi-cuisine restaurant, gym, coffee shop and laundry ensure a comfortable stay.

Fortune Kences　　　　Hotel ₹₹

☏ 0877 2255855; www.fortunehotels.in; opp APSRTC bus terminal; d from ₹3100–7000 (incl of full board) Fortune has a coffee shop and in-house restaurants, while its rooms are lavishly fitted.

Udayee International　　Hotel ₹

☏ 0877 2266581; www.udayeeinternational.com; No. 13-6-771/20; d ₹2108–4497 (incl of full board) With the trappings of a big hotel, this doesn't burn your bank. It isn't very plush, but has spacious rooms and comforts like hot water.

Sindhuri Park　　　　　Hotel ₹

☏ 0877 2256438; www.hotelsindhuri.com; 14-2-118, 119, TP Area; d ₹2631–4159 (incl of full board) Besides a reasonably-priced and comfortable stay, Sindhuri Park provides an excellent view of an old pushkarni (temple pond). The courteous staff compensate for the lack of plush furnishings and facilities.

ASR Guest House　　Guesthouse ₹

☏ 0877 2251501; www.asrguesthouse.blogspot.in; 19-9-4 A1, Old Tiruchanoor Rd; r ₹1360 ASR fits the bill for buget options with its clean and spacious AC rooms. It is a short drive away from the railway station and bus stand. Hot water is available only on request.

TIRUMALA

TTD Guest Houses　　Guesthouse ₹

☏ 0877 2277777; www.ttdsevaonline.com; d ₹100–₹2000 (incl of full board) The no-frills TTD-operated guesthouses are ideal for those willing to rough it out. Book well in advance (90 days). Though dormitories are available, the ₹1000-plus rooms offer more privacy and comfort.

Eating

Greens, Tirupati　　Multi-Cuisine ₹₹₹

☏ 0877 2255855; www.fortunehotels.in; opp APSRTC bus terminal; 7am–10pm Part of the Fortune Kences hotel, this restaurant offers decent vegetarian food.

Woodside, Tirumala　Multi-Cuisine ₹₹

Ring Rd, near Museum; 6am–10.30pm Great for a quick north/south Indian meal or snacks, after you have completed the temple trail in Tirumala. .

Sandeepa, Tirumala — Multi-Cuisine ₹₹
Ring Rd, near Museum; 5am–midnight Low on ambience but high on taste, Sandeepa buzzes with weary, hungry pilgrims, who come to devour sumptuous south and north Indian meals and snacks like idlis and dosas.

India Coffee House Tirumala — Coffee House ₹
Lepakshi Rd; 6am–10pm Next to Lepakshi showroom, this dingy but clean cafe is good to grab a quick, relaxing cup of coffee and snacks.

Activities

Walk to Tirumala
Depending on your stamina enthusiastic tourists and pilgrims climb to Tirumala from Tirupati. It's a four hour trek. Start at the Garuda Circle, and take the 3550 steps (11km) to Tirumala. This route closes between 12am and 3pm.

Sri Venkateswara Zoo
☏ **0877 2249235; www.svzoo.org; Pudipatla Post; adult/child ₹15/5; car ₹250; camera ₹75 (additional charge of ₹25 for safari inside); 8.30am–5.30pm** About 16km from Tirupati, this zoo is a good stopover if you are travelling with children. It is very well maintained, and you can drive around in your car.

Souveniers on sale around Sri Venkateswara Swamy Temple

Chandragiri Fort
₹10; photography prohibited; 9am–5pm Fri closed Less than 15km from Tirupati, the Chandragiri Fort is an impressive reminder of ruler Krishnadevaraya Raya of the Vijayanagar kingdom. The 11th-century fort now serves as a museum. A lawn and lake add to its beauty.

🔒 Shopping

Lepakshi — Handicrafts
☏ **0877 2277246; www.lepakshihandicrafts.gov.in; Tirumala Hills; 10am–9pm** Balaji-themed curios, jewellery, key chains, statues, wooden toys and more line the congested shop in the town centre of Tirumala. The elaborate wooden sculptures are a big buy.

Shilparamam — Handicrafts
Tiruchanoor Rd; ₹10; camera/video ₹100/150; 10am–8.30pm This arts and crafts village is a good place to pick up regional handicrafts.

Index

A

Abbi Falls 101
Abdul Kalam's House 377
accommodation
  Alappuzha 226–8
  Ananthagiri 462–3
  Andaman Islands 440–2
  Araku Valley 462–3
  Badami 178
  Bandipur 94
  Belur and Halebidu 128
  Bengaluru 64–6
  BRT Wildlife Sanctuary 96
  Chennai 308–9
  Chettinadu 364–5
  Chidambaram 331
  Chikmagalur 120–1
  Coimbatore 408–9
  Coonoor 425–6
  Coorg 108–10
  Dandeli 164–5
  East Coast Road 309–10
  Ernakulam 246–7
  family hotels 41
  Fort kochi 247–50
  Gokarna 162–3
  Hampi 186–7
  Hassan 128
  Havelock Island 440–2
  Hospet 186
  Hyderabad 482–4
  Kabini 96
  Kanchipuram 310
  Kanyakumari 390–1
  Karwar 163–4
  Kollam 230–1
  Kotagiri 426–7
  Kovalam 208–10
  Kozhikode 278
  Kumarakom 228–30
  Kushalnagar 110
  Kutta 109–10
  Lakshadweep 288
  Madikeri 108–9
  Madurai 379
  Mamallapuram 328–9
  Mangalore 142–3
  Masinagudi 95
  Mattancherry 247–50
  Munnar 264
  Mysore 82–3
  Neil Island 442
  Ooty 424–5
  Periyar Tiger Reserve 265
  Port Blair 440
  Puducherry 329–30
  Rameswaram 380–1
  Sakleshpur 121–2
  Srisailam 497
  Thanjavur 346–7
  Thiruvananthapuram 204–6
  Tiruchirappalli 354–5
  Tirupati 504
  Tranquebar 331
  Udupi 143–4
  Valparai 409
  Varkala 206–8
  Vijayawada 470
  Visakhapatnam 460–2
  Wayanad 279
Achyutaraya Temple 185
activities. See individual locations
Adi Kumbeswarar Temple 340, 342, 343
Agastya Lake 173
Agumbe 141
Aihole 55, 170–9
  getting there 170
  highlights 170, 176–7
Airavateswarar Temple, Darasuram 345
Akka Mahadevi caves 494
Alagar Kovil 374–5
Alappuzha 216–33
  accommodation 226–8
  eating 231–2
  getting there 216
  highlights 216, 217–21
  shopping 233
Amritapuri 225
Ananthagiri 453
  accommodation 462–3
  eating 464
Andaman Islands 434–45
  see also **Havelock Island; Neil Island; Port Blair**
  accommodation 440–2
  eating 443–4
  getting there 434
  highlights 434, 435–9
Anderson's Church 298
Andhra Pradesh 15, 447–505. See also **Araku Valley; Hyderabad; Srisailam; Tirupati; Vijayawada; Visakhapatnam**
  best trips 449
  eating 35
  getting there 31, 447
  highlights 450–1
  map 448
  shopping 39
  why go 447
Anegundi 54, 181, 185
Anjengo Fort 201
Annegudde Sri Vinayaka Temple 138
Anshi Dandeli Tiger Reserve 152
Anshi National Park 160
antique market, Karaikudi 362
AP State Archeology Museum 478–9
Araku Valley 452–65
  accommodation 462–3
  eating 464
  getting there 452
  highlights 452, 458
archaeological museum, Badami 173
Arikamedu 335
Arjuna's Penance 319
Armenian Church 303
Ashtamudi Lake 224
Athangudi Palace 361–2
Athirappally Waterfalls 240
Attukal Waterfalls 260
Auroville 325
autorickshaw travel 29, 30, 31

Ayurveda 22, 201
Ayyanakere 117
Azhiyar Dam 406

B
Baba Budangiri Hill 114
backwaters 18
   Kumarakom 222
   Poovar 203
   of Supa Dam 159
Badami 55, 170-9
   accommodation 178
   activities 179
   eating 178-9
   getting there 170
   highlights 170, 172-4
   shopping 179
Baindur Beach 140
Balaramapuram 198
bamboo raft cruise 193
Banagudi Shola (Sacred Forest) 423
Banashankari 177
Banasura Sagar Dam 276
Bandipur 86-97
   accommodation 94
   activities 97
   eating 96-7
   getting there 86
   highlights 86, 88-9
   shopping 97
Banerghatta National Park 63
Bangalore Boulevard 42
   Bangalore Palace 58-9
Bangaru Kamakshiamman Temple 339
Bay Island Driftwood Museum 221-2
beaches
   Baindur Beach 140
   Black Beach 201
   Cherai Beach 241
   Chowara beach 203
   Corbyn's Cove Beach 436
   Devbagh Beach 158
   Elephant Beach 437-8
   Elliot's Beach 300
   Eve Beach 202
   Gokarna Beach 152
   Grow Beach 202
   Half Moon Beach 154
   Hawa Beach 202
   Kappad Beach 274
   Karwar Beach 157
   Kaup Beach 140
   Kollam Beach 224
   Kozhikode Beach 274
   Kudle Beach 153, 155
   Lighthouse Beach 202
   Majali Beach 159
   Malpe Beach 140
   Manthara Beach 201
   Maravanthe Beach 140
   Marina Beach 299-300
   Mattu Beach 140
   Murudeshwar Beach 131, 139
   Odayam Beach 201
   Om Beach 152-3
   Panambur Beach 136
   Papanasam Beach 200-1
   Paradise Beach 154, 324
   in Puducherry 324
   Radhanagar Beach 437
   Reppo Beach 324
   RK Beach 454-5
   Rushikonda Beach 456
   Serenity Beach 324
   Shankhumugham Beach 199
   Someshwar Beach 132-3
   Suratkal Beach 136
   Tannir Bavi Beach 136
   Thirumullavaram Beach 225
   Thundi Beach 286
   Vijaynagar Beach 438
   Yarada Beach 457
Beach View Park, Kanyakumari 389
Bear Shola Falls 397
Belavadi Temple 116-7
Belur and Halebidu 119, 124-9
   accommodation 128
   eating 129
   getting there 124
   highlights 124, 126-7
   shopping 129
Bengaluru 24-5, 56-76
   accommodation 64-6
   activities 74-5
   eating 66-72
   getting there/around 56, 58
   highlights 56, 58-62
   nightlife & entertainment 72-4
   shopping 75-6
Bengaluru Habba 85
Berijam Lake 397
Betta Byreshwara temple 119
Beypore 271
   boat-building yards 272
Bharathi Park 324
Bhoganandeeswara Temple 63
Bhuta Kola 147
Bhutnatha Temple 173-4
Big Mountain Loop 114
Biligiri Rangaswamy Temple 92
Biological Park 132
bird sanctuary, Kumarakom 221
birdwatching 89, 90
Birla Temple 480
Bisle Reserve Forest 119
Black Beach 201
Black Thunder theme park 405
Boat House 417
Borra Caves 458
Botanical Gardens, Ooty 416-7
Brahmagiri trek 106-7
Brahmotsavam festival 342
Brihadeeswarar Temple 338
Brindavan Gardens 80
BRT (Biligiri Rangaswamy Temple) Wildlife Sanctuary 86-97
   accommodation 96
   getting there 93
   highlights 86, 92-3
Bryant Park 394
bus travel 28, 29, 30, 31

C
camping 107
canoeing 107
Cathedral of Our Lady of the Immaculate Conception 321, 322-3
Catherine Falls 422

cave temples, Badami 172
Cellular Jail, Port Blair 435–6, 437
Chakrapani Temple 343–4
Chamundeshwari Temple 79
Charminar 450, 474
Chennai 296–315
  accommodation 308–9
  churches 303
  eating 310–2
  entertainment 313
  getting there 296
  highlights 296, 298–302
  nightlife 312–3
  shopping 313–4
Chennakesava Temple 125, 126
Cherai Beach 241
Chettiar Park 395
Chettinadu 295, 358–69
  see also **Karaikudi**
  accommodation 364–5
  activities 367
  eating 365–7
  getting there 358
  highlights 358
  shopping 367–8
Chettinadu cuisine 26, 369
Chidambaram 325–7
  accommodation 331
Chikmagalur 54, 112–23
  accommodation 120–1
  activities 122–3
  eating 122
  getting there 112
  highlights 112, 114–7
  shopping 123
children
  travelling with 40–1
Chilukur Balaji Temple 479
Chinese Fishing Nets 192, 242
Chinnar Wildlife Sanctuary 260
Chithirai 374
Chitrasanthe 85
Cholamandal Artists' Village 304
Chowara Beach 203
Chowmahalla Palace 477
Chunnambar Boat House 324

churches
Anderson's Church 298
Armenian Church 303
in Chennai 303
Church of Our Lady of Light 303
Church of the Sacred Heart of Jesus 323
Edappally Church 239
Eglise de Notre Dame des Anges 322
Lady of Lourdes Church 352
Milagres Church 134
in Puducherry 322–3
Schwartz Church 339–40
Shettihalli Church 126–7
St Andrew's Church 303
St Francis Church 242–3
St Mary's Church 303
St Stephen's Church 418–9
Tucker's Church 298
Vasco Church 242–3
Church of Our Lady of Light 303
Church of the Sacred Heart of Jesus 323
climate
  when to go 8–9
Coaker's Walk 394–5
coastal Andhra cuisine 451
coffee 36, 113
coffee plantation 21, 118–9
Coffee Yatra 116
Coimbatore 402–13
  accommodation 408–9
  eating 410–1
  getting there 402
  highlights 402, 404–6
  shopping 411–2
Coin Museum 137–8
Coonoor 295, 414–33
  accommodation 425–6
  eating 429
  getting there 414
  highlights 414, 419–21
  shopping 431
Coorg 21, 55, 98–111.
  See also **Kakkabe; Kushalnagar; Kutta; Madikeri**

accommodation 108–10
adventure activities 106–7
eating 111
getting there 98
highlights 98, 100–4
shopping 111
Corbyn's Cove Beach 436
Crocodile Bank 305
Cubbon Park 61

D
Dakshinachitra 304
Dakshinamnaya Sri Sharada Peetham 141
Dandeli 150–69
  accommodation 164–5
  activities 168–9
  eating 167
  getting there 150
  highlights 150, 159–61
  shopping 169
Dandeli Wildlife Sanctuary 160
Daroji Sloth Bear Sanctuary 185
Devarajaswami Temple 307
Devbagh Beach 158
Dhanushkodi 377
Dhyanalinga Isha Yoga Centre & Temple 406
Dodda Basavanaguddi (bull temple) 59–60
Doddabetta Peak 416
Dodda Sampige Mara 92
Dolphin Nose, Yarada Beach 457
Dolphin's Nose, Coonoor 420
driving 11
Droog 420–1
Dubare Elephant Camp 104
Dudh Gadi View Point 161
Durbar Hall Art Centre 237
Durga Temple Complex 176–7
Dutch Cemetery 243
Dutch Palace 244

E
Eachanari Vinayagar Temple 405
East Coast Road (ECR) 296–315
  accommodation 309–10

INDEX

eating 312
getting there 296
highlights 296, 304–5
eating 32–5, 41. *See also* individual locations
Edakkal Caves 277
Edappally Church 239
Ekambareswarar Temple 307
Elephant Beach 437–8
Elephant Junction 262
Elliot's Beach 300
Eravikulam National Park 258–9
Ernakulam 234–55
accommodation 246–7
eating 250–1
getting around 236
highlights 236–41
shopping 253–4
Ernakulam Shiva Temple 238
Etikoppaka 465
Eve Beach 202

F
Farahabad 496
Floriculture Centre 259
Fort Dansborg 327
Fort Kochi 192, 234–55
accommodation 247–50
activities 253
eating 251–2
entertainment 252
highlights 242–4
shopping 254–5
Fort Museum 298
forts
Anjengo Fort 201
Droog 420–1
Fort Dansborg 327
Golconda Fort 476
Kondapalli Fort 468–9
Manjarabad Fort 118
Mirjan Fort 155
North Fort 174
Shivaganga Fort 339
Thirumayam Fort 361
French Quarter, Puducherry 25, 317

G
Galaganatha Temple 175

Gandamadana Parvatham 376
Gandhi Memorial 388
Gandhi Memorial Museum 372–3
Ganesha Ratha 320
Ganesha Temple 59–60
Gangaikondacholapuram 345
Gangamma Devi Temple 61
gardens. *See* parks & gardens
GD Naidu Museum 404–5
George Town & around 298
Gokarna 150–69
accommodation 162–3
activities 168
eating 165–7
getting there 150
highlights 150, 152–5
Gokarna Beach 152
Golconda Fort 476
Golden Temple 103–4
Gorur Dam 127
Goubert Avenue 322
government mueseum
Bengaluru 60–1
Chennai 298
Puducherry 323
Green Park 262
Green Valley View Point 396–7
Grow Beach 202

H
Half Moon Beach 154
Hampi 54, 180–7
accommodation 186–7
activities 187
eating 187
getting there 180
highlights 180, 182–5
shopping 187
Hanuman Temple, Anegundi 185
Hassan 124–9
accommodation 128
eating 129
getting there 124
Havelock Island 20, 436–7
accommodation 440–2
eating 443–4
highlights 436–8

Hawa Beach 202
health 9–10, 41
Hebbe Falls 114–5
H.E.H The Nizam's Museum 477–8
Heritage Centre & Aerospace Museum 62
Highfield Tea Estate, Coonoor 421
Hill Palace Museum 236–7
Himavad Gopalaswamy Betta 89
Horanadu Temple 116
Hospet
accommodation 186
houseboats 192, 218, 223
Hoysaleswara Temple 125, 126
Hussain Sagar Lake 478
Hyderabad 472–91
accommodation 482–4
activities 489–90
eating 484–8
entertainment 489
getting there 472
highlights 472, 474–80
nightlife 488–9
shopping 490–1

I
Igguthappa Temple, Kabbe 102–3, 104
Indira Gandhi Zoological Park 454
Indo Portuguese Museum 242
INS Kurusura Submarine Museum 455
International Society for Krishna Consciousness (ISKCON) temple 59
Internet 8

J
Jain caves 375
Jain temple
Alappuzha 221
Pattadakal 175
Wayanad 277
Jalli Kattu 374
Jambulinga Temple 175
Janardhana Swamy Temple 200

Japali Hanuman Temple, Tirumala 501
Jawaharlal Nehru Planetarium 62
jeep safaris 88, 92–3
Jog Falls 156
Jomlu Teertha Falls 139
jungle treks, BRT wildlife Sanctuary 93

K
Kabini 86–97
　accommodation 96
　getting there 91
　highlights 86, 91–2
Kabini Dam 91
Kadmat 282–9
　getting there 282
　highlights 287
Kadri Manjunatheswara Temple 133–4
Kadu Malleshwara Temple 61
Kailasagiri 456
Kailasanathar Temple 306
Kakkabe 101
　highlights 102–3
Kalaripayattu 206
Kalhatti Falls 115
Kallur Peak 423
Kalpetta 270–81
Kamaraj Memorial 388
Kanaka Durga Temple 467
Kanan Devan Tea Museum 258
Kanchi Kamakoti Peetam 307
Kanchi Kamakshi Temple 306
Kanchi Kudil Heritage Museum 306
Kanchipuram 296–315
　accommodation 310
　activities 313
　getting there 296
　highlights 296, 306–7
　shopping 314
Kaneri River Dam 160
Kanyakumari 23, 386–91
　accommodation 390–1
　eating 391
　getting there 386
　highlights 386, 387–9
Kapaleeswarar Temple 301–2
Kappad Beach 274
Karaikudi 358–68
　getting there 358
　shopping 367–8
Karkala 137
Karnataka 12–3, 51–187. See also **Aihole; Badami; Bandipur; Belur and Halebidu; Bengaluru; Chikmagalur; Coorg; Dandeli; Gokarna; Hampi; Kabini; Karwar; Mangalore; Masinagudi; Mysore; Pattadakal; Sakleshpur; Udupi**
　eating 32–3
　festivals 85
　getting around 28–9, 51
　highlights 54–5
　map 52
　shopping 36–7
Karwar 150–69
　accommodation 163–4
　activities 168
　eating 167
　getting there 150
　highlights 150, 157–9
Karwar Beach 157
Kasu Brahmananda Reddy National Park 477
Katiki Waterfall 458
Kaup Beach 140
Kavala Caves 161
Kavaratti 282–9
　getting there 282
　highlights 283–5
Kaveri River 344
Keelakuyilkudi 375
Kemmanagundi 114–5
Kerala 13, 189–289. See also **Alappuzha; Ernakulam; Fort kochi; Kochi; Kollam; Kovalam; Kozhikode; Kumarakom; Lakshadweep; Mattancherry; Munnar; Periyar Tiger Reserve; Thiruvananthapuram; Varkala; Wayanad**
　eating 33
　getting around 29–30, 189
　highlights 192–3
　map 190
　myths & legends 203
　shopping 37–8
Kerala Folklore Museum 236
Keralam, Museum of History & Heritage 43, 196
Kerala Science and Technology Museum 196–7
Kochi 234–55
　getting there 234
　highlights 234
　travelling within 244
Kochi-Muziris Biennale 43
Kodaikanal 392–401
　accommodation 398–9
　eating 399–400
　getting there 392
　highlights 392, 394–7
　shopping 401
Kodaikanal Lake 393, 394
Kodanad Viewpoint 422
Kodnad Elephant Camp 241
Kollam 216–33
　accommodation 230–1
　getting there 216
　highlights 216, 224–5
Kollam Beach 224
Kondapalli Fort 468–9
Kondapalli Toy Village 468
Konkan Coast 19
Kotagiri 414–433
　accommodation 426–7
　eating 429
　getting there 414
　highlights 414, 422–3
　shopping 432
Kotikal Mandapam 320
Kovai Kuttralam Falls 404
Kovai Kuttralam Waterfall 405
Kovalam 194–215
　accommodation 208–10
　eating 213–4
　getting there 194
　highlights 194, 202–3
　shopping 215

Kozhikode 270–281
  accommodation 278
  eating 279–80
  getting there 270
  highlights 270, 272–4
  shopping 281
Kozhikode Beach 274
Krishna Mandapam 320
Krishna Menon Museum 273–4
K Sreenivasan Art Gallery & Textile Museum 405
Kuchipudi 469
Kudle Beach 153, 155
Kudroli Gokarnanatha 134
Kudroli Jamia Masjid 135
Kumarakom 216–33
  accommodation 228–30
  eating 232–3
  getting there 216
  highlights 216, 221–2
  shopping 233
Kumari Amman Temple 387–8
Kumbakonam 336–49
  accommodation 347
  eating 348
  getting there 336
  highlights 336, 340, 342–4
  history 342
  shopping 349
Kumily 257, 262
  getting there 256
Kunjarugiri Sri Durga Devi Temple 138
Kurinji Andavar Temple 395
Kurumgad Island 158
Kuruva Island (Kuruvadweep) 276
Kushalnagar 101
  accommodation 110
Kutta 101
  accommodation 109–10
  adventure sports 106

L
Ladkhan Temple 177
Lady Canning's Seat 420
Lady of Lourdes Church 352
Lake Garden 132
lakes
  Agastya Lake 173
  Ashtamudi Lake 224
  Berijam Lake 397
  Hussain Sagar Lake 478
  Kodaikanal Lake 393
  Pookot Lake 271, 277
  Sasthamkotta Lake 225
  Vembanad Lake 192, 217, 219
Lakkundi Utsav 85
Lakshadweep 26–7, 282–8. See also **Kadmat; Kavaratti; Minicoy**
  accommodation 288
  eating 288
  getting there 282
  highlights 282
Lal Bagh Botanical Gardens 61
Lamb's Rock 420
languages 8
Lighthouse Beach 202
Lighthouse Island 157
Lighthouse, Minicoy 286–7
Loam's View Point 407
Lotus Mahal 183
Lulu Shopping Mall 43, 254
Lumbini Park 478

M
Madikeri 98–111
  accommodation 108–9
  eating 111
  highlights 100–2
  shopping 111
Madikeri Fort & Palace 100
Madras Museum 298
Madurai 24, 370–85
  accommodation 379
  eating 381–3
  getting there 370
  highlights 370, 372–5
  shopping 384–5
Mahabaleshwar Temple 154
Mahakuta 177
Mahamaham Tank 342
Mahanavami Dibba 183
Maharaja World theme park 405
Mahatma Gandhi Park 224
Mahisasuramardini Mandapam 320
Main Beach, Kavaratti 283–4
Majali Beach 159
Malabar River Festival 42–3
Mallela Teertham 496
Mallikarjuna Temple 175
Malpe Beach 140
Mamallapuram 294, 316–35
  accommodation 328–9
  eating 331–2
  getting there 316
  highlights 316, 318–20
  shopping 335
Manakkula Vinayagar Koil 323
Mananthavady 271
Manasa Amusement Park 132
mandapams, Mamallapuram 320
Mangaladevi Temple 133
Mangalagiri 469
Mangala village walk 89
Mangalore 130–49
  accommodation 142–3
  activities 147–8
  eating 145
  getting there 130
  highlights 130, 132–6
  shopping 148
Manjarabad Fort 118
Manjehalli Falls 118
mansions, Chettinadu 295, 363
Manthara Beach 201
map 16–7
Maravanthe Beach 140
Margi Kathakali Institution 199
Mariamman Teppakulam 373–4
Marina Beach 299–300
marine aquarium, Kavaratti 285
Marine Drive 238
Mariyamma Temple 133
Masinagudi 86–97
  accommodation 95
  eating 97
  getting there 90
  highlights 86, 90
Matanga Paravath 182–3
Mattancherry 234–55
  accommodation 247–50
  activities 253

eating 251–2
entertainment 252
highlights 242–4
shopping 254–5
Mattu Beach 140
Mattupetty Dam 260
Mecca Masjid 475
Meenakshi Sundareswarar Temple 24, 371, 372, 374
Meguti Hill 176
memorial for B.R Ambedkar, Puducherry 322
microlight flying, Coorg 42, 106
Milagres Church 134
Minicoy 282–89
getting there 282
highlights 286–7
Mirjan Fort 155
mobiles 8
money 8
Monkey Falls 405
Moodbidri 137
Mookambika Devi Temple 138
Mosale 127
Mudumalai Sanctuary 88
Mukombu Picnic Spot 353
Mullayangiri 114
Muniyara Dolmens 260
Munnar 193, 257, 256–69
accommodation 264
activities 268
eating 266
entertainment 267
getting there/around 256, 258
highlights 256
shopping 268–9
Murudeshwar Beach 131, 139
Murudeshwar Temple 131, 138
Museum of Kerala History 239
museums
AP State Archeology Museum 478–9
archaeological museum, Badami 173
Bay Island Driftwood Museum 221–2
Coin Museum 137–8
Fort Museum 298
Gandhi Memorial Museum 372–3
GD Naidu Museum 404–5
Government Museum (see Government Muesum)
H.E.H The Nizam's Museum 477–8
Heritage Centre & Aerospace Museum 62
Hill Palace Museum 236–7
Indo Portuguese Museum 242
INS Kurusura Submarine Museum 455
Kanan Devan Tea Museum 258
Kanchi Kudil 306
Kerala Folklore Museum 236
Keralam 43, 196
Kerala Science and Technology Museum 196–7
Krishna Menon Museum 273–4
Madras Museum 298
Museum of Kerala History 239
Musuem of Anatomy & Pathology 139
Pazhassi Raja Museum 273–4
Pudukkottai Museum 362
Puthe Maliga Palace Museum 198, 199
Rajaraja Museum 340
RKK Memorial Museum 218
Salar Jung Museum 477–8
Seemanthi Bai Government Museum 136
Southern Naval Command Maritime Museum 243
Tribal Research Centre Museum 419
Victoria Jubilee Museum 468
Visakha Museum 455
Museum Theatre, Chennai 298
Musuem of Anatomy & Pathology, Udupi 139
Muthanga Wildlife sanctuary 277
Muttukadu Boat House 305
Mylapore 301
Mysore 78–84
accommodation 82–3
activities 84
eating 83–4
getting there 78
highlights 78–80
history 79
shopping 84
Mysore Palace 79
Mysore Zoo 80

N
Nagarhole National Park 86–97
Nagarjuna Sagar Dam 481
Nagarjunasagar Srisailam Interpretation Centre 495
Nageswarar Temple 342–3
Nalnad Palace, Kabbe 103
Nandeeshwara Temple 61
Nandi Hills 63
Nataraja Temple 325–6
National Art Gallery 298
National Gallery of Modern Art 58
Necklace Road, Hyderabad 478
Neelakurinji blooms 260
Neendakara Fishing Harbour 224
Nehru Park 423
Nehru Zoological Park 474–5
Neil Island 438–9
accommodation 442
eating 444
nightlife & entertainment. See individual locations
Nilgiri Mountain Railway, Ooty 18, 419
North Fort 174
Nrityagram 63
NTR Gardens 477

INDEX

O
Oachira Parabrahma Temple 225
Odayam Beach 201
OED Gallery, Mattancherry 255
Om Beach 152–3
Omkareshwar Temple 101
One Tree Point 153
Ooty 414–33
 accommodation 424–5
 activities 430
 eating 428
 getting there 414
 highlights 414, 416–9
 shopping 430

P
packing 10
Padampuram Botanical Garden 458
Pakshipathalam 275
palaces
 Bangalore Palace 58–9
 Chowmahalla Palace 477
 Madikeri Fort & Palace 100
 Mysore Palace 79
 Nalnad Palace 103
 Thirumalai Nayak Palace 373
 Tipu Sultan's Palace 60
Paladhara Panchadhara 495
Pamban Bridge 377
Panambur Beach 136
Pancha Rathas 318–9
Papanasam Beach 200–1
Papanatha Temple 175
Papavinasanam, Tirumala 501
Paradise Beach 154, 324
Pardesi Synagogue 244
parks & gardens
 Bharathi Park 324
 Botanical Gardens 416–7
 Brindavan Gardens 80
 Bryant Park 394
 Chettiar Park 395
 Cubbon Park 61
 Green Park 262
 Kasu Brahmananda Reddy National Park 477
 Lal Bagh Botanical Gardens 61
 Lumbini Park 478
 Mahatma Gandhi Park 224
 Nehru Park 423
 NTR Gardens 477
 Padampuram Botanical Garden 458
 Pilikula Nisargadhama 132
 Raja's Seat
 Rose Garden 418
 Sea View Park 220
 Sim's Park 419
 Thread Garden 417–8
 Vijay Park 220
Parthasarathy Temple 299
Patal Ganga 495
Pathiramanal Island 219
Pattadakal 55, 170–9
 getting there 170
 highlights 170, 175
Pazhassi Raja Museum 273–4
Pazhayannur Bhagvathi Temple 244
Pedana 469
Periyar Tiger Reserve 27, 193, 256–69
 accommodation 265
 eating 266–7
 entertainment 267
 getting there/around 256, 258
 highlights 256, 261–2
 shopping 269
Perur Patteeswarar Swamy Temple 404
Pethakal Bungalow 422–3
Phoenix Market City Mall, Chennai 42
Pilikula Nisargadhama 132
Pillaiyarpatti Vinayagar Temple 360
Pillar Rock 396
Planters' bungalows, Munnar 193
Pochampally 481
Pookot Lake 271, 277
Poovar backwaters 203
Port Blair 434–45
 accommodation 440
 eating 443
 getting there 434
Pudhu Mandapam, Madurai 384
Puducherry 25, 316–35.
 See also **Auroville; Chidambaram; Tranquebar (Tharangambadi)**
 accommodation 329–30
 activities 334–5
 beaches 324
 churches of 322–3
 eating 332–3
 getting there 316
 highlights 316, 321–4
 nightlife 334
 shopping 335
Pudukkottai Museum 362
Punnainallur Mariamman Temple 339
Puthe Maliga Palace Museum 198, 199

Q
Quad biking 107
Queens' Bath 184
Qutb Shahi tombs 476

R
Radhanagar Beach, Havelock 437
rafting 106, 148, 168
Rajahmundry 465
Rajaraja Museum 340
Raja's Seat 100
Ralliah Dam 421
Ramaswamy Temple 344
Rameswaram 370–85
 accommodation 380–1
 eating 383–4
 getting there 370
 highlights 370, 376–7
 shopping 385
Ramoji Film City 480
Ranganathittu Bird Sanctuary 81
Rangoli Metro Art Center (Bangalore boulevard) 58
Ravanaphadi 177
Regional Science Centre and Planetarium 272–3
Reppo Beach 324

RK Beach 454–5
RKK Memorial Museum 218
Road safari, Masinagudi 90
Rock Fort Temple 351–2
Rosario (Portuguese) Cathedral 134
Rose Garden 418
Ross Island 436
Royal Palace 339, 340
Royal Tombs 102
Rushikonda Beach 456

S

safety 9–10
Sakleshpur 112–23
  accommodation 121–2
  activities 123
  getting there 112
  highlights 112, 118–9
  shopping 123
Salar Jung Museum 477–8
sanctuaries
  BRT Wildlife Sanctuary 88
  Chinnar Wildlife Sanctuary 260
  Dandeli Wildlife Sanctuary 160
  Daroji Sloth Bear Sanctuary 185
  Gudavi Bird Sanctuary 156
  Kumarakom Bird Sanctuary 221
  Mudumalai Sanctuary 88
  Muthanga Wildlife Sanctuary 277
  Ranganathittu Bird Sanctuary 81
  Tholpetty Wildlife Sanctuary 275
Sangmeshwara Temple 175
Sankaram 457
Santa Cruz Cathedral Basilica 243
Santhome Basilica 300–1
Sarangapani Temple 343
Saraswathy Mahal Library 340
saris 36, 37, 38, 39
Sasthamkotta Lake 225
Sasthamkotta Temple 225
Schwartz Church 339–40
scuba diving 20, 148, 289, 322, 439
seafront, Kanyakumari 389
Sea View Park 220
Seemanthi Bai Government Museum 136
Serenity beach 324
Seyyid Muhammad Shareeful Madani dargah 135
Shankhumugham Beach 199
Sharavu Ganapathi Temple 133
Shettihalli Church 126–7
Shila Thoranam, Tirumala 501
Shivaganga Fort 339
Sholaiyar Dam 407
shopping 36–9. See also individual locations
Shore Temple, Mamallapuram 294, 318
Shravanabelagola 127
Silent valley view 395–6
Silidaphadi 174
Silver Cascade Falls 397
Simhachalam Temple 457–8
Sim's Park 419
snake boat races, Kerala 220
snorkelling 20
Someshwar Beach 132–3
Someshwar temple 132–3
Southern Naval Command Maritime Museum 243
Spice Coast Open, Kovalam 43
Sree Padmanabhaswamy Temple 196, 197–8
Sri Aurobindo ashram 321
Sri Jambukeswarar Temple, Srirangam 353
Sri Jayachamarajendra Art Gallery 80
Sri Kalahasti 502
Sri Kalyana Venkateswara Swamy Temple, Narayanavanam 503
Sri Krishna Mutt 131, 138
Sri Krishna Temple Ambalappuzha 218–9
Udupi 137
Srinivasa Perumal Temple, Nachiar Koyil 345
Srinivasa Ramanujam house 344
Sri Padmavathi Devi Alayam (Alamelu Mangapuram), Tirupati 502
Sri Parasurama Temple 202
Sri Poornathrayeesha Temple 237
Sri Ramanathaswamy Temple 376, 377
Sri Ranganathaswamy Temple, Srirangam 352–3
Srirangapatnam 81
Srisailam 451, 492–7
  accommodation 497
  eating 497
  getting there 492
  highlights 492, 493–6
  shopping 497
Srisailam Devasthanam 493–4
Sri Varahaswamy Temple, Tirumala 501
Sri Venkateswara Swamy Temple, Tirumala 20, 499, 500, 503
St. Philomena's Cathedral 80
St Aloysius Chapel 134–5
St Andrew's Church 303
St Francis Church 242–3
St George's Cathedral 303
St Mary's Church 303
St Mary's Island 140
St Stephen's Church 418–9
St Thomas's Mount 303
Suchindram Temple 389
Sultan Bathery 135–6
Supa Dam 159
Suratkal Beach 136
surfing 147, 333
Swamimalai 341
Swami Vivekananda Memorial Wandering Monk Exhibition 388–9
Sykes Point 160
Syntheri Rocks 159

T

Tali Temple 273
Tamil Nadu 14, 291–445.

INDEX

See also **Andaman Islands; Coimbatore; Coonoor; East Coast Road (ECR); Kanchipuram; Kanyakumari; Kodaikanal; Kotagiri; Kumbakonam; Madurai; Mamallapuram; Ooty; Puducherry; Rameswaram; Thanjavur; Tiruchirappalli; Valparai**
   eating 34
   getting around 30–1, 291
   highlights 294–5
   map 292
   shopping 38
Tannir Bavi Beach 136
taxes 11
taxi travel 29–30, 31
tea estates, Valparai 407
tea factory & museum, Ooty 416
tea tasting, Coonoor 295
temple complex, Pattadakal 175
temple museum, Tirumala 503
temples
   Achyutaraya Temple 185
   Adi Kumbeswarar Temple 340, 342
   Airavateswarar Temple, Darasuram 345
   Alagar Kovil 374–5
   Annegudde Sri Vinayaka Temple 138
   Bangaru Kamakshiamman Temple 339
   Belavadi Temple 116–7
   Betta Byreshwara 119
   Bhoganandeeswara Temple 63
   Bhutnatha Temple 173–4
   Biligiri Rangaswamy Temple 92
   Birla Temple 480
   Brihadeeswarar Temple 338
   cave temples, Badami 172
   Chakrapani Temple 343–4
   Chamundeshwari Temple 79
   Chennakesava Temple 125, 126
   Chilukur Balaji Temple 479
   Devarajaswami Temple 307
   Dhyanalinga Isha Yoga Centre & Temple 406
   Dodda Basavanaguddi 59–60
   Eachanari Vinayagar temple 405
   Ekambareswarar Temple 307
   Ernakulam Shiva Temple 238
   Galaganatha temple 175
   Ganesha Temple 59–60
   Gangamma Devi Temple 61
   Golden Temple 103–4
   Hanuman temple, Anegundi 185
   Horanadu temple 116
   Hoysaleswara Temple 125, 126
   Igguthappa Temple 102–3, 104
   ISKCON 59
   Jain temple 175, 221
   Jambulinga temple 175
   Janardhana Swamy temple 200
   Japali Hanuman Temple 501
   Kadri Manjunatheswara Temple 133
   Kadu Malleshwara Temple 61
   Kailasanathar Temple 306
   Kamakshi temple 306
   Kanaka Durga Temple 467
   Kapaleeswarar Temple 301–2
   Kashivishvanatha temple 175
   Kudroli Gokarnatha 134
   Kumari Amman Temple 387–8
   Kunjarugiri Sri Durga Devi Temple 138
   Kurinji Andavar Temple 395
   Ladkhan temple 177
   Lakshmi Narsimha Temple 61
   Mahabaleshwar Temple 154
   Mallikarjuna temple 175
   Mangaladevi Temple 133
   Mariyamma Temple 133
   Meenakshi Sundareswarar Temple 24, 371, 374
   Mookambika Devi Temple 138
   Murudeshwar 131, 138
   Nandeeshwara Temple 61
   Nataraja Temple 325–6
   Oachira Parabrahma Temple 225
   Omkareshwar Temple 100, 101
   Papanatha Temple 175
   Parthasarathy Temple 299
   Pazhayannur Bhagvathi Temple 244
   Perur Patteeswarar Swamy Temple 404
   Pillaiyarpatti Vinayagar Temple 360
   Punnainallur Mariamman Temple 339
   Ramanathaswamy Temple 371
   Ramaswamy Temple 344
   Ranganathaswamy Temple 81
   Sangmeshwara temple 175
   Sarangapani Temple 343
   Sasthamkotta Temple 225
   Sharavu Ganapathi Temple 133
   Shore Temple 294, 318
   Simhachalam Temple 457–8
   Someshwar temple 132–3

Sree Padmanabhaswamy Temple 196, 197–8
Sri Jambukeswarar Temple 353
Sri Kalahasti 502
Sri Kalyana Venkateswara Swamy Temple, Narayanavanam 503
Sri Krishna Temple 137, 218–9
Srinivasa Perumal Temple, Nachiar Kovil 345
Sri Parasurama Temple 202
Sri Poornathrayeesha Temple 237
Sri Ramanathaswamy Temple 376, 377
Sri Ranganathaswamy Temple 352–3
Sri Venkateswara Swamy Temple 20, 499, 500
Suchindram Temple 389
Tali Temple 273
Thayumanaswamy Temple 352
Thirumala Devaswom Temple 243
Thirunelli Temple 275
Thiruparankundram Temple 374
Thiruvenkadamudaiyan Temple 360
Trimurti Cave Temple 320
Ucchi Pillayar Vinayagar Temple 352
Ulavi Channa Basaveshvar Temple 161
Uppiliappan Kovil 345
Vaikom Mahadev Temple 222
Vaikuntaperumal Temple 307
Venkataramana Temple 133
Vijaya Vittala Temple 184–5
Virupaksha Temple 175, 182

Temple Street, Malleshwaram 61
Thangaserry Fishing Village & Lighthouse 224
Thanjavur 336–49
  accommodation 346–7
  eating 347–8
  getting there 336
  highlights 336, 338–40
  shopping 348–9
Thayumanaswamy Temple 352
Thekkady 262
Thenparankundram Cave 375
Theosophical Society 302
Thirumala Devaswom Temple 243
Thirumalai Nayak Palace 373
Thirumayam Fort 361
Thirumullavaram Beach 225
Thirunelli Temple 275
Thiruparankundram Temple 374
Thiruvaiyaru 341
Thiruvananthapuram 194–215
  accommodation 204–6
  eating 210–2
  getting there 194
  highlights 194, 196–9
  shopping 214–5
Thiruvenkadamudaiyan Temple 360
Tholpetty Wildlife Sanctuary 275
Thotlakonda 456–7
Thread Garden 417–8
Thundi Beach 286
tipping 33
Tipu Sultan's Palace 60
Tiruchirappalli 350–7
  accommodation 354–5
  eating 355–7
  getting there 350
  highlights 350, 351–3
  shopping 357
Tirupati 498–505
  accommodation 504
  activities 505
  eating 504–5

getting there 498
highlights 498, 500–3
shopping 505
Toda Shrine 422
Topslip 406
Top Station 259
tourist information 11
Townhall 287
Toy Train, Ooty 419
train travel 28, 29, 30, 31
Tranquebar (Tharangambadi) 294, 327
  accommodation 331
trekking 106–7, 157, 281, 407
Tribal Museum of Habitat 458
Tribal Research Centre Museum 419
Tribhuvanam 345
Trimurti Cave Temple 320
Triveni Sangam 389
Tucker's Church 298

U
Ucchi Pillayar Vinayagar Temple 352
Udupi 130–49
  accommodation 143–4
  activities 147–8
  eating 146
  getting there 130
  highlights 130, 137–40
  shopping 148
Ujra Mosque 285
Ulavi Channa Basaveshvar Temple 161
Undavalli Caves 467–8
Uppada 465
Uppiliappan Kovil 345
Uttarayan 342

V
Vaigai Dam 393
Vaikom Mahadev Temple 222
Vaikuntaperumal Temple 307
Vajra Waterfall 161
Valparai 402–13
  accommodation 409
  eating 411

getting there 402
  highlights 402, 406–7
  shopping 412
Varadarajaperumal Temple 307
Varaha Mandapam II 320
Varkala 194–215
  accommodation 206–8
  eating 212–3
  getting there 194
  highlights 194, 200–1
  shopping 215
Varma, Raja Ravi 197
Vasco Church 242–3
Vattakanal Village 396
Vazhachal Falls 240
Veli Tourist Village 199
Vembanad Lake 192, 217, 219
Venkatappa Art Gallery 60–1
Venkataramana Temple 133
Victoria Jubilee Museum 468
Viewing Tower, Kanyakumari 389
Vijaya Vittala Temple 184–5

Vijayawada 466–71
  accommodation 470
  eating 471
  getting there 466
  highlights 466, 467–9
  shopping 471
Vijaynagar Beach 438
Vijay Park 220
Virupaksha Temple 175, 182
Visakha Museum 455
Visakhapatnam 450, 452–65
  accommodation 460–2
  eating 463–4
  getting there/around 452, 455
  highlights 452, 454–8
  shopping 464
Vivekananda House 300
Vivekanandapuram 389
Vizhinjam Harbour 203

W
Wall of Wonder, Lakshadweep 26–7

Wandering Monk Exhibition, Swami Vivekananda Memorial 388–9
Warangal 481
Waterfalls, Wayanad 277
Wayanad 270–81
  accommodation 279
  activities 281
  eating 280
  getting there 270
  highlights 270, 275–7
  shopping 281
Wesleyan Chapel 298
Wonder La 240, 241

Y
Yakshagana Festival 85, 147
Yanam 465
Yana Rocks 154, 155
Yarada Beach 457

Z
Zoological Gardens & Museums 196

NOTES

PICTURE CREDITS

Placement key: T=Top, TC=Top Centre, TR=Top Right, TL=Top Left, C=Centre, B=Bottom, BC=Bottom Centre, BR=Bottom Right, BL=Bottom Left.

Although we have done our best to credit all the copyright holders of the photographs used in this book, we apologise for any unintentional omissions. If informed of any further acknowledgements we will definitely include them in future editions of the book.

Lonely Planet would like to thank the following photographers, organisations and picture libraries for permission to reproduce their photographs:

Ambady Estate: 265B.

Amruthum Ayurvedic Village Resort: 204B.

Anirban Mahapatra: 54T.

Anns Residency: 250T.

Art of Bicycle Trips: 269B.

Art of Living: 74T.

Blue Matsya: 142B.

Casa Cottage: 65B.

Chandrika Arul: 307B, 313B.

Corbis: Demotix/ Aji Jayachandran 317T; Dinodia 361T; Hemis/ Gardel Bertrand 12 – 13T; National Geographic Society/ Randy Olson 21T; Robert Harding World Imagery/ Marco Cristofori 450T.

Cultural foundation: 358B, 362T.

Daiwik Hotel: 380B.

Department of Tourism Tamil Nadu: 2 – 3T, 11T, 18B, 23C, 24T, 40C, 149B, 293B, 294B, 295B, 299T, 302T, 319T, 320B, 326T, 327B, 334T, 338B, 344T, 345B, 349T, 350B, 351T, 352B, 359T, 363TR, 363B, 368T, 371T, 372B, 375T, 376B, 386B, 387T, 388B, 391T, 392B, 393T, 394B, 396T, 397B, 403T, 404B, 407B, 415T, 417B, 418T, 433TR, 433B.

Destiny Farmstay: 424B.

Dhole's Den: 97T.

Dr Srinidhi Chidambaram: 315B.

Emerald Bay: 163B.

Flameback Lodges: 121T.

Flickr: Creative Commons/ Abhijit Shylanath 169B,/ Ronald Tagra 220T.

Gecko Café: 331B.

Getty images: Flickr/ Indira Nair 115T,/ James Adaickalasamy 46 – 47,/ Madhu Kannan 274B,/ Mahesh Telkar 50,/ Neeraj Murali 297T,/ Rajesh Vijayarajan 118B,/ Samyak Kaninde 99T,/ Sk.fotography 14 – 15B,/ Vinod Kumar Photography 131T,/ Yug_and_her 450B; Gallo Images/ Travel Ink 304B; Hemis.fr/ Guiziou Franck 151T; Lonely Planet Images/ 8C, 36B, 78B, 146T, 176B, 180B, 318B, 488T, 167T, 185B, 233T, 280T, Anders Blomqvist 290,/ Christer Fredriksson 193B,/ Graham Crouch 444T,/ Richard l'Anson 39B; National Geographic/ Martin Gray 451T\ 494B; Photolibrary/ Felix Hug 446; Photononstop/ Frédéric Soreau 453T; Stringer/ Noah Seelam 464T\ 468B.

Gowri Nivas: 109T.

Harivihar Heritage Homestead: 278T.

Heritage Resort: 178B.

Hindustan Beach Retreat: 207T.

Hornbill river resort: 164B.

Hoysala Village Resort: 128B.

Imli: 70B.

Indiapicture: Alamy/ Ajayclicks 184T, Anders Blomqvist 214B, Angus McComiskey 261B, Aruna Bhat 100B\ 102T, Ball Miwako 294T, Bon Appetit/ Lehmann, Jörg 369B, David Pearson 80T,

ACKNOWLEDGEMENTS 521

dbimages 199T,/ Amanda Ahn 503B, Eldred Lim 451B, ephotocorp/ Mihir Sule 284B,/ Vikram Hoshing 161T, Eric Nathan 322T, Imagery India 241B, John Bennet 475T, Maurice Joseph 272B, Pep Roig 125T, Robert Harding Picture Library Ltd/ Michael Runkel 436B, Ruby 341B, Sajith Sivasankaran 31B, Saptarishi Saigal 88C, Simon Reddy 22BL\ 26C\ 32C\ 232B\ 252B\ 324T\ 325B\ 463B, Steve Davey Photography 239B, Stuart Forster 30TL\ 10B, SuperStock/ V. Muthuraman 301T, Szefei Wong 35T, Terry Whittaker 27B, Tibor Bognar 321T, Tim Whitby 155B, Travel Pictures/ Pictures Colour Library 197B\ 225B, Travelib Asia 241T, Travelib Environment 25C, Travelib India 385T, Universal Images Group Limited/ Education Images 285T, Vivek Sharma 53B, Yadid Levy 2T; AWL RM 367TR; Axiom 183T; Hemis 55B; Image Broker 91B; IP-Black 6 -7\ 38T\ 77B\ 133B\ 174T\ 182B\ 303B\ 343T\ 459B\ 499T; IP-Zero 03 266B; Luca Tettoni 63B; Monkey Business 245B; Photononstop RM 456T; Tips 34B\ 81B; Wilmar Photography 323B.

Karnataka Tourism board: 130B, 140T, 152B, 158T.

King's Cliff: 428B.

Kerala Tourism Board: 3B, 18T, 28B, 42T, 191B, 192B, 193T, 195T, 198B, 200T, 201B, 202B, 217T, 221B, 223B, 235T, 237T, 238T, 257T, 262T, 263B, 267T, 271T, 276T.

La Closerie: 328B.

La Maison: 427B.

Lazy Hills: 426T.

Le Meridien: 408B.

Like That Only: 66BL.

Lonely Planet images: 490B.

Lymond house: 429T.

Madras Talkies: 44BL, 45B.

MGM Eastwoods: 309T.

Monkey Bar: 68T.

Ohri's: 487T.

Old Harbour hotel: 246B.

Phil's Bistro: 383B.

Planters Bunglow: 54B, 112B.

Prahlad Kakkar: 20C, 435T, 438T, 439B, 442T, 445B.

Priya Aiyappa: 105B.

Puneetinder Kaur Sidhu: 103B.

Random House of Canada Limited: 44T.

Royal Orchid: 82B, 186B.

Sangam hotel: 355T, 379T.

Saratha Vilas: 364B.

Sharan Saikumar: 283T, 286B.

Sheema Mookherjee: 209B.

Shutterstock: Jool-yan 181T; Noppasin 57T\ 479T; Pikoso.kz 19C; Thomas Kauroff 138T; WITTY234 411B.

Sinclair's Bay View: 441T.

Sumer Verma: 27T, 282B, 289B.

Supriya Shegal: 21B, 55T, 60T, 86B, 87T, 89T, 90T, 106B, 107T, 113T, 116T, 117B, 126B, 134B, 135T, 136B, 139B, 150B, 170B, 171T, 219B, 222T, 258T, 295T, 413B, 421T, 430B, 449B, 500B, 501T. 505T.

Sxc.hu: Dave Dyet 24B.

Taamara: 229T.

Tanjore Hi: 346B.

Tharavad Heritage Home: 230T.

The Carlton: 398B.

The Fern Creek: 399T.

The Park hotel: 460T, 482B.

The Serai Bandipur: 94B.

The Wild Orchid: 440B.

Tom's Old Mansion: 249T.

Vani Ganapathy: 85B.

Vembanad House: 226B.

Vikram Sathyanathan: 336B, 339TR.

Villa Maya: 210B.

Villa Urvinkhan: 120B.

Wikipedia: Creative Commons Attribution 2.0 Generic license/ albany_tim 242B,/ Arian Zwegers 337T,/ earnest.edison9 423B,/ Jean-Pierre Dalbéra 469T,/ mehul.antani 188,/ ukanda 497T,/ Venkatesh K 434B; Creative Commons Attribution 2.5 Generic license/ L. Shyamal 93T,/ Balaji Rakonda 141B; Creative Commons Attribution 3.0 Unported license/ PriyaBooks 470B,/ Ramesh Meda , Sonarpulse 154T; Creative Commons Attribution-Share Alike 2.0 Generic license/ Charles Haynes 145T\ 212T,/ Karan Verma 485B,/ Manvendra Bhangui 287T,/ Stu Spivack 356T,/ Technofreak 124B,/ Yashima 310B; Creative Commons Attribution-Share Alike 3.0 Unported license 43B\ 56B\ 59T\ 156B\ 273T\ 467T\ 473T\ 492B\ 493T\ 496T\ Luc Viatour/www.Lucnix.be in 110B,/ Pratheepps 73T,/ Rajeshodayanchal at ml.wikipedia 62T,/ Arun Suresh 259B,/ Balajirakonda 466 B,/ Dilli2040 104T,/ Dineshkannambadi 173T\ 172C,/ Femto 148T,/ Mail2arunjith 254T,/ Mohan Krishnan 296B,/ Raj srikanth800 452B,/ Ramesh Ramaiah 465B,/ Sanyambahga 476B,/ Sureshiras 457B,/ Vasanth S.N. 98B,/ Cephas 405 480T; Creative Commons Attribution-ShareAlike 3.0 License 332T\ 454B\ 498B; Public Domain 175B\ 234B\ 244T\ 381T\ 481B\ 495T.

Cover Images:
Front – Indiapicture: Alamy/ Muthuraman Vaithinathan. **Back** - Getty:hemis.fr

THIS GUIDE HAS BEEN RESEARCHED AND AUTHORED BY:

Supriya Sehgal has a penchant for travelling 'mapless and ungoogled'. Over the last eight years, she has willingly got lost a number of times in the most obscure places of India. She lives on a healthy diet of anecdotes and tea with auto drivers, copassengers and bewildered locals. Supriya currently runs a Bangalore-based travel photography outfit called 'Photography Onthemove' and writes regularly on travel. For this book she has covered Kerala, Andhra Pradesh and a few portions of Karnataka as well.

Smita Tripathy was bitten by the travel bug at a young age and she has managed to satiate her wanderlust even while juggling her different roles of being a journalist and a mother. Currently she divides her time between her parental home in Delhi and her adopted state of Tamil Nadu, which she's written about here. Over the years, she's learnt to appreciate much more than just a well-made dosa here.

Janaki Venkataraman is a Chennai-based journalist with over 35 years of experience. She travels around the world frequently but her favourite pit stops continue to be the many known and unknown pockets of Tamil Nadu and hence she has written a couple of chapter on the state.

Contributions also by:
Sudha G. Tilak, Puneetinder Kaur Sindhu, Karuna Ezara Parikh, Bikram Ghosh and Sharan Saikumar.

LONELY PLANET INDIA TEAM

Commissioning Editor Pallavi Pasricha
Design Manager Kavita Saha
Designer Ayesha Sarkar
Layout Designer Arun Aggarwal
Picture Researcher Shweta Andrews

Although the authors and Lonely Planet have taken all reasonable care in preparing this book, we make no warranty about the accuracy or completeness of its content and, to the maximum extent permitted, disclaim all liability arising from its use.

PUBLISHED BY

Lonely Planet Publications Pty Ltd
ABN 36 005 607 983
1st edition – January 2014
ISBN 978 1 74321 967 6
© Lonely Planet January 2014 Photographs © as indicated 2014
10 9 8 7 6 5 4 3 2 1
Printed in India
All rights reserved. No part of this publication may be copied, stored in a retrieval system, or transmitted in any form by any means, electronic, mechanical, recording or otherwise, except brief extracts for the purpose of review, and no part of this publication may be sold or hired, without the written permission of the publisher. Lonely Planet and the Lonely Planet logo are trademarks of Lonely Planet and are registered in the US Patent and Trademark Office and in other countries. Lonely Planet does not allow its name or logo to be appropriated by commercial establishments, such as retailers, restaurants or hotels. Please let us know of any misuses: lonelyplanet.com/ip.